You're a Human Being—
What's That?

You're a Human Being—What's That?

The Scientific Answer

Frederick R. Bauer

Author of Logical Fictions and
James vs Darwin

iUniverse, Inc.
Bloomington

You're a Human Being—What's That?
The Scientific Answer

iUniverse books may be ordered through booksellers or by contacting:

iUniverse
1663 Liberty Drive
Bloomington, IN 47403
www.iuniverse.com
1-800-Authors (1-800-288-4677)

ISBN: 978-1-4620-5290-5 (sc)
ISBN: 978-1-4620-5291-2 (ebk)

Printed in the United States of America

iUniverse rev. date: 09/23/2011

CONTENTS

Epilogue

A MORE DETAILED TABLE OF CONTENTS

Part Two: Applied to "What is a Human Being?"

Introduction: The Question.

I. Mind-Body Theories as Answers to "What am I?" First-person approach. Consciousness is central.

II. Five-Concept Model. Semantic problems. A.Act. B.Object. C.Power. D.Habit. A note on maturation. A note on IQs. E.Agent. III. Phenomenalism. The strengths of the phenomenalist position. The radical-empiricist principle. Having a concept vs making an inference.

IV. Materialism in General. Materialism as a genus. Avoiding pseudo-problems. Two common arguments for the soul. Conclusion.

V. Materialism I: Radical Behaviorism. Preface. Short historical background. Radical behaviorism and consciousness: a thought experiment. Applied. Strengths of radical behaviorism. Contemporary obfuscation. Appendix: methodological vs radical behaviorism.

VI. Materialism II: Brain-Mind Identity. Preface. The argument. Strengths of Brain-Mind Identity theory. Strengths of the Brain-Mind Identity theory. Conclusion. Tests.

VII. Materialism III: Epiphenomenalism. Transition. A bit of history. Strengths of epiphenomenalism. The brain. Consciousness. Three errors to be avoided, anthropomorphism, the correlation=identity fallacy, and the correlation=causality fallacy. Conclusions regarding epiphenomenalism. A postscript on all materialisms. Transition.

VIII. Berkeley's Idealism. The first major alternative to Descartes. Berkeley re the self. Berkeley's challenge to materialists.

IX. Two-Substance, Sharp Dualism, beyond St.Thomas to Descartes. Introduction. Materialism is not a scientific answer. More background history. Descartes. Representationalism again. Science. Soul & body: two central idea-thoughts. The origin of ideas. Back to "What am I?" First, why St.Thomas? St.Thomas, Plato, and Aristotle. The five-concept model again. The unity of your conscious-agent self. What St.Thomas didn't know. Two approaches to "You are a soul." Addendum re animals.

X. Jamesian Quintalism. Introduction. Quintalism. James and souls. The 'common-sense principle.' The ultimate question. Ten concluding notes.

For a provost

With the same vocation

ABOUT THE AUTHOR

Frederick R. Bauer is an associate professor of philosophy at Assumption College in Worcester, Massachusetts, and has been teaching various courses in philosophy since 1967. Besides his Ph.D., he holds an MA in counseling psychology. Dr. Bauer lives in Worcester, Massachusetts, with his wife.

PART ONE

The Evidence
According to Modern Science

A. INTRODUCTION: The FOCUS

Stated somewhat overdramatically, the object studied in this text will be . . .

you!

Each one of us has something very basic in common, namely, that he or she is a member of that most interesting species, *homo sapiens*. What, though, makes us *homo sapientes* what we are? To understand some of the key parts of the full answer to that question is our goal. In other words, to understand some of the key elements in your own makeup. To understand you. In short, to answer a question you must ask and answer for yourself. That question is . . .

What am I?

No other topic can compete with this in interest and importance. Its interest lies chiefly in the fact that there is nothing that is quite so close to us as our selves. Its importance stems from the role that our understanding of our selves plays, not only in how we should live our own lives, but in deciding what goals our generation should set for itself in preparing a world hospitable to future generations.

Another approach to this inquiry is to say we're seeking the scientific answer to the question, "What is the nature of a human being?" Of course, there are different opinions about what science is and about what is the scientific answer to the question, "What is the nature of a human being?" The author of this text believes his answer is 'the' scientific one. Otherwise, he'd change his opinion.

Then, too, reference to "a nature" raises large questions, such as, "Do natures or essences exist?", "Is there a nature common to all humans?", and so on. But questions about human nature can be broken down into other questions: "What things can be said of all humans?" "What do humans have in common with inanimate objects?" "What do they have in common with other living things?" "What is distinctive about them?" "What is their origin and ultimate destiny?" Etc.

The Western tradition. Perhaps never before has there been so much disagreement about humans' nature as there is at the present time. For most of the last two thousand years, Western culture was dominated by a view of humans that resulted from a synthesis of Greek philosophy and Judaeo-Christian religion. According to this tradition, humans were believed to be composed of two distinct principles or components, a material body and a spiritual soul. Because their soul gives them the ability to reason, humans were regarded as superior to all other creatures. In fact, according to the traditional view, the physical universe was thought to exist specifically to serve humans and their temporal needs.

This view was non-evolutionary. Though the body originated from matter, the spiritual soul, it was maintained, was created immediately by God who was himself purely spiritual in nature. This belief implied that each and every individual human soul was created according to the same general blueprint, was endowed with the same general potentialities, and was intended for the same general destiny, namely, an unending existence in the presence of the Creator after the death of the body. It was recognized, however, that individuals by their own free choice could frustrate that intention.

Attacks against the tradition. This sketch, admittedly a crude one, of certain ingredients of the traditional Western view of humans has come under heavy attack in modern times. None of these attacks is entirely new, but the reason why they have recently succeeded after mostly failing in the past is that they are now grounded on modern scientific theories generally accepted even by the traditionalists.

There are several prongs to the attack on the traditional view. One prong of the attack comes from Darwin's theory of evolution. To use the words of Calvin Hall, "before Darwin, man was set apart from the rest of the animal kingdom by virtue of his having a soul. The evolutionary doctrine made man a part of nature, an animal among other animals. Man became an object of scientific study, no different, save in complexity, from other forms of life." (C. Hall, 1954, p.11)

This attempt to demote humans from a position superior to the animals to the rank of simply the most complex of animals has been strengthened by the study of animals themselves, the study named "ethology." Traditionalists who argue that humans transcend the purely animal kingdom have claimed that humans alone are capable of tool-making and language communication, and of the symbolic conceptualization and the logical reasoning that these presumably require. (Cfr. M. Adler, 1967) However, recent investigations have led many to believe that not only are some animals tool users, but that they also display powers of generalization (conceptualization) in certain experimental situations and are capable of acquiring the power of language communication (the chimps) or even that they already possess such powers (the dolphins). Frans de Waal, a prominent researcher, has drawn attention to the unsuspected capabilities of animals.

The attack also comes from the newer sciences of biochemistry and biophysics. Whereas Darwin's theory of evolution allegedly traces human ancestry back, not to an immaterial Creator, but to more primitive forms of life, advances in modern biology have led many to trace life itself back to forces that are immanent in matter itself. Here again, the challenge is an old one, but it is recent discoveries that have lent a high degree of credibility to an older challenge. Processes within the living organism that were formerly attributed to a nonphysical life-principle or soul are now found to be describable as precise physical events occurring at the microscopic and submicroscopic level. This has been taken as evidence for the conclusion that, in the words of one scientist, the living organism and more especially the human organism "is a machine, but he is a very complex one." (B. F. Skinner, 1969, p.63) The work of Harold Urey and his graduate student, Stanley Miller, who synthesized some of the basic building blocks of life from completely inanimate material within the laboratory, taken together with later experiments in synthesizing cellular components inside the test-tube, have led many to agree with G. Simpson's assertion that "studies demonstrate not only the possibility but also the probability that life arose from the inorganic spontaneously, that is, without supernatural intervention and by the operation of material processes." (G. Simpson, 1949, p.340).

Additional ammunition for the challenge to the traditional view comes from those investigations that relate to consciousness. The theories of Sigmund Freud were heralded as a breakthrough in the effort to understand human behavior scientifically. Those who were reluctant to accept Freud's work as sufficiently scientific were offered an alternative in the theories and experiments of behaviorism. According to the foremost spokesman for this school of thought, B. F. Skinner, cited above, the single factor preventing us from predicting human behavior as accurately and as unfailingly as we can predict the behavior of other machines is the almost infinite complexity involved. His thesis is reinforced by contemporary research on methods of altering consciousness with drugs and with electrodes implanted in the brain.

Finally, research on the brain, neuroscience, has become the strongest challenge to traditional views of human beings. Dean Wooldridge sums up this view that sees humans as machines whose behavior is guided by electronic circuits in the brain: "All intelligence, whether of computer or brain, is the natural consequence of the powerful symbol manipulating capabilities of complex switching networks and therefore the ordinary laws of the physical sciences are adequate to account for all aspects of what we consider to be intelligent behavior." (D. Wooldridge, 1968, p.128) R. Watson, Descartes' biographer, is convinced that "When humankind finally faces the fact that the mind is the brain, that there is no independently existing mental soul to survive the death of the body, . . . there will be a revolution in human thought the like of which none has gone before." (R. Watson, 2002, p.327)

Today, then, there is no unanimity of opinion, nothing that even approaches it, with respect to the nature of the human being. The clash between the traditional Western view and the conclusions drawn by many from modern scientific advances has produced increasingly diverse attempts to harmonize the facts. Whatever verdict one arrives at on the question, "What does it mean to be a human being?", therefore, can only be arrived at after much careful weighing and sifting of evidence.

Some practical ramifications. As mentioned earlier, the effort to answer the question is imperative. High stakes ride on the answer to the question, both for one's own life and for society as a whole. According to the traditional body-soul view, an individual's life has two aspects to it that, though they interpenetrate each other, are quite distinct. On the one hand, the physical body imposes on them a concern for adequate food, protection from the elements, and a measure of material conveniences. On the other hand, the intellect-endowed soul or spirit imposes the need to pursue a transcendent wisdom, to observe various ethical norms, and to establish a proper relationship to the Creator.

This dualistic view of humans contends that the demands of the body are of a temporary nature, whereas those of the soul have an eternal significance. This is because the soul will endure long after the body has gone to its grave, and its (the soul's) condition will be happy or miserable depending on how well the person will have attended to its needs during its sojourn in the flesh. Adherents of the traditional view may disagree with the precise formulation of these points, but it is obvious that their position regarding life's priorities will differ radically from those who believe that the body alone is real, that there is no soul and hence no existence beyond the death of the body, and that all higher wisdom and religion is illusory. If the latter view were correct, then humans' biological or animal instincts and their attendant pleasure would be the final criteria of what is important during life.

Similar radical disagreements on practical matters emerge when proponents of these different views discuss methods of dealing with neurotic, psychotic, and criminal behavior. The disagreement revolves not only about matters already mentioned, but also about the question of whether humans have the ability to choose freely or whether their choices are ultimately determined by their physiological makeup and their environment. Traditionalists maintain that the fulfilled, healthy person is one who recognizes and develops his moral and spiritual potentialities and that is it is within his power to do so. Orthodox psychoanalysts and behaviorists tend to look on such concerns as expressions of infantile, regressive, or simply meaningless tendencies. More than this, those who regard humans as free insist that they can surmount environmental and biological pressures and can actively mold their own future, whereas those who favor the "humans are machines" theory hope for nothing more than that individuals consciously face, with unrepressed self-awareness, the forces responsible for their behavior or, at best, submit to programs that will recondition their responses. With respect to criminal behavior, it suffices to refer to the debate as to whether the lawbreaker is responsible for his actions or is merely the victim of irresistible impulses.

The debate carries over into the social arena as well. Shall society be established on the premise that humans should be free to establish their own values, even religious, so long as they do not trespass on one another's rights, or are social institutions to be engineered with a view to furnishing human robots, devoid of freedom and dignity, with what is necessary to keep them biologically fit and content? The conflict and its vital importance can be appreciated by examining, not only the theoretical arguments put forward by the spokespersons for the opposing views but, perhaps even better, by reading and comparing literary works that paint vivid pictures of the results anticipated from the adoption of the differing social "recipes." Examples of the latter are B. F. Skinner's *Walden Two* and K. Vonnegut's *Player Piano*.

Philosophy? Or Science? What, then, is human nature? What follows will undoubtedly be regarded at first as 'philosophy,' not 'science.' But the author realized, more than a quarter of a century ago, that all attempts to 'do' philosophy unscientifically or to 'do' science unphilosophically are absurd. Any so-called 'philosopher' who ignores what he or she regards as 'scientific facts' is ignorant, and any 'scientist' who thinks he or she is not building on a 'philosophical' foundation is self-deluded. Plato, the first great psychologist, didn't believe in such a distinction, nor did Aristotle who wrote the first psychology textbook.

Belief in the historically *recent* (and mythical) distinction that most people make between psychology and philosophy has become an enormous impediment to reaching the goal of a grand unifying system. Even though the amount of knowledge needed to become a well-educated person in this new millennium is unbelievably enormous, and even though it has become convenient, even necessary, to 'divide' knowledge up in order to allow some people to specialize in mastering certain 'slices' of the knowledge-pie and to allow others to specialize on other topics, it is essential to recognize that such distinctions are really imaginary. This text, then, will make use of whatever facts are important and relevant to answering the question, "What is a human being?" But, because of its special focus, a few words are in order to delineate somewhat the boundaries of the present work.

The primary focus is the individual human being, as opposed to groups (e.g., social, political, cultural, etc.) supposedly 'made up' of individual human beings. Beware of claims that sociology, anthropology, history, and politics autonomous sciences, as if they are not constructed on implicit theories about the nature of individual humans.

Yet, in referring to the individual, this should be taken to mean, paradoxically, "the individual in general," if it is permissible to use such a phrase. The goal is to understand better that which makes any individual being human, that which the individual has in common with other individuals, not the factors which make one individual human different from another, as for example, Tom Smith from Mary Jones. In studying humans, of course, it will be necessary to speak also of material objects, plants, and animals, inasmuch as, besides what makes him different, there are also things which he and they have in common.

Ontology? The focus can be further refined by stating that the focus is not everything that humans have in common, but chiefly what is often referred to as their "ontological" or "metaphysical" nature. Do not think of those as names for strange, esoteric inquiries. Not in this text, at least. The quest here will be different from such things distinguished, purely for convenience, as anatomy, physiology, and empirical psychology. For instance, it is left to specialists on anatomy to ask how many vertebrae are contained in the human backbone and to the specialists in physiology to determine the workings of the respiratory, digestive, or reproductive systems of humans. The lines between philosophical and empirical psychology are somewhat as follows. An empirical psychologist may study the relation between the ability to remember and the ability to perform on IQ tests, or he may inquire into the strength of pure retention (e.g., by the ability to remember nonsense syllables) as opposed to the strength of retention aided by association, or he may try to find methods for memory improvement. In all of these instances, the empirical psychologist can carry out his work without bothering to ask just what memory is in the first place. When he does ask this question, his question becomes what has traditionally been regarded as "philosophical." Is memory a function of the brain or does it reveal properties that can only be understood as somehow transcending matter and the brain? Are the things that we remember, i.e., memories, actual past events somehow surviving in the present or are they psychic images that refer to past realities or are they complex molecular formations or faint electrical potentials stored in the brain or are they none of these? It is these latter questions that will be asked in the present work.

In other words, the objective here is to go beyond the phenomena that can be observed (in some sense of that term) to the underlying structure or reality that makes them possible. The word "*meta*physical" connotes this notion of "going beyond", whereas the word "*on*tological" suggests that what is arrived at is the ultimate reality or being that is involved. ("Meta" means "beyond," while "to on" is the Greek word for "being.")

Method. What approach or method will be used in what follows? We will make use of whatever data or alleged facts are relevant to our question. From those data we will seek a reasoned answer to it. Since the person who is ultimately responsible for any judgment is the one who makes or accepts it, this means that each individual must decide for himself what are the data, that is, things that are intuitively recognized as facts that can only be accepted and not logically demonstrated, and what further truths follow reasonably, that is, logically, from those data.

In other words, no 'special method' will be used. The facts that will be appealed to will be facts that any 'ordinary thinking' person can verify for him—or herself. Einstein wrote that "The whole of science is nothing more than a refinement of everyday thinking." Einstein (Ideas and Opinions, p.283). Theories about 'special methods,' whether scientific, philosophical, or theological, are self-defense afterthoughts invented to protect beliefs that cannot be defended on everyday-thinking terms. (Illustrations of the interminable debates fostered by attempts to pinpoint boundary lines between philosophy and science can be found in the anthology entitled *Readings in the Philosophy of Nature*, edited by H. J. Koren, pp. 3-99. See also my 2008 *The Wonderful Myth Called 'Science.'*)

To summarize, then, our question is "What is a human being?" The question is both highly controversial and important. A complete understanding of any individual would require not only philosophy, but history, anthropology, literature, empirical psychology, biology, etc. Our principal focus will be on the underlying ontological structure of the human being. Our method will consist in gathering whatever certain data are relevant in order to arrive at a logically reasoned answer to our question.

IMPORTANT INSTRUCTION

Some philosophy texts are written for beginners. Others are written for the expert. The following pages are written for both. Philosophy, though, is not chiefly the study and analysis of texts. Above all, it consists in personal reflection. Unless the beginner makes a serious commitment to this personal reflection, it is certain that he will never gain access to those vast worlds of reality explored by the greatest minds of history. Anyone who merely reads out of idle curiosity or with the desire to argue glibly about any and every subject will always remain a foreigner looking in from the outside.

The following pages should be regarded, therefore, only as a guide or a map designed to facilitate your own personal reflections. Unless you, the reader, spend more time in reflection than in reading, you can expect little profit from your labors. A student was once given this advice by his instructor: "Do not think that the time you spend simply looking out the window, thinking about what you have read, is wasted. It is the most important part of becoming a philosopher."

As you read, then, be careful to stop from time to time. Mull over what you have read. See how it fits your own experience—your own most intimate convictions about life, people, the world, yourself. Where the text mentions one example, think of others. Examine them. Think up your own thought experiments. But *do not*—let it be repeated—*do not merely read and memorize*. Even using the time to sleep might be more profitable.

Your efforts may not always be easy. You will be asked to radically re-examine ways of looking at things that are so entrenched after years of unquestioning acceptance that it may be difficult at first even to understand any other view. Some discussions will appear abstract in the extreme, far removed from everyday, down-to-earth affairs. There are rewards awaiting you, however. The greatest of these will be a far greater sensitivity to previously unsuspected facets of reality and a richer appreciation of some of the answers to life's riddles. But they are yours only on condition that you use the right currency to purchase them: your own sustained and patient reflection.

B. EVIDENCE: THE DATA

What "data" means. Where shall we begin, then, in our inquiry about "What is a human being?" Where will we find the evidence that supports the true answer?

Shall we begin by writing down all of the things we have *personally* discovered about people during our own lifetime of personally observing them? Or shall we glean the records of the past, collecting from the work of *historians* those traits that have been common to human beings down through the ages? Perhaps we can bypass these inventories and begin with the studies made by *sociologists*, since they have been systematically observing diverse groups of humans and cataloguing their customs.

Before deciding where to begin, it is worthwhile pausing a moment in order to understand how important beginnings are. It is obvious, of course, that for every inquiry there must be some starting point. Such starting points are frequently referred to as "data," which is a word taken from the Latin and meaning "the things which are given." In other words, some facts are regarded as given or conceded; the inquiry consists in moving beyond these to some acceptable answers or conclusions.

It takes but little reflection to realize that the initial data, that is, the undisputed facts (or alleged facts) that will serve as the foundation upon which the diverse theories and answers are built, are extremely important. Though it is by no means the *only* reason why people investigating the same problem arrive at entirely different answers, the fact that they start with different facts or data is one of the most important reasons.

Here in Part One, then, rather than immediately attack the question, "What is a human being?", we are going to *first state a thesis* about the data we, in imitation of certain giant thinkers of the past, will use in answering the question. Then we will offer three sets of reasons or arguments for accepting that thesis.

In any piece of writing, basic assumptions are present. No author sits down and commits to paper some of his own notions on a subject without already having arrived at certain conclusions. Nor is he, if he is properly critical, unaware of the way he arrived at those conclusions, i.e., at his starting points or assumption-premises, and of the connection between them and his conclusions.

More importantly, however, the starting point for determining the 'ontological' nature of a human being is, in some way, far more determinative with respect to this text's conclusions than is the case with many other inquiries. The initial thesis here deals with knowledge, human knowledge, all human knowledge. That humans are capable, not just of knowing, but of knowing what knowing is and is not, humans' knowledge is one of the most fundamental things about them.

Much more might be said about the problem of starting with the correct data. Decisions about starting data or facts versus inferences and logical conclusions based on them are inevitably controversial. The decision made by this author is best understood in retrospect. Part Two will make the reasons for this text's starting-point decision utterly clear. Now it is time to simply state the initial thesis and then to offer reasons in its favor.

Section 1. The Thesis: Representationalism.

History. Where do we begin, then? We begin with our own stream of consciousness or, with what we might call, for want of a better term, the "contents" of our consciousness. This is Descartes' representationalism.

Descartes, the most revolutionary thinker of all time, was the first to use modern discoveries to show that, contrary to our common-sense convictions, we have no direct experience of anything except the realities in our own mind. Earlier thinkers—Plato, Aristotle, and St. Augustine—had already described such mind-contained or mental realities as ideas, images, desires, and passions. After him, other great thinkers—Locke, Leibniz, Berkeley, Hume, and Kant—explored the mind's contents in ever greater detail. Descartes, however, was the first to set forth a radically new worldview that recognized that our conscious experience is cut off from realities lying out beyond the perimeter of our mind.

Up-to-date science. Any clinging to common sense, i.e., any refusal to accept Descartes' discovery, deserves to be called by its proper name: "pre-scientific, pseudo-science." Bertrand Russell, in the mid-twentieth-century, described the thesis as follows:

> We all start from 'naive realism,' i.e., the doctrine that things are what they seem. We think grass is green, that stones are hard, and that snow is cold. But physics assures us that the greenness of grass, the hardness of stones, and the coldness of snow are not the greenness, hardness, and coldness that we know in our experience, but something very different. The observer, when he seems to himself to be observing a stone, is really, if physics is to be believed, observing the effects of the stone upon himself. Thus science seems to be at war with itself; when it most means to be objective, it finds itself plunged into subjectivity against its will. Naive realism leads to physics, and physics, if true, shows that naive realism is false. Therefore naive realism, if true, is false; therefore it is false. (B. Russell, *An Inquiry Into Meaning and Truth*, Introduction)

When Albert Einstein commented on this passage of Russell's, he lumped naïve realism with the belief that human thought is limitless and referred to it as a "plebeian illusion":

> [The] more aristocratic illusion concerning the unlimited penetrative power of thought has as its counterpart the more plebeian illusion of naïve realism, according

13

to which things "are" as they are perceived by us through our senses. This illusion dominates the daily life of men and of animals; it is also the point of departure in all of the sciences, especially of the natural sciences. (A. Einstein, *Ideas and Opinions*, p.30)

Carl Jung, after discussing contemporary controversies regarding human nature, put forward Descartes' thesis as the premise for psychology:

> Without a doubt, psychic happenings constitute our only immediate experience. All that I experience is psychic. Even physical pain is a psychic event that belongs to my experience. My sense impressions—for all that they force upon me a world of impenetrable objects occupying space—are psychic images, and these alone are my immediate experience, for they alone are the immediate objects of my consciousness. (C.G. Jung, 1933, pp. 59-60)

As can be seen, this thesis has both a negative and a positive side to it. The negative side consists in a rejection of the common-sense assumption that the human mind has direct access to the objective world of physical objects, including one's own body. It likewise denies that we have direct access to the consciousness of other people. The positive side of the thesis contends that what a person does have direct and immediate access to is his or her own sense impressions, memories, beliefs, convictions, and the like. These latter are the data, the starting points, the evidence upon which the answer to the question, "What is a human being?" must be based. They are, in fact, the ultimate data with which one must work in trying to answer any question.

Representationalism. The mental contents Descartes was most interested in were ideas or concepts. Because he adopted the traditional theory of truth, he thought of ideas as representations of the things they were ideas of. A true idea or thought would be an accurate representation, one that was in some sense 'a copy' that matched or corresponded to an external reality.

As a result, his theory has come to be known as "representationalism."

Two-World Theory. For the sake of emphasis, as well as pedagogy, we will adopt a metaphor in referring to this initial thesis. We will speak of it as "the two-world theory." When we open our eyes and look around us, we ordinarily believe that what we directly experience is a world of reality outside our own mind and independent of it. We will refer to this object of immediate experience as "the naïve or everyday world." Instead of accepting this immediately perceived world as the actual objective world, our thesis states that it is a reality within one's own consciousness, and that the objective world is in some sense an additional world often said to be located "behind" the naïve world. Because we distinguish, therefore, between the naïve world within consciousness and the world of objective reality outside it, we speak of this as "the two-world theory."

Epistemological Dualism. We can also designate this theory as "epistemological dualism." It is a dualism, i.e. it holds that the objects of our knowledge are two and not only one, namely, the world within the mind and the objective world outside. And by adding that it is epistemological dualism, we distinguish it from other forms of dualism. For instance, the theory that the human being is constituted of two principles, soul and body, is called "dualism" in psychology. And the more general thesis that in the universe we find two distinct principles, spirit and matter, is a metaphysical or ontological form of dualism. Because we are dealing with human knowledge, and because the philosophical investigation of the nature and validity of human knowledge is known as "epistemology" (from the Greek word meaning certainly true knowledge), the two-world theory is a form of epistemological dualism.

Let us sharpen our focus here. Readers may not be fully aware of the significance of the thesis as yet, but such awareness is indispensable. In asking readers to begin by giving serious consideration to the two-world theory or to epistemological dualism, we are asking them to consider *a radical reorientation in their attitude toward reality.* The two-world theory is not a trivial notion regarding some peripheral facet of existence. Rather, it deals with the very core of one's being. The thesis holds, in effect, that one's experience and the immediate objects of that experience—in fact, what might be labeled "one's whole world"—is radically different from what it seems to be. A more concrete and descriptive introduction to the theory is the following lengthy passage found at the beginning of W. Kohler's work, *Gestalt Psychology*:

> There seems to be a *single starting point* for psychology, exactly as *for all the other sciences*: the world as we find it, naïvely and uncritically. The naïveté may be lost as we proceed. Problems may be found which were at first completely hidden from our eyes. For their solution it may be necessary to devise concepts that seem to have little contact with direct primary experience. Nevertheless, the whole development must begin with a naïve picture of the world. *This origin is necessary because there is no other basis from which a science can arise.* In my case, which may be taken as representative of many others, that naïve picture consists, at this moment, of a blue lake with dark forests around it, a big, gray rock, hard and cool, which I have chosen as a seat, a paper on which I write, a faint noise of the wind which hardly moves the trees, and a strong odor characteristic of boats and fishing.
>
> But there is more in this world: somehow I now behold, though it does not become fused with the blue lake of the present, another lake of a milder blue, at which I found myself, some years ago, looking from its shore in Illinois. I am perfectly accustomed to beholding thousands of views of this kind which arise when I am alone. And there is still more in this world: for instance, my hand and my fingers as they lightly move across the paper. Now, when I stop writing and look around again, there

also is a feeling of health and vigor. But in the next moment, I feel something like a dark pressure somewhere in my interior which tends to develop into a feeling of being hunted—I have promised to have this manuscript ready within a few months.

Most people live permanently in a world such as this, which is for them the world, and hardly ever find serious problems in its fundamental properties. Crowded streets may take the place of the lake, a cushion in a sedan that of my rock, some serious words of a business transaction may be remembered instead of Lake Michigan, and the dark pressure may have to do with tax-paying instead of book-writing. All these are minor differences so long as one takes the world at its face value, *as we all do except in hours* in which science disturbs our natural attitude. There are problems, of course, even for the most uncritical citizens of this first-hand world. But for the most part, they do not refer to its nature as such; rather, they are of a practical or emotional sort, and merely mean that, this world being taken for granted, we do not know how to behave in the part of it which we face as our present situation.

Centuries ago, various sciences, most of all physics and biology, began to destroy the simple confidence with which human beings tend to take this world as *the reality*. Though hundreds of millions still remain undisturbed, the scientist now finds it full of almost contradictory properties. Fortunately, he has been able to discover behind it another world, properties of which, quite different from those of the world of naïve people, do not seem to be contradictory at all." (W. Kohler, 1947, pp. 7-8; most italics added.)

What we find in this passage from W. Kohler is a concrete description of the naïve world. As he mentions, it is up to each reader to substitute a description of his or her own situation in place of Kohler's. Before going on, let us pick out some salient facts about this naïve world, or, in less metaphorical terms, about our common-sense view of things.

The common-sense foundation. To begin with, we might note, as Kohler does, that *all science and all philosophy take their start from the common-sense view of things*. It means, in fact, that long before one writes a book that begins by stating that the naïve world is a world within the mind, one originally believed that that world *was* the world of objective reality.

Each of us—at some period between birth (when we entertain no conscious views whatever) and the age of six or seven—develops a set of convictions about himself and the world around him. This set of convictions is acquired in an unpremeditated, unnoticed, unlearned manner. Saying that they are acquired in an unlearned manner must not be confused with saying that they are themselves unlearned, only that we do not first have to learn how to learn them. It is as if "nature" herself teaches them to us. Or, better, it seems that our nature is programmed in such a way that we automatically acquire *these* convictions if we acquire any convictions whatever.

Among these convictions are the following: each of us is a living being, possessing a body, situated at a definite point in space and time. Each of us is located on this planet, earth, which is part of a universe that also contains sun, moon, other planets, and stars. Making up our environment are many other physical realities, such as mountains, forests, rivers, cities, homes, etc. As for the time-dimension, much history preceded the birth of anyone of us and, presumably, much history will follow our death. This objective reality into which each of us is born exists without any dependence upon us or our awareness of it. Even more, the things that surround us, such as trees, animals, buildings, tables, telephones, and the like, have properties such as size, shape, weight, color, odor, temperature, etc., that likewise do not depend upon us or our awareness of them.

Included in this set of common-sense convictions about ourselves and the world is a concept about the way we know this world. We regard the infant mind as an originally empty tablet. The infant's senses, however, put it into direct contact with its environment, so that, gradually accumulating more and more information from this sensory contact, the mind is able to recognize and sort things out and thereby to build up a set of ideas that matches the outside world.

The important fact to keep in mind, however, is that all human speculation, whether it be physics, biology, psychology, sociology, philosophy, or theology, originates in a mind that at some early stage in life took the common-sense view of things for granted.

A second important fact is that not only do these systems of knowledge grow from the soil of common sense, but *they cannot even sever their connection with that soil.* We may come to reject some of the convictions of common sense, but we will never be able to dispense entirely with the concepts and language of common sense, even if we use these concepts merely as a foil for our own, newer ideas, that is, as something to which we can contrast our own ideas. The older generation of thinkers is able to teach their abstract concepts to their young disciples only by means of examples described in terms of everyday, common-sense experience. Even among themselves, experts with different 'technical' vocabularies can communicate only because they can translate these back into the ordinary language of common sense which they share. Werner Heisenberg, well known for his contributions to the quantum theory which is far removed from the common-sense view of things, saw the connection between the common-sense concepts of plain language and the validity of scientific theories as being so close that he argued:

> Even for the physicist the description (of scientific discoveries and ideas) in plain language will be a criterion of the degree of understanding that has been reached."
> [1] (Heisenberg, 1958, p. 168.)

The third noteworthy point regarding the common-sense view of things is that, as Kohler reminds us, we all—scientists and philosophers and psychologists alike—revert back to it in our off-duty hours, and we do so automatically, without effort, and without exception. Outside the laboratory or classroom, we ordinarily act toward apples and ants, bananas and birds, just as we did before we learned any science or philosophy or psychology.

Here, then, is the naïve "world", the everyday way of looking at things. It constitutes a major portion of our mental landscape. It justifiably lays claim to an ineradicable priority in our thinking. Some philosophers have been so impressed with this priority that any attempt to question or doubt common sense—that set of basic convictions that are "obvious from the common experience of men"—is regarded by them as intellectual suicide. In fact, our own attitude toward common sense will be a very positive one. While not believing that it is intellectual suicide to critically examine our common-sense convictions or even, if needs be, to conclude that *some* of the convictions that common sense regards as "obvious" are, in fact, mistaken, it must be stated here at the outset that *no conviction of common sense will be surrendered unless there are preponderant reasons for doing so.* That claim is so important that we will call it "the common-sense principle."

Nevertheless, the reader is being invited here at the outset to weigh the claim that in at least one important respect, common sense is wrong. Rather than being in direct, immediate contact with objective reality, as we ordinarily believe, our two-world thesis states that we have direct contact only with a subjective reality, that is, a reality within the mind itself. The reason for saying this is that the common-sense "world" that we take to be the objective one turns out to be a subjective reality. The objective world, to the extent that it is known, is known only indirectly.

Some illustrations. Though elements of this two-world theory have a long ancestry that can be traced back to the earliest Greek philosophers, it is only in modern times that they have gained widespread support. This support has come from many directions, from the researches of modern physics, from psychology, from philosophy, etc. Some brief sampling of the suggestions that have come from these sources may encourage the reader to venture out beyond the familiar shoreline of common sense, by showing him that he is far from alone in this venture.

For instance, modern physicists have done as much as anyone to show that reality may be quite different from our ordinary ideas about it. Thanks to the spread of universal education and the marvels of mass communication, the average reader will already be familiar with enough ideas from modern science to be able to appreciate this statement. Who is there, for instance, who has not heard it said that matter is composed of minute atoms, that atoms are mostly empty space, that if the matter constituting the human body were compressed the product will be no larger than the head of a pin? This by itself contradicts our usual way of regarding things such as the human body, which appears quite solid and continuous. But the contradiction is even more complete if we accept what Galileo, Newton, and a host of scientists since them have claimed, viz., that the colors, sounds, odors, tastes, and other sensible qualities which common sense insists are part of the physical world, actually exist only in the mind and that matter itself is quite devoid of such qualities. If one were to pause and reflect on this, he would realize that there are here two pictures of two different worlds. In line with what Kohler has written, one twentieth-century scientist, Arthur Eddington, wrote quite forcibly about the contrast:

> I have settled down to the task of writing these lectures and have drawn up my chairs to my two tables. Two tables! Yes; there are duplicates of everything around me—two tables, two chairs, two pens. One of them has been familiar to me from earliest years. It is a commonplace of that environment which I call the world. How shall I describe it? It has extension; it is comparatively permanent; it is coloured; above all it is *substantial*. By substantial I do not merely mean that it does not collapse when I lean upon it; I mean that it is constituted of 'substance' and by that word I am trying to convey to you some conception of its intrinsic nature. It is a *thing*, not like space, which is a mere negation; nor like time, which is—Heaven knows what!
>
> Table No.2 is my scientific table. It is a more recent acquaintance and I do not feel so familiar with it. It does not belong to the world previously mentioned—the world that spontaneously appears around me when I open my eyes, though how much of it is objective and how much subjective I do not here consider. It is part of a world which in more devious ways has forced itself on my attention. My scientific table is mostly emptiness. Sparsely scattered in that emptiness are numerous electric charges rushing about with great speed; but their combined bulk amounts to less than a billionth of the bulk of the table itself. (Eddington, 1928, pp. xi-xii)

Some philosophers have found support here, in the fact that people can live with such conflicting views and to a degree accept both of them as objectively valid (reflect: does not the average citizen accept both the common-sense and the scientific accounts as valid?!), for the theory that there are not one or two, but many worlds. Phenomenologists devote attention to the fact that our frequently diverse interests and attitudes towards a particular reality can lead us to make from it two or more distinct objects. Each of them is then situated within larger conceptual frameworks of similarly motivated constructions, so that in the end we have several entire "worlds" distinct from one another. W. Luijpen explains:

> The worlds of the farmer, the professor, the revolutionary, the traveling salesman, the hermit, the politician, etc., are fundamentally very different because the modes in which these human beings stand in the world differ fundamentally from one another.
>
> Omitting provisionally the meaning of love and of history as standpoints, as well as the fundamentally diverse interests of the various sciences, we may offer a few very concrete examples. What is water for me? It is that which is regularly used for washing and drinking. Let us suppose however, that I love bathing. In this case water would show itself quite different to me. I would refer to it as 'the cooling waves.' If I were a fireman, water would again be something else—an extinguisher. I would never be

able to affirm this meaning if I did not know what a fire is and what is meant by extinguishing a fire. For a fisherman water is neither a cooling wave nor an extinguisher, for a fisherman faces water with a quite different intention, so that it has an entirely different meaning to him. Anyone who in wintertime has the misfortune to break through the ice and is carried underneath the frozen surface sees the most fearsome aspect water can show. No one, however, ever froze to death in 'the cooling waves.' Finally, to terminate with another arbitrary example, there is a single standpoint from which water is H^2O—namely, that of the chemist. One who asks water what it is by means of analytic techniques will receive the answer: H^2O. Outside this standpoint of the chemist, water, of course, is not just H^2O—just as water is not 'the cooling waves' for the non-bather or for one who refuses to place himself in the 'world-meaning' which constitutes being a bather. (W. Luijpen, 1960, pp. 31-32.)

It is not only in our diverse approaches to the world of physical reality that reflection discovers the existence of many "worlds," in addition to the one objective universe. When we turn to an individual's views of people, we discover the same phenomenon. To what extent do we know the reality of other people? Each of us has had sufficient experience of interpersonal relationships to have learned of the gulf that frequently exists between our concept of another person and his or her reality.

There has never before in history existed such an abundance of literature to document the thesis of epistemological dualism. Sociologists and psychologists have devoted much of their efforts to studying the subtle ways in which our largely subjective views of other people are habitually formed. And it is the subjective view, not the reality, which governs our response to others. One of the most striking illustrations of this is the case of lovers at the beginning and at the end of an affair. Initially willing to go to the ends of the earth for each other, they may later on refuse to go as far as the corner drug store. Interestingly enough, our emotions shape our constructions at the same time that they are shaped by those constructions. The loved one, as perceived by the lover, is largely the projection of an imaginary ideal generated by the sweet stirrings of passion, just as the subsequent, less flattering image of the other may be a caricature projected on the basis of wounded feelings, deep-seated grievances, and the like. But, whatever the explanation, our ideas of people are largely subjective, at odds with their inner reality, and this is one reason why we often disagree vehemently about the character and merits of the same individual.

But, although the reader may nod agreement when attention is focused on physical objects and other people, it may still come as a shock to discover how far our concepts of our own self may be from the objective reality. We might be reluctant to make the discovery, since our self-image is so vitally essential for us.

> We have noted . . . how important it is for individuals to see themselves as basically in control of their behavior—including their emotions, cognition, and

actions. Essential to this perception of self-control is the assumption that we have an integrated, consistent personality, a central core which represents our essential, unique nature. This "personality" provides a basis for perceiving a continuity of ourselves over time. We see meaning in present experiences in terms of frames of reference established in the past and we attach significance to them in terms of their likely future consequences. Situations change, time passes, even our attitudes and values may change, yet we hold firm to the belief that we are the same person throughout. It is this constancy of self which provides for most people a firm, reliable yardstick against which perceived change in the outer world is measured, interpreted, and evaluated. (Ruch-Zimbardo, P.582)

In spite of the importance of having an accurate self-image, there often exists such a discrepancy between one's idea of him—or herself and one's real self that psychoanalysts and philosophers have come to speak as if they were different selves altogether. William James for example, calls the real or objective self the "pure ego." It is looked upon by most psychologists as existing, for the most part, somewhere beneath the surface of consciousness. What we call our "self" is ordinarily only an image or concept that we construct in our mind, on the basis of our own intuitions and the feedback which we receive from others. Thus, in contrast to the "pure" ego, W. James speaks of various "empirical" ego's, the "material me," "the social me," and the "spiritual me." (Cfr. W. James, 1892, chapter 12)

The process by which the growing child develops an integrated concept of himself is a complex one. The process in some cases is never quite achieved and, in others, collapses under extreme stress. We obtain a better understanding of the difference between the objective or "pure" self and the self-concept that constitutes our "empirical" self by reflecting on this process as it occurs in human development. Fascinating accounts of it are available; see for instance, M.Sechehaye's *Autobiography of a Schizophrenic Girl*, or R.D. Laing's *The Divided Self*, and similar works.

All of this adds up to one conclusion: whether we are speaking of the world of material things, of other people, or of our very own self, modern research suggests that we must always distinguish between reality and appearance, between what things and people are and how we perceive them. Epistemological dualism attempts to account for the situation by maintaining that the appearances and perceptions are "within the mind," that they have to do with the psychic happenings which Jung says are the only objects of our immediate experience, and that the world of objective reality is distinct from and in many respects different from the world of appearances.

Interestingly enough, the world of appearances, the perceptions and concepts that individuals have of the things and people around them, are far more important to individuals than the world of objective reality. Some people dismiss subjective thoughts and perceptions with the phrase that they are "*mere* ideas" existing "only in the mind." Such an attitude is singularly naïve. The overwhelming truth of the matter is that what is most real to persons, "the" reality in terms of which they make their choices and direct the course of their lives, is not the objective world outside the perimeter of their consciousness, not the world as it is, but the world as it appears to them, their own subjective view of the world. The popular proverb, "What you don't know won't hurt you," gives a negative twist to this insight. Quite plainly, that which in no wise penetrates our consciousness is for us just as if it did not exist. (One must add of course, that it may someday enter our consciousness, so that our unawareness of something is no argument against its objective reality.) Similarly, something that exists only in our own consciousness will be completely real for us so long as we do not suspect that it exists only there. To illustrate: a man who walks into a crowded room, not realizing that the seat of his trousers is split, is not at all uncomfortable, whereas, on the contrary, a perfectly intact seam would not in the least lessen his discomfort if he *believed* his trousers were split in the seat.

Arguments: transition. More than enough has been said now to help readers understand that this text's Part One will stand as a challenge to their ordinary attitude toward the world. But this has been merely a sketch of the thesis that will be presented. What reasons or arguments are there sufficiently strong to persuade readers to renounce their comfortable, long entrenched belief that, when they open their eyes, what appears is the real world just as it is? What arguments are there to show that what immediately presents itself is a world within their own consciousness?

Section 2. Three Arguments for Representationalism.

Preface. It is to such reasons or arguments that we will now turn, in the main section of Part One. Three different lines of reasoning, about three different but related topics, will be presented. Each of the three will challenge some widely held fallacy, some conviction that would easily deserve the label "common sense." After the facts have been reviewed and the alternatives to common sense put forward, it will be seen that the three alternative views mesh into one overall argument in favor of epistemological dualism. The immediate implications of this will form the final section of Part One.

In order to reach a basically different orientation to our knowledge of reality, we are proposing to take the route of patient, intellectual analysis. Many of our contemporaries would suggest that the same goal can be arrived at much more quickly through the use of drugs. (See, for example, the books written by Carlos Castaneda.) In the long run, however, the route of understanding or critical reflection is more secure than the drug route. For one thing, it is a fact that psychedelic drug experience too often leads to tragic results to be anything better than a high-risk gamble. But there is an even more important reason. Whereas drugs induce a sudden leap from one world into another, leaving wholly unexplained (from the viewpoint of the user's subjective experience) the relation of the two, the person who patiently climbs the ladder of reasoned argument keeps that ladder intact as a connecting link between the different worlds, and can at will travel back and forth between them, knowing all the while what is going on. No one, to our knowledge, has argued so convincingly for the advantages of understanding as compared to drug-use as Jerome Lettvin in his widely-publicized debate with Timothy Leary before an MIT audience. (The debate is now available on the internet.)

Argument One.

Non-Sensory Objects

The predominance of non-sensory modes of consciousness and the special nature of their objects.

A gradual exposition. The project of becoming aware of the 'world' within the mind and its non-identity with objective reality is one that has several stages to it. The stages consist of a series of critical reflections or arguments. Each of these reflections must be pursued separately, and yet it will be found that they overlap in many essential areas. Often, the same argument will produce two (or more) important conclusions that are simply different sides of the same coin.

In fact, the following three arguments are intended to converge in the realization that the reality with which we are in immediate contact is a subjective reality and that this reality is distinct from objective reality. In a sense, it will be a process of coming to know that what we mis-took as a single reality is actually two.

Each argument will begin, as was emphasized earlier, by an examination of our common-sense, uncritical views. Philosophical and scientific discoveries, unlike the insights obtained from drug-induced or mystical or dream experiences, ordinarily come about in this manner. Many common-sense facts, accepted on the basis of ordinary experience, are brought together and examined for consistency. It is when they are found to be in contradiction with one another that a new theory is adopted which, it is hoped, will bring them into harmony. (Recall Kohler's remark, to the effect that scientists have found the naïve world "full of almost contradictory properties.") We can bring these remarks into line with the "two-world" metaphor by saying that it is only *by means of an 'internal critique,'* that is, by finding contradictions within the one-world view, that we learn of the existence of a second world within the mind.

The first argument will focus on showing that consciousness involves far more than simply seeing, hearing, touching, smelling and tasting—i.e., far more than simply sensing—and then on showing that the immediate objects of non-sensory consciousness have a remarkable property: they are independent of objective reality or extra-mental existence.

More than just sensing. Probably no one would argue seriously that consciousness consists entirely of sensing. Everyone has an immediate awareness of pleasure or pain, being contented or sad, loving, desiring, hating, being angry, remembering, imagining, speculating, and so forth. This acknowledgment of the existence of non-sensory modes or facets of consciousness is, in fact, part of our common-sense conception of ourselves. Why say, then, that a realization of it is a step which will help to detach a person from his or her common-sense view of things?

The reason is that most people, while acknowledging the existence of non-sensory cognition, fail to appreciate the fact that it constitutes a much greater part of cognitive experience than sensation does. And, failing this, they fail to notice the true nature of the *non-sensory objects*. It is not the admission that cognition involves more than simply sensation that is contrary to common sense; it is the consequence of this admission, viz., the unusual nature of the objects of non-sensory knowledge, that in many respects runs counter to common-sense assumptions.

Before speaking of the objects, however, it is first of all necessary to pause and become more aware of the predominance of the non-sensory facets of our cognitive experience. The average citizen, unless attention is drawn to it, makes the mistake of implicitly identifying human knowledge with sensation. The great philosopher, Plato, regarded this mistake as one which was so prevalent and so harmful to a true understanding of human knowledge that he devoted a large part of his dialogue, the *Theatetus*, to an argument demonstrating that there is more to knowledge than mere sense perception.

In fact, essential as sensing is, it constitutes a far smaller percentage of our total conscious experience than initially seems to be the case. In order to understand this better, we must devote some effort to distinguishing the different facets of experience. Experience *seems* to be a single, albeit complicated process. There are even some contemporary psychologists and philosophers who, in reaction to the tendency of their predecessors to perhaps overemphasize the distinctness of the various conscious functions, would like to argue that all such distinctions are misleading. (Cfr. for example, R. Firth, 1949-1950, pp. 204, ff.) Yet, even though we may agree with them that experience seems to be a single, unified whole and that the various functions are integrated into a unique kind of totality, the fact remains that it is not only proper but indispensable that we make distinctions.

Cognitive vs non-cognitive. To begin with, it is necessary to distinguish the cognitive from the non-cognitive functions of the mind. Remembering, imagining, and reasoning—as well as sensing—can be grouped together as cognitive functions, that is, they are forms of knowing, whereas pleasure, pain, contentment, sadness, loving and hating are types of affective or appetitive processes. The plain fact that we can know something without loving it or hating it is evidence enough for the assertion that the knowledge and the affective attitudes are somehow distinct.

Even within the area of cognitive functions, distinctions are easily recognized. Seeing and hearing are in some way distinct, otherwise there would be no difference between being blind and being deaf. (How they are distinct will be taken up later.) Our focus, however, is directed toward the distinction between sensing and the other cognitive functions of the mind. Plato used a rather easy argument to show that the mind has other powers than merely those of sight, hearing, touch, taste and smell. We are, he pointed out, able to understand the difference between sight and its objects, on the one hand, and hearing and its objects, on the other. Yet, it is not by any of the senses that we are able to determine this distinction. For instance, the distinction is not made by sight: the eye does not see both colors and sounds, is not aware of both seeing and hearing, yet to make the distinction between the two, it is first of all necessary to know and compare both. The same holds true for the other senses. The conclusion, therefore, is that some new, additional power of the mind must be acknowledged, since it is a fact of experience that we all do know the difference between sight and hearing. Without trying to be more specific about the matter, we can simply state that this new, additional power is non-sensory, distinct from any one of the kinds of sensation.

In order now to obtain a better appreciation of the fact that sensing makes up only a small fraction of the total bulk of our cognitive experience at most moments of our lives, let us reflect on what that experience would be like if it consisted entirely of sensing. To begin with, notice what it would be like if we had no *memory* to go along with sensing. We would be in the condition of newborn infants (or even younger fetuses, since it seems certain that the fetus begins to experience and remember while still in the womb). William James has compared this condition to that of being presented with "one big blooming buzzing confusion." (Cfr. W. James, 1892, p.29) Without memory, experience would consist of a stream of momentary, fleeting sensations. There would be no suspicion that objects were anything more than surfaces or shells, for by the time that we perceive the previously-unperceived back of an object, the just-sensed side is turned away. There would be no speech or music: we never actually hear more than a syllable of speech nor more than a single note or harmonious chord of music at a time, so that *all we would ever be aware of would be one syllable or note, then another, then another*. In addition, each thing that we sense would be for us entirely strange and unfamiliar: without memory, we would have nothing with which to compare or associate the present sensation. Pursue this line of reflection and soon you will realize that it is next to impossible even to imagine what an experience narrowed down to pure sensing would be like. Psychologists are correct in maintaining that such an experience rarely, if ever, occurs except at the earliest moments of life. Which is accounted for partially by the fact that memory plays an overwhelmingly large role in our experience.

What would experience be like, were it to consist only of sensing plus memory? Again, it would be quite difficult to visualize. Sensing deals only with the present, memory with the past. Yet our consciousness is also a large measure directed toward the future.

And most of our future will consist of encounters with events, objects, people, etc., which are new or different from what we have experienced in the past or are experiencing at the present moment. Our ability to *anticipate* and to cope with these new or different realities is possible only to the extent that we are capable of recognizing a likeness or similarity between them and the things we have previously experienced. What other way is there to explain why it is that we have known what to expect when we approach a complete stranger on the street in order to request directions to some destination? Why do we not ignore the stranger as we would a lamppost and, instead, ask directions of the small infant in the baby carriage or the dog walking beside it, neither of whom we have ever met before? Is it not obvious that the explanation lies in the fact that, even before we meet the stranger or the infant or dog, we already have formed something like general concepts of human adults, infants and dogs, and so are able to recognize these three beings whom we have never encountered before. Thus, it is not a question of remembering them—and having some idea how they will act or react.

Of course, memory is intimately associated with this ability to project the future, but even when that future involves encounters with familiar realities, there is more than just memory. For instance, no friend or acquaintance is ever exactly the same in the new encounter: their clothes are different, their physical features may be somewhat different, their conversation is about new topics, and yet we are able to cope with these novelties because our concepts even of familiar objects incorporate more than just exact reproductions of previous encounters with them. It includes a thick margin of possibilities, so long as these are consistent with the general concept under which our mind files them.

Furthermore, this ability to orient ourselves toward an unsensed and unremembered future includes a creative faculty of mind. The architect who designs a radically new and different kind of edifice, the artist whose novel style initiates a change in trends, the writer composing a work of fiction—all of these exemplify this power of creativity by conceiving and planning things which never existed before. Yet these are only the extreme examples: each of us calls upon our creative abilities whenever we plan for the next day or even when we simply daydream.

It would be possible to go on and on with facts that demonstrate the predominance of non-sensory over sensory mind functioning, but we will limit ourselves to one final reflection. Mention was made earlier about the mind's power to form *general concepts*. It is this power to form general abstract concepts and to reason logically with them that accounts for one of the most significant features of our contemporary world: science and scientific technology. Such science is possible only because the mind has the power to go beyond the maze of apparently order-less phenomena perceived by the senses and recorded by the memory in order to detect hidden patterns and regularities. Galileo and Newton did not make their momentous discoveries because they sensed things that no one else had ever sensed before. They made them, in large measure, because their minds were able to recognize non-sensible relations between things that no one previously had recognized. They were able to compare, to (mentally) look beyond surface differences, and detect similarities, to form abstract concepts of gravitation, motion, acceleration, momentum, force, and the like, etc.

Reflection on these matters should lead to a much more balanced estimate of the relative parts that the non-sensory modes of consciousness play in our cognitive experience. Sensing may still be regarded as basic. It is required to trigger off the other activities; a person perpetually deprived of sensation would, in our present human condition, never attain consciousness at all. In addition, sensing is constantly needed if we are to have the clues necessary for knowing our environment and how to respond to it. But for mature consciousness, sensing makes up only a small percentage of what goes on within the mind.

We turn now to the more important consideration of this section, namely, the remarkable fact that the objects of non-sensory cognitive experience are independent of objective, extra-mental existence. By this is meant that, once we have acquired certain ideas or concepts, they lead a life of their own with respect to the world of objective reality. Our ideas of trees, rivers, mountains, planets, other people, and the like, *once we possess them*, no longer require the physical existence of trees, rivers, mountains, planets, or other people in order to exist.

Before proceeding, it is only fair to warn the beginner in philosophy that much controversy surrounds this issue. This is the case, however, with practically every philosophical position a person may hold. Not that this is a great secret. Philosophers are notorious for disagreeing about everything. The warning is mentioned here because the existence and nature of mental objects has been a subject of particularly vigorous disagreement in twentieth century philosophy.

Bypassing these controversies for the present, then, we will present a positive argument for the statement that there are objects of non-sensory cognitive experience which are independent of the objective world. The objects discussed here are images and concepts. (An important note. Later on, it will be argued that our knowledge of concepts might much more properly be understood as knowledge of meanings, propositions, or complete thoughts. But this further understanding requires a sophistication that the reader perhaps lacks at present. Even if talk of mental concepts is somewhat simplistic, however, much of what is said of their type of existence can be transferred later to meanings and propositions. End of note.)

Bipolarity, intentionality. Consider, once again, non-sensory cognition. Remembering, imagining, and conceptualizing are like sensing, in that they never occur unless they have an object. We cannot remember, imagine or conceptualize without remembering, imagining, or conceptualizing *something*, just as we cannot sense without sensing *something*. This is what is meant by the statement that cognitive activities are *bipolar* or *intentional*. They are *bipolar* or two-poled. That is, the cognitive *act*, one of the poles, is always accompanied by an *object*, the other pole. To say that they are *intentional* does not mean that they are deliberate, but that they are always directed at some object. (The Latin word "intendere" means, among other things, "to tend or stretch towards.") Whenever remembering or imagining or conceptualizing occurs, one will find a remembered, imagined, or conceptualized object. Act and object, though distinct, are intimately related.

Notice the special kind of reality possessed by *the objects of non-sensory cognition*, however. Once we have come to know them, they no longer require any support from the external, objective world. Someone might wish to qualify this by insisting that they at least require the existence of the mind which knows them and that the mind itself is a part of the objective world. A discussion of this point would involve us in another recurring controversy: do ideas depend on individual minds or do they have some unsuspected objective reality of their own? The common-sense view is that they depend on individual minds, and this view will form part of the basis for the arguments in the following section. For the present, the controversy does not affect our argument that, at any rate, their existence does not require the existence of the concrete, physical world of rivers and mountains, forests and lakes, etc.

The key to an appreciation of this fact lies in an understanding of the difference between non-sensory cognition and what we ordinarily take to be the nature of sensation. Most people believe—and it is one of the most difficult common-sense convictions to shake—that when we see, hear, touch, smell or taste, the object of that experience is some physical reality (and/or its sensible qualities) belonging to the world external to the perceiver. Do we not instinctively feel that, when we pick up an apple and eat it, it is a physical apple that we see, feel, taste, and smell, and that it is the sound made by the crunch of our teeth into the apple that we hear? Combined with this common-sense view is the conviction that the apple, prior to our eating of it, had an objective existence of its own. Let us sum up the situation as most of us initially understand it: the object of sense experience is a physically existing, extra-mental object. *No third intervening entity* comes between the act of sensing and the physical object.

Prior to serious reflection on the subject, people tend to believe, for the most part, that the same holds true for the non-sensory modes of cognition and their objects. When we remember, we seldom question the fact that what we remember is the same physical reality that we previously sensed. When we imagine or picture something to ourselves, we rarely pause to note that we often (usually?) imagine or picture something that does not exist except in our own minds. And the same thing happens when we conceptualize: we ordinarily do not ask whether what we are thinking of exists in the physical world or only in our own mind, and very often we would give the first answer if we did ask.

On the contrary, the thesis here is that, in many instances, what we are dealing with cannot be objective reality. Furthermore, a simple experiment will show that in the remaining instances, *even when we are dealing with objective reality, it is only indirectly*. There always is present a subjective object and it is this which is known directly.

Consider the *objects of memory*. What is it that we remember, after we have eaten the apple? It cannot be the apple, since it no longer exists. If there is an object for our memory, that is, unless we conclude that what we are remembering is nothing, then it is apparent that the object in this case must be something that does not exist physically in the external world. This conclusion rests on another of our robust common-sense convictions, namely, the belief that the only real, physical apples are the ones that exist in the here and now.

One may attempt to escape the admission that what we are remembering is not a physical apple by asserting that we do remember the physical apple, that is, the apple that did exist—and did exist physically. Here we might embark on a long debate about time, plus memory and its objects. It will have to suffice for the present to insist that, according to common sense, the only things that exist are things that exist now, in the present. It is absurd to believe that the objective universe is actually a string of changeless worlds, each constituting one moment in time—including, therefore, the world of five minutes ago before I ate the apple, other worlds corresponding to each bite I took from the apple, and the present world in which the apple no longer exists—and that each of them, after waiting for eons in the limbo of the future, momentarily has the spotlight of "now-ness" thrown upon it and then remains forever afterwards in the shadow of the past.

If that highly imaginative view is rejected, as this author believes it must be, we may return to the common-sense notion that the only objective, physical universe in which the apple (which did exist but now has been eaten) could possibly be found is the universe that physically exists here and now, and it is certain that the apple that did exist cannot be found in it. This does not simplify the task of determining what actually is the nature of the object of our memory, except that it does support the position taken here, that that object is *not* part of the external, physical universe. More importantly, nothing that happens in that physical universe can affect the subjective existence of our remembered apple, unless, as was mentioned earlier, it is something that happens to our mind and its ability to remember. (Anyone interested in pursuing further the nature of time—past, present, and future—may consult R. Gale, 1967.)

Understand what is being said here. When it is claimed that the object of memory is *independent of physical reality*, this does not mean that it did not at one time depend on physical reality in order to become a remembered object. It means that it is *now* independent of the physical reality that exists *now*. One of the usual arguments for the existence of an external physical world is that the world within the mind requires an original cause and that this cause must be the external physical world itself. This is not an unimportant matter, but it is not relevant to the issue at hand. We are not inquiring into the origin of the world of memory and thought, but into its present mode of existence.

This independence possessed by the objects of memory in relation to the present physical universe is easily seen to carry over to the *objects of imagination*. A good example of imagining is the practice of fantasizing. We can create the wildest fantasies, we can daydream to our heart's content, without ever worrying that the real world will in any way affect our fantasies or daydreams. Our experience of reality may change our desire to fantasize, it may cause us to indulge in different daydreams, but so long as we *desire* to entertain our original fantasies and daydreams, they will be there for us to entertain. This power of fantasy is closely associated with our anticipations of the future. In fact, the chief difference between imagining and anticipating the future may be largely one of terminology, except for the added fact that in trying to anticipate the future we attempt to rely more closely on memory and to tailor our anticipations to what we can realistically expect to happen. However that may be—and, admittedly, these few remarks merely scratch the surface of another complex subject—the important fact is that, at any given moment, the objects of our fantasies and anticipations of the future do not physically exist. They exist in our mind.

What about the *objects of thinking* as opposed to remembering, imagining or anticipating? These latter may not be as distinct from "mere" thinking as our discussion has led us to believe. They may not be distinct at all, except perhaps from the point of view of their objects. We do speak, for instance, of thinking about the past (remembering) and thinking about the future (anticipating) and thinking about castles in the air (imagining). Nevertheless, the aim here is not to delve at length into the precise nature of different non-sensory cognitive processes, but rather to show that their objects are independent of or—to put it another way—indifferent to physical existence. Now it is a fact that most of us instinctively believe that when we are *thinking about present reality* as opposed to remembering, etc., it is the actual physical world that is the object of our immediate awareness.

The first step in subjecting this belief to critical scrutiny involves a restatement of the difference between sensing and thinking. They are not the same thing. We may be seeing the apple in our hand, but our thinking may or may not be directed at the apple. We may be thinking about the football game that is on television in the next room or about the high price the supermarket down the street is demanding for apples. Suppose that we are thinking of the apple itself, though. The question is: accepting for the present the validity of our conviction that we directly *sense* the physical apple, is it also the immediate object of our *thinking* about it? Most likely, our initial answer will be an affirmative one.

Two experiments, one actual and one imaginary, should help to undermine this answer and to replace it with the answer that, although we can think about physical reality, it is an indirect object, the immediate object of thought being one which is indifferent to physical existence.

First, *the actual experiment*. Two persons are required, as well as a table, a lighted candle, an ashtray, and a small piece of paper. One person is asked to look at the piece of paper and to think about it. Then he is asked to close his eyes, while continuing to think of the same piece of paper. The only difference is that, whereas in the first moment he was both seeing and thinking about the paper, in the second moment he is only thinking about it. The object of the thinking appears identical in the two cases: whatever he could think about the paper with his eyes open he can think just as easily with his eyes closed. That is, he can think of the paper's being white, being thin, about its being something a person can write on, etc. The object, it appears, is still the piece of paper on the table before him.

But is it? If the second person noiselessly lights the paper with the burning candle flame and lets it turn to ashes in the ashtray, what happens? Although there is no longer any piece of paper, but only some ashes, does this in any way affect the first person's thinking or what is consciously present to his mind? On the condition that he has not heard any suspicious sounds and is completely unaware of what has transpired, his conscious experience will be completely unaffected by the change in the paper, and he will continue to believe that what he is thinking about is the same piece of paper that he began thinking about. Yet it is impossible for him to be thinking of the actual paper on the table, since there is no paper on the table to be thinking of. What *is* this object of which he is thinking now? Certainly it is a puzzling kind of object, but at least it can be described in negative terms: it is an object which does not exist physically, it is an object which cannot be seen or touched, and it is an object which will not be changed so long as he wishes to continue thinking about it.

The important issue, of course, is whether or not the immediate object of the person's thinking changed when the physical piece of paper was burned. Working backwards, we first ask whether the object that he was thinking of with his eyes shut, while the piece of paper was on the table, is the same object he is thinking of after the paper was ignited and placed in the ashtray. The answer is that, if the object was initially the physical piece of paper but later was some nonphysical object, *this cannot be proven by the person's own experience*. In fact, since he will never be able to tell at what point the physical object was replaced by the non-physical one, his personal experience is a far stronger argument for the theory that even at the outset the immediate object of his thinking was non-physical. Certainly it is non-physical in the later period, if the observations concerning memory were correct. And, since his personal experience seems to indicate that the object before and after the burning was identical, then even during the earlier period the object was non-physical. Going yet further backwards, we must either contend that the immediate object of thought changed when he closed his eyes, which does not seem to be the case once one has learned to distinguish clearly between sensing and thinking, or else submit to the same argument as before: even with his eyes open, the immediate object of his *thinking* was non-physical.

Additional facts tend to strengthen the latter argument. For example, there are the facts of perceptual illusion. A flat, rough-surfaced piece of plastic might have been used in place of the paper. If the subject were told that this was a piece of paper, he unquestionably would have believed it. In such a situation, the object of his thinking will have been something not physically real, namely, "the piece of paper on the table." The object of his sensing would be one thing (the piece of plastic), the object of his thinking another (the non-physically-existent piece of paper). The strongest fact of all, however, is one which will be taken up in the third argument for epistemological dualism, the argument that not even sensing gives us direct access to physical reality. Even the white rectangular-shaped object that presents itself when the person's eyes are open and directed towards the piece of paper (or plastic) exists only within his consciousness. That argument must be postponed until later.

The imaginary experiment which, following tradition, we will call a "thought experiment" is the following. With your eyes open, think about the world presently beyond reach of your senses. For someone sitting in a room, reading these lines, this means thinking about the other rooms in the house or building, the other buildings in the vicinity, the open lawns and gardens and trees and fields surrounding these buildings, one's absent friends and acquaintances, etc. Imagine that—whatever hypothetical explanation might be dreamed up for the catastrophe—everything in the physical universe except what is within reach of one's senses at this moment is suddenly annihilated. Again, on the condition that one has no intimation of the disaster, one's thoughts about all those previously real and unseen but now annihilated rooms, buildings, lawns, gardens, etc., will be utterly unchanged. Apart from those objects for whose existence one has present sensible evidence, there is not one single thing in the physical universe for whose existence he can have absolute certainty. That is, so long as there is nothing in his present sense experience to contradict it, it is conceivable that any one of those objects whose silent annihilation (if such a thing is possible) or whose non-silent destruction (provided the destruction is far enough away) no longer physically exists. With respect to any of these thoughts, therefore, the object will be indifferent to physical existence for the same reasons as before. Once we have acquired knowledge of anything, our thinking about that object does not depend on the facts of objective reality. Nor does the object of such thinking, if we are correct in believing that thinking always has an object, depend on objective reality.

The above facts, obvious upon the slightest reflection, can be multiplied indefinitely. Do you want to know whether the U.S. president is alive. Thinking of him—as you just did—would prove that he is still alive, i.e., has not been assassinated in the last five minutes, would prove it, IF what you are directly conscious of is the president rather than a concept or thought. Is your car still in the parking lot where you left it, as opposed to its having been stolen and then 'totaled' in an accident? If you're directly aware of it rather than your idea or concept of it, just try to think of it, and that will give you your answer. Does God exist? Santa? Etc.

The arguments given above have a limited objective. They deal directly with the objects of non-sensory cognition. Nothing said thus far is incompatible with the conviction that our senses provide us with direct and unmediated awareness of the physical world. The arguments deal only with *the immediate objects of non-sensory cognition.* Furthermore, no denial is made that, in addition to its immediate objects, non-sensory cognition allows us to know objective reality indirectly, that is, through the non-sensory objects known directly. Above all, the arguments in no way lead logically to the view that there is no objective reality or that objective reality is never, in some sense, similar to or like our subjective reality.

It is necessary to underline these last points. Recall that all of our arguments begin with common sense. It is certainly one of the most solid convictions of common sense that there is an objective universe. Now, as was pointed out in the preceding paragraph, none of the arguments so far affects the conviction that *sensation* gives us direct access to objective reality. Furthermore, a little reflection will show that, ultimately, the strongest of the above arguments presuppose that there is an objective universe, for it is precisely the discrepancy which common sense discovers between (what we believe about) objective reality and the objects of one's immediate non-sensory experience that leads to the conclusion that the two are distinct. For instance, it was our ability to remember the apple we have eaten even though the objective world is now minus that apple that was the basis for the first argument. It is the common-sense conviction that the golden palace of our daydreams as well as the still unrealized future nowhere exists in the actual world that led to the second argument. And it is the conflict between the objective change of paper to ashes and the lack of change in the object of immediate experience that gave force to the other argument.

Although one contends that such facts support the thesis that the immediate objects of remembering, imagining, and thinking are nonphysical, it is still possible to argue that, *when these objects match objective reality*, we know both them and objective reality. This is one facet of the philosophical position labeled "representationalism." (The other facet pertains to the nature of sense knowledge.) According to representationalism, the objects of thought are—in some mysterious and perhaps impossible-to-fully-define manner—representations or likenesses of reality. This theory has a long and distinguished philosophical ancestry. It has also given rise to the usual multitude of disagreements, qualifications, refinements, and distinctions that one familiar with the history of philosophy would expect. One controversy focuses on the exact meaning of "match" when it is a said that, to some extent, the nonphysical object of *thought matches objective reality*. Another controversy centers on how to use the terms "direct" and "indirect" when speaking of the contact between non-sensory cognition and its objects

Without going into the matter of propositions (though, as noted above, it the only satisfactory way of dealing with the objects of intellectual cognition*), it can be said that a large portion of traditional philosophy explains the nonphysical objects of knowledge in terms of images and concepts. The difference between these latter is important. (*See Appendix B)

Images versus concepts. The word "image" is comparatively easy to grasp. For our purposes, *an image can be defined as a reproduction or copy of a sensed object.* For instance, after looking at an apple or piece of paper, we can close our eyes and in our memory or imagination—here, it matters little which we choose—reproduce or picture for ourselves what we just saw. This reproduction is an image. Images are not restricted to visual impressions, however. We can also reproduce in our imagination faint echoes of sounds we have heard, we can recreate smells, tastes, and tactile sensations.

Images, however, are distinct from concepts. The best introduction to the notion of a concept or idea would be one of the standard discussions indexed under the heading, "Universal Concepts." Many philosophers have argued that all concepts are universal concepts.

(i) Mention was made earlier of the mind's power to generalize. Consider, for instance, the idea of an apple. After we have had sensory contact with many different individual apples, for instance, we form a general concept of apple. This is possible because we can compare the different apples we have seen and eaten and learn to isolate those factors which they have in common from those features peculiar to different individuals. Our concept of apple will specify that it is a fruit which is somewhat round, firm, white on the inside, and edible: it will not specify exactly the color of the outside (except that it probably will be green, yellow, or red) nor the size (though here again, there are limits), nor the exact taste. We can think and talk about apples without including any but the first set of specifications, and—when we do—we have before our mind the concept of apple. That this idea or universal concept is distinct from any image is sometimes argued on the grounds that an image, being the reproduction of a sense impression, must always include these particular specifications of color, size, etc. Because we have seen only green or yellow or red apples, we can imagine only green, yellow, or red apples, not—as in the case of our universal concept of an apple—an apple of no particular color. Or, if—as many believe—there are vague images (e.g., of apples with no specified color) we can introduce other arguments for the distinction.

(ii) Rene Descartes used the argument that when we try to form an image of solid figures, we cannot go very far before our powers of imagination give out. For instance, although we may be able to form an *image* of a three-sided figure which is notably different from our image of a four-sided figure, this becomes more difficult when it is a case of a nine-sided figure relative to a ten-sided one, and by the time that we reach a 999-sided and a 1000-sided figure we are probably producing nothing more than identical roughly-rounded images.

This is in contrast to our *concepts*: there is not the least confusion in our mind that when we are thinking about a 999-sided figure, we are thinking of something quite distinct from a 1000-sided one. The imaged figures are the same, the thought-about ones are distinct. Conclusion? Images and concepts are distinct.

(iii) Additional ammunition comes from the fact that we seem able to have concepts of things that are entirely unimaginable, such as moral goodness, justice, human rights, laws, and the like. If these cannot be sensed, and if images are reproductions of sensations, it follows that when we think of such things, we are not thinking of images. Other, more sophisticated arguments may be omitted here.

It can now be understood why there is a question concerning how the nonphysical objects match physical realities. In the case of images, we say that there is a likeness, that the images are copies of the things we have sensed. They are also unlike, however. The physical object is precisely that, physical. It is (often) solid, tangible, accessible to everyone, has an existence outside our mind, etc., whereas the image has none of these features. When it comes to concepts, the likeness is of an entirely different nature. The best attempt to explain the match in this case was that provided by the scholastics who utilized Aristotle's theories of form and act. Perhaps the easiest way to deal with the idea here is to say that a true thought is one that (vaguely, in some way) 'corresponds' to reality. (E.g. consult J. Maritain, 1959, chap. lll, J. Royce, 1961, chap. 11; R. P. Phillips, 1950, vol. I; etc.) Whether one is speaking of images or concepts as the objects of non-sensory cognition, it is clear that these, being nonphysical entities within the mind, are in some manner *distinct* from physical realities outside the mind; "distinct" here means that they constitute two sets of entities.

The other controversy centers around the meaning of "direct" and "indirect" or around "immediate" and "mediate." It is maintained here that the objects of direct or immediate non-sensory cognition are not external realities but nonphysical ones. Some philosophers, notably the scholastics, argue that—although in other respects their position is similar to the usual forms of representationalism, at least insofar as they acknowledge, in addition to physical realities, nonphysical or mental images and concepts—the evidence demands that the mediate and immediate objects are exactly the reverse of what is stated here. Not all of the objectors use the same terminology, but this is entirely subordinate to the major issue that can be stated in a fairly clear manner as follows. *According to their objection, experience proves that it is the external, objective world that is known first of all and therefore, directly or immediately.*

Initially, the argument for this objection sounds impressively convincing. It is beyond question and as clear as daylight that the infant or child is, *or seems to be*, aware of his mother, her breast, the crib, his playthings, his own body, long before—*long* before!—it is ever aware of images and concepts or realizes that there are such things as images and concepts. Nor is it only infants and children whose experience seems to confirm the argument that we know reality directly or first of all and ideas (concepts) only later or indirectly by means of an arduous process of reflection. For instance, there are relatively few adults who are not extremely vague about what an idea is, and it certainly seems that we as adults ordinarily think directly about reality and not about our own ideas.

Moreover, philosophers, even after a great deal of reflection on images and concepts, express strong disagreement among themselves not only about the nature, but even the existence of images and concepts. This last fact, the argument runs, seems to reinforce the view that we know reality much better and more directly than mental images and concepts, for, if we were immediately aware of the latter, then we would expect much less disagreement about their nature and existence.

To do full justice to this debate would require volumes. It is this author's frank opinion that the nature of human knowledge involves such difficulty that, even after surveying all of the explanations that previous generations of philosophers have given on the subject, one is left with the conviction that none of them are adequate. So many paradoxes emerge that knowledge must be declared something of a mystery—however distasteful we rationalists may find the word "mystery."

Ideas-as-thought-objects. Yet, there is a crucial distinction that can be introduced at this juncture which not only will provide the reader with a better insight into the complexities of human knowledge and into the two-world theory, but will also serve as a very simple answer to the above objection. First of all, the debate really centers around concepts, so we will dispense here with images. Secondly, we will use the term "idea" in place of "concept." The distinction, then, is this: when we say that ideas, not objective realities, are the objects of our immediate non-sensory awareness, *this must be taken to mean ideas-as-thought-objects, not ideas-as-ideas.*

What philosophers call ideas or concepts are unusual entities, and to speak with any kind of consistency about them it is necessary to look at them from two very different angles. i) When we speak of them as ideas (ideas-as-ideas), we are looking at them from the point of view that they exist in the mind and are distinct from or indifferent to objective, physical reality. From this point of view, they are alike: they are all equally in the mind, etc. ii) But we can also look at them from the point of view of what is frequently called, in metaphorical terms, their "content", and here they are different from one another: one is the idea of an apple, another is the idea of a piece of paper, another is the idea of a mountain, etc. We will call them, when they are spoken of from this point of view, "ideas-as-thought-objects".

A comparison may help. Three wood carvings, one representing a man, another representing a dog, the third representing a boat, may be viewed from the same two angles: from one angle, they are all alike, i.e. wood carvings, while from the aspect of the objects represented they are distinct. Epistemological dualism does not contend that we first become aware of ideas *as ideas.* The scholastics are correct: many people go to their graves never suspecting that the ideas of which they are aware are ideas. Rather, the two-world view maintains that we are aware of ideas *as thought-objects.* These we ordinarily MIS-take to be physical objects, not realizing their true nature. Most people, faced with the piece-of-paper-experiment will confidently assert, after the paper has been burnt, that what they are thinking about is the same (physical) piece of paper they saw lying on the table a moment earlier. Only a wary philosopher would hesitate to make this assertion. But the fact remains that what such a person is thinking about cannot be a physical reality, since the entire physical universe can be searched without that piece of paper being found. This negative fact, that the object of thought in this case—if there is an object, as we have agreed to believe—is not something physical, is the first meaning of the statement that the immediate object of thought is an idea. But it is an idea ordinarily taken—or MIS-taken—to be a physical reality.

From this point on, the objects of our immediate non-sensory intellectual awareness will be regularly called "thought-objects", since this designation can be understood as combining the two facets of ideas or concepts. They will also be referred to, in conformity with twentieth-century philosophy that has been influenced by the theories of Brentano and Husserl (who were, in turn, influenced by earlier scholastic theories), as "intentional objects."

Further obscurities will be left untouched for the present. Once more, for instance, we will not go into the theory that it is more proper to treat the object of intellectual cognition as propositions rather than as concepts. Such a discussion might make it necessary to revise somewhat what has been said till now about remembering, imagining, and thinking.

Terminology. Before concluding this first argument in favor of the two-world thesis, a final paragraph may be helpful for interpreting such terms as "real," "physical," "subjective," and the like. Only one rule can be given: look to the context in determining the meaning of such terms. More will be said later on about the absolute necessity that exists for the reader to interpret the two-world view from his own personal standpoint, but the effort to do so must be made from the outset.

For instance, the phrase "outside the mind" must be read as meaning "outside *your* (the reader's) mind." The "objective" universe is, therefore, the universe outside your (the reader's) mind, just as "subjective" reality refers to what is inside your (the reader's) mind. (Is it necessary to add the obvious, but extremely important qualification that "subjective" as used here does not mean—as it does in other contexts—"an idea that is groundless or even false," but only that it exists in the mind of the subject who is doing the knowing?) One can see, therefore, that *what is subjective reality for one person constitutes part of another person's objective world.* (That is, my mind and its thought-objects are outside your mind.)

The term "physical" is particularly equivocal. At times it may mean "material" or "corporeal," in contrast to "immaterial" or "mental." At other times, it is used somewhat synonymously with "objective," to signify that reference is being made to actual reality outside and independent of one's mind.

Lastly, it should be understood without difficulty that to say that something is real may sometimes mean that it exists, not in someone's mind, but in the objective universe, whereas at other times it may merely mean that it exists—period!—whether in the mind or outside it. My dreams may be unreal or merely fictitious or purely imaginary insofar as nothing in objective reality corresponds to them, but from another angle they are very real: dreams really do occur and my dreams are real ones.

Summary. The purpose of these pages is to show reason for the assertion that, though there is a world of objective reality that we can learn about, the primary reality for each of us or the "world" of our immediate experience is a "world" within our own minds. This inner world is constituted partly, in terms of this first argument, of images and thought-objects. This inner world of images and thought-objects is not some thin, tenuous, bloodless affair. On the contrary, it is so real that for the most part we mistake it for the physical world itself, not realizing that they are distinct. For us, it is *more*, not less, real than the physical world. This inner world is built up gradually in our minds as our experience increases. The construction process may go astray, as when we form distorted ideas of the physical universe, of other people, even of our own "self." But, until now, we can assume that, thanks to the fact that we have senses in addition to our memory, imagination, and intellect, we can always check by a direct sense observation to see that our inner world conforms to objective reality. The above reflections should aid, however, in becoming more aware of the inner world, despite the fact that many of the reflections demand an effort to think "abstractly"—meaning by this an effort to think about things that are invisible and intangible. Even more help in discovering the inner world will be found in the second and third arguments or sets of reflections. (Have you heeded the 'Instruction'?)

Till now, our objective has been to distinguish between subjective and objective reality, between things as-they-exist-in-the-mind and things as-they-exist-in-themselves. The point of making this distinction is to lay the groundwork for arguing that we have direct access only to things as they exist in the mind or to things as thought-objects.

But our world of thought-objects is an enormously rich one, containing as it does such things as rivers, forests, cities, sun, moon, stars and the like, but also Santa Claus, Romeo and Juliet, mermaids and a host of other, similar things, in sum, every single item which we can presently remember, fantasize about, or create by dreaming it up. There are those thought-objects that we take to be "real", those we label "merely imaginary," and those which we classify as "doubtful." How are we to account for this very important fact in the context of representationalism or epistemological dualism? We do it by making an important distinction . . .

Fact: We understand more than we believe. *Having an idea of something vs assenting to the thing's existence.* The easiest way is to take note of the obvious difference we experience between merely forming an idea of something on the one hand, and assenting to or withholding assent from the thing on the other hand.

1. *Forming an idea . . . being aware of . . .* The mind originally, at birth, is apparently blank, empty. Then gradually we acquire or form ideas about things. We may form ideas on the basis—so it seems—of direct sense experience of things, such as rivers, forests, or the like. We

may also form ideas of things on the basis of what others tell us. Such seem to be our ideas of distant lands, people with whom we have no acquaintance, events from the past, etc. Or we may form ideas of things for ourselves, in our dreams or fantasies. Of these there is no end. By the time we begin to reflect on epistemological questions, our once-empty minds are filled with countless worlds of thought-objects.

2. *Role of assent.* We do not merely have ideas, however, we also have convictions about them: we assent to some, withhold our assent from others, or adopt a doubtful attitude to others. What does this amount to except the following? In the case of those things we assent to, that is, in the case of those things we regard as "real", we judge that the ideas in our mind are matched by objective counterparts in the real world outside our mind. For example, to say that the sun and moon are "real for me" is to say that I believe that, not only do I have ideas of the sun and moon in my mind, but there exist objects outside my mind corresponding to those ideas. In the case of Santa Claus, Romeo and Juliet, mermaids, and similar "unreal (for me)" or "merely imaginary" objects, i.e., things from which I withhold my assent (concerning their existence), I judge that the ideas which obviously exist in my mind are not matched by anything in the objective world. In the case of "doubtful" things, I lack evidence or reasons to make the judgement that my ideas are matched by anything outside my mind. P.S. Descartes, in *Meditation Three*, made great use of this distinction.

Once the crucially important difference between merely having an idea of something and making a judgment about its existence (i.e., about the existence of an objective counterpart to the subjective idea) is grasped, it is clear in what sense we have some control in "making our own reality." By assenting to the (objective) existence of something, it becomes "real" for us, whereas by withholding that assent we render it "unreal" or "merely imaginary" for ourselves. In fact, we spend much of our lives shifting things from one status category to another. As a child, Santa Claus was part of "reality (for me)", but later experience led me to relegate it to the category of "unreal (for me)" or "fictitious". Some ideas are such that we spend a lifetime trying to make up our minds about: God, the soul, UFO's, life on other planets, etc. But, regardless of objective reality, the things we assent to become 'real' for us, while those things we refrain from assenting to are excluded from reality for us.

Argument Two.

Language

The privacy of the inner world is shown by the fact that ideas are not transmitted by language.

Preface. This next section will concentrate on an analysis of language. How critically important the subject of language is can be grasped by reflecting on the fact that the knowledge each new generation inherits from an earlier generation is supposedly 'passed on' or 'transmitted' via language. At least that is our customary way of thinking.

The first part of this analysis will consist of an attempt to distinguish the different kinds of entities that are referred to in global fashion as "language," and to situate them in their relationships to each other and to the rest of reality. Parts two and three will then be devoted to a defense of two other theses with respect to language. The overall aim of the section will be to reinforce the reader's awareness of his or her own inner world and of the degree to which it is his or her own and no one else's.

Because the focus here is limited, many facets of language either will not be mentioned at all or will be treated only in an abbreviated manner. Anthropologists, grammarians, linguists, translators, psychologists, and others have all conducted extensive, enlightening and interesting research on this complex subject, and it has been one of the predominant topics of debate among twentieth-century philosophers. What is discussed in this section relates both directly and indirectly to these other researches and will be presupposed when some of them are taken up in later parts of our inquiry into the nature of the human person. For our present purposes, however, attention will be focused on two questions: "What is language?" and "Is language the source of ideas?"

First thesis. *"Language" refers to different realities*. To begin with, we are able to situate it in the context of the previous reflections. According to the two-world view, there is a world of objective reality, consisting—according to common sense—of rivers and forests, trains and skyscrapers, animals, people, etc. In addition, each of us has an inner world within our own mind, consisting at least partially of the images and ideas that, we hope, in some way match those objective realities. As long as we speak in such a context, we can then view language—especially spoken or written language, consisting of individual words—as signs or symbols whereby we communicate to each other our ideas about realities. Thus, an apple is an objective reality to which there corresponds our idea of an apple, and we have the word "apple" which serves among English-speaking people as the symbol for that reality and that idea.

This is an extremely simplified approach to a complex subject and one that has been challenged by many philosophers. Yet, *the three-fold distinction between reality, thought, and language* fits quite nicely into the common-sense view of things and is the only suitable way of setting the stage for the further, more difficult questions.

That objective reality is distinct from both our ideas of that reality and the language which we use to communicate those ideas is basic to the common-sense outlook. We regard objective reality as "being there" independently of our knowledge of it. Presumably, the universe existed long before any humans were present to think or talk about it, just as it exists now and is what it is regardless of how we think or talk about it.

Then, too, our ideas are distinct from our language. The major objections to this assertion come from those who deny the existence of ideas or concepts or anything like them in the first place. This is not the place to defend the contention that ideas or something like them do exist. What was discussed in the previous section must suffice for the time being as warrant for that contention.

Once such a contention is agreed to, however, the distinction between thought and language presents no great difficulties. We need only survey the various groups of people who think and speak, and note that, although these groups speak very different languages, they think enough alike that they can communicate through the mediumship of translators. The point can be illustrated with rather simple examples: though the English, French, Germans, and Italians make use of different words to symbolize the color red (those words are, respectively, "red," "rouge," "rot," and "rosso"), there is no reason to doubt that the idea which one group forms of that color is any different from the ideas formed by the other groups. If thought-objects (ideas) and language were identical, then either these groups should all use the same word (since their ideas are the same) or else they should have different ideas (since the words are different).

It is necessary to add that people's general conceptualizations of things—particularly when it is a question of less tangible realities, such as time, the soul, the deity—do often differ, so that translation from one language to another cannot always be so straightforward as in the instance of the color red, yet there is no evidence that their concepts are not often identical when it is a question of simple, concrete realities. That sentences made from contemporary languages can be found which will symbolize the same thoughts (even highly abstract ones) expressed in such different and long-unused languages as Sanskrit, Aramaic, Hebrew, etc., is the basic assumption underlying the life-endeavors of many scholars.

More importantly, perhaps, the realization that thought and language differ is essential even when the parties to the communication process speak the same language. Many arguments revolve around the fact that people can use the same word or phrase to mean different things (i.e. to express different thoughts). Such arguments are more verbal than real. The lesson is brought out quite well in the following story told by William James:

Some years ago, being with a camping party in the mountains I returned from a solitary ramble to find everyone engaged in a ferocious metaphysical dispute. The *corpus* of the dispute was a squirrel—a live squirrel supposed to be clinging to one side of a tree trunk; while over against the tree's opposite side a human being was imagined to stand. This human witness tries to get sight of the squirrel by moving rapidly round the tree, but no matter how fast he goes, the squirrel moves as fast in the opposite direction, and always keeps the tree between himself and the man, so that never a glimpse of him is caught. The resultant metaphysical problem now is this: Does the man go round the squirrel or not? He goes round the tree, sure enough, and the squirrel is on the tree; but does he go round the squirrel? In the unlimited leisure of the wilderness, discussion had been worn threadbare. Everyone had taken sides, and was obstinate; and the numbers on both sides were even. Each side, when I appeared therefore appealed to me to make it a majority. Mindful of the scholastic adage that whenever you meet a contradiction you must make a distinction, I immediately sought and found one, as follows: "Which party is right," I said, "depends on what you practically mean by 'going round' the squirrel. If you mean passing from the north of him to the east, then to the south, then to the west, and then to the north of him again, obviously the man does go round him, for he occupies these successive positions. But if on the contrary you mean being first in front of him, then on the right of him, then behind him, then on his left, and finally in front again, it is quite as obvious that the man fails to go round him, for by the compensating movements the squirrel makes, he keeps his belly turned towards the man all the time, and his back turned away. Make the distinction, and there is no occasion for any farther dispute. You are both right and both wrong according as you conceive "the verb 'to go round' in one practical fashion or the other. (W. James, 1907, beginning of Lecture Two.)

The reason why James was able to solve the dispute over which the two parties were deadlocked was that he instinctively dissociated the words (language) "go round" from their meaning (thought). One might reasonably expect that nobody who has ever opened a dictionary and seen multiple definitions listed under a vast number of the entries would fall into the trap of verbal arguments, but what is reasonable and what humans do, often fail to coincide. Too many people display an exaggerated reverence for language, acting as though certain uses of words possess some divinely sanctioned authority—particularly their own use of those words.

These reflections suffice to situate discussion of 'language' in a general context. In terms of the discussion thus far, words are signs of thought-objects that are believed to match objective realities. This is only a beginning however. The term" language" can itself symbolize a number of different kinds of realities. Sometimes the term refers to purely physical realities, sometimes it refers to what will be called "sense-data," and sometimes it refers to psychic images or reproductions of those sense-data. It is essential for what follows that the distinctions be made clear. i) Language involves what one might regard as *purely physical realities.* There are several varieties of these. We have approached language basically as a means for communicating, and there are many ways in which communication takes place. Typically, we think of the spoken and the written word when we think of language, but people also communicate with each other by means of gestures, facial expressions, and tones of voice. Recently, much has been written about "body language," those subtle and often unconscious forms of behavior that nevertheless convey messages. The several art forms—dance, sculpture, painting, music, etc.—are also commonly thought of as media for communication. And, if we accept as valid the saying that actions speak louder than words, this broadens even more the range of things that might be included under the umbrella-term of language: the fact that someone refuses to speak or otherwise communicate with us is something that itself communicates a message.

Following is a list of the various physical realities that can in certain circumstances become symbols that serve the purposes of communication. Physical objects: ink—or pencil-marks on paper (written language), punctures or elevations in paper (Braille), chalk marks on blackboards, scratches on plastic disks or magnetic traces on plastic tapes (recordings), etc. Physical entities or forces: light-waves (ship-to-shore or ship-to-ship or lighthouse-to-ship communication), air vibrations (audible speech), etc. Physical behavior: body-language, facial expressions, gestures, semaphore, sign language (for the deaf), etc. This is only a partial listing of the purely physical realities commonly used for the most precise, unambiguous types of communication, and omits those used for the more ambiguous forms of artistic expression.

The important thing to note is that all of these things are, first of all, merely physical realities. *They have a reality of their own apart from their function as signs or symbols.* Anyone of them can exist without exercising any communication purposes and, in many instances, do so exist. Blotches caused by spilt ink, accidental scratches in plastic disks, light waves from the sun, exercises performed in the interests of muscular fitness are all examples of such physical realities which do not serve to communicate. Later on, we will take up the question, "Are those physical realities used in communicating essentially different from those which are not?", and reasons will be given to show that the answer is "No." Even if someone answered, "Yes" to this question, that would not falsify the assertion that the physical realities used for communicating are, first of all, physical realities. If they are different from other physical realities, this is by virtue of something additional which presupposes the physical dimension. ii) There is a second class of things which must be considered when speaking of language. These are the *psychic*—in contrast to the physical—*sense-data* or phenomena which constitute perceived language. The contention here is that merely physical "language" acts as nothing more than an external stimulus for the perceived language we become directly aware of. This—perceived language—consists almost exclusively of visual, auditory, and tactile sense-data. Recall that the physical elements of language spoken of previously are physical realities. As part of the objective universe, they exist outside the perceiver. In order to be perceived, they must produce some effect within the perceiver's consciousness. These effects, referred to here as perceived language, represent one portion of the entire battery of sense-data which, at any particular moment, are produced within the perceiver's consciousness by all of the stimuli entering the latter's senses from the external environment. We are here anticipating the thesis to be presented in the next section (Argument Three) which treats of the sense-datum theory, but, according to that thesis, what we are directly aware of in sensation are psychic effects and not, as is usually believed, their external stimuli. That is, the speech-sounds we hear, the patterned, colored shapes (e.g. of letters) we see, the tactile impressions we receive, are entities within the mind, distinct from the air vibrations, the light waves, the physical pressures, which cause them.

Just as the "physical language" spoken of earlier is basically identical. in nature with non-linguistic physical realities, so this perceived language in itself consists of sense-data which are not different in nature from other sense-data. Before functioning as symbols, the sounds that we hear when someone else speaks to us (to take but one example) are no different, as sounds, from sounds we hear when someone slams a door or hammers a nail into a wall. The difference, as will be argued, consists in our different interpretations of the various sounds, which in turn depend in large measure on acquired habits of association. In themselves, sounds are sounds, colored patterns are colored patterns etc. iii) The final class of entities to which the name of language can be applied embraces those *psychic images* sometimes referred to as "inner speech" or "inner language." These are memory-images corresponding to the sense-data mentioned above. In the previous section, we spoke of images. These can be defined as *less vivid and forceful reproductions of more vivid and forceful sensations* (sense-data). Depending upon which type of sense-data serves a person as their most basic type of language, there will ordinarily be present in their mind, while they are thinking explicitly about some matter, inner speech to clothe their ideas. While thinking in silence, the average person's inner speech probably consists of sound-images. For a deaf person, it may be visual images of hand gestures (sign language). For the person who is both blind and deaf, as Helen Keller became, it will be some sort of tactile images.

A few passages from a condensation of Helen Keller's account of the relationship between Annie Sullivan and herself will illustrate what is meant by inner language. Speaking of herself, she begins:

> Here was a small human being who at the age of 19 months had moved with appalling suddenness not only from light to darkness but to silence. My few words wilted, my mind was chained in darkness, and my growing body was governed largely by animal impulses . . . A sorrier situation never confronted a young woman with a noble purpose than that which faced Annie Sullivan. I recall her repeated attempts to spell words—words which meant nothing—into my small hand. But at last, on April 5, 1887, about a month after her arrival, she reached my consciousness with the word "water." It happened at the well house, where I was holding a mug under the spout. Annie pumped water into it, and when the water gushed over onto my hand she kept spelling w-a-t-e-r into my other hand with her fingers. Suddenly I understood. Caught up in the first joy I had known since my illness, I reached out

eagerly to Annie's ever-ready hand, begging for new words to identify whatever objects I touched. Spark after spark of meaning flew from hand to hand and, miraculously, affection was born. From the well house there walked two enraptured beings calling each other "Helen" and "Teacher." . . . To this day I cannot "command the uses of my soul" or stir my mind to action without the memory of the quasi-electric touch of Teacher's fingers upon my palm. (*Reader's Digest* condensation of a chapter from the book, *Teacher*, by Helen Keller.)

The last paragraph of Miss Keller's account confirms the claim that, even while we are silently thinking to ourselves about something, there accompanies our thinking the images of our dominant type of language sensations. This is more than the sub-vocal speech of which some psychologists speak, for what they are referring to are the faint movements of the speech muscles that slow readers often make as they read.

An experiment can be conducted that will help the reader, if his dominant type of speech is auditory speech, to notice the presence of these images. Look at the following sentences:

There is a copy of the book up on the shelf. Yes, the red one. If you'd like to read it, take that copy. I've already read it.

There are three words in those sentences that are pertinent: "red," "read," and "read." Careful reflection will show that, when you saw the first and the last words, which are different, you "mentally pronounced" them the same way. By contrast, even though the second and third words look exactly alike, you "mentally pronounced" them differently. This "mental pronouncing" is not strictly an activity of throat muscles. Nor is it an activity of intellect or reason. It is merely the reproduction within your consciousness of images, images of the sensations you would have heard had someone (even yourself) been speaking those words aloud as you were reading. What occurs is that, because of the association between those visual sensations (the written words which you saw) and certain auditory sensations (heard language), the perception of the first automatically triggers off images of the latter.

Summarizing this first portion of our discussion of language, we see that language is basically—though not exclusively—an instrument for communicating with one another. The term "language" does not refer, however, to one single type of entity. On the contrary, the term is applied either collectively or separately to at least three different kinds of realities: certain physical realities, and two kinds of psychic entities, namely, sense-data and images of them. Having considered these matters, we are now in a position to move on to a defense of two further, additional theses concerning language: first, there is no such "thing" as language, and second, ideas are not transmitted via language.

The first additional thesis, *that there is no such thing as language,* follows quite logically, once the previous discussion has been accepted. This assertion must be understood literally. It states that there is no such thing—with the accent on the *singular* form of the noun—as language. As we have seen, there are many things—in the plural—which are used in communicating with one another. There are ink marks, sound waves, hand gestures, etc. The thesis is not a denial of the reality of such things. Quite the opposite: the thesis argues that such realities—in the *plural*—are the only realities designated by the term "language."

What the thesis denies is that there is, over and above the different sounds, ink marks, gestures, and the like, any additional invisible or intangible reality which we might call "a" language. If someone looks about for a chair or a tree, he may be able to put his hand on some single, concrete object. When one searches for a visible, tangible object named "language," all that he will find are such things as ink marks on paper, sounds from humans' mouths, hand-gesturing by the deaf, etc. Apart from such concrete realities, all of them particular, historically-conditioned marks, sounds, and gestures, there is nothing that anyone can point to as language.

Someone might point to a dictionary or to a grammar book as something that "contains," say, the English language or the French language, but a closer analysis of the matter should make it clear that any dictionary we point to is only one collection of ink-marked pieces of paper out of millions of such collections. If a dictionary did contain a language, then it would have to contain either the entire language or only part of the language. Either alternative leads to insuperable difficulties.

No dictionary contains only part of the language. No one would say, for instance, that the English language gains or loses something (part of itself) when any single dictionary is printed or destroyed.

Nor does any dictionary contain the entire language. First, this would mean that there are as many English languages as there are dictionaries. The alternative to this would be to say that each of them contains the one, single English language: the same individual English language contained in this large dictionary in this city also exists simultaneously in a thousand other cities where large, small, and in-between-size dictionaries are to be found. As if this were not paradoxical enough—the print is different, the number of entries is different, etc.—one who held such a thesis would probably argue that, even if every dictionary were destroyed, the English language would still exist. That's because most people who hold such a thesis would argue that, even prior to the printing of dictionaries, the English language would have been contained, not in books such as dictionaries, but in the heads of those who spoke the English language.

Further problems would then arise. Should we say that there are different English languages, viz., Old English, Middle English, British English, American English, etc.? *One book on the English language has fifty-six entries under the heading, "English."* If they are all 'descendents' of a single, original English language, where can we find 'it'? What will happen after the last survivor of English-speaking people dies? Will the English language go on to exist in some nether world populated by all the other "dead languages" used by past generations.

Anyone familiar with the problem of universals will recognize the difficulties involved in maintaining that there is any such reality as "the English (or French, etc.) language" over and beyond the countless ink marks, speech sounds, hand gestures, etc., to which we refer collectively, for purposes of convenience, by the singular term, "language." One difficulty consists in trying to explain the nature of such an intangible, invisible entity. A greater difficulty lies in any and every attempt to explain the meaning of "is contained," when it is said that the language is contained in certain books or in the heads of certain people. One of the oldest (and still useful) discussions of such difficulties is Plato's dialogue entitled *The Parmenides.*

But the strongest argument against the theory may consist, not in the difficulties that beset it, but in the fact that all of the important facts about communication can be explained *without any need for the theory that language as such exists.* What happens when two people communicate can be understood in terms of the individual physical and psychic entities spoken of above, if and when these are taken together with the individual habits of association and the individual ideas of the persons who are communicating. The theory that language is some *additional*, Platonic essence is useless, for it adds nothing to our understanding of the process of communication. This negative argument, that the theory of invisible and intangible language is not needed to explain any facts and is therefore groundless, is a form of the argument known as "Ockham's Razor" (named after the philosopher, William of Ockham).

All that is necessary now is to explain how communication can occur without resorting to anything beyond the physical and psychic entities mentioned earlier, if and when they are taken together with the individual habits of association and individual ideas of individual human beings. Our defense of the second thesis concerning language will be a third thesis.

The third thesis states that *no ideas are transmitted through language.* Instead, each of us is equipped with internal mechanisms whereby we obtain all of our ideas by means of our own personal, private experiences. Again, the thesis must be understood *literally.* It states that no ideas pass from one person to another via language. It does not mean that books and speech and gestures external to us are not important in the process whereby we form our ideas. They *are* important, but only as triggers, stimuli, or catalysts which put into operation our internal thought-producing mechanisms. If we were looking for an analogy, we might consider what happens in an automated factory: the operator, external to the factory, must push the correct buttons in order to send the proper current to the proper machines at the proper time, but the manufactured product comes, not from the operator, but from inside the factory itself. The light reaching your eyes from this page is merely triggering your own internal mechanisms to produce the thoughts which you are now thinking.

One of the essential keys to understanding language is an awareness of the phenomenon of *association.* This is a multi-faceted phenomenon which pervades our conscious life. For the most part, the mechanisms responsible for it operate automatically, that is, they require no deliberate effort of our own. They occur almost unconsciously, though the least bit of reflection suffices to make us aware of them. In a moment, if you continue reading, you will see a word that, possibly, you have not seen for some time. At the same instant that you see it, a thought will come to your mind so instantly and automatically that you will be powerless to prevent it. The word?

Elephant.

Countless other words would have served the purpose. So, why did only one out of thousands of possible ideas come to your mind when you looked at that word, at that set of letters? Not because there is some metaphysical connection between that set of letters and that idea. There is not, for instance, any similarity in shape, color, size, etc., between that word and that idea, any more than there is between that word and those animals we decided to label "elephants." Not because your mind is so constructed that the so-called English word rather than the Italian "elefante" or the Russian "slon" is the best trigger for that idea. Nor did the idea arise in your mind because it was contained in that word: if you had never seen or heard the word before, and above all if you had not formed the idea at some previous time in your life, you could have sat and looked forever at that word without having the idea come to your mind. (Are you certain that "slon" really is a Russian word and not just a trick 'word' designed to deceive you? Can you tell just by looking at it?) The truth does not lie in any of these false explanations, but in the fact that, having heard or seen this word simultaneously with the sensations (probably visual) you experienced while looking toward a particular kind of animal or a picture of one, your mind now automatically re-experiences the images of those sensations and the idea connected with them whenever you see or hear that word.

Philosophers refer to this phenomenon as "association." By analogy with the process whereby atoms become associated to form molecules, they speak of a process whereby the mind forms bonds between such things as words, sensations, images, and ideas. This is only an analogy—the underlying mental mechanisms are profoundly obscure—but it is an aid in referring to the unmistakable fact that *after the mind has actually experienced several things simultaneously, renewed contact with just one of them tends from that time on to be accompanied or followed by a re-experiencing (through memory or imagination) of the others.* The important thing is that the associated images and ideas that are re-experienced come, not from the present experience, but from previous, remembered ones. The idea of an elephant did not come from seeing the word now, but—to use another comparison—was brought to the forefront of consciousness from your memory where it was stored from previous experience.

Associations are formed between several different mental contents. The result is a network of crisscrossing links. There are associations between ordinary sense-data, between them and/or their memory-images, between the latter and our concepts, and between all of these and the psychic sense-data and images which we call "language." These associations are complex and subtle, and many important questions can be and have been raised with respect to the entire subject, but since this is not a treatise on the imagination a few simple examples will have to suffice to introduce these complexities.

Associations are formed between ordinary sense-data. At any moment, our consciousness is at least partially constituted of a welter of sense-impressions pouring in from each of our different senses, sight, hearing, touch, etc. Yet, we learn gradually to isolate certain sense-impressions and to connect them with certain other selected or isolated impressions. For instance, we can sit next to a grandfather clock in a room filled with other objects. There may be several sounds reaching our ear (cars driving by, low music coming from the radio, etc.). Yet when we isolate or attend to the ticking sound of the clock, we associate it, not with just any of the things we are seeing, but with one particular object isolated from our entire visual field. Examples can be multiplied almost endlessly. E.g., you are even now associating what you see and what your hands feel and thinking of them both as coming from one thing, a book.

Similarly, these associated sensations generate associations in their memory-images. Having sensed data relating to the visual, auditory, and tactile qualities connected with clocks, we form in our mind image clusters or complex images of clocks. At this moment, it may be possible to recreate in one's imagination the combined appearance, sound and feel of a typical grandfather clock, or of a small travel-alarm, or of an electric desk-clock, a wristwatch, etc.

Once the links between the individual ingredients of these complex images have been forged, it is possible for just one of the original sensations to excite the memory of the others. If someone is handed a watch and, with eyes shut, turns it over in his hands, he can anticipate both what it will look and sound like before opening his eyes or putting it to his ear. Some philosophers and psychologists have given prominent recognition to this phenomenon by formulating a law for it, *the law of association.* It states that whenever certain sensations have been experienced either simultaneously or in close temporal proximity, there is produced a condition within the mind such that, when only one or two of the sensations are afterwards experienced, they tend to recall the remainder of the original complex.

Along with this process of association goes another. At the same time that the complex images are being formed, the person is learning to associate with them the names (words) ordinarily used by the people in whose midst he or she lives to refer to the objects represented by those images. For the infant, much trial and error precedes the correct associating of name (itself a perceived "sense-impression) and complex image. Multiply these associations and we have the beginnings of language acquisition.

The final set of associations of which we will treat are those which link the world of images and their associated sense-data symbols (words) with the world of concepts and ideas. Gradually, the mind achieves what we have been treating as the formation of general or universal concepts, and then learns to recognize temporal, causal, and logical relationships. At this latter stage, associations are formed, not so much perhaps between complex images and language-sounds, but rather between complex thought-patterns and language-sounds (there is no simple complex image associated with the words "if," "then," "again," "sometimes," etc.).

A full treatment of the above associations and how the mind acquires them, over and beyond this oversimplified account, would not only require additional volumes, but would lead into areas only recently begun to be investigated. For one thing, the process whereby connections are made or seen between different sense-data selected from the mass of impressions pouring in at any one moment is now believed to require certain innate perceptual mechanisms, what some adherents of the theories of gestalt psychology view as pre-wired circuits. Another complication comes from the fact that these processes of association take place simultaneously and exercise reciprocal effects on each other. For instance, it may be true that some image clusters are formed prior to the time that names are attached to them (Helen Keller, seems to have formed many such image clusters—perhaps concepts as well?—prior to learning their tactile "names" from Annie Sullivan), but it is likewise true that the mind must intervene by means of its conceptualizations to isolate the less visible and tangible facets of situations before any label can be attached to them (e.g., when it is a question of learning the meaning of "good," "early," "far," "the reason why," etc.). A third complication would take us back to the earlier-mentioned problem of whether or not the intellect's functions involve, not so much the formation of ideas or concepts, but rather of propositions, and this would lead to the investigations of contemporary linguists who believe that the acquisition of language involves innate 'grammar' mechanisms. Added to these problems are the studies of anthropologists and sociologists that demonstrate the ways in which one's physical and social environment shapes one's inner world: these suggest, among other things, that there are additional, intricate, criss-crossing, reciprocal effects of sense-impressions, language, and conceptualizations. Finally, to mention but one more of the complexities which affect this whole matter, philosophers and psychologists disagree concerning the ultimate basis of psychological associations: are those bases causal ones such as similarity and temporal proximity or do they also include purely logical relationships?

Such matters are beyond the scope of our present concern which is to answer the question, "Are ideas transmitted by language?" Nevertheless, it is to be hoped that enough has been said about association to make the reader aware of the basic phenomenon. We can now return to the third thesis.

The third thesis, recall, is that *no ideas are transmitted from one person to another by means of language*. The best way to make this thesis clear is to relate it to education. There are two ways to think of what teachers do. The common-sense view is that teachers put knowledge into students' minds. The true interpretation is that teachers draw knowledge out of their students' minds. Call those two views i)the piggyback theory and ii)the eduction theory.

The piggyback theory. For pedagogical reasons, let us label the common-sense belief *"the piggyback theory."* People often imagine that in some vague manner ideas can be conveyed from one mind to another, riding piggyback on the words spoken by one person and heard by the other. For instance, ask the ordinary person how he originally got his idea of God. The answer that is usually given goes something like this: "I got it from my parents (or from the minister, priest, or rabbi in church, or from a teacher, etc.)." Few, if any, will answer that they received the idea from their own personal experience. How many people claim to have seen God or heard him speak or felt the touch of his hand? Just as few claim to have had inner religious experience concrete enough to enable them to give a definite description of that experience. The only alternative that occurs spontaneously to people asked this question is that they got the idea, by means of language, from someone else. The situation is the same for many other ideas which people do not believe they could have obtained from their own personal experience.

Not only is there no more than circumstantial evidence for the theory that words can bring ideas from another person's mind to our own, however, but there are many facts that directly militate against it.

At first it may seem too strong to say that there is no more than circumstantial evidence for the opinion that ideas are transferred from one mind to another by language. The empirical evidence for the opinion is, in fact, as strong as the evidence for many scientific theories about the laws of cause and effect operative in the physical world.

Here is an example. QU: On what grounds do scientists claim that cigarette smoking causes lung cancer? AN: To a large extent on the grounds of statistics. In a striking number of cases, the people who do in fact smoke do develop lung cancer. And this statistical evidence is sufficient to make many scientists feel justified in concluding that smoking causes lung cancer, even before researchers have directly observed the physiological or chemical mechanism whereby the two are linked. The evidence is not conclusive, though, and therefore smokers and cigarette manufacturers, impelled no doubt by vested interests which lead them to hope that the theory is mistaken, are the first to point out that, until some direct link is discovered, the theory cannot be regarded as proven. Why not? Because there are other possible explanations that the evidence has not ruled out. For instance, many people smoke till their nineties and never develop lung cancer, whereas others who have never smoked do develop lung cancer. (See J. S. Mill's 'Canons of Induction.')

The same applies to the piggyback theory. It is beyond question that each of us has a vast amount of knowledge that we would not have if we had been isolated from all other language-using human beings who already had that knowledge. So many of our ideas come to us when we are listening to others speak or looking at what they have written, that we naturally infer that the one is the cause of the other, i.e., that the speech and the writing cause the ideas. Our conversation contains many expressions of this hypothesis: "I got the idea from so-and-so," "books transmit ideas from one generation to the next," and so on.

Yet, a closer examination of the evidence reveals that the only thing we can prove is that many of our ideas emerge in our minds *when* we are listening to other people speak or reading what they have written. Inferring from this temporal conjunction between two events that the one is the cause of the other is an example of what is called the "post hoc, ergo propter hoc" (after this, therefore because of this) fallacy. Thoughts and ideas are intangible and it would be impossible to empirically demonstrate that they are somehow contained inside the air-molecule vibrations that travel from one person's vocal chords to another's eardrums or that they are resting on the page along with the ink marks and travel, via light waves, from the page to the eye. Not only is this argument for the piggyback theory inconclusive. The evidence against it is surprisingly extensive.

To begin with, the image of one person getting an idea from someone else is obviously metaphorical. The metaphor is based on the notion of physical giving, as when one person gives another person a watch or something similar. There is an important difference in the two types of giving. In the case of giving physical objects, the person who gives no longer possesses what he gave. In the second case, the giver retains every bit of the idea that he had at the beginning. What, then, would "giving someone else an idea of ours" or "receiving an idea from someone else" mean?

A thought-experiment will furnish a second argument against the common-sense theory. Imagine an infant lying in its crib. Let some learned theologian enter and begin discoursing lengthily about God. The result? It is obvious that the infant will not be one step closer to having an idea of God than it was before the speech began.

Some might object that this is simply because the infant's intelligence is not sufficiently developed to enable it to understand such an abstract concept. Our next experiment, then, is to introduce this English-speaking theologian into a group of adults in Cairo, Egypt, who speak only Arabic. At the end of an hour's discourse in English, they will not be one step closer to understanding his notion of God than they were at the outset. In fact, unless they have been told beforehand, they will not have the slightest idea what the subject of his discourse was, even if they already possess elaborate ideas about God! The reason is simple: they have never learned or acquired the *habits of association* which would make it possible for the sounds they hear to recall from their memories the ideas associated with those words. Of course, if the theologian accompanies his talk with gestures, pointing to the heavens, making a profound bow, and the like, some in his audience may guess that he is speaking of God or religion or worship or some similar subject, but this communication will be possible only because they have learned to *associate* such gestures with such ideas.

Pause to absorb the significance of these facts. Were the theologian to have used the Arabic language, that is, were he to have made those sounds which his adult audience had learned to associate with such ideas as those of God, religion, worship, and the like, communication would have taken place without any more than the usual difficulties. Ordinary communication via language, if it is to occur at all, presupposes that the receiver of the communication already possess at least some ideas and some associative links between these and the perceived language which are similar to those which the communicator has learned. If for ordinary communication to occur ideas must already be present in the listener's mind, then how can it be the speech that puts the ideas in the mind in the first instance?

To this, the only answer for the present must be that a person's original ideas are acquired from his own experience. Another person's gestures (or some similar intervention) may be a stimulus for an individual to acquire certain ideas, but the latter must—by using his own inductive powers of intelligence—discover *for himself* both the idea and the connection between the idea and the other's gestures.

But, once having acquired a fund of ideas from our own personal experience, is it not possible for us to acquire *new* ideas from someone else? Again, if the question is understood literally, the answer is "No." New ideas can be had on the occasion of hearing someone else speak, but they come from within the mind itself. Taking a cue from Plato's famous theory that "Learning is recollection" (see Plato's *Phaedo*), Aristotle—in his *Posterior Analytics*, Book One, Chapter One—wrote, "All instruction given or received by way of argument proceeds from pre-existent knowledge." That pre-existent knowledge is in the memory of the learner whose mind has the inborn ability to put remembered ideas together to form new ideas or, as we say, to put two and two together and get four.

This can happen even without outside intervention. Whenever someone, while taking a walk, lying in bed, showering, etc., puts together previous information and is rewarded with a new insight, we have an example of the process operating spontaneously. This actually occurs continuously in all of our lives, but most famously, perhaps, in the case of scientists whose sudden inspirations lead to novel discoveries.

When such new knowledge is obtained on the occasion of listening to someone speak or looking at what they have written, we have the same process, only it is stimulated or triggered by sense-impressions (heard or seen sense-data) produced through the intervention of the external speaker or book. But it is, fundamentally, the same process: whether we combine the old ideas spontaneously for ourselves or whether the ideas are combined under the stimulus of the speech sensations we hear—and in an order linked to the order of the speaker's words—the new thought or idea does not come from the outside, but emerges from within the mind itself.

The "eduction" theory. Here, then, is the alternative to the piggyback theory. Language does not take ideas from one person and put them into another person's mind. Rather, language serves to *draw knowledge from* another's mind. By virtue of the listener's habits of association that link certain sounds (or other sense-data) to certain thoughts, the sounds evoke from his mind the ideas already acquired by him from his own previous experience. In addition to its power to recall former ideas, the order in which the words evoke the former ideas can stimulate the mind to form new ideas by virtue of its own innate mechanisms.

This alternative to the 'piggyback theory' is called in this text "*the eduction theory*" of language communication. The term "eduction" comes from the Latin term meaning "to lead or draw out of." It is worth noting that *"eduction" and "education" have the same Latin root*. Somewhere along the way, educators realized the truth of Aristotle's view that they were not putting knowledge into the learner's mind but rather aiding his mind to bring knowledge forth from within itself.

The reader may have noticed that only two or three arguments were presented as evidence against the piggyback theory. At that point, the alternative, eduction theory was presented. Initially, however, we stated that there is a great deal of evidence against the piggyback or transmission theory. The justification for presenting the second, alternative view before speaking of any further evidence against the first is that the arguments against the first are simultaneously evidence for the second. Return now to some of the additional evidence.

53

First, notice that it is impossible to convey to a blind person, through language, the idea of color, or to someone who is anosmic, through words, the idea of taste, or to a deaf person, through signs, the idea of sound. That is, no one will ever know what color is who has not seen it for himself, no one will ever know what sound is who has never heard it, nor will anyone ever learn what heat is who has never felt it. The meaning of spoken words that refer to such ideas can only be learned, if in addition to hearing the words spoken, the person simultaneously experiences the reality to which such words refer. Your parents do not teach you the colors. They teach you only the colors' names. You must see the colors for yourself.

Recall the experience related by Helen Keller. What was happening when suddenly she understood the meaning of the tactile sensations coming from her hand? It was not a case of her simply noticing those sensations for the first time. Annie Sullivan spent many long and seemingly-fruitless hours of such tactile-sensation-producing efforts before Helen "caught on." Rather, Helen's excitement came from the fact that, suddenly, her mind saw the connection between those tactile sensations originating in the contact of Annie's hand with hers and the sensations of the water gushing over her other hand. (If her story records her actual experience, it would seem that she had a more explicit awareness of that initial "language" connection than the average infant has.)

Notice, too, how the critical association habits are formed. The process requires specific time-related sensations. The infant will never connect the sound "Mama" with a particular body-shape-plus-soft-voice-plus-gentle-touch if the sound "Mama" is heard randomly, i.e. sometimes when the mother is present, sometimes when only the father is present, sometimes when the baby-sitter is putting on a dry diaper, etc. Both the object to be named and the sound of its name must be experienced simultaneously in order for the association between the two to be formed and then solidified into a habit of association. Some philosophers, called "empiricists," have concluded from these facts that all ideas must be traced back to sense experience. This is an unwarranted conclusion. Nevertheless, their position at least shows a sensitiveness to the fact that we do not gain our original ideas from language.

Further evidence can be found by returning to the question, "Where do we get our idea of God from?" If it does not come from language or from personal experience, then where does it come from? The answer is that, in a sense, it does come—or is created!—from personal experience. At least our original idea of God is based on ideas received from experience. An incident that occurred in the working district of Paris some few years ago will explain what is meant. After listening to a newly-ordained and zealous young priest deliver a sermon on the theme of God as our Father, his pastor, an older, more experienced man stopped him in the sacristy and asked: "What effect do you think your sermon had on the men in your audience, when most of them dislike their fathers as domineering drunkards, hardly interested in their family and children?" The pastor may have been overly cynical, but he understood something about our idea of God that perhaps the younger priest did not. Our idea of God is one that is formed out of our own personal experience, but an experience that is ordinarily not of God himself, but of things we liken God to. When a parent introduces the idea of God to his child, he or she makes use of ideas the child already has. God is a certain person (just as the child's parents and relatives and neighbors are persons), God lives up in heaven or in the church (though, like the characters in the child's favorite fairy-tales, God makes himself invisible), God watches what the child is doing (just as his parents do), God is either pleased or angry with the kid's behavior (just as his parents are), etc. If the child does not know beforehand what a person is, what being in a place is, what it is like to watch or to be pleased or to be angry, then what his parents tell him about God will be as meaningless to him as the theologian's discourse was to the infant.

Incidentally, we find here further confirmation of the theory of epistemological dualism. It is a notorious fact that people have very different ideas of God. And that each behaves toward God in conformity with his own idea. A person's idea of God is God to him. J.B. Phillips wrote an interesting little book on this subject, entitled *Your God is Too Small*, in which he described the different Gods that different people worshipped. Fortunately, he concluded, the real God is quite another thing from these caricatures. The best religious traditions tell us that, in fact, the real God is quite beyond the grasp of our ordinary concepts, perhaps beyond the grasp of human concepts altogether. This is the significance of so-called "negative theology": it analyzes the shortcomings of every human concept of God, concluding—far too skeptically!—that the most we can know is what God is not.

Other facts confirm the thesis that ideas do not come via language. First of all, there are the instances where someone misunderstands what is said to him. The speaker has one set of ideas. He believes that he is expressing himself quite clearly; and yet, when the listener relates to some third party what the speaker said, it is apparent that the ideas he took from the words was something quite different. (Anyone who has ever taught for a while learns to accept such "misquotations" as one of the normal risks of his chosen profession.) Or we come across a paragraph that puts a new idea or even a favorite old one of ours into well-chosen language, and we make a mental note to remember that passage for future reference. But when we return and excitedly reread the passage to someone else, we suddenly discover that the author was not saying quite what we thought he was saying. In these instances of misunderstanding, the point is not only that the language did not put into our minds the only ideas that someone could claim were contained in it, but the additional fact that ideas obviously not in the words presented themselves to our consciousness as effortlessly and naturally as any ideas we ever received through communication. Is it possible to argue that the ideas come from the words in one instance but do not come from the words in another instance that is, experientially, indistinguishable from the first? Or is it not rather that in neither case do the ideas come from the words? Misunderstandings are explainable on the second hypothesis. As will be seen further on, our acquired habits of association and other factors screen or filter our sensations, so that, in a sense, we may not even perceive the exact words communicated but those which we impulsively anticipated the speaker would speak (were he thinking the same thoughts that sprang to our mind). This is a summary of many, different situations, but the conclusion is plain. Our ideas do not come from language; rather they come from our personal experience, become associated with language sensations, and are later evoked or educed by the appropriate language, i.e., auditory sensations.

A reverse situation occurs. There are instances where communication occurs, though the words correspond to neither party's ideas. A person gets confused in his search for the right words to use in conveying what he wishes us to understand. Words tumble out of his mouth that say exactly the opposite of what he is thinking. And yet, both he and we know just what he meant. The same happens in technical, highly abstract writing. A philosopher tries to express his thoughts on a complex subject, but each concept fits tightly into a vast network of other ideas. Were he to qualify each statement, to preclude misunderstandings with respect to all of the related matters, his every statement would fill a page. In addition, he may be setting down his ideas for beginners. So he writes sentences that serve to convey his notions on one subject, though he may at the same time make use of expressions that refer in passing to other matters on which he holds ideas diametrically opposed to what his words literally state. Some of his readers, who think along his lines, will understand his meaning, in spite of the surface appearance of certain of his statements.

Thus, contrary to common beliefs, ideas are not carried from one mind to another on the backs of the sound waves or the ink-marked paper that may travel from place to place. Sound waves crossing the open spaces separating one person from another derive their power of "communicating thought" from something inside the listener, namely, his habits of association (or, at least his capacity for forming them) and from his ability to form new ideas from old ones, and not from something mysteriously contained in the sound, waves themselves, such as an invisible, intangible "meaning."

A note. Before concluding, let us add a footnote to the foregoing discussion. There are still some who might contend, as Aquinas does, that the air vibrations and ink marks used as language possess something additional that other air vibrations and ink marks do not possess. Aquinas writes: "There is, in the sensible sound, an immaterial power ["virtus" in Latin] of exciting the mind of the hearer, since it—viz., the sound—proceeds from a conception in the mind of the speaker" (cfr. *Summa Theologiae*, III, q.62, a.4, ad 1). As was contended in the preceding paragraph, this theory explains nothing that is not explained by the alternative theory without invoking any "immaterial power." We therefore apply Ockham's Razor to it.

For instance, look at the following set of letters: BLITIRI. Does it have any meaning inside it? The word is not found in the English dictionary, so most people would conclude that it does not. It is a simple thing to "give" it a meaning, however. We might agree to call the next discovered subatomic particle a "blitiri." Or we might shorten the word to "blit" and announce that henceforth it will refer to "a group of four persons, made up of two men and two women." There is no evidence whatsoever that our "giving to the word a meaning" changes anything in the word (that is, in the ink marks). The only observable change is a change in us: we form an association between the sound made by some one who pronounces that word (that is, makes the sounds customarily associated with those ink marks) and a particular idea. What is more, we could, if we wished, go to the beach and "write" those letters in the sand. But we would not be putting something into the sand; we would merely be removing some sand. Also, God did not add something to the nature of the rainbow when he told Noah that henceforth it would be a sign of goodwill toward humankind. To make something a symbol is not to add something to it, but to form a psychological association in us. End of note.

It is true, nevertheless, that there must be something in the vibrations or the ink marks. At this moment, the reader has as many habits of association, practically speaking, as he had while he was reading the previous sentence. Nothing has changed in him or his habits, yet he is now thinking different thoughts than he was thinking two sentences earlier. Certainly the difference lies in the ink marks on the paper. Is it not a difference similar to that which distinguishes what we call nonsense sounds, such as "lauwn jepher na duztib," from what we call intelligible speech? Is it perhaps something similar to what makes theologians distinguish the religious phenomenon of speaking in tongues from prophecy? The answer is "yes and no."

Yes, there is something different about the air vibrations or the ink marks themselves. But, no, it is not some mysterious reality present in the one and absent in the other. (The experiment with the word "blitiri" showed this.) Even before we "gave meaning" to the word "blitiri," that set of letters was already different from any other set of letters. The difference consists in the overall shape and arrangement of the letters. 'b' has a shape different from 'd.' And the arrangement, what is called today the "gestalt," of p, l, u, and m in "plum" is different from the arrangement in "lump," though both are formed from the same four letters.

Logical positivism. This analysis of language and of the origin of the ideas that come into our minds when we are engaged in conversation or reading has important consequences. The fact that there is no such thing as "a language" puts us on our guard against uncritically accepting the theory of some contemporary researchers who maintain that a person's language shapes his ideas.

For instance, during the twentieth century, there arose huge debates about language and meaning. One group of thinkers called "logical positivists" argued that some language—used particularly by writers known as theologians and metaphysicians—is meaningless. Unintelligible. It should have been obvious from the start that, with regard to language we call "intelligible" and language we call "meaningless," the important difference is not in the sounds or ink marks. It is something extrinsic to the sounds or marks, namely, the association-habits of language-users. Sounds and ink marks are not distinguished intrinsically into intelligible and meaningless, though they may be different sounds or differently shaped and arranged ink marks.

Sociology. There is another reason why this analysis of language—this application of Ockham's Razor—is important. It is not uncommon to see statements like the following even in popular magazines. (This one appeared in the pages of one of the last issues of *Look Magazine*.)

> Psychologists say all higher levels of thinking depend on language. But at the same time, the structure of whatever language we use affects the way we see the world—influences, in fact, our attitudes and thought processes themselves.

Those familiar with the theories of B.L. Whorf will recognize the source of such statements. Interpreted literally, the passage implies that there are such things as languages that the members of a particular society share in common. It further suggests that this language, a sort of structured block of words, imposes its structure on our perceptions, our attitudes, and our thought processes—all of which are treated as if they are distinct from the imposing body of language. Thus, the structure of the English language, something that is assumed to pre-exist the infant born into a particular society that uses the English language, causes him to perceive and think about reality in one way, while the Chinese language, for instance, will cause another infant to perceive and think about reality in another.

There is, of course, a valid and important insight wrapped up in the passage, but it is important to disentangle the insight from the confusing form in which it is expressed. First, language must be demythologized. That is, it must be seen for what it is, shaped and arranged ink marks, air-molecule vibrations, gestures, psychic sense-data and their memory-images. Then it will be seen that language is not a reality distinct from perceptions, but—to the extent that it consists of sense-data and their memory-images—is part of them. More importantly, certain features attributed by the theory to language ("its structure"), such as the subject-predicate form, certain verb-tense forms, etc., actually are part of the innate thought-mechanisms of the mind.

The really valid insights of the theory can be expressed better in other, less misleading ways, even though they lose some of their dramatic, attention-drawing force. Under the impact of the order in which his ideas are evoked (by virtue of the order of words spoken to him), an individual in one society will form different associations that will produce different attitudes. Finally, and this is a matter that will be taken up in a later discussion of reductionism, we can be misled into isolating certain words from the context of a valid proposition, inventing concepts (often concepts of fictions), and into building dubious philosophical theories on them. (These and the following remarks may mean little to the beginner, but will serve to indicate how other researches that he may subsequently pursue will fit into the theory of language presented in this section.)

Conclusions vis-à-vis representationalism. First, any references to "a body of knowledge common to a group of people" must be 'unpacked' or 'critically analyzed.' *There are only individual thoughts of individual people,* and though one person's thoughts may be exactly similar to those of someone else, they do not cease to be his own thoughts. Our everyday way of speaking sometimes generates the opposite view. Instead of saying that the learned men of each generation acquire more correct or more extensive knowledge than the learned men of previous generations, we sometimes speak metaphorically and assert that "mankind's knowledge" increases with each subsequent generation. Instead of speaking of stores of information contained in the different minds of individual contemporary scientists, we talk about "the rapidly accumulating body of scientific knowledge." Often, the same people who say these things simultaneously accept the contradictory position that thoughts and ideas are not self-sustaining realities but are the kind of thing that can exist only in someone's mind. If this latter view is correct, then reference to a common body of knowledge, somehow hovering in our midst, in which we all participate by some sort of osmotic process, is an example of poetic license.

Secondly, if there is some common body of knowledge—as Plato, the Averroists, and other "objective idealists" have maintained—it is not what the man in the street thinks about when he refers to a common body of knowledge, nor is our acquaintance with it acquired in the way people ordinarily believe our knowledge is acquired. That is, if—as people ordinarily believe—whatever comes into our minds must enter by the gates of sensation, this common body of ideas would be inaccessible. Ideas cannot be sensed. Only those symbols of ideas, namely, spoken or written words, can. And we have seen that these are not the source of our ideas.

One final conclusion is this. Each of us, like Helen Keller, must acquire all of our ideas—all of them!—for ourselves. First in the darkness of the womb and later outside it, it is up to us to make sense of the flood of sensations that pours in through the separate senses. When other people speak to us, the only thing this adds to our ordinary sensations is more sensations, i.e. more heard sounds. When they write letters to us, all the letters add are more sights of shaped and arranged ink marks. When Annie Sullivan 'communicated' with Helen Keller, all Helen received were more tactile sensations. Etc. The language sensations, no matter whether they are produced by the most brilliant or the most unlettered of our contemporaries, are only so much more raw data that we must somehow make sense of. Or, if you prefer, they are only so many additional stimuli that, hopefully, will trigger our innate mechanisms into adding to that coherent world-view, our inner world.

To fully appreciate this, it is essential to become aware that the key to the contrast between infancy and a mature ability to "speak and understand a language" is the formation of *innumerable habits of association*. If, many years ago, this piece of paper had been held before your infant eyes, you would have seen exactly what you see now: hundreds of small figures against a white background. You may have stared at it for a moment or it may not have held your attention even that long. In either case, you would have comprehended nothing, not even that this was a page of writing that you could not understand. Now, although you see nothing more than you saw then, what you see is a spark, setting off a chain of reactions that occur in such a split second that they are almost undetectable except by patient reflection. The difference between then and now lies in the stupendous changes that have occurred within your own mind. An infinitely complex thought-world, supported by and supporting an infinitely complex system of image-associations, has been built up, little by little, through thousands upon thousands of waking hours. Thanks to those habits of association, certain bits of that thought-world are lit up, brought back to the forefront of consciousness as you run your eyes over these lines of small black marks.

As was noted in Argument One, this inner thought-world is at your disposal, *no matter what happens now to the outside world.* You can relive memories of your home, its rooms, the furniture that makes them comfortable. You can relive experiences with good friends. You have countless worlds of imagination to wander through, ranging from Snow White and the Dwarfs to the most recent movie you have seen or novel you have read. There are past historical eras you have learned about, as well as the infinite spaces of astronomy and the incredible world of events taking place within the atom. You can dream dreams of the future.

This inner world, parts of which were paraded onto the stage of your explicit consciousness just now because you saw certain tiny black marks, is a world within your own mind. (Your past, your fantasies, the heavens, the interior of the atom, probably have nothing to do with the room in which you are seated as you read this.) *What is the bridge,* the connection, between this inner world and the outer world of objective reality? Tiny black marks re-awakened portions of your inner world just now, but how do you know that anything in that inner world corresponds to the real world?

Most people would answer: by means of the senses. "If I wish, I can put down this book and experience the real world by looking, listening, smelling, tasting, and touching." What if you are mistaken in this belief, however? What if your "ordinary" sensations—as opposed to these "language" sensations—are themselves only signs and symbols of external reality, another language to be deciphered, rather than direct contact with that reality? This is the question to which we will now turn, in an effort to complete your realization of the fact that, in a sense, each of us lives immediately in the personal, private 'world' of our own minds, and only indirectly in a common, objective, physical universe.

Argument Three.

Sensory Objects

Sensed objects are private psychic entities that exist only in the mind of the individual who experiences them.

Preface. The thesis of epistemological dualism, it will be recalled, is that the data that you must use in answering the question, "What is a human being?", are the 'contents' of your own consciousness. We are omitting in Part One all of those facets of consciousness that are non-cognitive, and focusing instead on cognitive psychic processes and their objects. Until now, the discussion has dealt chiefly with the non-sensory cognitive processes and their objects. For convenience, the non-sensory *acts* have been listed as thinking, remembering, and imagining, and the *objects* of non-sensory knowledge have been identified as images and intentional thought-objects. Our overriding concern has been to make the reader aware of the vast universe of images and thought-objects stored in his conscious and subconscious mind and linked together with each other by thousands of intricate cross-associations.

In this third and final argument in favor of epistemological dualism, the two-world theory, or representationalism—three names for one theory—we turn our attention to sensation. The term "sensation", as it is used here, is an abbreviation. It is convenient to use this one word to refer to what are five—or more—specific processes, namely, seeing, hearing, tasting, smelling, and tactile feeling. There is not some single, general phenomenon, sensation, over and above these several distinct processes. Or, if there is, some other term should be used for it, such as, "awareness."

Our concern with sensation, in this section, is not to analyze sight, hearing, taste, etc., in all of their complexities. Rather, we will limit ourselves to just one question: *"What and where are the objects of sensation?"* Though many other facets of sensation will be dealt with in the course of our discussion, they will be treated only insofar as they relate to this one type of question. What do we see? What do we hear? What do we smell? Etc.

Before proceeding, let us take a moment to note the importance of sensation and some of the ramifications of the different theories about its objects.

Sense experience's importance. There is no need to try and prove the importance of sensation itself. The senses appear to be the mind's gateways to the world. To lose even one of our senses represents a serious loss. The blind person's access to the world is severely curtailed by the loss of sight. The deaf person, though in some respects less unfortunate than the blind person, is still handicapped by his inability to detect sounds. It is difficult to imagine what it would be like to be deprived of all sensation, but if such a thing were possible, it would be worse than complete solitary confinement. Plunged into the dark, silent dungeon of sensationless existence, a person so deprived would be cut off from all contact with reality.

If going to sleep is—as most of us believe it is—a radical shut down of our sense mechanisms, then the permanent loss of all sensation would be the equivalent of never being able to wake up again. The result would be either a perpetual dreamlike sleep or a total comatose unconsciousness.

This view, that the senses are the mind's gateways to the world and that the loss of the senses cuts us off from that world, is the common-sense view of sensation. If we ask what this view implies about the *objects* of sensation, the answer is simple. The objects of the senses, that is, the things we see and hear and feel, are objective realities such as books, desks, chairs, walls, people, and the like. Furthermore, the average person who has not previously given much attention to the matter would probably describe the relation between sensation and its objects as "direct contact." Such a person most likely will have heard or read or studied something about light and sound waves and about nerve impulses, and will know that these are somehow involved in sensation, but rarely would he even mention these things when asked the question, "What do you see (or hear or feel)?" Though light and sound waves and nerve impulses may be prerequisite conditions for sensation it seems that seeing, hearing, feeling, and the like put us is immediate touch with the outside world.

Whether it comes as a surprise to him or not, the student soon learns that not everyone holds this common-sense view. However, a recent psychology text has this to say:

> Some existentialists have held that man is ultimately isolated from his fellow man because all of his contact with other humans is indirect and mediated by the senses. No information from the environment ever reaches the brain without first getting by the sensory receptors and the neural pathways; man never has immediate knowledge of the world's objects, other people, or anything. Psychology has thus come to consider the physical world as *stimulus*, its effects on a person as sensation, and his interpretation of the effects as perceptions. (CRM Books, *Psychology Today: an Introduction*, p.255)

Not only existentialists and psychologists hold such opposed-to-common-sense opinions about sensation, however. The opinion held by a wide variety of thinkers today is that the senses are not so much as gateways or windows onto reality, but only carriers of messages from reality to the mind that must then interpret them in order to know reality. A memorable presentation of this alternative view of the senses can be found in a long passage from a book by the nineteenth-century scientific writer, Karl Pearson, entitled *The Grammar of Science*.

Pearson compared the mind or self to a clerk in a central telephone exchange, receiving messages from the outside. This clerk, who must be imagined never to have been outside the telephone exchange, receives messages from several different subscribers, and on the basis of what they tell him, he forms his opinions about the events taking place in the world outside his office. In a similar manner, the sense organs, set in motion by stimuli from the outside environment, transmit signals via the nerve pathways to the brain. The signals that arrive at the brain (and then—as we shall see—at the mind) are distinct from the outside realities, just as the sounds received over the telephone by the clerk are distinct from the outside events. It is the *effects* that these signals produce in the mind, that we will call "sense-data," that the mind is directly aware of when the senses perform their functions.

On the basis of the sense-data that are no more than clues, the mind—aided by its own innate mechanisms—fashions for itself a picture of the outside world. Jerome Bruner, a contemporary psychologist, expressed this thought when he said: "You never get a direct test on reality. You must take scraps and test them against your mental model of the world." (Conversation reported in *New York Times Magazine*, Nov. 29, 1970, p.32. The passage from Pearson's book can be found in *An Introduction to Philosophical Analysis*, by John Hospers, 1967, pp. 502-504.)

This alternative to the common-sense opinion about sensation has a long history to it, but it became commonly accepted only at the time of Galileo, Descartes and Newton, the era that saw the advent of modern science. At one period, the common-sense view was so widely rejected by educated persons that the philosopher, David Hume, felt safe in making the following statement:

> It seems evident that men are carried by a natural instinct or prepossession to repose faith in their senses . . . (and) when men follow this blind and powerful instinct of nature, they always suppose the very images, presented by the senses, to be the external objects, and never entertain any suspicion that the one are nothing but representations of the other. This very table, which we see white and which we feel hard, is believed to exist, independent of our perception, and to be something external to our mind which perceives it . . . *But this universal and primary opinion of all men is soon destroyed by the slightest philosophy.* (David Hume, *Enquiry Concerning Human Understanding*, Chapter XII, italics added.)

Many contemporary philosophers vigorously deny that philosophy undermines common sense. There were several attempts in the twentieth century to reinstate the common-sense view. But that "Revolt Against Dualism" was motivated more by the desire to avoid the *consequences* of representationalism, however, than by any solidly-refuted errors in the facts on which representationalism is based. (For an account of these recent revolts and their weaknesses, see the work *Revolt Against Dualism*, by Arthur Lovejoy.)

What are these consequences? The first is that it puts the final plank into the theory of epistemological dualism. It is not just the objects of immediate non-sensory cognition that are within the mind, but the objects of immediate sense awareness are also in the mind. According to this anti-common-sense or—as we shall call it—"sense-datum" theory, what you see when you open your eyes are not things on the other side of your eyes but things within your mind, and what you hear are not more and less distant sounds but sounds within your mind, etc. Your entire immediate world is an inner, subjective world.

The reverse side of this contention is the one that worries most those philosophers who, because of it, try to reinstate common sense. If the objects of all direct knowledge are within the mind, then we never have direct knowledge of the external, objective world. The thought-objects and images and sense-data that make up the objects of direct cognition come between our mind and the world, effectively acting as a curtain or screen cutting off our view of objective reality. If that is so, then it raises questions, not only about the possibility of knowing what the real world is like, but even about the possibility of proving that it exists. Earlier, we compared the loss of one's senses to the loss of all contact with the world and said that this would produce, at best, a dream-like state of consciousness. There are many people who feel that the sense-datum analysis of sensation produces the same result. If it is true, they say, then it may be that our entire life is one long dream.

This fear is reinforced if one looks at the history of modern philosophy since the time of Descartes and the scientific and philosophical attacks on the common-sense theory of sensation. Descartes, sometimes called "the father of modern philosophy," after raising doubts about sensation, asked the question: "How do I know that, even when I seem to be awake, my experience is not simply a dream?" And he took this question so seriously that he felt he had to elaborate a long demonstration that the world, God, and other people do in fact exist.

The views of Descartes set in motion a long series of novel views that destroyed whatever consensus had ever existed among earlier philosophers. Some pointed out the weaknesses of Descartes' proofs for the world's existence and tried to improve on them. Some concluded that no proof could ever be given. Most of those who continued to believe that an objective world does exist, admitted that there is little if anything that we can know about it except its existence. Others went so far as to say that the objective world as we ordinarily think of it does not exist after all.

Such are some of the important consequences that we set out to consider before getting into the actual arguments about the objects of sensation. That is, we will delay for a moment longer any discussion of the actual arguments in favor of the sense-datum theory. The reason is that, around this time, some novices in philosophy will have become nervous. (Not all do. Some shrug off the entire matter as "nonsense to be expected from philosophy.") There is not really any reason to fear that all the rugs are being pulled from beneath your feet, even if it may be difficult to avoid feeling that they are.

For instance, if there *are* any arguments against the existence of an objective reality that is knowable, even if indirectly, they do not come from the attack on the common-sense view of sensation. As has been emphasized repeatedly, the arguments all begin from the assumption that there *is* an objective universe. The discussions that follow will begin from that same assumption. In fact, it is precisely our common-sense view about what things in the objective world are like that is the foundation for the theory that we do not directly sense them. If there is no objective, physical universe, many—and some philosophers would say all—of the arguments for the sense-datum theory would fall.

In order to show that the sense-datum theory does not make it necessary to question the existence of the real world or to doubt that we can learn something of what it is like, let us compare the role that sensation plays in our overall knowledge, as that role is seen by the common-sense theory and as it is seen by the sense-datum theory.

In both theories, sensation is fundamental for at least two purposes. It is necessary to trigger consciousness, first of all. Neither theory maintains that the mind would ever have any knowledge if it had no sensations. A person who was born, deprived of all his senses, would—so far as anyone knows—remain in a perpetual coma, in all probability lacking even dreams. Secondly, both theories regard sensation as essential if we are to have any way of checking which of our non-sensory conceptualizations—which of our "mental models of the world" (to use Jerome Bruner's phrase)—is correct.

This second assertion is the important one for our purposes. If what has been argued in Argument One about the nature of the objects of non-sensory cognition was correct, then the second assertion follows quite logically. It will be recalled that the first argument stated that the non-sensory modes of consciousness do not put us in direct contact with the external world. Even when it is a case of thinking about something like a piece of paper on the table in front of us, the immediate object of thought is an immaterial thought-object in our mind.

Now, whichever theory of sensation one holds, it is sensation that provides the link between our worlds of images and thought-objects and the real world. A person may entertain all kinds of suspicions about what is happening on the table in front of him. He may begin to wonder whether the piece of paper is still lying where it was originally or whether, unknown to him, it has been destroyed. In either case he will have to resort to some kind of sensation in order to assure himself of the truth. In the common-sense theory, this check will be made by opening one's eyes and looking directly at the table and what is on it. In the sense-datum view, the check will be made by opening his eyes, letting the light set up impulses to his brain, thereby producing a visual sense-datum that was not present when his eyes were closed.

The indirectness of the sense-datum check should not cause as much concern as it sometimes does. Even someone who holds the common-sense theory will realize, if he reflects on it, that a great deal of life is conducted on just such an indirect basis. i) Our family relationships are important to us, yet our certainty that we were born on a particular day to particular parents will never be more than indirect, because we were not conscious of what was happening when it happened and it is impossible now to turn the clock backwards to watch it. ii) Our knowledge of the thoughts and feelings of others is always indirect. Such things are not visible, and our often instantaneous judgments about what they are thinking and feeling must be based on such clues as their gestures, facial expressions, the sounds they make (language), etc. iii) Most of science—the science that infiltrates every corner of our lives by producing the countless machines, appliances, and goods that we use—is verified only indirectly. No one has ever seen electricity or a single light or sound wave or an atom. iv) And consider how much of our knowledge of the world has come from books, newspapers, magazines, radio and television. All of it is indirect.

We need only refer to the previous section on language to realize this. Someone might think that television is an exception, that it "brings the world right into our living room." This is an illusion, however, if we take it literally. Nothing enters the living room except invisible, high-frequency electro-magnetic radiations. These in turn are used to produce, possibly thousands of miles from the original events and objects (which do not move from their initial location!), the pictures that we see—if we see anything in the living room.

Furthermore, the indirectness of this large portion of our worldview (only a few examples were mentioned out of thousands) does not in any way affect the realness we attach to it. For us, the portion of our world-view based on indirect clues can be just as real as beliefs that we judge to be founded on direct sense observation. For instance, consider again our knowledge of other people's thoughts and feelings. Even though the youth being interviewed for his first job is directly aware of the physical walls, the desk, the chairs and the outward appearance of the man conducting the interview (that is, if the common-sense view is correct, he directly senses these things) and only indirectly infers the interviewer's thoughts, these latter are for the moment the only reality that exists for him. Even when these purely thought-objects (which can never be objects of the senses) completely lack any correspondence to objective fact, they are utterly real for the person thinking them. A graphic proof of this occurred on October 30, 1938, during a famous radio broadcast by Orson Welles that dramatized a purely imaginary attack by Martians upon the earth. So real were 'the Martians' and their 'invasion' to some people whose only clues were some noises coming from a radio loudspeaker, that widespread panic occurred.

What this demonstrates is not that there are no significant differences between the common-sense and the sense-datum theories of sensation, but that indirectness is not by itself an argument against the validity of knowledge and the reality of what is thus indirectly known. If we were able to know nothing but what we immediately *sense*, then we should deny that other people have thoughts and feelings. Each of us should regard himself as the only person in the world with thoughts and feelings and all other people as mere bodies or robots. Similarly, any such idea as that of God or of spirits living beyond the grave should be rejected as utterly fictitious. None of these can be seen, heard, or touched. If one continues to believe in the reality of other people's thoughts and feelings and even of God and spirits of the dead, despite the fact that our knowledge of them is based only on indirect clues, then our situation, even if the sense-datum theory is correct, is not so terribly desperate. Acceptance of the theory will be, if the argument to follow is not mistaken, only a recognition of an indirectness that extends further than was previously suspected.

However that may be, the *fear* of initially uncomfortable consequences should not outweigh the acceptance of *the facts* if these can be shown to be true. The argument for the sense-datum theory claims to show that there is direct evidence that contradicts the common-sense view of sensation.

Let us, then, examine that argument. It deals, as was pointed out earlier, with the object or objects of immediate sensation. What do we see? What do we hear? What do we feel? The argument is a long and involved one, consisting of preliminary clarifications as well as careful analysis of crucial experiences.

The *first clarification* that is basic to the entire argument is the distinction between sensation and non-sensory interpretation. We can attack the distinction by reviewing the difference between sensing something and thinking about it. Look at any object you choose. An example might be this piece of paper you hold in your hands. As you look at it, you notice that your mind is free to think many different thoughts about it. You can, without moving your eyes, think about the fact that the paper is white. You can mentally compare this color, white, with the colors of other objects: the colors of snow or of clouds or of cats that are also white, or the colors of apples, oranges, or trees that are different from white. You can concentrate on the shape of the paper and how it differs from circular, oval and square shapes. You can think of how the paper was manufactured, what it is made of, its weight, its size relative to other things, the contrast between its apparent solidity and the scientific view that it is mostly empty space, the fact that it has writing on it, etc. If you keep your eyes focused on one portion of the paper, you will notice that though your thinking is continually changing as it ranges over a wide variety of topics, your sensation remains almost identical. Neither the color, the shape, or the size of what you see, nor your visual contact with it change. On the basis of such facts, we can conclude that sensing something and thinking about it are distinct.

When this thinking is instantaneous and nearly subconscious, it is often called "perception." We prefer to call it "interpretation." You turn the corner in the clothing department and almost bump into someone. At least that is your first interpretation. A moment later, you smile to yourself. What you thought was "someone" is only a store-dressed manikin. Your initial impression was instantaneous, unreflecting. It gives way, in an almost equally instantaneous, unreflecting way to the realization that this is a manikin, not a live person. But what you see and your sensation remain unchanged. The manikin does not change color or size or shape, nor does the clarity with which you sense these things. What changes is something distinct from both, your interpretation of what you see. This is what is meant by the distinction between sensation and non-sensory interpretation. Our concern is with the objects of sensation.

The *second clarification* refers to the distinction between act and object. The general notion of object should be clear from Argument One. In all cognition, we distinguish between act and object, e.g. between the act of remembering and what is remembered, between the act of imagining and what is imagined, between thinking and thought-objects.

There are some philosophers who have argued that there is no such act-object distinction in the case of sensation, but if we begin with the ordinary common-sense approach to it, the distinction is obvious. According to common sense, it is certainly true to say that the piece of ink-marked paper you are looking at now existed for a considerable time before you first laid eyes on it. That there is something white, rectangular, and covered with black figures present to you now is beyond doubt. The change that has occurred between the time when this paper was unseen by you and the present is not in the paper but in you. This change can only be described as a change from your not sensing it to your sensing it. Whereas formerly there was only the paper or object, there is now your added act of sensing. It is difficult to find any better word for this act than "seeing." We can describe it as *being aware* of the white, rectangular, covered-with-black-figures object, so long as we do not include in the awareness any of the added non-sensory factors of attention or interpretation. Important modifications of the common-sense view will have to be made before analyzing any crucial experiences, the most important being that we suspend judgment about the nature of the white, rectangular, covered-with-black-figures object while asking "What do we see?", but there can be no question whatsoever of the fact that, according to common sense, the distinction between the act of sensing and its object is obvious.

Next, it is essential to underline the fact that truth and error have absolutely no application to sensing. Truth and error pertain only to the interpretations that we make in reference to what we sense. Some philosophers have argued that all sensation is at least partially illusory, that our senses constantly deceive us. Rene Descartes sometimes argued this way, though on occasion he also took pains to point out that in speaking this way he was really referring, not to the sensing itself, but to the judgments we make in connection with sensing.

In sensing, the alternatives are either that we sense or we do not sense something, not that we sense it rightly or wrongly. When we almost walked into the manikin, there was no fault in our sensing. We saw what we saw. The error lay in our automatic interpretation of what we saw.

This contention, that sensing is never false—nor is it ever true in the most basic sense of that term—is fundamental to the sense-datum theory. In a way, it can even be regarded as the most vital link in the chain of reasoning that establishes that theory. It is only fair to point out that, because it is so critical, the contention has been attacked by many of the opponents of the sense-datum theory. A little further on, this issue will be examined further, therefore. For the moment, it is sufficient that the reader has been alerted to the issue.

Four proposed classes of objects. We will examine four possible answers to our question, "What do we sense?" The first answer states that we sense external physical realities such as books, chairs, desks, people, etc. This is the ordinary, common-sense view. The second answer is that we sense objects produced within our sense organs themselves. We will refer to this theory as the "intra-organic theory" ("within-the-organ theory"). A third proposal is that sensation consists in an immediate awareness of the patterns of nerve impulses produced in our brain by the external stimuli. For that reason, it will be called the "nerve-impulse theory." The final alternative, that sensation is an immediate awareness of non-physical or psychic objects produced in our consciousness by the brain impulses, is the answer given by the sense-datum theory and is the one we will argue for.

These are not the only answers ever proposed, but they are the four major ones that philosophers during the past four centuries have given. Nor must the reader think that philosophers holding one or other of these theories have not added important qualifications to their answers, even though, since this discussion is only an introduction to the problems of sensation, these qualifications will generally be ignored here. The reader who wishes to investigate the entire subject further is invited to consult the selected bibliography given at end of Part Two.

The core of the argument for the sense-datum theory is basically a process of elimination. It revolves around an analysis of actual experiences, in an effort to see if the objects of those experiences match up with the description that each of the theories predicts. When the object fails to possess the qualities that one theory predicts, attention is given to the next theory. In this way, it is shown that only the fourth, the sense-datum theory, enables us to explain the facts of sensation while simultaneously leaving most of our common-sense convictions about the world intact.

In order to perform the required analysis and comparisons, though, it is necessary to know beforehand what each of the theories predicts about its candidate for the object of sensation. A brief review of some of the commonly accepted accounts about what takes place before and during sensation will help to understand the various theories and what they say about the object.

1. The *common-sense* view is that held by all of us before we learn anything about physics or physiology. There is no need to elaborate on the common-sense view, since this was explained at the outset of this section. What we see, hear, taste, smell, and feel are realities in the objective world, things such as apples, pieces of paper, manikins, etc. The only thing that should be added before going on to the next theory is that, according to our common-sense view, the objects that we sense are ordinarily believed to be unaffected, unchanged by our sensations. The root of this belief may be the fact that *we ourselves are unchanged when someone else looks at us.* If we were altered when someone enters a room and watches us, it would be impossible for anyone to spy on us. Reversing this insight, common sense leads us to believe that our looking at anything produces no alteration in that object. Qualifications must be made when the sense under consideration is taste (we must bite into what we taste) or touch (unless the object is hard enough to resist the pressure of our touch), but this is the kind of consideration that the reader can easily adjust to in his own reflections. In any concrete situation, though, there are limits to the change that common sense will recognize as occurring in sensation. The change is ordinarily either minimal or nonexistent. To sum up: the common-sense theory holds that the objects of sensation are the physical objects constituting our external environment and that these are unaffected by our sensation.

2. The *intra-organic* theory, on the contrary, maintains that the objects that we directly sense are within the sense organs themselves. The following is a typical expression of this view:

> Only the objects touching the sense organs . . . are immediately perceived through external sensation. What is immediately seen is just the object that touches the retina, what is immediately felt is the inner surface of the skin in contact with the nerve ends, what is heard immediately is only the sound within the ear, and so on. (J. Owens, 1963, pp. 219-220)

The intra-organic theory builds chiefly on facts that have been the concern of modern scientific inquiry, particularly—though not exclusively—those which deal with light and sound transmission. Science has destroyed our naïve belief that sensing is an extremely simple, uncomplicated affair. We now realize far better than ever before in history that countless "invisible" events take place in sensation. One of the most important events, according to this theory, is the formation of objects within the sense organ. An appreciation of the intra-organic object theory can be had from reflection on the following facts.

To begin with, it is clear that there must be something akin to physical contact involved in order for any sensation of an external object to take place. Sometimes this physical contact is immediate, at other times a bridge must exist to provide the proper stimulus to the sense organ.

In the case of tactile sensation, no bridge is ordinarily required. There is direct contact between the observer's body and the felt object. You hold the paper in your hands, you touch the wall, you kick the stone in your path. The same is true of the sense of taste. The food must make actual contact with our palate before we experience the taste.

But, with the remaining three senses, smell, hearing and sight, it seems logical to expect that some bridge is required: your ears do not literally reach out to the person speaking in the next room, nor do your eyes stretch down to the paper in front of you, etc. The bridges in these cases are not ordinarily observable. Today we believe, of course, that tiny molecules of whatever distant object we smell are traveling through the air and finally making contact with our olfactory nerves at the moment that we begin smelling. We take it for granted that sound and light provide the bridge between our auditory and optic sense organs and their objects. But we do not usually see molecules floating in the air, nor do we see sound waves, nor is light itself visible in the space between us and the distant objects we are looking at.

Yet, these bridges are suggested to us by common experience. Who is there who has never seen cigarette smoke spread throughout an area and "gotten the smell" of it only when the smoke visibly reached his nostrils? Or who has never seen the beam of a searchlight or a pair of headlights penetrating a night haze, or the rays of the sun as it streams through a window into a darkened room and reveals dust specks dancing in the air, or at least the beam of a small flashlight as it cuts through the dark, illuminating just those objects on which it falls?

Such experiences are more remote with respect to sound but again there are certain common experiences that set us thinking. The sound of a guitar is obviously connected with the vibrating strings and a building vibrates when some very heavy object is dropped onto concrete or when thunder roars close-by, suggesting that hearing may involve the transmission of vibrations, just as sight involves the transmission of light. These are all common experiences that, along with other experiences that curious men have searched out for themselves, form the basis for the well established view that in each case of sensation, there must be some sort of direct contact between the sense organ (eye, ear, nose, tongue, skin) and either the object sensed or else some entity that travels from the object sensed to the sense organ.

For the actual experiments that have provided these further experiences, a book on physics (optics, acoustics, etc.) or on general psychology (usually under the heading of "The Senses") should be consulted. Unfortunately, too many of these works present the reader with the conclusions rather than with the experiments and the reasoning based on the experiments that led to the conclusions. But in the case of the three senses mentioned, the general facts concerning the transmission of "something" from the distant object to the sense organs are so well established that it is legitimate to assume them for the present.

Returning, then, to our treatment of the different theories regarding the objects of immediate sense awareness, we find that the second theory to be explained, the intra-organic theory, builds on these modern "scientific" facts concerning the physical processes involved in sensation. Some contact is required for sensation to occur, and when this contact is not direct, then some bridge must exist between the person who senses and the distant physical object. In every case, however, whether a bridge is required or not, the contact creates a new entity within the sense organ (eye, ear, etc.). As will be seen, it is this intra-organic object and not the external one that is—according to this theory—the object of immediate sense awareness. Since the outermost layer of our bodies is a layer of dead skin, the tactile nerves do not make direct contact with objects, but must be stimulated by pressures created under the skin. Consequently, the immediate object of the tactile sense, according to J. Owens (quoted earlier) is "the inner surface of the skin in contact with the nerve ends." What is smelled are only those particles of matter that travel to the olfactory nerves located within the head, at about the level of the eyes! What is tasted are those dissolved food particles that seep into the openings of the tongue to make contact with the taste buds embedded beneath the tongue's surface. What is heard are only those vibrations that, *after* traveling the intervening spaces, reach the inner ear. And, finally, what is seen directly and immediately are the images (patterns of light waves) that are projected onto the retinas at the back of the eyes.

Since the stimuli that create these intra-organic objects may be altered, we might say "distorted," by factors that intervene between the external object and the sense organs, this theory predicts that, even when the extra-organic objects do not change, the intra-organic objects may. For example, the particles from two quite different odor-producing objects may combine in the air and produce a sensation not similar to either one. Sound vibrations that must pass through a barrier will arrive at the ear in a different condition from that which we find when the barrier is removed (we say that they are "muffled" or "flattened" or some such thing). Similarly, distorted window panes, heat rising from an asphalt pavement, magnifying glasses, and the like, create corresponding alterations in the retinal images.

3. The third theory, the *nerve-impulse* theory, focuses on yet another set of facts, gleaned by modern science, but generally accepted even by those who reject the nerve-impulse theory. For sensation to take place, it is not enough for the external sense organ to be stimulated. The stimulus must travel from the sense organ to the brain, either directly or (in the case of touch) through the spinal column. But what travels is not the original stimulus. Instead, the original stimulus—itself something distinct from the external object—must create a new entity, an electro-chemical impulse (in reality, something akin to a chain of explosions along the nerve fiber), and it is this impulse that reaches the brain. Since it takes time for the nerve impulses to travel (it might require about one-fiftieth of a second for an impulse from the toe of a man six feet tall to reach his brain), a new impulse may be forming at one end of a nerve when an earlier one is reaching the brain. Finally, incoming nerve impulses must actually be received into the brain itself, where they are integrated into larger patterns of excitations.

This theory that seems to have impressed many contemporary philosophers, contends that what a person is immediately aware of in sensation is just the nerve impulses or the patterns of excitation in the brain itself. (The brain, it is said, then interprets these incoming signals in order to learn about the external environment.) The theory predicts, therefore, that, as in the preceding theory, various intervening factors, can affect the immediately-sensed objects. It is hypothesized, for instance, that each moment of experience leaves memory-traces in the brain, and these may very well modify the incoming stimuli. (In fact, our brain may have something like inborn "pre-wired circuits" that modify or structure incoming stimuli from the moment of our birth.) Changes in the receptor nerves as well as in the transmitting neurons may modify the incoming stimuli. Similarly, drugs (e.g. alcohol, LSD, etc.) distort the incoming signals, thus altering the objects of our immediate sense awareness. In these instances, the external objects and even the intra-organic objects may, without changing, produce different sensed objects (nerve impulses or patterns of nerve excitation in the brain).

4. The fourth and last theory that we will concentrate on, is what has come to be widely known as the "*sense-datum* theory." According to this theory, of which there are different versions, we have no immediate sense awareness of any of the preceding types of object. Though many—perhaps most—of those who hold this theory believe that external objects, intra-organic stimuli, and nerve impulses exist and that they are even necessary for sensation to occur, they maintain that there is *an additional set of entities* whose real nature most people never suspect, produced by or at least in some way dependent upon the nerve impulses in the brain, and that these are what we directly and immediately sense. The sense-datum theory offered here contends that, corresponding to nerve impulses received into one part of the *brain* and lacking color themselves, there are produced within the *mind* or *consciousness* the

broad field of shaped colors (or colored shapes that we sense visually, and that, corresponding to nerve impulses received into another part of the brain and themselves soundless, there are produced within the mind the sounds we are aware of, and that something parallel occurs with each of the senses. There *may be* colors, sounds, odors, flavors, heat, cold, etc., in the outside world that are like those in the mind, but, if the sense-datum theory is correct, we can never directly sense them. The only colors, sounds, and so forth that we directly experience sensibly are those in the inner world of our own consciousness. Because these are the immediate objects of sense awareness, *given* directly to the senses, they are called "sense-data" (i.e., "sense-givens"). In addition, they are psychic (pertaining to the mind), not physical, in nature.

Basic form of the argument. How does one go about determining which theory is correct? Is there some *method* for finding out whether we directly sense external objects or only intra-organic objects or only nerve excitations in the brain or none of these but only sense-data in the mind?

There is such a method, and it can be summed up in two words: *compare* and *eliminate*.

First, compare i) *what one senses* with ii) each of these *alternative objects*. Where we find a discrepancy, we eliminate that candidate, until, when we find a match between *what is sensed* and one of the alternatives, we elect that candidate as the-sought-after answer to our question.

Such comparing may seem easy (or, again, it may not!), but there are several preliminary notions implicit in the description of it that must be brought into the light.

The first and perhaps most important preliminary lies in the phrases "what one senses" and "what is sensed," and this is the reason for underlining them above. How is it possible to separate what one senses from each of the four candidates? Is this not making five things out of four? If what we sense is one of the above, does it not follow that, once we are certain what we sense, we already have the answer to the above question? That is, will we not then know, with no further problem, whether it is an external physical object or an intra-organic one, etc.?

The solution to this difficulty, which may not be noticed upon a first reading of the "method," is a critical turning-point for anyone who undertakes a radical examination of sensation. Upon it hinges a very large part of whatever answer one gives to the question, "What and where are the objects of immediate sense-awareness?" The solution is utterly simple and yet utterly obscure, for it requires an effort to suspend one of our most deeply rooted common-sense convictions, namely, the conviction that what-we-sense is physical things—stars, trees, books, apples, etc.—things that exist in the external physical world. In order to carry out this suspension, it is necessary to focus one's attention intently on the objects of sensation in order to describe them as accurately as possible, *while simultaneously refraining from thinking of them as physical objects.*

An example may help. Suppose that it is the *object* of visual sensing (sight) that is being examined. In order to describe this object, we do what we have done since the day we were born: we open our eyes. What appears, with all of its undeniable colors, shapes, and other qualities, is the object of immediate sense awareness. But notice. It is not just one "thing" that appears, but an entire field of "things." Hence the statement earlier, when describing the sense-datum theory, that the object of sight is a *field*. This point should be kept in mind, even though—for purposes of convenience—we will usually speak only about one part out of the entire visual field at a time, usually that part more or less at the center. At this moment, then, you might describe the object of your immediate visual awareness as a rectangular-shaped, white object, having black figures within its borders and arranged in horizontal rows. In line with the previously mentioned suspension, however, you *refrain* from adding that it *is* a piece of paper. You may be certain that it is a piece of white paper covered with black print, but if you ever wish to understand the reasons why many philosophers argue that the entire world of immediate awareness, of sensation as well as of imagination, memory, and thought, is within one's consciousness, it is essential to temporarily make this suspension of your life-long common-sense convictions.

> When we speak of *what is sensed*, therefore, this phrase must be taken to refer to all of the colors, shapes, odors, tastes, etc., that you have always seen, heard, smelled, tasted, and that you will continue to see, hear, smell, taste, or otherwise sense.

It is about such things as the rectangular-shaped, white object, with black figures within its borders, figures arranged in horizontal rows, that we speak when we speak of what is sensed. The question then will be, "Is the rectangular-shaped, white object actually a physical piece of paper held between your two hands as you ordinarily believe, or is it perhaps something else?" If it is something else, then without a doubt the true nature of your experience is something quite different from what you have always believed it to be!

Aristotle's three-part distinction is of enormous help here. Or, we might add, of indispensable help. In his text, *On the Soul*, Bk.II, Ch.6, he laid out three facts about our everyday, common-sense ideas of what-we-sense. Sometimes, we think we see a bird, but it turns out to be a plane. (Or Superman?) But we know we saw *something*. Or we think we see something small, but it turns out to be huge. A bird is small, a Boeing 747 is huge. Still, we know we saw *something*. Finally, Aristotle notes that, if we did see something, it could only be because it has a color. The air around us is invisible because it has no color. With these and hundreds of similar experiences in mind, Aristotle concluded that, if we want to be precise, we should say that (i) the first class of objects we can be most certain about are the objects *'proper'* to each sense: color for sight, sound for hearing, odor for smell, flavor for taste, and hot or cold, hard or soft, etc., for touch. He gave the name *'common'* to (ii) the second category of sense-objects: size, shape, rest or motion, etc. As for (iii) the group of things we can be most often mistaken about—e.g., is it a bird, a plane, a UFO, etc.—Aristotle called *'incidental.'* You will notice that the examination of the four different theories regarding "What do we sense?" run along the common-sense lines Aristotle sorted out more than two thousand years ago.

Once the effort has been made to carefully *notice* and *describe* what you sense (see, hear, etc. and so forth), but without saying whether it is a physical object or something in your eye or ear or a set of nerve excitations in your brain or something in your mind, then—as the method prescribes—you *compare* it, for example, with the actual piece of paper in your hands and the pattern of light waves on your retina(s) and with the nerve excitations in your brain.

Another question will arise in your mind if you think over the implications of what has been said thus far. If the way to discover what we sense is to carefully attend to what we see, hear, smell, and the like, and to describe it while suspending certain of our spontaneous or impulsive convictions (this, by the way, is what many philosophers have called "phenomenological description"), then how are we to know the things we are to compare the sensed objects with? If we ever do actually imagine that what we see are patterned colors in our mind then how can we compare them with things we never have and never could see, namely, the external piece of paper, the retinal image, or the nerve impulses in our brain? This difficulty, which many philosophers have raised against any questioning of sensation, brings us to the second notion that we said was implicit in the method.

The second implicit notion that must now be made explicit is this. The critical, scientific examination of sensation and its object *must begin with the basic principles of our original, common-sense belief-system*, the set of beliefs that every normal person develops by the age or five or six. In our comparison, we simply accept, without question for the present, what we know—or *think* we know—about the external world, about light waves and the eye or about sound waves and the ear, and about the operations of the nervous system. For most educated people, beliefs such as the following, that light exists, takes time to travel, can be focused into patterns called images, that there are retinas and optic nerves and nerve impulses . . . such beliefs have acquired such certainty that they are nearly on a par with our other basic common-sense convictions. In fact—and this is a significant point for those who doubt the validity of any tampering with our common-sense convictions about sensation to ponder—it is not only easy to explain such theories about the light waves and sound waves, about retinas, inner ears, optic and auditory nerves, nerve impulses, and the like—given enough time to do so, of course—but almost every critical sense realist, phenomenologist, phenomenalist, idealist, or anyone else who discusses sensation, arrives at his position after implicitly assuming the validity of such theories at some earlier period of life. And many of those who reject the intra-organic, nerve-impulse, or sense-datum theories in favor of common-sense realism, continue to accept as literally true the scientific theories about light, sound, the nervous system and the like. The result is what we like to call "theoretical schizophrenia," namely, the simultaneous acceptance of contradictory beliefs.

Be that as it may, the answer to the question raised above is that we *accept* our common-sense convictions about the external world, about intra-organic objects, and about the nervous system, and *then* compare i) what we sense with ii) each of these assumed realities. This is in line with the principle adopted earlier: no conviction of common sense will be surrendered unless there are preponderant reasons for doing so. At the moment, there are none with respect to the convictions spoken of here. Further, the remarks made at the beginning of Argument Three about the indirectness of much of our knowledge provide a clue for understanding how we might be able to know about the external world, about intra-organic objects, and about the nervous system, even if the objects of our immediate sense awareness are within our consciousness.

This brings us to a third preliminary notion implicit in our description of the method to be employed here. We do not proceed to compare what we sense with just any of the four candidates. There is an *order* to be followed. We might, if we wish, call it "the order prescribed by common sense." That is, we begin with the hypothesis of common sense itself. We begin by comparing what we sense with objects in the external physical world, for it is just these which common sense tells us we sense. Only if they do not match do we move on to the next candidate, the intra-organic objects. And so on.

This third notion of order explains the second word of 'the method' employed here: *elimination*. The road to the sense-datum theory is traveled by *a method of elimination*. Anyone who does not follow this road will not come even close to fully realizing what are meant by "sense-data." You may have thought you grasped what was said earlier (under "Four proposed classes of objects") about psychic objects produced in our consciousness by the brain impulses. You may already understand what is meant by external physical object, by intra-organic object, and by pattern of nerve-excitation, but it is nearly certain that you will not fully comprehend what is meant by "sense-datum" (as opposed to having some vague idea about it) until after you have examined the first three alternatives in order.

Warning. Often, sense-data are referred to as "images," and there is no harm in this, *as long as* it is understood that these are not invisible images *of* the colors we see, silent images *of* the sounds we hear, odorless images *of* the odors we smell, etc. It is colors themselves we see, sounds themselves we hear, odors themselves we smell, and so on. This warning will be particularly important to keep in mind when reading about 'images' created by light reflected to the eyes (the intra-organic theory). Colors may have the form of images, but what is seen is colors. (End of warning.)

The final preliminary notion that must be made explicit is this. When it is said that we must see whether what we sense matches or does not match the objects predicted by each of the theories, this must be taken in a broad sense. It is not sufficient to make an examination of just one or two cases. We are looking for *general* matchings or *general* discrepancies. With respect to the only example mentioned till now, the rectangular-shaped, white object you see at this moment, a comparison of this individual object with the piece of paper in your hands might lead you to conclude that their properties are the same. This is only a single case, however. What is intended by the method is a comparison of a wide range of cases. It will be assumed that our senses work the same way, no matter which objects we are sensing. The alternative is believing that, in some instances we sense external objects, in some instances we sense intra-organic objects, in still others, excitations in the brain, etc., and at times we might even sense all four types of objects simultaneously! Unless our senses constantly shift gears, it seems reasonable to expect that their objects will all belong to just one of the outlined classes.

1b. Examination of the common-sense view. Recall that the common-sense view is that what we sense directly are ordinary things in the external world: moon, stars, mountains, lakes, forests, animals, cars, people, and pieces of white paper covered with print. Nothing seems more obvious. We open our eyes and there they are, *with nothing at all between us and them*! We listen, and we hear the radio, cars, birds, motors, and such things. We bite into an apple and it is the apple we taste.

There are two ways of disputing this "obvious" conviction. The method most commonly used is to turn the facts gathered by modern science against common sense. The physical and physiological processes involved in sensation are shown to lead to the impossibility of common-sense realism. The second method is to use a more direct comparison of various sensed objects with what is believed by common sense about the external physical objects involved in order to bring out the discrepancies between the two. In actual practice, however, the two ways of arguing against the common-sense view are really one, because the 'scientific' facts are conclusions derived from problems with common sense itself.

The line of reasoning that has led so many thinkers to give up the common-sense view of sensing and its objects can most effectively be begun by reexamining the type of contact involved in the sensing process. It is easy to believe that immediate contact is required in the cases of touch and taste sensations. We can neither feel nor taste anything when it is distant from us, no matter whether the distance is a mile or an inch. With the other senses, the case is not so clear.

It seems certain that not only are the objects we see distant, but Aristotle long ago pointed out that it seems impossible to see anything unless it *is* distant. For example, you can read this page as long as you hold it away from your face, but when it is flush against your face it is impossible to read. Similarly, is it not obvious that we can hear sounds from a great distance? (The eye and the ear are, in fact, often called "distance receptors.") And everyone knows that it is not necessary to sit on a pile of garbage in order to smell it.

Closer examination of the facts, as well as a survey of a wider variety of facts, dispels these easy assumptions that we can smell, hear, and see objects that are distant from us. Reference was made earlier to the example of cigarette smoke. If a person lights a cigarette and directs a puff of the smoke toward us, we can note that the smoke is perceptible only when the puff reaches us. Whoever has been near an outdoor blaze can recall being able to "get out of the way of the smoke" by moving: we smell the smoke when it is passing as long as we stand in its way, but when we get out of the way we can no longer detect it, unless, of course, some of it has gotten into our clothing. Or consider the case of Limburger cheese. After someone has brought a piece of this cheese into the room, a few moments must elapse before we can begin to detect it. But if it has been allowed to stand in the room long enough, it will remain detectable, even though in the meantime it rests at the bottom of our stomachs! Advertisers of room deodorants sell their products by hinting that unless we use Brand X our neighbors will know what we had for supper the night before. Only one explanation seems to put such disparate facts into a neat, consistent pattern, and that is the theory that various objects "evaporate," that is, that minute particles of these objects are continually separating themselves and floating away. The sensation of smelling does not occur until these particles are drawn into our nostrils and make contact with our olfactory nerves. Likewise, even though the original object is removed or destroyed (e.g. eaten), some of the evaporated particles may remain in the air, causing us to perceive the same sensation as before.

Just what does this explanation prove, however? There are many who feel that nothing more is required in order to conclude that we cannot smell objects distant from us, and that, consequently, the only objects we ever smell are the particles within our nostrils. The facts do prove this, but not without drawing out their implications further than the above account has done.

For instance, some defenders of common sense insist that the facts referred to deal only with the physics of smell perception, but that, since sensation is a psychic activity (in Aristotle's language, it involves a measure of immateriality), such facts do not even touch on the issue of sensation proper. Such a reply is partially based on the unquestioned *assumption* that Aristotle's common-sense view of knowledge is correct. (Aristotle's explanation of sensation appears in his work, *On the Soul*, which builds on theories established in his work, *The Physics*, which—in turn—unquestioningly takes direct realism for granted.) May it not be the case that the presence of the odorous particles within our nostrils is only a condition for sensation, and that once the *condition* is fulfilled we smell the distant object after all? In other words, how can we maintain that, just because the facts show that we cannot smell an object *before* its emanations reach us, we cannot smell the object, period? What is said here of smell can be paralleled by the sense of sight. There are few educated people who are not convinced, from their own experience, that light is an essential prerequisite for seeing things. Seal up the windows and the cracks around the doors, turn out the lights in the room, and nothing is visible. If light is necessary for sight, and if, in addition, the light must reach our eyes before sight occurs, this still does not seem to rule out the possibility that, when the light does reach our eyes, we see the distant objects and not the incoming light. In fact, to common sense this possibility is a certainty. Thus, the defender of common sense argues that discussing the physics of sensation is discussing only its material conditions. These have nothing to do, they claim, with sensation proper and its true objects.

Such an objection will not rescue common sense, but close attention to it can further our understanding of the argument against common sense and of the complexity of the argument.

We have already pointed out that the objection assumes that common sense is correct, that is, that what we smell and see are distant objects. What if one were to ask, though, whether or not the particles are real objects in their own right? There are numerous reasons for believing that they are. This is not the place to delve deeply into such matters, but a thorough discussion of the contention that smoke and cheese particles are real would show that anyone rejecting it must also reject much larger blocks of present-day scientific knowledge as well. (Curiously, many of the most staunch defenders of common sense also accept more of modern science as literally true than do many of the adversaries of common sense.) But if, to repeat, one were to admit that smoke and cheese particles exist in their own right, that is, that they become independent of the original object once they have detached themselves from it, then there is absolutely no reason whatever to believe that it is not they, but the original object that we smell. Even if we admitted that the smell of the cheese particles is exactly like the smell of the piece of cheese, this in no way condones the belief that, in smelling them, we are really smelling the odor of it (as many who advocate Aristotle's theories argue).

After all, even if all of the cheese in the world smelled the same, would anyone feel justified in arguing that in smelling one piece of cheese, he was smelling all of the cheese in the world? (This would convert sensing individual things into sensing universals!) It would seem, then, that if anyone admits that odorous particles are beings in their own right, it is these that we smell and not the distant objects.

This is not the most essential part of the difficulty with the argument about "conditions," however. For that, we return to the matter of comparison. Is it possible to compare what we smell and the physical objects and to find them agreeing in all respects? The answer is "No."

A small step toward understanding this can be made by considering the question of intensity: the closer we approach to the original object, the more intense the odor ordinarily becomes. We are so accustomed to this that we immediately think "So what? Isn't this precisely what one would expect?" Pause, however, and ask whether this is a logical expectation. After all, according to common sense, we believe that the odor of the block of cheese remains constant. *It* does not become stronger and weaker. Why, then does the odor that we smell become stronger and weaker? On the other hand, if particles are real, the explanation is obvious. The closer we are to the source of the evaporating particles, the more numerous they are, so that more of them make contact with our olfactory nerves, the more individual olfactory nerves are stimulated, and the more intense are the impulses sent to the brain. On the other hand, if the particles are dispersed uniformly throughout the room, the smell will be no more intense in one spot than in any other. The belief that what we smell are only the particles in direct contact with the olfactory nerves has at least this advantage over the common-sense view: it is simpler, and it is easier to understand.

Larger discrepancies occur at other times. After a piece of fish has been baked long enough, it begins to lose its "fishy" smell. The original odor lingers in the kitchen, but when we get close to the piece of fish itself, we notice that it may have little or even no odor at all. What, then, is the object we smell when we step back from the now odorless fish? Not the fish's original odor, which in no way can be attributed now to the actual piece of fish! The difficulty vanishes, of course, if we acknowledge that the original "fishy" particles of the fish, which remain dispersed in the air, are what we smell.

But the most extreme discrepancy imaginable is found in the cases of the eaten cheese and the burnt incense. For a good time after the Limburger has been chewed, mixed with the digestive juices, and rests inside the stomachs of people who, let us suppose, have left the room, the odor of the cheese hovers in the air. Or—to make the lesson even more obvious—long after the piece of incense has burned to an ash, the odor of incense persists. In these cases it is impossible to identify what we smell with the cheese or the incense, since these no longer exist. It is not now a difference between a strong odor and a faint one, or between a fishy and a non-fishy one, but between an odor that exists and one that is non-existent. Unless someone believes that he can smell non-existent odors, it is clear that he cannot be smelling the original cheese, fish, or incense. The intra-organic theory—it should be obvious that the alternative presently being opposed to the common-sense view is the intra-organic theory—explains these cases with no difficulty at all. We never do smell the fish, the cheese, or the incense, but only particles from these objects, suspended in the air, and these do remain long after the fish is baked, the cheese is eaten, and the incense burned.

It cannot be repeated too often that the crucial feature of the argument against common-sense realism is the discovery, by careful comparison, of discrepancies between the properties of what is actually sensed and the properties of the external physical objects involved in the instances under examination. This does not mean that the so-called "scientific" arguments (so-called, because they represent an application of the most common-sense logic to observations that frequently are not only available to anyone interested in experiencing them but are also indistinguishable, as observations, from any others that we ever make) are not relevant. In fact, they are, because—though we cannot pause here to establish the point—they are originally based on just such discrepancies between observation and what common sense predicts as we are discussing presently. In the end, however, the arguments that decisively undermine the common-sense theory of sensation deal, not with the physical conditions or prerequisites for sensing, but with the fact that the objects immediately sensed have properties that are at odds with the properties of external physical objects. In such cases, it is perfectly logical to identify the sensed objects, which have properties that the physical objects do not have, with other candidates which do have them (in the above cases, with the intra-organic objects).

Hearing. A review of the argument against common sense will show that, until now, *only three senses* have been dealt with in the attempt to show that it is not possible to sense anything that lacks immediate contact with our sense organs, that is, with anything distant from those organs. *Hearing* and *sight* have yet to be analysed.

Hearing is the easier of the two to examine carefully. To begin with, a close examination of very common experiences reveals the not very astonishing fact that sound, though it travels much more swiftly than odorous particles through the air, does take time to travel. For instance everyone has witnessed instances in which two objects are brought into violent contact and noticed that, as one stands farther from the collision, a longer and longer time interval elapses before one hears the sound. Whether it is a carpenter's hammer striking a nail or a pile hammer driving a post into the ground, or a marching drummer's sticks banging into the sides of his drum, the farther away one is, the more out of synchronization is what we see (the contact) and what we hear. The only plausible explanation ever offered for such experiences is that the initial physical contact sets up vibrations in the air and that these vibrations or waves of vibrations (physical sound waves) travel outwards, requiring time to pass from one place to the next, specifically *from* the vibrations' cause *to* one's ears.

That explanation is confirmed by the numberless other experiences that it illuminates. For example, echoes become understandable. When we shout and then listen for the echo, we hear two sounds: we hear the sound of our voice at the very moment that we shout, and we then hear the echo. This is explained when we realize that the vibrations created by our vocal chords affect our eardrums almost instantaneously, and this accounts for the first sound that we hear. Then they continue to travel outwards. Except when there is some obstacle, say, a mountain or a closed set of walls that bounce the vibrations back, they continue traveling outwards indefinitely. The obstacles that reflect the vibrations back to us are responsible for echoes, and it is the "same" sound that we heard originally that we hear for the second time as the echo, only now it is weakened and possibly even distorted. Similarly, it is now possible to understand why, the farther we are from the atmospheric disturbances that create thunder and lightning, the more time elapses before we hear the sound of the thunder. This is because, though the thunder and lightning occur at the same time, the sound waves travel much more slowly to our ear than the light does to our eye, with the result that the time lag in sound's travel is less or is more apparent depending on how close we are to the scene.

What such experiences reveal is, first of all, that it is impossible to hear any sound before the sound waves reach our ears. Sound waves, essentially, are vibrations, at least when it is physical sounds that are referred to. (The reason for making this qualification will become clearer later on.) What is important to keep in mind is that by the time one vibration reaches our ear, either many new ones have been produced back at the original site, unless of course there are no longer any at all there.

Turn back to the examples already given. We presume that the carpenter heard the sound of his hammer striking the nail almost the very instant that contact was made. We hear the sound, say, one second later. Only, when we hear the sound, the carpenter is already drawing his hammer back for another strike, and he is hearing no sound at that moment. The sound waves reaching our ears are not *conditions* required for us to hear some sound one thousand feet away (since none exist there to be heard), but *are themselves the sound that we hear*. At least we can accept this conclusion until the intra-organic theory is examined.

The argument is even more clear-cut in the example of the thunder. A person one mile from the original atmospheric disturbance will hear the sound of the thunder approximately five seconds later. Since signals travel much more quickly through a telephone wire, it would be possible for someone to hear the thunder twice if he or she happened to be speaking to someone much nearer to the scene: the sound could be heard first over the telephone, and then coming through the air. Such things have, in fact, been experienced. In such instances, it is clear that, by the time the thunder reaches the hearer's eardrums the second time, all is quiet back at the original site. Here we have instances of the total discrepancy that we found earlier, when speaking of smell (in the cases of the eaten cheese, the baked fish, and the burned incense), a discrepancy that dissolves when the sensed sound is compared with the intra-organic object (the vibrations within the ear itself).

Of course, there are cases where there are sounds at the original site and where they are merely different from the sensed sounds, not entirely non-existent. The Doppler effect is an example of this. When an external reality is emitting a sound while traveling rapidly toward or away from us, the vibrations that reach our ears will have a different frequency from the frequency that they have at the traveling source itself. The altered frequency creates an altered quality in the heard sounds, and this quality is referred to as the pitch of the sound. An experiment can be set up. Two observers can be stationed along rail tracks one mile apart. When the speeding train is between them, its whistle is blown. The trainman will hear a sound with a steady pitch, the observer whom the train has passed will hear a falling pitch, and the third person farther up the tracks will hear a rising pitch. (The observers could be replaced with tape recorders, with similar results.) The fact that they hear three different sounds is evidence that three different sounds exist, and the only suitable way to account for this is to recognize that the sounds each one hears are similar to the sounds in contact with his own eardrums.

Or consider the surprise each of us feels when we listen to a tape recording of our own voice for the first time. Invariably, we say "That doesn't sound like me!" Equally surprising to us is the answer of others listening to the recording: "That sounds *just* like you!" What we mean is that the sound we hear from the recording is different from the sound we hear at the moment we are speaking, even though it may be like the sound others hear when we speak. Are there, then, two sounds when we speak, the one we hear and the one others hear? Which is the sound of our real voice?

The intra-organic theory claims that there are, indeed, two different sounds: we hear the vibrations produced inside our own ears (many of which do not travel out of our mouth through the air to our ears but remain within the head and are slightly modified in the process) and others hear the somewhat different vibrations inside their own ears.

These are not different conditions for hearing the same sound. They are cases of different sensed (heard) sounds. This distinction, which is crucially important, has been the subject of endless debates. Some critics would argue that in the cases discussed in the previous paragraph people hear the same sounds (the sound of the train whistle in one instance, the sound of someone's voice in the second), adding that, of course, the sound *seems* to be different.

Many answers are possible. First, such a criticism does not touch the cases in which there is no longer a distant sound at the original site to be heard. Secondly, it does not explain why the three tape recorders capture three different sounds (though some, unable to break the spell of long-entrenched common sense, would stubbornly insist that even these three sounds only *seem* to be different). Thirdly, it bypasses the fact that the only way to explain why people, in these instances, say that the sound *seems* to be rising or falling, i.e., changing (in the case of the train whistle) is that the sound they hear *is* rising or falling.

People do not always use the word "seem" to mean the same thing, nor do they use it only in situations similar to those under discussion. But the reason the term is used here is because people ordinarily think in common-sense terms, that is, they believe that the external sound and the sound they hear are one and the same. Because they know that the external pitch of the train whistle itself is not actually rising, though the sound they hear is, they seek a compromise by saying that the train whistle only *seems* to be rising. The compromise becomes unnecessary as soon as it is realized that we are dealing here with two sounds, one of which truly is rising in pitch and one of which has a steady pitch. In fact, we never hear the external sound; rather we infer its nature from the sound we hear. We do not *sense* the distant sound; our *mind* infers its nature on the basis of the sound within the ear.

If the discussion is beginning to make sense to you, it is possible for you to grasp more fully the importance, referred to earlier, of learning to focus on what is sensed while simultaneously refraining from thinking of it as something physical. Persons insistent on believing they hear the train whistle itself simply won't allow themselves to notice that the sound they hear is actually rising or falling, because it is assumed that the train whistle itself gives out a steady-pitched sound. Some authors believe such persons have not yet acquired the ability to distinguish a sound (what is sensed) from its unsensed source.

Sight. We come now to the most difficult sense of all, sight. There are countless people who accept the intra-organic object theory for touch, taste, smell, and hearing, but who balk when they are asked to consider the possibility that they never see anything that is further away from them than their own retinas. All of us have the feeling that, no matter what we may believe about smell and hearing, it is perfectly certain that, when we open our eyes, we see things distant from us: the clouds and trees outside the window, the doors and walls across the room, etc. There is probably no common-sense conviction more difficult for people to examine open-mindedly than the conviction that the brightly colored, distinctly shaped objects or *field of objects* that they see directly are inches, feet, often miles away from them.

Nevertheless, if someone does wish to critically examine this conviction, certain preliminary considerations will be of help. To begin with, let us discuss retinal images. The eye has often been compared to the camera. Both are enclosed structures (sometimes referred to as "boxes," though with quite distinct shapes), both have an opening to admit light, both have lenses at the opening that focus the light into patterns on the surface opposite the opening, and both have some mechanism for registering the light patterns (the camera has photographic film, the eye has a retina made up of millions of nerve receptors). The pattern of light formed on the retina is called an "image." Though some authors challenge the suitability of saying that there is an image on the retina, their objection is groundless as long as we do not think of it as a static thing, but as light rays or waves that have a pattern to them.

It is extremely helpful to become familiar with this notion of optical images. It can be done best of all, perhaps, by using a camera with a piece of ground glass (sanded or roughened glass) in place of the film. If you have ever had an opportunity to examine one of the large cameras used by photographers to take studio portraits—the kind that used to have the black hood under which the photographer hid his head for "a moment" while focusing the camera—you know what an optical image is. (In this third millennium, digital cameras that provide picture-screens make it easier than ever to understand what an optical image is.)

Lacking those mediums, a small magnifying glass and a blank sheet of paper can be substituted. You stand inside a room that has a window opening onto the outdoors. The darker the room and the sunnier the day outside, the better. Holding the magnifying glass between the window and the sheet of paper, you will find that, by experimenting with the distance between the magnifying glass and the paper, you can produce an image of the outdoors, e.g. trees, etc. Several things are to be noted about the image. To begin with, it is a reality that is distinct from the object that it is an image of. The latter is on one side of the magnifying glass, is outdoors, and is upright. The image, on the other hand, is on the opposite side of the magnifying glass, is indoors, located where the piece of paper is, and is upside-down. However much they may look alike or resemble each other, they constitute two realities, not one. When you turn your head to look at the sheet of paper, it is the image that you see, not the objects outdoors. Seeing one is not seeing the other, any more than smelling particles of cheese suspended in the air is smelling the piece of cheese on the table (or in your stomach).

In addition, the image can be changed without altering the outdoor objects. It is already different in some respects. For one, as was mentioned, its spatial orientation is the reverse of the object. There may be no absolute up and down in the universe, but, relative to our own bodies at least (unless you are standing on your head), the object outdoors is upright, and the image is upside down. Secondly, the image is much smaller than the object that it is an image of. It can be further changed. By widening or shortening the distance between the magnifying glass and the paper, the image can be blurred, with no change in the distinct contours of the object outside the window. By tilting the magnifying glass, the image can be distorted in shape, again with no change in the outer object's shape. Your imagination can supply other examples. (E.g. heat waves rising from a radiator below the window can, if strong enough, create small "wavings" in the image.)

Once the nature of the retinal image is grasped, the intra-organic theory is easily understood. According to it, the often bright-colored and usually distinctly-patterned objects that we see when we open our eyes are not actually distant from us—as they inevitably seem to be—but are as close to us as our own retinas.

Another preliminary notion is helpful, though. The image is formed from the light rays impinging on our retinas. But—and this is a fact that the staunchest defenders of common sense find difficult to deny—it takes time for light to travel from the distant object to the eye.

For a long time, it was easy to believe that light travels instantaneously. Aristotle argued that, if light took time to travel, then we should see it travel across the sky at dawn. The sky is a vast stretch of space, but the fact is that at dawn each part of the sky and landscape seems to become lighter at the same time, that is, light does not seem to reach some places more slowly than others nearer the sun. Our own experience seems to confirm this. Though the sound of the carpenter's hammer observably requires time to travel to our ear, it seems that we observe the hammer strike at the very moment the carpenter does. And when we flip on the light, the room instantaneously lights up, just as it instantaneously is plunged back into darkness when we flip off the switch.

The first concrete, empirical evidence for the finite speed of light was obtained only in 1676. That year, Olaus Roemer predicted that the eclipse of one of Jupiter's moons would appear ten minutes later than rival astronomers were expecting. He explained it by saying that, because the earth would be sixty million miles further from Jupiter than at other times, it would take the light that much longer to reach the earth.

Modern observations have so solidly established the finite speed of light that it now forms the very foundation for various parts of modern science. The reason why it was only late in human history that we learned definitively of this phenomenon of nature and the reason why we never notice it at all in our daily lives is because, even though light does take time to get from one place to another, the speed with which it does so is incredibly fast, about 186,000 miles per second. Not per minute, but per second! This means that a ray of light could theoretically travel around the equator seven times in one second.

This fact has had enormous consequences for philosophy, so much so that one historian of ideas, Arthur Lovejoy, mentions the omission of Olaus Roemer's 1676 discoveries from philosophy texts as evidence of how poorly many histories of philosophy are written.

Perhaps as much as anything else, the proof that light travels with a finite speed helped to undermine the common-sense view of visual sensation. Why? Because it now makes it possible to apply the same arguments to sight's immediate objects as were applied to those of smell and hearing: the argument that we can see and smell things long after the distant external object has perished. More of that later, however. For now, let us simply note that the light that reaches our retinas (and that forms the retinal image) has left the vicinity of the distant object at least some time before it reaches our retinas, even if the time is measured in billionths of a second. Further, if light travels in waves, whether waves in the luminiferous ether—the existence of which is denied by many scientists today (or replaced by the space-time continuum!)—or whether merely as waves of photons, then by the time one set of waves reaches our retinas, other waves are already being generated at the distant object.

Having established these clarifications, we are now in position to discuss the fatal defects in the common-sense view of visual sensation. We concentrate on noting the properties of what we sense—in this case, what we see—while suspending judgment about its physical nature, and then compare these properties with the properties that we believe the external objects to possess.

There is no one who has not had the experience of looking into the night sky and of observing those thousands of white pinpoints that we call stars. Astronomical observations and the calculations built on them have confirmed the fact that they are almost infinitely more distant than men living before 1500 A.D. believed. By the time of Aristotle, one astronomer, Aristarchus of Samos, had estimated the distance of the stars from the earth to be about 100 million miles, which we now know is the approximate distance to the sun-star (93,000,000 miles). Copernicus merely enlarged this by about twenty times.

Today, these figures are replaced by others so large that they nearly defy imagination. It is reckoned that the next nearest star, Alpha Centauri, is more than four light years away*. This means that Alpha Centauri, the closest star after our sun, is so far away that it takes more than four years for a ray of its light to reach us. By contrast, a ray of the sun's light crosses the 93,000,000 miles that separate it from us in merely eight minutes. Other stars are millions of light years away, i.e. their light must travel for millions of years before reaching our retinas. (*One light year is the distance covered by a ray of light in one year, that is, 186,000 X 60 X 60 X 24 X 365$^{1/4}$ miles, i.e., a little less than six trillion miles.)

Once these facts are grasped, we can understand it when astronomers, after formulating hypotheses about the birth and death of stars, tell us that by the time the light from some distant stars reaches our eyes, the star itself may have exploded or burned out. (This was the case with Supernova 1987A.) As long as the light, still traversing the vast reaches of space between the now burnt-out star and the earth, reaches our retinas, it will be focused into a star image and we will see the white pinpoint that we (mis-)take to be a distant star. Only it cannot *be* the distant star that is no longer a bright ball of flame. "It" is the white pinpoint we see when we open our eyes, the white pinpoint that seems to be distant, "out there." *That* is what we see. But that is not, as we common-sensically believe it to be, a distant star, for there no longer is any distant star in that direction. This is an argument identical in outline to that used with the eaten cheese, the burnt incense, and the sound of the thunder.

The incompatibility of the finite speed of light and the common-sense view of sight's objects can be exploited by a thought-experiment. Suppose that the sun could be replaced with a cold, dead planet—just long enough for the experiment, of course. If an astronaut landed on this planet and, say, at 10:00 fired off a flare that burned for one minute, some interesting things would happen. By focusing our most powerful telescope on the event (since this experiment is entirely imaginary, we can also imagine that our telescope is strong enough to zoom right in on the tiny figure of the astronaut), we on earth would see nothing at 10:00 when the flare is fired. We would continue to see nothing during the entire minute that it burns. Only at 10:08, seven minutes after the flare has burned out, do we first see the burst of light, and we will continue to see it until 10:09. The explanation is simple. Eight minutes are necessary for the initial rays coming from the burning flare to travel the 93,000,000 miles to our retinas. Each succeeding wave radiated during the next minute requires the same eight minutes, the last one reaching our eye just one minute after the first.

The significance of those facts is monumental. The light waves reaching our retinas are not merely prerequisites to enable us to see the distant flare. The flare no longer exists by the time the light reaches our eyes. What do we see? Only direct experience, not theory, can enable us to describe it: that is, whatever we see, we will see simply by letting the light fall on our retinas. What will be seen will look exactly like a man standing beneath a burning flare. And it will look like it is far off, as distant as any far off objects seen through a telescope. It will no more look like an object flush against our retinas than the white pinpoint we see when we look toward the burnt-out star does. But it cannot be a man standing beneath a burning flare. What looks like the man and the flare, what *seems* to be distant from us, we now know can *actually* be no further away than our retinas. There simply is nothing more distant from us than that to serve as a candidate for what we see now, the image of a flare.

Several things must be noted. The strength of this argument rests on another common-sense conviction that was mentioned under "Argument One," namely, the conviction that the past no longer exists, that the only things that can be found in the universe at this moment are things that exist at this moment. Things existing now may have existed in the past and may be different from what they were then, ourselves for instance. But nowhere will anyone searching the universe this moment find, in addition to you as you are now, another you as you were five minutes ago and a third you as you were a year ago, and so on. This common-sense conviction is utterly at odds with the "answer" that some give to the above argument: they say that what we see is not the retinal image, but the flare that did exist (even though it no longer does). But unless our universe can contain things that no longer exist, then it is impossible for us to see them, for what we see does exist, and it exists now. We must give up one or other of these common-sense convictions. The argument against common sense's theory of sensation is based on a retention of common sense's conviction about time and the perishing of the past.

Secondly, and it is impossible to overemphasize this point, the *depth* or apparent distance of the object that is seen is in no way affected by the fact that it cannot be physically further from us than our retinas. A moment's recall of *the similar fact about heard sound* will make clear what is at issue. There is no way of accepting the ordinary theory about sound waves without also accepting the conclusion that we never hear any sound that is further from us than our eardrums. Though the vibrations from the carpenter's hammer, from the atmospheric disturbances, and from the snap of one's fingers next to his ear may have originated at points distant from us, the sounds we hear, at the moment we hear them, *are* equally close. Yet it is next to impossible for it not to *seem* that the thunder sound is much further away than the finger-snap-sound. Our habits of interpretation are so habitual, not to say instantaneous, that even after one realizes that the sounds are not physically distant, *they will continue to seem so.* In fact, experts in acoustics, with special equipment and placing arrangements can recreate within one's ear the stimuli usually only produced by distant objects and can cause in the experimental subject the illusion of hearing distant objects. With special instruments, too, they can feed sound waves coming from one direction into the ear on the opposite side of one's head and similarly reverse the input from the other direction, with the result that one will locate sound sources, instinctively and inescapably, in the wrong places.

Just as we cannot avoid the impression that sounds that we think "can't be," *are* distant, *so we cannot avoid having the impression that the things we see are distant,* even though facts show that they *cannot* be. An excellent demonstration of this is the stereoscope. Every Christmas, parents are urged to buy View-Masters for their children. Looking through them, we see scenes that have a full three-dimensionality. It is impossible to have the impression of seeing two two-dimensional transparencies, and yet it is quite certain that the only physical realities before our eyes are two entirely flat color transparencies. No single physical object in the scene is further from us than any other, but the impression that some are is unavoidable. The famous rooms designed by A. Ames are additional demonstrations of the fact that visual depth (the apparent distance of what we see) does not coincide with physical objects' distances.

Note well, then: when it is said here that you see, not a distant physical star, but rather an image of the star, this does not mean that, instead of the apparently-distant white pinpoint, you see some invisible image somewhere between that pinpoint and your eye. That *apparently* distant, white pinpoint is *itself* the image. And when it is said later on that what you see when you turn your eyes in the direction of the white piece of paper you hold in your hand is not the paper but an image, it is the *apparently* two or three-feet-distant white, rectangular-shaped object you see that *is* the image.

Anyone interested further in the factors that are held responsible for the apparent depth of the objects we see may profitably consult a psychology text dealing with the various cues that the mind uses in its perceptions.

The third point to be noted with respect to the thought-experiment is that, though the case of the man with the flare is entirely imaginary, it only illustrates the principles at work in countless real cases. The eclipse of Jupiter's moon is one such case. For ten minutes, astronomers saw what looked like a distant *illuminated* body in the sky, even though, at that very moment, part or all of the actual heavenly body was plunged into darkness. The brightly lit orb that they saw could not have been the distant physical object. But there was, of course, a round pattern (image) of light striking their retinas during that period. Similarly, short bursts of light (laser beams) have been directed at our moon and been reflected back to earth by special reflectors left there by astronauts. The reflections are seen as spots on the moon, but not until a matter of seconds has passed, and by then the spot on the moon has become dark again. The radio signals conveying photographic and other information from rockets sent to explore Venus and Mars take time to travel back to earth—radio waves are electromagnetic waves similar to light waves except in frequency. Etc.

(*Further note for those unfamiliar with light.* Although most people are dimly aware of the fact that light is required for vision, many do not understand how different reality is from their ordinary ways of thinking about it. We ordinarily think of the night sky surrounding the moon as being quite dark, and for most this would be equivalent to saying that there is not much light in the sky. Similarly, most people seldom reflect on the fact that the space between their car's headlights and distant objects, at night, is filled with light. In fact, however, the space before our eyes is ordinarily filled with incredible amounts of light, traveling in every direction. Look again at the moon. The sun, hidden from us by the earth's rotation, floods the night sky with light, except for a corridor of darkness that constitutes the shadow thrown by the earth. The reason why the remainder of the sky appears dark to us is that none of this light reaches our eyes except for that which is reflected back by the moon. The nighttime driver sees none of the light thrown by his headlights except the light that is reflected back to his eyes by distant objects. If there is a fog, however, the billions of tiny vapor droplets each reflect a bit of the light before it can reach the distant objects, thus effectively cutting off those distant objects from our gaze. But it is never the moon, the distant objects, or the fog droplets that we see, but only the images produced by light reflected back from those objects to our eyes. It is never sufficient for light to fall onto some object in order for us to see it; the light must bounce from that object in order to form retinal images. A beam of light can pass directly before our eyes at night, but if the atmosphere is clear and none of the light is reflected into our eyes, we will see nothing. The reason we can "see objects in an ordinary room" from any point of the room is that light is bouncing from those things in every direction. That is why it was said earlier that the space before our eyes is ordinarily filled with incredible amounts of light, traveling in every direction. Of course, the lenses of our eyes are required to focus the criss-crossing light waves into neat patterns or images on our retinas, and it is these, not the physical objects in the room, that we really see. These and similar facts lend further support to the by now common conclusion that we can never see anything until light has reached our eyes. Such facts support the further conclusion that we cannot see the distant objects at all. End of note.)

Someone, though admitting that it seems that we cannot directly see *distant* objects like stars and the sun (since the time for the light's travel is significant), may wonder whether it is not possible for us to say that we can see *nearby* objects where the time-lapse is measured in billionths of a second. This is ruled out for various reasons. First of all, it would mean that for someone looking toward the setting sun the object that seems the farthest away (the sun) is really the closest (on his retina), while the objects that seem the closest (nearby trees, etc.) are further away. Even worse, it would mean (as above) that vision follows different sets of laws: one set for distant objects, another for closer ones.

Once a person has become familiar with images and particularly with the facts of *apparent depth*, it becomes easier to apply the method of comparison to nearby objects and to see why they fail to match what we see. For example, think of the oft-discussed straight stick that is half immersed in water. What exists, physically? In other words, what are the qualities of the external stick? Common sense tells us that it is straight when it is out of the water, and that it retains this shape when it is in the water. What are the properties of what we see? Three answers are ordinarily given. "What we see is straight, period." "What we see appears to be broken or bent at the place where the stick enters the water." "What we see really is bent." Which answer is given is critical. At present, we are considering only two of the four possibilities, namely, the external physical object and the retinal image. (The nerve-impulse theory and the sense-datum theory are not yet in view.)

Common sense gives the first two answers together. Convinced that we see the physical stick and that the stick is straight, the common-sense theorist *must* say that what we see is straight. There is nothing bent (distant from him) to see. He adds, however, that it *seems* or *appears* to be bent. The intra-organic object theorist answers that this is a misdescription of what is seen. What is seen very obviously *is* bent, and anyone who was not aware of the physical stick's straightness would unhesitatingly give this answer. It is only when the person learns that the stick is straight that he begins to change his description of what he sees, so that his description will harmonize with his belief about the stick. According to the intra-organic theorist, the obscurities created by common sense's desire to retain all of its convictions simultaneously are dissipated once we realize that there are two things involved here, a straight stick and a bent image. We see the bent image, not knowing that it is an image, whereas we think we see the straight stick, not knowing that there is a bent image. Convinced that the same thing cannot be at once straight and bent, we compromise by saying that what we see *is* straight, but *appears* bent. Now, however, realizing that two things exist, we can say what is true: what we see is bent. We know about the straight stick, not with our eyes, but by inferring—from other experiences!, such as the straight image we see later on when the stick is drawn out of the water, by running our hand along the stick while it is in the water, etc.—its properties with our mind.

Many persons miss the force of the above reasoning because they unconsciously *"change the subject."* For example, when discussing the case of the stick that is partially immersed in water, they not only reply that the stick merely *appears* to be bent, but they add: "That is no difficulty, since we know that light is refracted (i.e., because it travels more slowly through a medium like water, its path or direction of travel is altered) and *causes* the stick to appear bent." In other words, the discussion switches from the question "What and where is the object being immediately sensed?" to the question "*Why* is that object (or *why* does that object appear to be) bent?" Many believe that facts concerning different causal conditions, whether physical or physiological, answer the first question when, in fact, they are frequently not even directly pertinent to it. Thus, M. Lean, in his work, *Sense-Perception and Matter*, replies to C.D. Broad's assertion that physical and physiological explanations are irrelevant in determining whether we see the stick or something else by writing that "these facts about different refractive indices of different media do explain the phenomenon of the bent appearance of the stick" (*op. cit.*, p.180). We might say that if Lean recognized the "appearance" as an entity distinct from the stick, what he says would be true; but he goes on, as most people do, to deny that we sense anything distinct from the stick itself.

Without going into the matter further here, let it be said that the only really plausible explanation why we see something bent even though the stick remains straight is light-refraction. But, to repeat the charge made above, an explanation regarding the reason *why* what we sense is bent does not answer the questions, *What* do we sense? (Incidentally, it is worth remarking that direct sense realists, who object to the introduction of scientific theories when these are used to attack sense realism, immediately turn to such theories as light refraction in order to *defend* sense realism! Contrary to appearances, however, the only support that such theories provide to direct sense realism is illusory.)

A more careful description of what we actually see, unbiased by notions about what we should see, begins to reveal that everything we see has properties at odds with the properties of external physical objects.

For instance, find a magazine-photo that has, for instance, a nearby object that looks much larger than a distant object that is actually larger than the nearby object. Suppose you find a photo with an image of a nearby person's head and an image of a distant auto. The distant auto appears smaller than the human's head. But we know that the auto is the larger of the two. That is the real reason we say that the auto only "appears" smaller. But if you look and describe what you actually see, i.e., the relative sizes of the 'things' in the photo, without making any prejudgments about their relative sizes, what would you say? Is it not a fact that the image of the human's head is larger than the image we take to be the auto?

The sizes and shapes of what we see continually change as we walk about just as they do in videos. So do the sizes and shapes of the images on the retina. The sizes and shapes of the external objects do not, however. This is the reason why the intra-organic theorist claims that a close inspection of even the ordinary things we see reveals that the common-sense view of sensation is mistaken.

Other examples abound. When what we would call a *white* object (e.g., a white sheet) has *colored* light projected onto it, the only light that the screen can reflect is the colored light. This creates in the eye, not a white image, but a colored one. Common sense would say that we actually see a white object, but that it appears colored. The intra-organic theory points out that we see a colored object (and only infer from other experiences—from what we see when full light is thrown on the sheet—that the physical sheet itself is white). Whether what is seen is white or colored is something that each one must consult their direct experience to answer. Try it the next time you go to the theatre to watch a Technicolor movie. Do you see colors or a white screen? Do you believe that the screen changes its color with each different wavelength of light that is projected onto it?!

When we look in the direction of a distant object, but hold one of our fingers about five inches from the center of our face, we can pay attention to a very startling phenomenon. If we focus on our finger, everything in the background doubles. If we focus on a distant object, we suddenly have two fingers! More correctly, in each case we will see one of one thing, and two of another. But we *know* that physical objects, whether cars or fingers, do not suddenly multiply, so that there are two where before there was only one. Keep in mind, however, that there are always two retinal images. A study of a text that discusses retinal disparity will explain that we will see *as one* those images that occupy relatively the *same* portions of the two retinas. Focusing on the distant object really means (partly) bringing the two images to the central part of each retina. But doing this causes the images of other things to occupy different parts of the retinas, with the result that we now see both images separately. (Notice that closing one eye immediately eliminates one of the doubled objects.) The question pertinent here is, "When the finger is doubled, do you see one thing that appears to be two, or do you see two things?" Your answer will determine whether you recognize the inadequacy of common sense or not.

Now for a final example. If a large board is painted with tiny squares of yellow and blue paint, arranged as on a checkerboard, an observer at a distance from the board will claim that it appears to be green. When asked if what is seen is green or only appears to be green, the answer will probably depend upon whether or not the observer knows how the board is actually painted. Because the lenses of the eyes do not separate the light wave patterns sharply enough and because the portion of the retinas covered by the image is so small, the retinal image will be a mixture of the two wavelengths. (This is an oversimplification of the wavelengths, but more careful description would lead to similar results.) A camera pointed in the same direction would yield the same green image. We may say, therefore, that the distant object is not green, but only yellow and blue, whereas the retinal image is green. Which is really seen, therefore? Only a careful, unbiased description of the color of what is actually seen will give the correct answer.

The reason for introducing this final example into an already overlong discussion of the common-sense view is that it provides an opportunity to examine one more unsuccessful dodge of common sense. Many people, faced with this situation, will claim that the distant board *is* green, because, as everyone knows, yellow and blue form a combination that is green. Now, while this may be true in a few instances, as when we mix yellow and blue paint so thoroughly that the yellow and blue no longer exist separately (one wonders what the mixture would look like under the microscope), this is not the case here. There is no combination out at the board, as a closer examination would disclose. Aristotle and Aquinas discussed similar cases and declared that such mixtures are mixed "only to the eye," i.e., that no true mix has occurred. The only colors that exist at the board are yellow and blue, and if these are not seen, then the color of the board is not seen. But, points out the intra-organic theorist, the colors *are* combined at the retinas to form green! The correct inference to be drawn is clear.

This concludes our examination of the common-sense theory of the objects of sensation, though, in fact, the sense of touch has hardly been mentioned at all. This will be remedied in the next section.

It is only right to warn the reader that common sense is still not without defenders, despite the arguments marshaled against it here. The defenses have been both many and ingenious, but they often involve theories of metaphysics and of language that are too abstruse to be treated in a brief discussion. Some neo-Aristotelians defend common sense by theorizing about knowledge as the immaterial reception of forms. K. Gallagher has registered a justifiable complaint against such an approach on the grounds that the defense is erected on a dogmatic assumption that common sense is correct. (See K. Gallagher, "Some Recent Anglo-American Views on Perception," in the *International Philosophical Quarterly*, vol. IV, pp. 122, ff.). That is, *if* the common-sense view were correct about what we sense, their defense would be valid.

But we must first examine to see if its views about our sensing external objects is correct, and in this the starting facts, the facts to be explained, turn out to be different from common sense's expectations. Other neo-scholastics propose a theory of virtual common-sense realism that can be shown by careful analysis to be identical, not with common sense, but with a Kantian-type phenomenalism. (For an exposition of the theory and a critique, cfr. K. Gallagher, 1964, pp. 108-119.) For examples of defenses built on language theories, see the contributions of W. H. F. Barnes and G. A. Paul in R. J. Swartz (1965) and by J. L. Austin and G. Ryle in R. J. Hirst (1965). An excellent discussion of the various theories can be found in J. Hospers (1967), Pt.8, pp.493, ff.

2b. Examination of the intra-organic-object theory. It is not unusual that students, having been confronted with the arguments against common sense, concede that it is indeed impossible to see, hear, smell, taste, or feel physical objects distant from them. They find their minds overwhelmed by the endless supply of facts, ordinarily unnoticed, that militate against the usual view. But a factor that is perhaps even more convincing is the almost aesthetic neatness with which the intra-organic theory fits all of these facts together. In other words, the experiences that argue against the common-sense view, because the common-sense view *cannot* explain them, simultaneously increase the strength of the intra-organic theory because it *can* account for them. One author writes:

> It is argued that the intuitionist [i.e., common sense] view would oblige us to attribute contradictory predicates to the same realities: for since the colour, size, and shape of objects vary according to their distance from us, the angle from which they are looked at, and the media through which they are viewed, it will follow that we shall have to say that they are simultaneously of different sizes, shapes and colours: e.g. a penny will be at once half and a quarter of an inch in diameter, both light and dark brown, circular and oval simultaneously. It is, however, plain that according to our theory we do not sense the penny on the table but the projection of light reflected by it to the eye, and this intra-organic object is in fact of different dimensions, shapes and colours according to the point of view from which the penny is looked at. Since, moreover, we cannot regard it simultaneously from more than one point of view it is plain that there can be no discordance between those objects which we actually and immediately see. The same answer will evidently apply to any difficulty which urges that the use of a medium will alter the object—so a microscope will make us see a strange monster when unaided vision will only show us a flea—for the external object, the insect, does not change, but only the object in contact with the eye changes; and this is, in the one case, a large and horrible shape, in the other, a tiny speck. (R.P. Phillips, 1950, vol. II, pp. 70-71.)

We have seen that the intra-organic theory not only explains the variations in what we see, but also explains the variations in the sounds we hear and the odors we smell. Similarly, if what we taste are the food particles dissolved in the mouth's juices, then alterations in these juices (caused by illness, etc.) would explain why things that ordinarily have a pleasant taste are experienced differently at other times.

Many halt their inquiry into sensation and its objects at this point. Nevertheless, a close inspection of other experiences reveals large numbers of phenomena that even the intra-organic theory cannot cover. Surprisingly, it turns out that we do not see retinal images, nor do we hear the air-molecule vibrations within the ears, nor do we smell, taste, or feel objects in contact with the extremities of our olfactory, gustatory, or tactual nerves.

A reason frequently offered for this opinion is that we can never sense anything until the stimuli reaching the external sense organs have been transformed into nerve impulses, the nerves have transmitted these impulses to the brain, and the impulses have been received into the brain and organized by its internal structures. The necessity for these events within the nervous system, which intervene between the time the stimuli contact the external organs and the time sensation proper occurs, is shown by the fact that if any of the nerves leading from any sense organ to the brain are physically severed, the normal sensations associated with that sense organ are disrupted, whether or not the stimuli continue to reach the external organ. The same cut-off in normal sensation can be produced by using drugs to block the functions of the nervous system. We make practical use of the latter fact in surgery: the pain that cutting and similar physical mutilation ordinarily involves is prevented by the employment of anesthetics. To many, such facts are sufficient evidence for the conclusion that what we actually are aware of in sensation is not the external physical world, nor the stimuli in contact with the sense organs, but the patterns of nerve excitations within the brain itself.

A bit of reflection similar to that used earlier shows, however, that such facts may not convince everyone that, by themselves, they prove that we do not sense the external stimuli. All that the facts demonstrate is that we cannot sense the stimuli until the impulses are received into the brain. They do not show that when the nerve impulses are received in the brain, it is the nerve impulses that we sense. It may be that they furnish only the prerequisite conditions for sensing the external stimuli.

A better argument is made by drawing attention to the fact that, according to modern research, some time must elapse between the time the stimuli reach the external organ and the moment the resulting impulses are received into the brain. Although the time required for these previously-unsuspected events is measured, not in light-years or in entire seconds, but in millionths of seconds, still by the time the impulses produced by earlier stimuli are received into the brain, new stimuli have arrived at the external sense organs.

A defender of the intra-organic theory might counter this argument by saying that what is sensed is not individual light or sound waves, etc., but their overall gestalt. If the overall gestalt of the earlier and the later stimuli are similar, it might be argued that the time lapse does not affect the theory that what is sensed is the gestalt of the external stimuli.

Now, while this counter-argument offered by the intra-organic-object theorist might appear to be a good one, a close analysis and comparison of the nature of the stimuli and the events in the nervous system, taken together with an analysis of the phrase "same gestalt," would show that it actually is much weaker than it appears and that it assumes what it attempts to demonstrate. Nevertheless, none of the facts mentioned above are needed in order to show that the intra-organic theory is mistaken. Attentive comparison of what is sensed with the intra-organic objects is sufficient by itself to discredit the theory.

For example, it is obvious that the objects that we see have the same spatial orientation as we attribute to our own bodies. When we direct our eyes toward someone else, the body-shaped object we see (which we take to be the other person) is upright with respect to ourselves. The "head" of the object is nearer to what we take to be the ceiling, and the "feet" are nearer the floor. (Since we have ruled out the common-sense view, we now use the phrase "direct our eyes toward someone" rather than "see someone.") Nevertheless, the retinal images are upside-down with respect to our own bodies: the "head" of the retinal image is closer to the floor, whereas the "feet" in the image are nearer the ceiling. This striking discrepancy between the intra-organic objects (the retinal images) and what we see undermines the theory that what we see are the retinal images.

Someone familiar with the experiments conducted by G.M. Stratton and others* may argue that what we see is not upright, but only appears upright, or that, although we ordinarily see the upside-down retinal images "as right-side up," we can also learn to see them as "upside-down." In other words, they would argue that what we see really has the spatial orientation that the retinal images have, though we may not always see them that way. (*In the experiments, persons wearing special instruments that re-inverted the retinal images were able to adapt to the new situation so well that some even claimed that what they saw actually became upright again *after a period of adjustment.* Controversy surrounds the actual reports of what was experienced.)

A serious mistake is made in describing what we see as being only "apparently" upright, however. There is no uncertainty about the way that ordinary persons would phenomenologically describe the uprightness or invertedness of what is seen in relation to their ordinary perception of their own bodily orientation. (But, as will be seen later, what is perceived immediately is the orientation of one's body-image rather than of the physical body itself). Ordinarily, what is seen clearly is upright or upside-down in reference to one's own perceived orientation. Of course, if Stratton's account is correct, namely, if what he saw gradually changed, during the period of adaptation, from being initially upside-down to being upright, this by itself would disprove the intra-organic theory, inasmuch as it is obvious that the retinal image(s) did not change their orientation during the period of adaptation.

There are other facts to be considered as well. The experience of colorblind people shows that they, at least, often see things that are not on their retinas. The most common type of color blindness is the inability to distinguish red and green. This does not mean that such people see nothing at all when red or green objects are on their retinas: they do not see empty gaps or patches of black (many think that black is the absence of any color). Rather, when red or green images are on their retinas, they see corresponding "patches" of gray. That is, they see something that is as gray as anything gray that other people see. Here again we find a discrepancy between what is seen and what is on the retinas, namely, the discrepancy between what is gray and what is red or green.

Experimenters have found that a similar discrepancy can be created for people who are not colorblind as well. Whereas the painter must mix yellow and blue paint if he wishes to produce green, yellow and blue lamps directed onto the retina will cause a person to see the color white. (Helmholtz, in R.J. Hirst, 1965, p. 62.) Similarly, experimenters using the anomaloscope have discovered that when a combination of monochromatic red and monochromatic green light is allowed to fall onto part of a person's retinas, that person will see a yellow spot that is indistinguishable from another spot created by monochromatic yellow light falling onto another part of the retina. Here we have the case of a person seeing two patches of yellow although the wave-lengths of the stimuli at the retina are entirely distinct.

Once again, it is important to keep in mind that the word "appears" has no place here. Someone might be tempted to say that, although one of the spots seen by the person *is* yellow, the other only *seems* to be yellow (though it actually is red and green). Both seen colors are equally yellow, so that, if someone who had never seen the color yellow asked to be shown that color, he could learn what yellow is by having the right combination of monochromatic red and green light flashed onto his retinas. Contrariwise, if he wished to know what red or green were, he would never learn it in this situation, unless he first adapted his eyes to one or other of the colors before having the combination focused on his retinas. Experiment has shown that a person who first looks into a bright red light, thus accommodating his retinas to the red, will then see only a bright green light when the combination of red and green light strike his retinas. And vice-versa. (Cfr. R.L. Gregory, *Eye and Brain*, 1966, pp. 127-29.)

Another interesting experiment that anyone can carry out concerns after-images. First, paste a small, one-inch square piece of brightly colored paper (with a uniform red, green, blue, or yellow color) over the Y below. Stare at it for about fifteen seconds. Then stare for fifteen seconds at the X below.

Y (patch)   X

People with normal sight will see a small, one-inch square 'patch' of color after staring at the X for a few seconds. That is called "an after-image." It will have the remarkable property of being "complementary" to the original color. For instance, if the color at Y is red, the after-image will be green, and vice-versa. If the color at Y is blue, the after-image will be yellow, and vice-versa. (Better yet, consult "After images" on the internet.)

Another phenomenon that the intra-organic theory is incapable of accounting for is the fact that, although we always have two retinal images, we do not always see two objects in our visual field. Only when there is retinal disparity, i.e., when portions of the retinal images do not cover "corresponding" parts of the retinas themselves, do we see two of whatever the portions represent. This fact was mentioned earlier in the examination of the common-sense view. If we hold our index finger five or six inches from the middle of our face, we will see two of the "things in the distance." (Of course, they are not really things in the distance. The fact that there is only one of each of the objects "out there" at a distance was used to refute common sense.) This is explained by the fact that there are two retinal images (or sub-images, since these are only parts of the entire retinal image fields). However, when both images cover the same part of each retina, we see only one object. There is only one flesh-colored, finger-shaped object. Similarly, as you look toward this page, you see only one of each letter*, though there are two separate retinal images of each letter, one on each retina. (*Unless you cross your eyes! Try it.)

Though such facts as the above (plus those to be mentioned later) taken together, form an argument of considerable weight against the intra-organic theory as it relates to sight, another experience by itself is enough to show that we do not see the pattern of light in contact with the retinas. We might call this experience "the filling-in of the blind spot." Most of us are familiar with the fact that there is one portion of the retina that has no rods or cones. It is known as the "blind spot" of the retina. Usually, the only factor mentioned in connection with the blind spot is that we cannot see whatever image falls onto that part of the retina. For example, *with your left eye closed*, look at the * below. Then move the book and the * about 10-12 inches away from your face, all the while keeping your open eye focused on the *, until the X off to the right of the * disappears. (The book and the page must be held horizontally and must be moved away and back slowly in order to find the position exactly suited to your eye.) What is significant is not the fact that the X disappears, however. That only tells us what we cannot see in this case. The more startling fact is that, in place of the X-image covering the blind spot, we do not see any gap. Rather, we see an unbroken continuation of the same color that surrounds the large spot, namely, *white* in the present instance. *The gap or "blind spot" is filled in* with a color that is not present on that portion of the retina or anywhere else in the physical world. (There is still a black spot on the retina as well as on the piece of paper.) The phenomenon is even more impressive when the area surrounding the * is brilliant red or orange, etc. At any rate, we have here an example of something seen that is entirely at odds with what is on the retina (white vs. black).

*   X

(It is now—in 2011—possible to study the blind spot experience on the internet. There are several web-sites listed under "Blind spot.")

Before discussing any further facts relating to the object of sight, let us turn now to a discussion of the sense of touch. Until now, little has been said about this sense, considered by many to be the most important of all. Aristotelians sometimes claim that touch is the most important sense of all by saying that it is involved even in sight, hearing, smell and taste. Their argument is based on a wholly non-phenomenological distortion of the meaning of "touch," however. That is, in saying that touch is fundamental to all of the senses, they are taking the word "touch" to mean "contact." In this sense, "touch" is fundamental to all sensation, as was pointed out above when speaking of the "bridges" that are required when immediate contact is lacking.

But *"touch" in the sense of "contact" is quite different from "touch" when the word is taken to refer to a separate mode of sensation*. Here, it would be preferable to use the word" feel." For example, while we are asleep, we are certainly touching the sheets, the pillow, the covers, etc., but we do not *feel* them! And when part of our body is anesthetized, it may touch many things and they may touch it, but we do not *feel* the things that the anaesthetized body-member touches. Unless the distinction is kept in mind, the attempt to find an answer to the question "What and where are the objects of sense awareness?" will become lost in a morass of ambiguities. When we speak here of touch or tactile sensation, we are dealing, not with mere *contact*, but with a type of sense *awareness* that is distinct from sight, hearing, and the like. Certainly no one would describe this experience of seeing these black marks against a white background as "visually touching" them except metaphorically.

A more usual reason given for regarding the sense of touch as the most important of all is that it provides us with an indisputable link with reality. Sight may be deceived by various illusions, but we can always fall back on the sense of touch in order to tell us what is the true state of affairs. For instance, it is the sense of touch, some would say, that guarantees that the partially immersed stick is not bent. (How many people have ever needed more than another look, when the stick is pulled out of the water, though?) Presumably touch provides the same guarantee with respect to the impressions of the other senses as well. The famous incident in which Dr. Samuel Johnson kicked a stone with his foot in order to prove the reality of the physical world outside the mind was ultimately based on this conviction that, even if doubts about the trustworthiness of the other senses are raised, the evidence of touch is irrefutable.

Instinctive convictions notwithstanding, the sense of touch does not reveal what Dr. Johnson believed it revealed. According to the intra-organic theory, what is felt is not anything on the outside of the body (physical objects such as chairs, pens, pieces of paper, and the like), but only various pressures and other phenomena beneath the surface of the skin. It can be argued, for instance, that the tactile nerves are never in touch with the external world, since the tactile nerves are embedded beneath skin: layers of dead skin cells stand between the tactile nerve endings and the outside world. Still, as long as the inner nerves are stimulated in the appropriate manner, we will have the sensation of "touching" something. For example, an object that is passed over part of the skin which has a lot of hair, but that strongly disturbs only the hairs without making actual contact with the skin itself, will cause us, unless we know otherwise, to believe that the object is touching us. The reason is that the hairs, when disturbed, in turn displace the nerve endings in contact with them below the skin. If auditory and visual clues were missing, we would be unable to distinguish the sensation produced by pressure from the tip of a small rod and that produced by a stream of air ejected with great force from the end of a small hose, since both create the same pressure against the nerves embedded beneath the skin. According to the argument based on such facts, what we feel, therefore, is not the external world itself, but the *effects* produced by the external world in the region beneath the skin's surface.

These facts by themselves do not create much of a problem so far as our confidence in the sense of touch is concerned. After all, if the intra-organic theory is correct, we are still aware of something quite physical and quite real, our own body, and we can still be certain that the very thin layer of microscopic cells that separate the tactile nerves from the outside world in no way undermines the objectivity of the sense of touch.

Another phenomenon that has been used to show that tactile sensation is not what we believe it to be hinges around the thermal sense that is closely associated with touch. Ordinarily, we do not even bother to distinguish the two types of sensation, so closely associated are they. For instance, when someone places their hand on a warm stove, they would say—if asked to describe what they feel—that they feel the warm stove. And even if we do distinguish the pressure from the warmth, for they are distinct, it is very important to note that *both are felt in the same place*. The importance of noting this fact becomes evident when it is shown that the warmth we feel cannot be within the skin itself, as the intra-organic theory would claim, and this becomes an argument against the intra-organic theory concerning the location of the felt pressure as well.

To begin with, what we refer to as 'felt temperature' (great heat, warmth, coolness, severe coldness, and the like) is not in the external object. A distinction must be made here between the *physical* temperature of external objects and *felt* temperature. We use thermometers to measure the first. We have merely our own sense awareness on which to base our reports of the second. Everyone is familiar with the experiences of stepping under a hot shower and of jumping into a pool of cold water. In both cases, the temperature we feel changes after a short time. The shower begins to feel merely warm—we may turn on more hot water, whereas the icy water of the pool may become so tepid that we wish it were colder. In neither case does the temperature of the water itself change significantly. Hence the discrepancy: no change in the physical temperature of the external objects, but a great change in the temperature we feel.

Another example brings out the challenge to common sense even more directly. Suppose there are three vessels of water, one extremely hot, another close to freezing, and a third about room temperature. If, after one hand has been soaked in the hot water and the other in the ice water, both hands are placed in the lukewarm water, one hand will experience coldness and the other, warmth. As G. Berkeley argued, it is contradictory to common sense to say that the lukewarm water is both hot and cold, therefore the coldness and heat one feels cannot be properties of the water itself (just as the shower did not turn cool nor the pool's water turn warm). But the felt coldness and the felt warmth are as real as any coldness or warmth we ever experience, so they must be somewhere other than in the water itself.

The intra-organic theorist claims that the felt coldness and warmth are within the skin. But this cannot be maintained, for it is the warm hand that feels the coldness and the cold hand that feels the warmth, just as it is the body warmed by the shower that feels coolness and the body cooled by the swimming pool that feels the warmth. They then tell us that what is felt is not any "absolute" temperature, but the "difference" between the outside physical temperature and the skin's temperature. The problem with this answer is that, when closely examined, it makes little sense, if any at all. For one thing, we are left wondering just what kind of property a "difference" is and to what reality it belongs. There is the physical temperature of the external object and the physical temperature of the body, and although we can *imagine* a third something that we call "the difference," this is merely a reification (projecting onto reality what exists only in the mind). We are comparing this case with cases in which there is a real difference. For instance, when we have a whole pie and someone removes half of it, we can still eat the remaining piece of pie that we describe as the difference between the original whole and the removed half. But a moment's reflection shows that the only difference here is the physical temperature that remains in the skin after part of its original kinetic energy (which constitutes, for the most part, what is called "physical temperature") is weakened, and as we have seen, this "difference" is warm when we feel the coolness and cold when we feel warmth!

Apart from the temperature of the external body and the temperature of the skin, there is no third entity to which we can attach the label, "the difference." If there were, one wonders to what it could belong, since it does not belong to the external object or to the skin.

If the felt temperature is not out at the skin, then where is it? The nerve-impulse theorist argues that what is crucial is that when impulses of a certain kind are triggered off and sent to the brain—no matter how they are triggered off, whether by warmer objects in contact with cooler hands or by cool objects in contact with warm hands—we will experience the resulting brain excitations in a particular way. Thus, according to this theory, it is the brain excitations that we sense, not some impossible-to-find congruent properties either in external objects or beneath the skin.

Perhaps the most powerful argument of all against the usual interpretations of touch's objects comes from what are called "phantom limb" experiences. Pause for a moment to become aware of what you call your body. With your hands stretched out at your sides, clench your fists and concentrate on the clenched feeling. Flex your muscles, taking note of the resulting sensations. Then do somewhat the same for the rest of your body, from your toes upwards. Is it possible, do you think, that you could experience sensations identical with these, if the corresponding limbs were amputated? Could you have a feeling like that which you experienced when you clenched your fist, even if you had no arm or hand?

At first, anyone who knows nothing of what amputees have experienced would, without hesitation, reply in the negative. To have that feeling under such circumstances would be equivalent to feeling one's fist when there was no fist to be felt. Just so, Dr. Johnson must have been convinced that he could not possibly have felt the jolt that he identified as the impact of his foot against the stone unless there had been both a foot and a stone involved.

The reason for raising questions here is that most people regard as absolutely obvious and unquestionable the fact that what they call muscular sensations, bodily aches and pains, and so on, exist where they seem to be felt: throughout one's physical body, i.e., in one's feet, legs, trunk, arms, hands, and the like. If that is where these feelings are, then to have the same feeling without the corresponding limb would be to have a feeling dangling in mid-air.

Analysis of thermal sensations has already shown that the heat and cold we feel are not where they appear to be, namely, in one's hands, skin, and so forth. The unimpeachable witness of thousands of amputees further undermines our instinctive certitude about the nature and location of these other bodily sensations. To have those sensations we are so certain are in our clenched fists or in our toes or in other parts of our body, it is not necessary that the fists or toes exist. Rene Descartes saw the implications of this fact at the beginning of the modern era. He recorded the case of a girl whose arm had to be removed because of an injury. The surgeon, desirous of breaking the unfortunate news to her gradually, wrapped up pieces of cloth to look like an arm beneath the bandages. Afterwards, the girl reported having pains, first, in one finger, then in other fingers of the hand which no longer existed. She was unaware of the amputation because she continued to experience sensations like those she had had before. Anyone interested in further details of phantom limb experiences may consult the article by R. Melzack in *Psychology Today*, Oct.1970. He writes of men whose legs have been amputated reporting quite distinct pains in their missing limbs, being able to describe which toes were affected. In fact, so indistinguishable are their sensations after the loss of their legs that amputees in wheel chairs have been known to fall while attempting to stand up on their no-longer-present legs. Descartes realized that a careful analysis of such experiences shows that just as heat and cold are not located where they seem to be, namely, in the body itself, so neither are pains, tickles, or other tactile and muscular sensations. The sensations are the direct result of the excitations to the brain, and given particular excitations—whether they originate in the limbs of the body or in the stump or somewhere else in the nervous system makes no difference—we will experience particular sensations. The nerve impulse theorists claim that the resulting brain excitations *are* the sensations (though the sense-datum theorists disagree, as will be seen).

Other experiences show likewise the fallacy of supposing that, because our pain seems to be in a particular place, this is an intuitive guarantee that it is in that place. Who is there who has never had the experience that we refer to as "hitting one's crazy bone"? A sharp blow directed at a suitable part of the elbow creates a sensation similar to an electric shock. Not in the elbow, however, but at one's fingertips. Chiropractors and others who specialize in the treatment of pain know that nerves, pinched at the spine, can create pains that seem to be distant from the site of the organic trouble.

The upshot of these experiences of pain, muscular sensations, and the like, taken together with thermal sensations, is that the only theory that puts them all into a single, consistent framework is that which recognizes that none of them exist out in the body itself, but only in the brain (or, according to the sense-datum theory, in the mind). The only alternative is to suppose that the sensations occur in haphazard fashion: sometimes in the limbs themselves (when these are present), sometimes retreating into the brain (after amputation), sometimes—well, where are the pains one feels in one's legs when a nerve in the spinal cord is pinched? And, even so, the "haphazard" theory does little to account for the thermal sensations.

One "out" that people, unaccustomed to carefully thinking about such matters, offhandedly resort to is the observation that amputees are not reporting actual sensations, but are merely *imagining* that they feel what they report. Now, while it may be correct to say that amputees are merely imagining that there is a *physical*, organic pain *in* their non-existent arm or leg, they are by no means merely imagining that there is a pain and that it is similar to the pains they have previously felt in connection with that limb.

To obtain a clearer notion of the error involved in this attempt to explain away the experiences of amputees, reflect on the difference there is between feeling a pain and merely imagining (or remembering) one. First simply *imagine* yourself clenching your fists or having your foot stepped on. Then follow this up by *actually* clenching your fists, etc. To claim that amputees, once they have lost an arm or a leg, have also lost the ability to know the difference between real pain and imagined pain is a mark either of arrogance or of ignorance. One has only to read, with care, the accounts of phantom limb experiences, to dispel the illusion that amputees do not feel what they report they feel. (A more conclusive experiment, of course, would be to cut off one's own arm or leg and experience the facts for oneself.)

As was said already, the advantage of the nerve impulse theory is that it puts all of the foregoing types of experience into a single, consistent framework. What is crucial in any sensation is the network of nerve excitations in the brain. When these are present, we will experience the corresponding sensation. At times, these excitations are produced by the impact of external stimuli, at other times they are produced in different ways. Soon after birth, we learn to translate the brain's excitations into a knowledge of our own physical body and its present condition. Later on, the same excitations, produced under unusual conditions, may automatically lead us into mistaken interpretations. In any case, when the brain excitations are the same, the sensations will be the same, for it is the brain excitations that we sense.

In the opinion of the nerve impulse theorists, that is!

3b. Examination of the nerve-impulse theory. Although the arguments against common sense were simultaneously arguments in favor of the intra-organic theory, the same is not quite so obvious in reference to the arguments against the intra-organic theory. Though the nerve-impulse advocate can legitimately claim that in all of the examined cases, there are nerve excitations in the brain, it is difficult to see immediately how these can themselves be the colors we see, the sounds we hear, the pains, pressures, and temperatures we feel. Some analysts will agree with K. Gallagher's comments on such a theory:

> Some will go so far as to assert that what I am aware of is inside my head, which
> is obviously nonsense. We have only to ask ourselves what is the comparative size of
> the table which I perceive and my head to convince ourselves that the perceived table

is not inside my head—if we are not convinced by the immediately given externality. (K. Gallagher, 1964, p. 86.)

Gallagher is correct in certain respects. The 'world' of immediate sensation certainly seems too spacious and voluminous to be identical with nerve excitations, even if they must be numbered in the millions, located within the hard bony structure we call our skull. Still, mention was made earlier, in dealing with visual and auditory depth, of the fact that things that are not distant may appear distant even after we concede their nearness, and not everyone would be convinced by Gallagher's objection that seems to presuppose the common-sense view.

The real strength of the nerve-impulse theory is that, in addition to raising insurmountable objections against the common-sense and the intra-organic theories when these are applied to various experiences such as phantom limbs, it also seems able to account for these within with a broad 'scientific' framework that embraces all other experiences as well. There is no common-sense or intra-organic theorist who denies that nerve impulses are received by the brain and excitation-networks created there.

Furthermore, this theory explains hallucinations, which are often used as a refutation of common sense. The subject of hallucination is a complex one. There seem to be some instances in which imagination is taken to be reality, at least occasionally. At other times, however, as in the case of hallucinogenic drug intake, persons actually experience vividly colored objects, sounds, and the like which cannot be found either in the external physical world or within the sense organs themselves. Again, unless persons who have taken these drugs lose their ability to make a simple distinction between imagining (or recalling) and sensing, they do not just imagine that they see unusual shapes and colors. They actually do so. The nerve-impulse theory explains this quite easily: the drugs produce unusual effects within the brain itself and these are experienced as the hallucinated objects.

Modern brain research has given strong support to this theory, or at least at first sight it appears to have done so. Brain researchers have found that all that is necessary to produce various colors, sounds, odors, pleasant and painful sensations, and the like, is to stimulate various parts of the brain directly with a small electric current. This has provided the basis for extensive research on methods that will enable blind people to distinguish shapes and deaf persons to hear sounds. Tiny TV cameras have been constructed whose output is fed directly into parts of the brain, with the result that the subject sees bits of light arranged in patterns. And tiny receivers transform air vibrations into electrical currents that produce sounds heard by persons who are deaf. Scientists have speculated, on the basis of such experiments, that if a brain were detached from the nervous system, kept alive with nourishing fluids, and fed the same currents which a man or woman's brain normally receives from the various afferent nerves, it would experience exactly the same sensations—patterned colors, sounds, body sensations, and all—that we now experience with the entire body attached.

Note: Incidentally, that is why, were brain transplants possible, the person whose brain was transplanted would receive a new body rather than the other way around. According to the nerve-impulse theory, we might say that the brain is, essentially, the person. In fact, that is precisely what J. Kluger wrote in *Time Magazine*'s cover story, "The New Map of the Brain," for January 29, 2007: "You have a liver; you have your limbs. You *are* your brain." (p.57) Thus, in the brain transplant, the memories, etc., would be those belonging to the person whose brain was placed in the new body. End of note.

Yet, when we apply our method of comparison to the nerve-impulse theory, it breaks down more completely and absolutely than either of the other two theories previously examined. This time, we can apply the "prerequisite conditions only" argument. That is, it is as nearly conclusive as a theory can be that the reception of nerve impulses into the brain and the creation of appropriate patterns of excitation are necessary prerequisites for sensation to occur, at least so long as we inhabit our bodies, but there is not even a single instance in which what we sense can be identified with patterns of nerve excitations in the brain.

The bankruptcy of the theory emerges when we notice that its proponents customarily use expressions such as were used above: "the brain senses certain excitations *as* color," just as "it senses other excitations *as* pain," etc. It is necessary to recall once again that we sense patterned colored objects, we hear sounds, we smell odors, we feel pains, and so forth. Moreover, once a person understands that we see, not some invisible images between us and the often bright colored objects 'in front of' us, but those very bright colored objects themselves, and that we hear, not some noiseless images of sound between ourselves and the sounds we hear, but the shrill or soft or thumping sounds themselves, etc., then it is beyond question that the colors we see are utterly different kinds of things from the sounds we hear. And both are distinct from the odors we smell or the flavors we taste. And none of them can possibly be confused with the pains we feel or with felt temperatures. All of these are utterly different kinds of entities. Otherwise, the blind person who can hear should know what color is, and the deaf person should know what sound is, and so on. Once we have learned to immerse ourselves in these experiences, to revel in them, and to 'taste' their obvious differences from each other, we know that it makes no sense to say that what we are experiencing are homogeneous, similar nerve impulses (MIS)*interpreted as* color, sound, etc.

Two facts are clear. First, that *the nerve-impulse theory of sensing's objects is an out and out denial that color, sound, odor, etc., exist;* it is a re-naming of colorless impulses by calling them "color," a renaming of silent impulses by calling them "sound," etc. Second is the fact that the surreptitious re-naming of "seeing," "hearing," etc., by calling it "interpretation," is an outrageous falsification and should be called what it is: "*mis*interpretation"!

Keeping those two facts in mind, we conclude by noting that the nerve excitations in the brain, as nerve excitations, do not differ! Even the impulses transmitted along the various afferent nerve pathways, viz., the optic nerve, the auditory nerves, the olfactory nerve, etc., are basically alike in nature. A small electric current applied, in an entirely dark room, to one part of a patient's brain, will cause that person to see a flash of light. Applied to a different part of his brain in an entirely dark and now soundless room, it will cause the patient to hear a sound. The flash of light has a color, and is utterly different from the sound, but the electric current is the same. The only fundamental difference in the brain's excitations is their different locations in the brain. This fact, that the objects sensed (colored patterned objects, sounds, pains, and the like) are totally *heterogeneous*, i.e. different in nature from each other, prevents any attempt to identify them with the brain excitations that are *homogeneous*, i.e., the same in nature. There simply is no flash of light in the patient's brain when the electricity is applied, yet the patient sees a flash. Nor is there any buzz or other sound in the brain, though the patient hears a sound. Lord Russell Brain has mentioned the further fact that the patterns or shapes of the sensed objects are not at all similar to the patterns or shapes of the brain's excitations, again proving that it is impossible to identify what we sense with what is in the brain when we compare the two. (Cfr. Brain's observations in R.J. Hirst, 1965, pp. 43-44.)

An extensive amount of literature has been produced by those who would identify mind and brain. When they do not attempt to identify the brain impulses and the objects we experience, such as colors, sounds, odors, tastes, pains, etc. (as J.J.C. Smart does, for instance), they tend to identify the act of sensing (the experience) with the processes in the nervous system, *thus eliminating the objects sensed*. The attempts to overcome this complete discrepancy between the facts of experience and the physical events within the brain itself multiply every day, as if people are determined to find some way of avoiding the disconcerting fact that mind and brain cannot be reduced to one and the same thing.

Only one answer is possible. Where logic fails to impress someone, patient, reflective immersion in experience itself is our sole resort. The visual datum described as the flashing red light atop the car of the state policeman idling on a dark street is completely silent, in contrast to the wholly invisible, colorless sound of the siren that initially brought the speeder to a halt. The magnificent panorama of color that we describe as a sunset has nothing in common with the sounds we hear as we listen, eyes closed, to Beethoven's Ninth Symphony. And none of them are one iota like the homogeneous nerve impulses shuttling *noiselessly* within the pitch *dark* interior of the skull of the person sensing any of them. In effect, the nerve impulse theory eliminates color, sound, odor, taste, heat, cold, and the like, instead of explaining what and where they are. The theory either is built on a blindness to the rich qualities of sense-data, or induces such a blindness in those who come to accept it.

4b. The sense-datum theory. At the outset, it was noted that the sense-datum theory is arrived at, essentially, by a process of elimination. Anyone well-versed in the history of philosophy will be conscious of the limitations of this brief introduction to the theory. Advocates of any of the first three positions that we have examined and rejected are fully capable of offering countless considerations in the form of reinterpretations, exceptions, qualifications, and the like, to show that their theory was not, in fact, eliminated by the arguments presented here. The refusal of philosophers to collectively relinquish their varying theories in favor of a single, uniform explanation of sensation is a matter of record, obvious to anyone who wishes to inquire into the matter. One author described the present state of affairs relative to this topic when he wrote that "it is not too much to say that the problem of perception remains the most unresolved in the whole of epistemology." (K. Gallagher, 1964, p. 122) Actually, the problem has been 'resolved' by various theories (correctly, we believe, by this text's Argument Three). What he probably meant was that there is no consensus vis-à-vis solving the problem.

The argument as presented in the preceding pages has focused on three of the clearest theories of sensation presented to date. Each of them more or less takes for granted the existence of an external physical world, of physical stimuli impinging on sense organs, and of the resulting excitations within the brain. Each argues that when we find the answer to the question, "What and where are the objects of immediate sense awareness?", the objects will fall into a single category, viz., one of the things presupposed by all the theories: either external objects, intra-organic objects, or patterns of brain impulses. By simultaneously using the arguments against one theory in order to establish the plausibility of the next, it was possible to leave aside any extended examination of the endless modifications that defenders of each view have employed to defend the attacked theory's "general" validity. It would be our contention that none of the modifications have been successful in defending any of the first three theories, but volumes would be required to support this contention. The same thing is true, in both respects, of the other alternative theories that individual thinkers have elaborated and of which little if anything has been said in the preceding pages.

In the remaining few pages, our aim will be to clarify the final import of the fourth and only remaining theory, the one that claims that the objects of immediate sense-awareness are sense-data, and to answer some of the difficulties that have been raised against it.

What are sense-data? There are two ways of approaching the question. One is to describe their most obvious "sensible" properties; the second is to attempt to set forth their objective or ontological status in nature, that is, in the entire scheme of things.

The first task, that of description, is somewhat easier. In fact, the entire argument thus far has built upon precisely such descriptions. To repeat, one must first distinguish quite carefully between seeing, hearing, smelling, etc. What we sense, then, is what we see, what we hear, and the like.

To avoid needless complications created by objections against other presentations of sense-data, the descriptions of 'what we see,' 'what we hear,' and so on, must be 'full-bodied.' For instance, what we see is everything that is present to us when we open our eyes. If you pause a moment to think about what you see at this moment (do not forget that the seeing and the thinking are distinct), you might be tempted to say only that you see a book. A full description, however, would surely include far more, namely, *everything in your total field of vision*. You most likely see what you think are your hands, other things in the area in front of you, etc. The only adequate way to describe what you see would be to think of it as a *Total Visual Field*. You see the white of the page, together with lines of black figures inside its borders, together with hand-shaped, flesh-colored objects at its right and left edges (probably). And so on. What you hear, if you hear anything, are various sounds. What you smell are odors. You taste tastes or flavors. You feel heat, cold, pressure, and the like. We often use material-object words (i.e., words referring to material objects) in our descriptions. This is required by the poverty of our language. With suitable qualifiers ("hand-shaped," or "flesh-colored," or "motor-like sounds," etc.), we can keep our descriptions neutral.

As for the second task, that is, explaining the nature or objective status of sense-data, we find ourselves confronted with something far more difficult. So far, the question has been answered only negatively. Sense-data are *not* physical realities, such as stars, trains, or pieces of paper, external to our bodies, *nor* are they inherent properties of such, *nor* are they stimuli or patterns of stimuli in contact with our sense organs, *nor* are they patterns of nerve impulses within our brain. We might wish to say, simply, that they are colors, sounds, odors, tastes, and the like, within the mind or consciousness and the like. But what are colors, sounds, odors, tastes, etc., if they are none of the above, as we normally think they are.

The first apparently positive answer to the question is contained in the statement that they are *psychic* entities. This is ordinarily interpreted as meaning that they are mental, pertain to the mind, belong to consciousness, and the like. The difficulty with this approach is that it, too, is a somewhat negative one. It may be argued that "psychic" ultimately means "in the mind" and that this really signifies "what is *not* in or part of the physical world." That is, we can hardly define what we mean by saying that sense-data are psychic without in the end contrasting them with physical things which they are not. The argument up to now, let us repeat, has been to show that sense-data are not external physical realities, physical stimuli or physiological nerve-impulses (which are also physical). They are 'something more.'

We cannot entirely escape the feeling that the term "psychic" is a negative description. A more promising approach is to say that sense-data are more closely related to thinking, remembering, and imagining, all of which are customarily identified as psychic or mental. However, thinking, remembering, imagining, and the like are acts, whereas sense-data are not acts, but the objects of sense awareness. We might compare sense-data with the objects of thinking, remembering, etc., which are not physical, and say that sense-data are psychic like the objects of the non-sensory cognitive functions. The difficulty now is that even the psychic nature of the thought-objects spoken of many pages ago was established by showing, not directly what they are, but what they are not, i.e., not physical objects in the objective world.

What is the point of all this? The point is that some have wondered whether there is any real meaning in saying that objects of consciousness are psychic. If this merely means that something is non-physical, does this not make the meaning entirely negative? (What positive meaning is there, for instance, in the term "non-square"?)

The answer is, first, that the terms "physical" and "psychic" are mutually needed to define each other, just as "top" and "bottom" are. Psychologists point out that the infant does not learn the significance of either "self" or "non-self" ("other") first: the meaning of each develops simultaneously, by contrast with the other. The meanings of "real" and "purely imaginary (non-real)" likewise develop together. Hume and others have shown that our concepts of "physical" and "outside the mind" are not quite so straightforward as they seem when we take only a superficial view. Secondly, we know at least that colors, sounds, odors, pains, tickles—collectively known as sense-data—are real. We are immediately aware of them, they exist, and when we discover that they do not exist in or as part of the physical world (if "physical" is understood in a common-sense way as referring to stars, planets, trees, squirrels, and so on), it forces us to realize that there is another dimension to the universe, which for centuries now has been designated as "within the mind."

In fact, however, further reflection on the discovery that sense-data are not physical can make us more sharply aware of their intrinsic properties or qualities. This reflection shows us that, for each of the senses, we must learn to more carefully distinguish the sense-data from their external stimuli, despite the linguistic convention which often uses the same words for each.

For example, the arguments show that the word *"heat"* can be used to refer to two quite distinct things, either to the physical heat of an object or to felt heat that we experience when our hand is acted upon by the physically hot object. If scientists are correct in believing that physical heat is another name for the kinetic energy of physical things, then it becomes even more obvious that there is no similarity between physical heat and felt heat. The same felt heat can be produced within our consciousness by external objects with quite different physical temperatures, by a red-hot stove as well as by a piece of dry ice.

So, too, with *"sound,"* the object of hearing. The word "sound" refers to entirely distinct things. It often is taken to refer to the physical patterns within the vibrations of air molecules. These we never directly experience with the sense of hearing. The sounds we hear are, we say, ultimately caused by the physical air vibrations. *Like any cause and effect*, they are separate entities. When the tree falls in an uninhabited forest, there is no doubt that the physical vibrations are there, nor is there is any doubt that a properly placed Sony would record those vibrations. There are none of those things we hear, namely "heard sounds," however, since these exist only within the consciousness of beings whose brains have been stimulated by the physical vibrations, and no such beings are found in the uninhabited forest. An interesting possibility is suggested by the speculations of some physicists, according to whom the air molecules do not ordinarily make any contact with each other (the nearer two molecules get to each other, the stronger the forces of repulsion between them). The more appropriate way to think of external "sound" would be to imagine it as a silent dance of molecules which never even touch one another.

The patterned colors we see are also strikingly different from their external counterparts. Newton studied the composition of light, using a prism, and discovered that a beam of "white" light can be broken up, that is, the various frequencies of the radiations can be separated (this results in the beautiful rainbow hues of the spectrum). When this light full of the entire range of frequencies strikes the surfaces of physical objects, what happens will depend on the physical light-absorbing and light-reflecting properties of those surfaces. Roughly speaking the surfaces will absorb those frequencies that match the vibratory state of their atomic or molecular structure, and reflect the remainder. If we spoke of the energy states of a surface (which remove from the incoming light the matching frequencies) as "the internal color of the surface," this would lead to the interesting speculation that ordinarily we see precisely the colors which the surface is not, that is, the colors produced by the rejected or reflected light frequencies.

An even more simplified description of this curious possibility would go as follows. We see the color red when "red" light (i.e. light with one particular frequency) strikes our retinas. What we *call* a red object, therefore, is one which does not absorb the "red" light, but reflects it, because its internal state is out of harmony with the "red" light. Were the object "internally" red, red would be the color we would not see when light reflected from it reached our eye!

The reason for writing "red" in quotation marks when describing light is that there is no reason for ascribing color as such to the electromagnetic radiation that we call visible light. Isaac Newton pointed this out many years ago. "Electromagnetic radiation" is a term used to cover a wide range of phenomena: radio waves are near one end, X-rays nearer the opposite end of the spectrum of electromagnetic radiations. "Visible light," that is, those radiations possessing the frequencies to which the human eye will respond, form only a small portion of the total electromagnetic radiations in the universe. In themselves, they are quite colorless and invisible.

Confirmation of the foregoing is this. A person operating a radio transmitter in the dark is surrounded by intense electromagnetic radiations of lower frequencies; therefore the retinas are not activated. Radiation in the "visible" portion of the spectrum is no more visible in itself than the radio waves. Unless it strikes the retinas, nothing will happen, which is why we see none of the light filling the night sky around the moon. Light is called "visible" simply because it has the capacity of setting up nerve impulses which will produce the color which we see and which is within the mind. (Pressure applied against one's closed eyes also sets up nerve impulses that produce bright colors within our consciousness, but we do not call the pressure "visible"!) If we reflect on these and the dozens of other interesting facts that physicists and psychologists have discovered about light and vision, we begin to understand what is meant when some claim that the physical world outside the mind, even at high noon, is as dark as the radio operator's room mentioned above.

Color as we experience it, therefore, exists only within our mind.

What we call the color of an external object might more properly be called the object's light-reflecting properties. Light itself is colorless electromagnetic radiations.

Note. Careful reflection upon the fact that the patterned colors we see, the sounds we hear, etc., are not in or part of the physical world also clarifies the ambiguity initially surrounding words such as "see," "hear," and the like. One friend tried using the term "see" to refer globally to the entire process which begins when stimuli from distant objects are transmitted to us, make an impact on our sense organs, set up nerve impulses to the brain, finally produce the sense-data within our minds, plus the most important element of all: our awareness of the resulting sense-data. (His dogged dodge would imply that it takes eight minutes to see, with a momentary glance, the sun.) Or we can use the term in the ordinary way to mean that, with our eyes, we do something (i.e. see) with respect to things that are located out beyond our eyes themselves. (This second view is also a mistake, as we have seen.) The most basic meaning of the term, it should now be clear, is to describe solely the relation between oneself and the colors produced within one's own consciousness: i.e. to be immediately aware of the patterned colors, or to have them directly present to oneself. (End of note.)

There still remain some questions about the nature of sense-data, however. Certainly, on any account, they are somewhat unusual entities. Do the colored patterns we see (the total visual fields) have another side to them? If we compare them to physical photographs, we might say that we see the side facing us—strange, though, what is the "I" that they face?—and that they have a "further" side to them! Then, too, shall we say that the various sense-data have spatial relations to one another? Do the sounds we hear exist somewhere off to the edges of the visual sense-data? How far from your visual sense-datum are the tactile sense-date you now associate with your toes? Again, if one accepts Aristotle's classification of reality into substance and accidents, then to which category do sense-data belong?

Perhaps it is not a good idea to assemble too many of the difficult questions about sense-data in a single place. Together, they reveal the extent to which our customary notions of things fail to prepare us for sense-data.

The feeling of "strangeness" which comes over us as we contemplate these questions makes us wonder whether our arguments against common sense and the other theories were actually correct. Before we allow this strangeness to overwhelm us, however, it is helpful to take note of some very ordinary experiences that we often think little about.

Is there anyone who has never experienced what we call "a ringing in one's ears"? Some individuals are afflicted with it constantly. Close analysis will reveal that these sounds which appear as if from nowhere cannot be located in the physical or physiological world. Neither can those flashing colors that we see when pressure is exerted against our closed eyes. Drug-induced hallucinations have been known for thousands of years, and we might say that the resurgence of drug use produced at least one notable side-effect: it has proven to many individuals that many things happen which a common-sense or pseudo-scientific outlook would declare absolutely impossible. Drug users do not merely imagine that they experience things that do not physically exist. They do experience them. Quite sober men, like the philosopher H.H. Price (well-known among British philosophers for his work on sense perception), have undergone experiments in order to "see for themselves" and have concluded that certain hallucinations are *not* just mistaken acts of *thinking* incorrectly. Who can explain away the sense-data (pains, tickles, twinges, etc.) experienced by amputees as "purely imaginary"?

No, despite the strangeness of sense-date, there is too much evidence to dismiss them as products of mistaken analyses of sensation. Even without the sense-datum theory, careful reflection on the above phenomena—plus reflections on remembered images, thought-objects, and the like—would reveal that the mind and its contents are already quite different from our customary conceptions of things. Ordinarily, we pay little attention to the contents of our mind or consciousness, because they are next to 'invisible' compared with what we see, hear, and so forth. Now, we find that the contents of consciousness include, not only the invisible, intangible images and thought-objects, but also spread-out, bright, patterned colors, loud and soft sounds, pungent odors and tastes, tickles, pains, and the like, all those entities we formerly took to be the external, objective world. The sense-datum theory, then, does not create a strange world. It merely enlarges somewhat our awareness of a world that is already full of marvels if we but take the time to notice them.

Instead of devoting further space to an analysis of the nature of sense-data, therefore, a few summary remarks will relate them to what is already recognized to be "within the mind." The visual sense-data are alike in nature to the colors one sees when pressure is applied to his closed eyes, or to the "stars" one sees after receiving a blow to the head. The sounds are similar in nature to the buzzing or ringing that most of us experience occasionally and which, though we say it is "in our ears," exists nowhere but in our consciousness.

Further, as has often been emphasized, our sense-data are experienced as spread out, as being distant at times and nearby at others. Because of this facet of our sense-data, some philosophers have described them as occupying "perceptual space," a kind of space within the world of consciousness itself—in contrast to the "physical" space of the external world.

The sense-data, apparently not created by the mind itself, but produced within the mind by something external, do not present themselves as the type of thing which we would describe as a property or accident of the mind itself. We do not 'turn blue' when we see a blue color. But if they are not properties of external things nor of the mind, are they then substances or beings in their own right? If one adhered to Aristotle's substance-accident metaphysics at this point, it would seem that we might look upon the sense-data as substances in their own right, at least as long as they exist. Admittedly, though, it is not easy to fit them neatly into a traditional framework, but all that this proves is that our theoretical models of reality—our philosophies—are not always adequate, as Hamlet long ago observed. Images, after-images, objective concepts, merely possible essences, and the like did not easily fit into older metaphysical systems, either.

"In the mind." To conclude these brief notes on the nature of sense-data a few remarks on the meaning of the phrase "in the mind" are necessary. The phrase is dangerously ambiguous. Consequently, when it is said, as it is here, that the things we have direct and immediate sense awareness of are "in the mind," this assertion may be misunderstood unless the ambiguity is exposed and then eliminated.

First, "in the mind" does not mean here, as it often means in other contexts, "imaginary." At the risk of sounding repetitious, let us recall the original reason for speaking of the object(s) of our immediate experience as an "inner world." Though this is a metaphor, it was introduced for the purpose of underlining the *reality* of what we experience. Our thought-objects and sense-data are the most real things in the universe for us, more immediately important than the physical universe itself. Customarily, when we say that someone's illness or pain, for example, is "only in his mind," we intend to convey our belief that there is nothing physically wrong with the person. Perhaps without thinking about it, we are also accusing him of merely pretending that he is in pain, and there may often be instances where this is so. When it is said in these pages that all pain is in the mind, however, this means that although the pain is most real—sometimes overwhelmingly so—it is not a physical thing located in the body, but rather a psychic effect produced by the stimuli reaching the brain. The pain of amputees is anything but imaginary, but it cannot exist in arms and legs that no longer exist.

Second, in order to properly understand the meaning of the phrase "in the mind," it is essential to distinguish the mind from the brain located inside the head. "In one's mind" is not a synonym for "in one's head." Any identification of mind with head must be avoided. Try to recapture your first reaction, probably a subconscious, gut-level one, to the news that Plato and (sometimes) Descartes maintained that a human being is, basically, a mind, or to the sense-datum theorist's contention that everything which we directly experience is in our mind. Wasn't your first reaction something like the following (if it had been put into words): "I'm not just a head or mind! My mind is up here in my head, up here where my brain is, up here where my eyes and ears, nose and mouth are. But I—me!—am mostly very real and solid and concrete down under my neck where my chest and lungs and stomach (with its occasional aches) and thighs and legs are. Most of me, in fact, is down inside my body. I do not begin at my neck and extend only upwards into my head. I also extend out into my arms and hands, down into my body that reaches to the floor. My mind (read "head") is very important to me, but my body (read "what is beneath my head") is just as much part of me. To say, then, that I am only my mind and that the body is not part of me is absurd. And, above all, when I hurt my knee or have a pain in my left side, for example, it is sheer nonsense to say that such pain is up around my eyes, that is, in my head!"

Repeat. To get a feel for the sense-datum theory—whether it is accepted by you or not—it is crucial that one overcome the natural tendency to identify mind with head. Most of us believe, without being aware of it, that the mind is some small, invisible "something" enclosed within the head that sits atop the shoulders. In fact, we probably picture it to ourselves as being slightly to the back of our head, certainly behind the eyes which look out at the world, and likely further back even than the ears. If there is such a thing as a mind at all!

To think "in the mind" in such a context means that everything we feel from our head on down is left out! What we feel is not in the mind (up around the eyes). And if "I" am the mind and only what is in the mind, this means that all of "that", namely, what I feel below my head, is not part of me. Such reflections, however, represent a failure to fully grasp the insight that the sense-datum theorists claim to have reached, an insight that says, in effect, that there is no spatial relation of "containment" between the head and the mind. The head does not contain the mind somewhere inside it.

One way to approach this new understanding of the mind is in a way to "expand" the mind. If it is impossible to bring the feelings of one's body—perhaps it would be better to say "one's body-feelings"—into the mind, it is possible to think of the mind or consciousness as a roomy, spacious thing which extends downwards to embrace those pressures, warmths, pains, aches, tingles, and the like which we associate with our body, but which, if the arguments regarding phantom limbs and similar experiences are correct, do not exist in the body itself. In fact, what one calls one's head, if this refers to what one *feels*, is not the physical head itself, but only the feelings caused by impulses coming to the brain from the head.

What we feel, then, or, alternatively, that part of our experienced reality which we call "our body" is not, in fact, our physical, biological body but a collection or structured set of sensations which have been called, in recent literature, our "body image." The tension, the straining ("muscle strain"), the tingling, the tickling, the pain, the itching, the pleasure and relief, above all the solidness, everything in our immediate experience which we ordinarily think of as the body—its inside and its extremities—all of it is a 'body image' which is just one part of this "inner world of the mind."

Third, such a conclusion obviously brings with it the need for further efforts to find a suitable terminology with which to describe the *inner* 'world' of the mind in contrast to the *outer* world. Unlike ideas or concepts (whose existence is established by an almost rarified intellectual effort), the body image is experienced as three-dimensional and solid. Whether it actually is so or not, it initially *seems* to be so. But, then, the visual sense-datum is also extended, at least in two dimensions. (Fichte and others were wrong in regarding the colors we see as unextended points.) As was mentioned earlier, some authors, in an effort to give credit to this "expansiveness" of the inner world, distinguish perceptual space (the "space" of the inner world) from physical space. No matter how hard we try, it is next to impossible to experience what we see or hear or feel any other way than as "spread out," even distant. These data are "in here", in contrast to the external physical world, but this "in here" is not experienced as a cramped little box inside the skull.

In fact, what the evolutionary materialist, Richard Dawkins, wrote comes close to the two-world theory:

> The problems raised by subjective consciousness are perhaps the most baffling in all philosophy, and solving them is far beyond my ambition. My suggestion is the more modest one that each species, in each situation, needs to deploy its information about the world in whatever way is most useful for taking action. 'Constructing a model in the head' is a helpful way to express how it is done, and comparing it to virtual reality is especially helpful in the case of humans. (R. Dawkins, *Unweaving the Rainbow*, p.283)

"Virtual reality" is an excellent way to think about what we sense-experience and mis-take for 'the external physical world.' Simply replace Dawkins' "head" with "mind."

What, then, are sense-data? For the present, what has been said here will have to suffice. The question can only be taken up in conjunction with broader questions about the nature of the self, the "I," which experiences them. Those questions will constitute the basis of Part Two.

C. FOUR CONCLUSIONS

Having immersed ourselves temporarily in just three of the lines of reasoning which tend to substantiate the validity of epistemological dualism, it is important to recall the purpose of studying that theory. Our purpose was not to study the human knowing process for its own sake. It was rather to set the stage for an investigation of the question, "What is a human being?" In these concluding pages on the theory of epistemological dualism, therefore, our effort must be to see how this theory relates to the more general question.

As was pointed out at the beginning, the theory of epistemological dualism concerns the starting point of the inquiry into the nature of the human being. It concerns the data with which our inquiry will begin. If the conclusions reached by our reflections on the objects of immediate or direct awareness are correct, this will have an essential bearing on all of our subsequent analyses.

1. First of all, the arguments for epistemological dualism establish the primacy of consciousness in our study of the human being. In the twentieth century, the mention of consciousness and the mind was often given "back-seat treatment" in discussing the human being, or even altogether eliminated. What took their place? Behavior replaced consciousness, the physiological organism replaced the mind. Psychology itself, which William James, at the turn of the century, regarded as the description and explanation of states of consciousness as such, gradually came to be treated as the study of human behavior. Today, many look for the answers to the question "What is a human being?" in those researches gathered under the heading, "behavioral sciences." Within the context of these sciences, the self or person is often looked upon as a convenient fiction, a logical construction. The reality underlying these fictions is assumed to be nothing more than the biological organism, with its complex patterns of behavior (among which must be listed its basically physical interactions with other biological organisms).

If epistemological dualism is correct, this is a radically mistaken inversion of the real facts. It is an inversion, an upside down way of viewing things, because it is our states of consciousness that we are immediately aware of, not the physical behavior of our bodies or the bodies of anyone else. To be even more precise, it is your own states of consciousness that you are immediately aware of, that is, the 'world' within your own mind. This is not a denial of the outer, physical body's existence. But these opening reflections show that you are never immediately aware of your own physical body. And if, as the body's "owner," you are never immediately aware of your body, certainly no one else is either. It is a strange procedure then, which insists on starting an inquiry into the nature of the human person by presuming that the body and its behavior are obvious and "scientifically certain" and that the existence of the mind and consciousness, through which know anything at all, are regarded are obscure and beyond the pale of scientific certainty. Bertrand Russell, many years ago, pointed out the mistake of adopting the behaviorist starting point:

> Even, therefore, when we assume the truth of physics, what we know most indubitably through perception is not the movements of matter, but certain events in ourselves which are connected, in a manner not quite invariable, with the movements of matter. To be specific, when Dr. Watson watches rats in mazes, what he knows, apart from difficult inferences, are certain events in himself. The behaviour of rats can only be inferred by the help of physics, and is by no means to be accepted as something accurately knowable by direct observation . . . To return to the physiologist observing another man's brain: what the physiologist sees is by no means identical with what happens in the brain he is observing . . . In a strict sense, he cannot observe anything in the other brain, but only the percepts which he himself has when he is suitable related to that brain." (B. Russell, 1927, pp. 140, 147.)

There is little difficulty in understanding the motive for the behaviorist inversion of certainties. The behaviorist starts, as all of us do, with a common-sense understanding of knowledge. He, like the rest of us, instinctively feels that what he sees and feels and otherwise senses is more obvious and trustworthy than what cannot be seen or felt. Psychic acts, consciousness, as well as ideas or thoughts: these are invisible and intangible. And since, according to common sense, what we see and feel are external bodies, it is natural to assume that we can be much more certain about bodies and their behavior than we can be about consciousness and its contents. It is precisely this common-sense assumption about sensation which analysis proves mistaken, however.

A note is called for here. What *is* our starting point for determining the nature of the human being? Common sense (i.e., our basic, instinctive beliefs about the world and ourselves) or the two-world theory? According to Kohler's statement about the naïve world, everyone's starting point is common sense. Here, though, it is argued that the two-world theory is our starting point. Are the two answers contradictions? The answer really is that both views are true. Common sense is the first philosophy we acquire. It is the foundation for all 'higher' learning.

The two-world theory, the conclusion from re-examining common sense, is the starting-point for the scientific answer to "What am I?" or "What is a human being?"

That is, common sense itself gives rise to epistemological dualism, which is a direct outcome of carefully analysing common sense. We begin with our common-sense convictions; there is no other starting point. But it is our awareness of the internal contradictions of common sense, the growing realization that certain common-sense convictions are incompatible with certain others, that leads us to accept epistemological dualism. Specifically, it is our refusal to give up our common-sense belief in an objective reality that doesn't depend on our knowledge or thoughts or perceptions of it that leads to an admission that, although it exists, we do not directly know that objective reality.

Careful analysis of common sense leads, therefore, to the distinction between the objective world and the 'world' of our immediate experience and to the conclusion that, in the words of Jung which were quoted on an earlier page, "psychic happenings constitute our only immediate experience." Descartes is correct in this, at least, that our consciousness and its "contents" are more certain to us even than the existence of the world of physical bodies.

2. The second point to stress is this. Our physical body, in fact all physical bodies, since they are part of the external universe, are not directly experienced by us. However, there is nothing in our analysis thus far that would cast any substantial doubt on the fact that our body exists. The existence of the body, of sense organs and the stimuli reaching them, of the brain and nervous system were all presupposed in the arguments used to establish epistemological dualism. Furthermore, nothing till now has been said about the relation between the body and the mind, though the arguments have shown that the mind and consciousness are not identical with the body. Whether either can exist without the other, how they interact with each other—these are questions that must be taken up later. One thing only is clear, namely, that we have no direct access to our physical bodies. No, one more thing is even more clear, namely, that we do sense immaterial colors, sounds, and other sense-data, all of which most certainly exist during the time that we sense them!

This conclusion runs contrary to much contemporary thought. Even apart from those materialistic currents of thought that deny the existence of mind altogether (thus identifying the human being with his or her body), other contemporary thinkers emphasize humans' in-carnate or em-bodied nature. They reject the body-mind dualism that is found in Plato and Descartes.

This rejection has even influenced Christian theology. Some have railed against body-mind dualism as if it were the most serious error ever to take hold in the cultural heritage of the West. According to them, it has inflicted serious psychological damage on untold millions by making them regard their bodies as enemies of the mind (or soul) and even as something to be ashamed of. Hence the present-day reaction emphasizes that our bodies are as much part of us as our minds and that they are not hostile or shameful.

Nevertheless, epistemological dualism is not identical with body-mind dualism. *These are different dualisms.* The conclusion that we have no direct access to the body does nothing, by itself, to prove that the biological body is not so intimately linked to the mind that the two cannot be looked upon as equally essential to the human being. But even if the two-world theory is later seen to have negative implications concerning the essentialness of the body to the human person, this need not be at all in conflict with the current emphasis on the natural goodness of the body.

The first, and less important, reason for this is the fact that the distinctness of the body from the mind is not logically connected with the notion that the body is shameful or inimical to the mind. No one condemns butterflies or stars simply because they are not essential parts of the human person. There are two separate questions here. The first concerns the precise relationship, either of distinctness or of unity, between mind and body. The second concerns the body's utility or hostility with respect to the mind. The first question is an ontological one, the second relates to ethics.

The essential reason why epistemological dualism is entirely compatible with the emphasis on the natural goodness of the body is that, even according to epistemological dualism, there was a serious error in much of the traditional theory of body-mind dualism. The older theory did not regard the biological body itself as the enemy of the human spirit. The true enemy was the passions and drives which tempt a person to neglect the pursuit of moral uprightness. Such passions or drives would be the instinct for biological survival, which might lead to moral cowardice, the sexual instinct, so often hard to bridle, and the desire for eating and drinking, which frequently are out of control. The reason why the older dualism seemed to lead logically to a dislike for the body is that the body was seen as the seat of these inimical drives. It was not the body itself, but the body as the seat of drives hostile to the soul, which was looked down on. This is a mistaken common-sense view, however, according to the two-world theory. Those passions, desires, and pleasures are not part of the body. They are within the mind, and they are neither morally good or bad. It is how we deal with them that is either good or bad.

Once again, it is essential to avoid the error of thinking that "in the mind," as understood here, means merely part of what we are conscious of. *All* of one's sense-data, including those which are referred to as the "body-image," and passions themselves, are psychic or in the mind. As was true of *everything* that we see, hear, taste, and smell, what we feel is not what we thought it was. In this case, what we feel is not our physical body. What it is is something within consciousness itself, our body-image. The actual physiological organism we call the physical body is outside, is part of never-sensed, objective reality.

3. A third consequence of the theory presented above is that, in a sense, each of us is partially responsible for 'creating' our own immediate 'world.' At first, our formation of ideas or thought-objects is done instinctively, with no deliberateness on our part. Inundated with sensations, our mental processes function automatically to construct a consistent framework

that will "make sense" of our experiences. At times, as with those who are retarded, autistic, or otherwise mentally handicapped, this inner-world-construction process goes awry. But, later on, some of this process is under our own control. If we wish to believe in something and devise plausible hypotheses to explain all the available experiential evidence in line with our wish, then that something will become real for us. Theodore Reik wrote of an extreme case of this 'reality-constructing' process. A Russian who believed that Princess Juliana of Holland was in love with him was convinced that snatches of conversation from passers-by were messages from the Princess: "Regards from the Princess," or "Write the Princess every Saturday." When she married and his frequent letters to her were returned, he ignored these facts. When two of his letters were lost, he interpreted this as proof that she held these two especially dear. On the other hand, if we repress or refuse to investigate the evidence for something we would prefer not to exist, then that thing becomes or remains unreal for us. Thus, within limits, our assent gives existence to, while our denial annihilates, things for us.

There are limits, of course. Although our interpretation of our sensible experience may be somewhat under our own control, the sensible experience itself largely is not. Philosophers have recognized in this fact one of the strongest indications of the existence of an objective reality. If our present experience reveals to us what we would describe as a drab room filled with shoddy furniture and a lack of companions, all the wishing in the world will not make it possible for us to shut our eyes and then open them onto the appearances of an expanse of white beach at the ocean's edge. Our interpretations may be our own, the raw experience which we interpret usually is not.

4. A final conclusion of the two-world view that is important here concerns other people, in fact, all consciousnesses other than our own. It is not only physical mountains and valleys, forests and lakes, cars and skyscrapers, that are "out there" in the objective world. Other people are as well. (St. Augustine, in his brief pamphlet, *Concerning the Teacher*, suggests that there is an important exception to this isolation from all other consciousnesses.) Once the true situation dawns on a person, yourself for instance, you achieved some beginning of that authentic self-awareness which the existentialists, following Kierkegaard, insist so strongly on. In addition to understanding the inescapability of having to take full personal responsibility for how you respond to your world, you grasp the reason why your bridges of communication with other people are so often very fragile things. Without a miracle, acquaintance with other minds is never direct. If it were, it would be an easy matter to determine when another is telling the truth or when he is lying. Juries, summoned to determine guilt and innocence, would be superfluous. Spying would be impossible. Tact would have no justification.

Of course, one does not have to accept epistemological dualism to learn this truth, but it does help us realize more fully that what we directly react to when it is a question of interpersonal relationships is not the actual, objective attitudes of other people, but what we believe those attitudes to be, our thought-objects of them. Theories of social interactionism, so common in contemporary speculation, must be carefully interpreted, therefore, in the light of this truth. It is precisely this indirectness of our awareness of other psyches that underlies much of psychotherapy: a great deal of the therapist's task consists in persuading his client to exchange his distorted views of others' attitudes for more objective ones. In fact, the entire behaviorist methodology is based on a recognition of this limitation of our immediate data, and, although we may disagree vehemently when the behaviorist denies the existence of consciousness, we can only applaud his insistence on the obvious fact that we do not directly observe the conscious experience of other beings, human or otherwise. Nor do those latest products of man's technology—lie detectors, EEGs, MRIs, PET-scans, and the like—give us direct access to the minds of other people. Even if our senses did give us direct access to these instruments, the only thing we would see would be the movement of needles across the faces of dials: we would still have to interpret them.

> The existentialist stress on the ultimate aloneness of the individual is a useful reminder for us . . . (It) alone makes more problematic and more fascinating the mystery of communication between alonenesses via, e.g., intuition and empathy, love and altruism, identification with others . . . We take these for granted. It would be better if we regarded them as miracles to be explained. (A. Maslow, on p. 57 of *Existential Psychology*, edited by R. May.)

Putting this final conclusion together with the third, we better appreciate the significance of passages from contemporary writers who very forcibly captured the basic human situation.

> (Man's) awareness of himself as a separate entity, the awareness of his own short life span of the fact that he will die before those whom he loves, or they before him, the awareness of his aloneness and separateness, of his helplessness before the forces of nature and of society, all this makes his separate, disunited existence an unbearable prison . . . The deepest need of man, then, is the need to overcome his separateness, to leave the prison of his aloneness. (E. From, *The Art of Loving*, ch. 2)

> This project of establishing communication, even if it does share somewhat the nature of a miracle, is more under control than other projects (e.g. discovering all of the secrets of nature through scientific investigation). It has always been recognized that the bridge, love, consists more in actions than in feelings or words; and our actions, how we live and behave with respect to others, are within our own power to be what we will them to be.

> Philosophy, we might say, begins with the recognition of aloneness in the existential sense. Obviously there is no demand that the individual make the experiment of

suspension or even bother about the significance of conceptual experimentation. The alternative is not ignorance but unwisdom. In fact, the force of mundanity (the common-sense attitude) is such that radical reflection on it is, if not a rarity, a rather scarce commodity. (M. Natanson, *The Journeying Self: A Study in Philosophy and Social Role*, p. 15).

PART TWO

The Evidence Applied

INTRODUCTION: THE QUESTION.

The prime objective of this text is to provide the true answer to the question: "What kind of being is a human person?" This question may look to some people like a simple enough question, but it is not. The question can be taken many different ways. It is sometimes interpreted with reference to society: Is the human person fundamentally a social being or are we aggressors instinctively poised to prey on our fellow-humans? Or, it might be understood as asking whether the human being is an innately noble savage or a sin-laden creature in need of salvation. It could also be taken as asking whether we are masters of our own destiny or pawns of an all-powerful environment.

Our central focus, however, goes beyond such interpretations of the question as these, to an even more basic one. It is intended to ask, What is the metaphysical or ontological make-up of the human being? This question is often referred to as the "mind-body problem." If we survey the history of Western Civilization, we find an uninterrupted succession of people who have taken it for granted that the human being includes in its make-up two distinct components. One component, the visible and tangible one, is called the "body," while the other one, invisible and intangible, is called variously "soul," "mind," or "spirit."

Despite the general consensus of Western peoples, however, there have always been individuals, sometimes groups of individuals, who subscribed to alternative views. Some denied the existence of the soul altogether. Others tended to deny the existence of the body, or at least to regard it as somewhat less than fully real. Others complained that neither was a being in its own right, and that only the composite of both, the human being, was most fully real. The most recent attack on the traditional debates about whether the human being is body-plus-mind, body alone, soul alone, etc., come from those who insist that such debates have all been a lot of hot air and/or wasted ink, that the "problem" was a pseudo-problem all along!

It is not our desire at the outset to adopt a specific stand on the mind-body debate. It is not even necessary at this point to explain why the debate is a vital one centering about a genuine problem and that it has not been much ado about nothing. It is sufficient to say that, in asking what kind of being the human person is, our aim is the same as that of the participants in the ancient body-mind debate, namely, to explore the metaphysical or ontological nature of the human person.

The outline for our investigation is as follows. Chapter One will introduce the special approach that we will adopt in investigating our question. Chapter Two will present a five-part conceptual framework, adapted from the writings of the Greek philosopher, Aristotle, which will be helpful in further explaining the approach discussed in Chapter One. Subsequent chapters will take up, one by one, several of the most influential theories that have been expounded by Western thinkers concerning the make-up of the human person. Each theory will be explained, along with some of the evidence and arguments proposed in its favor.

CHAPTER I

MIND-BODY THEORIES AS ANSWERS TO

"WHAT AM I?"

First person approach. In this text, the examination of the traditional theories concerning the nature of the human being will be given a special focus. First, the one asking the question will be you. Second, the human being you are to learn about is not the average human being, not the human being in general, but *yourself*. Instead of asking "What kind of being is a human person?", you must accustom yourself to asking "What kind of being am I?" And when examining any of the theories concerning the nature of the human person, your ultimate decision must rest, not on whether the theory fits people in general, but on whether or not it fully accounts for you and your experience of yourself.

There is a very good reason for this focus. It has to do with the matter of evidence. The theories we will be examining, each of them, are defended quite vigorously by someone. This means that the theories are not adopted simply on the grounds of personal taste or preference, but on the grounds that, to their supporters, they seem best able to explain those facts that count as evidence.

As was mentioned at the outset of Part One, disagreements about theories are ultimately traceable to disagreements about evidence or starting points. By focusing our inquiry onto the individual inquirer and his/her own personal experience, we focus onto what this author regards as the most important evidence of all. We will never allow it to be pushed from center stage for very long. The various theories will be presented as fairly as possible—taking into account the limits of time and space—as well as the facts urged in their favor. But it is important not to let the most central fact of all ever to be pushed into the background.

Consciousness is central. For a moment, consider the "most central fact of all." To begin with, the central fact is consciousness. If anyone should ask "Why consciousness?", it might be difficult to give a compelling logical answer. The answer does not lie with logic, but with a mature awareness, and such an awareness can be stirred up by asking a further question: "What good is anything without consciousness?" Nothing whatever gives us pleasure unless it is accompanied by consciousness. Even in a coma, we might be transported through a foreign country or to a concert (it does not happen, of course) almost as easily as we could be transported to a hospital (this might happen). And sleeping soundly at home is one way of relaxing (completely). But who would enjoy any such unconscious periods while they are occurring?

Nor is it an objection to point out that people at times flee from consciousness, either by self-destruction or by going to sleep. True, consciousness, pure and simple, does not constitute happiness. That much is obvious. There are periods when we can be conscious and, at the same time, miserable and in great suffering. At such times, we do, indeed, desire to escape from the misery and suffering, and if there is no way of doing this while remaining conscious, we may be driven to sacrifice consciousness itself. But we certainly cannot be said to enjoy the state of unconsciousness while we are in that state!

Reflection on an extreme situation will make the truth stand out clearly. Imagine yourself to have lived *your entire lifetime* without the slightest glimmer of consciousness. Newspapers often carry reports of individuals who lie suspended in a coma for days, weeks, even months or years, so the scenario is not totally inconceivable. For example, with a bit of inventiveness, you can picture yourself born in a coma, alive and breathing, but wholly unaware of anything at all. Further, you can imagine that, by virtue of modern medicine, you were fed intravenously and your body exercised, in such a manner that, biologically at least, you have managed to survive. Suppose that you existed in this totally comatose state for a hundred, five hundred, or a thousand years. Would it really matter to you whether or not you had ever existed? The answer is clear. If the entire span of your existence was devoid of all sensation, feeling, awareness, and thought, to-be-or-not-to-be would make no difference whatever to you.

To this most obvious of all obvious facts must be added another. The consciousness that is absolutely indispensable if your existence is to be worthwhile is your own uniquely personal consciousness. Your ancestors were in existence and conscious long before you were. Since you didn't exist, it made no difference to you. Conscious people can surround your bed and keep vigil while you sleep. The degree to which you are unaware of it is the degree to which it is meaningless to you. The human race can increase, multiply, and continue in existence for millions of years after you die. Again, it will not make the slightest difference to you. Yet, though it is impossible not to recognize the centrality of one's own consciousness in everyday life, philosophers through the ages seem often to have forgotten it.

Perhaps it is better to say that they have learned to forget it. Kierkegaard wrote about the Hegelian philosopher who forgot that he existed, so keen was he on getting an objective view of the whole universe and all reality! One of the paradoxes in our thinking is that we can,

126

even while thinking, become so absorbed in our thoughts that we lose sight of the fact that it is we ourselves who are doing the thinking. The point is important enough to dwell on a bit longer.

W. Somerset Maugham once wrote the following:

> To myself I am the most important person in the world; though I do not forget that, not even taking into consideration so grand a conception as the Absolute, but from the standpoint of common sense, I am of no consequence whatever. It would have made small difference to the universe if I had never existed. (*The Summing Up.*)

Take a moment to feel the impact of this reflection. Were I an eagle, I could look from a distance upon this planet-world of which I am a part. The planet-world is alive with teeming millions of people, each one a self just like me. From high above, however, my eye would be unable to pick me out from the rest. The number of people down on that planet who know my name is infinitesimal, compared with the number of people alive at this moment. If even four thousand persons down there know my name, that is only one millionth of the people presently alive.

To these dimensions of space can be added those of time. The universe has been around for a long, long time. Billions of years, scientists believe. During those eons of time, our sun was born and our planet came into being. Slowly this planet evolved, continents drifted apart from one another, glaciers and volcanoes left their marks, rivers cut deep canyons into the earth's surface. Scientists speculate that life will continue on this globe for some billions of years more, but eventually our sun will burn low, then go out, leaving the earth to freeze in an endless cosmic night. Situated amid this limitless river of time stretching from the distant past to the far off future, my lifetime is a fleeting instant. Momentarily my head emerges above the flow, but at death I sink again beneath the surface, as the waters close overhead, leaving no clue that I ever was. In history books, no one will ever read my name. A hundred and fifty years from now, I will be remembered by no one alive. There may be a slab of marble standing in a silent corner of some cemetery, able to tell the rare inquisitive visitor the name by which I was called, but even that will eventually be worn away by wind and rain. From the twin perspectives of space and time, my individual existence can be seen to make no difference to the universe. Such is the objective view of myself.

And yet. . . . That is an incomplete vantage point. All the while I was pretending to picture the earth from the eagle's lofty height, I did so only in imagination. In fact, my feet never left the earth. I remained down here, in the midst of these teeming millions. Physically speaking, I can never be anywhere but where I am. And that will always be at the center of my universe. It is from here, where I stand, that the universe begins. Space does stretch out infinitely in every direction, but from here! I can picture someone measuring off the universe from some other arbitrarily chosen center, but that center lies either in front of me somewhere, or behind me somewhere, or off to one side or above or below me. For me, that other center is located somewhere with reference to my center, which is my self! Similarly, time began for me at the moment I first opened my eyes and experienced the world. The past is measured with respect to me: the universe existed long centuries before me. The future is measured with reference to me: it will exist after me. Past, present, and future are all measured, ultimately, by me. Someone may speak of another date as central to all of history, but that moment itself is not "now." It is either past or future—as measured by my present.

In fact, there is a most important sense in which I am not at all insignificant to the universe. Without me, the universe is insignificant! What would it matter if a billion universes in succession had existed, each one more immense than the last, if I had never seen the light of day? What good were the glories of past civilizations that I had no part in? The only meaning they have for me is the meaning they derive from living now in my conscious awareness. Of what value will be some future golden age, if I am extinct by the time my contributions to unborn generations pay off? Of no value, except insofar as the dreaming of that far-off time adds a small edge of pleasure to my here-and-now experience. For me, the universe is real and possesses value only so long as I exist and am conscious of it. People are born equal, I maintain. But only one person is me, and all other people are precisely that—other! Can I honestly say that the existence of all other people combined has the significance to me that my own existence has? My existence, and my consciousness of it, is for me the prerequisite for their existence having any significance at all. Had I never existed, it would be completely indifferent whether anyone else had or not.

Such reflections bring one face to face with ultimate issues. We are able to be self-forgetful because of the very other-directedness of our conscious thinking. And when a person deliberately pursues "objectivity"—the outward directed attitude of cool observation so emphasized in science—it is finally possible for that person to play down the centrality of his or her own personal consciousness in determining the nature of the human being. So prevalent had this become in his own day that Kierkegaard devoted much of his writing to recalling individuals to the sense of their own being. The purpose of this chapter is to do for you what Kierkegaard tried to do in his work. So close is the parallel that it is appropriate to quote here a comment that the philosopher, A. Aiken, wrote in his anthology on nineteenth-century philosophers:

> Like Socrates, Kierkegaard is also a kind of gadfly who stings his audience until it performs the essential act of introspective self-knowledge. But it is you, the reader, who must do the essential work; all Kierkegaard does, or tries to do, is to shock you into facing the fact of your own existence as a conscious being. (*Age of Ideology*, p. 226)

In conclusion, be mindful of the fact that the most important thing for you is not brute, physical existence, but consciousness, and not someone else's consciousness, but your own. No theory about the makeup of the human person that fails to do justice to your conscious *awareness* and to your *conscious* awareness—no matter how brilliantly that theory sheds light on other facets of yourself—can ultimately be satisfactory.

As will be seen, our discussion of the various theories about human nature will bring up body-mind issues. These, however, must be translated into personal questions, such as, "Am I my body, period?" or "Am I my soul (mind)?" or "Am I both combined?" or "Am I . . . (whatever else is proposed)?" Your goal is not to understand the nature of the soul or body or composite, but the nature of yourself, the nature of that center of your universe.

CHAPTER II

THE FIVE-CONCEPT MODEL

SELF = ACT? OBJECT? POWER? HABIT? OR AGENT?

Semantic problems. Traditional controversies about the nature of the human being are bedeviled by a number of what many people describe as "semantic problems." There are moments when students, discovering the extent to which philosophers have used the same term to express different meanings and different words to express the same meaning, are tempted to dismiss the controversies themselves as "mere semantics," that is, terminological preferences. Since the readings used in this text come from a wide variety of writers, no two of whom used precisely the same terms in the same way, you may find yourself temporarily discouraged in attempting to understand them.

There is a solution to the problem of semantic confusion, however. The solution rests on some of the distinctions introduced in Part One. Most important for our present purpose is the distinction between reality, thought, and language, or between things, concepts, and words. Our concepts, presumably, represent objective *realities*, that is, things that exist, period! When this presumption is mistaken, when the concept but not the corresponding reality exists, we have what is called a fiction. Snow White and Santa Claus are fictions. They exist only as ideas or *concepts*. Concepts, in turn, are represented by *words* that are symbols for them. Semantic confusion is generated, largely, when the same word is used to symbolize different concepts and thereby to represent—through the concept—different things.

We are accustomed to the fact that different people use different words for the same idea. That is ordinarily the case with different languages. But we are not always so alert to the frequency with which the same word is used, in the same language, for different concepts and realities. To solve semantic confusions, all we must do is become more clear about the different concepts represented by the problem-words and make certain that we determine from the context which of the concepts is involved.

In this chapter, we will take up very briefly the word "self" and discuss some of the various meanings which the term has been given, i.e., some of the various concepts for which it has been used as a symbol. This will be advantageous, first, because it is a term used extensively in philosophical and psychological literature, and secondly, because it will help to sharpen the meaning of our basic question—more specifically, your basic question—"What kind of being am I?"

The word "self" is used extensively—and confusingly—in the literature dealing with the human person. For some, the word serves as a synonym for "person." John Locke, for example, used it this way, so that both words referred to "that conscious thinking thing, whatever substance it is made up of (whether spiritual or material, simple or compounded, it matters not)—which is sensible or conscious of pleasure and pain, capable of happiness or misery, and so is concerned for itself, as far as that consciousness extends" (Flew, p. 160; ignore the fact that Locke created much confusion with his misguided effort to give unchanging 'stipulative' definitions of substance, person, self, and man). Later on, philosophers began to speak of what W. James called the empirical self and the knowing self. Some treated these as two distinct selves, others—William James included—as two aspects of the same being. More recently, we find the self referred to as "an explanatory fiction, . . . a device for representing a functionally unified system of responses" (B.F. Skinner, *Science and Human Behavior*, 1953, p. 285). Others questioned the need for the concept: G. Allport, in his 1955 publication entitled *Becoming*, asked "Is the concept of self necessary?", while H. S. Sullivan regarded as an "almost inescapable illusion" the belief "that there is a perduring, unique, simple existent self." (H. S. Sullivan, in Ruitenbeek, 1964, p. 143)

Interestingly enough, though, the fact that these authors appear to disagree—the self is the person, there are two selves, the self is a fiction, the self is an "illusion"—this is by no means necessarily true. Quite often, their ideas are remarkably compatible, though their use of terms is not. The reverse side of the coin is that many of those who agree in the terms they use, disagree strongly in their thinking. Once again, it is imperative to sort out semantic differences from theoretical disagreements.

A surprising amount of clarification can be achieved with the aid of five simple concepts. These concepts already play an important though largely unnoticed role in our everyday thinking, and were seized upon long ago by Aristotle when he elaborated his common-sense philosophy. They are: act, object, power, habit, and agent. The five are closely interrelated, so that it is necessary to become acquainted with all five in order to be really clear about any single one. Note, however, that we are speaking of five concepts. We often use different words to refer to these five concepts, so beware of semantic confusion even as you lay the groundwork for overcoming semantic confusion!

A. Act. The concept of act is an easy one. We will call an "act" whatever anyone or anything does. Reading, playing checkers, lifting your foot, opening your eyes, breathing, are examples of acts. Do not confuse this use of the term "act" with the professional activity of movie actors or stage actors. The concept dealt with here is much broader, more nearly identical with the meaning of the word "action." We have many synonyms for the word "act": "deed," "activity," "operation," "function," "process," "performance," etc.

To determine whether or not it is appropriate to use the concept of act in a particular situation, simply ask whether anyone or anything is doing something. If yes, what is being done can be called an act. Such things as running, sewing, eating, and washing dishes obviously qualify as acts. Occasionally, however, we encounter cases that are less clear. We might hesitate to speak of seeing, hearing, remembering, thinking, etc., in the same way that we speak of the former instances. The reason is probably that the latter are not things that we can observe someone else doing. Yet, however different these latter may be from the former, a bit of reflection shows that we do conceive of them as things that people do: there is a big difference between someone who is asleep and someone who is awake and thinking, just as there is a difference between someone who is not hearing anything and someone who is.

More serious is the hesitation we might feel when referring to passive types of events. One person is shoved by another, a person is ordered to carry out a command, someone's fall is stopped by the ground beneath him. Aristotle would not call "acts" these things done *to* rather than initiated *by* someone. But even in the examples mentioned, there is some action which is a reaction to what is undergone. The person who is shoved (the shoving itself is an act performed by someone or something else) will subsequently move, and the motion usually will continue at least briefly after the shoving has stopped. The commanded person hears the order and initiates its execution. The hearing, motion, and execution are acts. Whether or not we wish to refer to the cessation of a fall as an act, we might still wish to call the consequent "lying there" an activity, though with this case our hesitation in applying the concept of act becomes severe. Correlatively, is standing still an act or the absence of the act of moving?! We often speak of an act or its omission. Is the omission nothing? The IRS prosecutes people for such omissions as failure to pay taxes. (In this case, the act is the decision to not pay them.) Nevertheless, these marginal cases are no cause for concern. The concept of act, which is indispensable for analysing the nature of the human person, is clear in itself and we will be dealing chiefly with fairly obvious applications of it. It is, moreover, sharply distinguished from the remaining four concepts.

B. Object. The concept of object is most easily defined with reference to act. The object is that upon which the act or activity bears. Simple illustrations are available. When a person exercises the act of eating, what he is eating is the object. When a person performs the act of sewing, the clothing being sewn is the object. When someone hears a sound, the sound is the object of the act of hearing.

As with the previous concept, so here as well we encounter some difficulties about the legitimacy of applying the concept of object in certain situations.

There need be no difficulty in such examples as the eating and the sewing. But what about the race which someone enters and runs? Is the race an object of the act of running, or is the word "race" simply a redundant term referring to the activity itself of running. One must look at the facts from as many angles as possible to see what makes the most sense, and in this case it makes most sense to regard "race" as a redundant reference to the act of running and not as an object of the act.

Other cases are more difficult. Philosophers are divided on the problem of act-vs-object as it applies to psychic activities. Some, like many phenomenologists, argue that psychic acts are not only distinct from their objects but that they are never without objects, while others deny that there are such things as acts distinct from the objects themselves. These are questions of fact, i.e., questions about reality, however. We can avoid the semantic problem easily enough by recognizing that, whatever the objective facts, we do have distinct concepts of act and object.

C. Power. The third concept that performs a basic role in our everyday thinking is that of power. The person who eats and who sews does not perform these activities all the time, but only intermittently. During those periods when the person is not performing them, we think of him or her as still retaining the power to eat or to sew. Synonyms for "power" are such terms as "ability," "capacity," "faculty," or "potentiality." Also, to distinguish this concept of power from that of mere force, we might speak, as some philosophers do, of an operative power. The concept of an operative power is the concept of some raw ability or root capacity, something real enough but something which only becomes manifested when it is put into operation, i.e., when the act which it makes possible is occurring.

We probably develop this concept of operative power in a very concrete way. People can walk and run. Most people, that is. Those who have lost their legs in an accident or through illness cannot, however. (Not unless they are fitted with prosthetic devices.) We say, therefore, that we walk or run by means of our legs. Our legs give us the power to walk or, we may say, they even constitute our power to walk. Similarly, our arms give us the power to lift, our eyes the power to see, our lungs the power to breathe, etc. Legs, arms, eyes, lungs, all of these are concrete, physical parts of our selves. It is only natural to extend the idea and to say that, since we can perform such acts as thinking, remembering, imagining, loving, and the like, we possess those powers. Even when we are not engaging in the activities, such powers or abilities remain part of us. Operative powers, then, are the means, the "limbs or organs" (literally or analogously), with which we perform particular acts.

In order not to get carried away with semantics, we must get beyond words to the ideas involved. For instance, it is apparent that the same root power can give rise to activities for which we have separate names. The human being stands, walks, skips, and jumps with the same pair of legs. There is no necessity to say that the person needs many different powers, one for each activity. Similarly, Aristotle traces the several activities of defining, dividing, opining, reasoning, questioning, etc., back to the single power of intellect or reason. So, too, we do all of our seeing, watching, viewing, scanning, and looking with a single visual power. In other words, the list of words for operative powers is much shorter than the list of words for acts.

As with the former concepts, there is much disagreement about the reality or realities to which the concept of power refers. Some disagree simply about the specific number of operative powers. Others will accept the concept as legitimately referring to legs, arms, lungs, and such physical realities, but will have nothing to do with non-physical psychic powers (intellect, reason, will, imagination, etc.). Others believe that these concepts are mere fictions, helpful enough in organizing our knowledge about the world and about people, but not literally representative of entities distinct from activities or agents (to be discussed in a moment). These often amount to purely semantic questions: should we say that a blind person has lost the ability to see or simply that there is some malfunction of his ability (if, that is, his ability to see is the "optic" portion of the nervous system)?

It is unnecessary to worry about these controversies here. The point remains that we do have a common-sense concept of operative power or ability and that we use it extensively. Our concepts of various beings, as Locke points out, are largely made up of concepts of those beings' powers. Neither the pillow on which a child sleeps nor the child while asleep display much if any visible activity. But this does not prevent us from believing that there is radical difference between the child and the pillow, namely, the fact that the child possesses all kinds of abilities or powers even while asleep, whereas the pillow never possessed those abilities in the first place. Or picture yourself confronted by three motionless objects, a rock, a turtle, and a sparrow. Our notions of the three go beyond their mere external appearance (shape, size, etc.); they consist far more of our concepts of their abilities. Proof for this would be the surprise we would experience, should the rock begin to inch forward, or the turtle to sing, or the sparrow to remain motionless as a stone for several days. Specific problems concerning applications of the concept of power or ability will be dealt with only when necessary.

D. Habit. It is interesting to note that, of the first three concepts, that of act is least controversial, that of object somewhat more so, and that of operative power the most controversial of the three. The concept of habit, though we use it a great deal, raises even more problems than the earlier ones.

We all know what habits are, of course. (!) We know that there are good habits and bad habits. Being kind, being honest, being polite, these are ordinarily considered to be good habits, whereas meanness, dishonesty, and impoliteness are bad habits. There are other habits that are neither good nor bad in themselves. For instance, skills are habits, such things as learning how to play the piano, how to type, how to play basketball, etc. We do not say, though, that a skilled typist is a good person or a concert pianist a bad person.

While we know many things which would count as habits, it is not so easy to know what exactly a habit in general is. Only metaphysicians generally would ask such a question. The scholastics, those men of the Middle Ages who were of all philosophers perhaps the most interested in metaphysical questions, did evolve a definition of habit which—whatever we may think of its ultimate validity—helps in clarifying this fourth of our common-sense concepts. They said that a habit is an acquired quality that modifies an operative power in such a way that the power is disposed to act with facility in a specific way.

Using this definition, we notice first of all that a habit is something acquired, in contrast to the power that is rather innate. Without this distinction, we might confuse power and habit, for both are referred to at times as "abilities." Take the example of typing. To say that someone has the ability to type can mean, first, that that person possesses the raw ability to punch the keys on a typewriter in the correct way. Anyone who has the usual complement of fingers, wrists, arms, etc., and who is not paralyzed, has the power or ability to type. Butterflies lack the power or ability. Generally speaking, humans are born with this power whereas butterflies are born without it. To say that someone has the ability to type can also mean that as a result of much practice, that person can now type with accuracy and facility. It means that the person has acquired a habit. Thus, of two people who have the ability to type (in the sense of an operative power), it may happen that only one of them has the ability to type (i.e., the habit). The operative power is something that usually is hereditary, whereas the habit is acquired only by the repetition of the appropriate acts, by practice. Furthermore, the habit can never be acquired unless there already exists the basic, raw operative power.

The twin concepts of operative power and habit lie at the root of the age-old "nature-nurture" controversies. There are many things which a particular culture takes for granted about people, such things as sex roles, family structure, marriage customs, race differences, etc. Quite often, such things are viewed as somehow natural, based on an unchanging, hereditary human nature. Women, for instance, are seen as possessing an innate talent for nurturing children during their early years, whereas men are regarded as naturally more adapted to working outside the home. Whites are deemed by many to be endowed with greater intellectual ability, blacks with greater natural aptitudes for some types of athletics. Such are the options of those who see sex roles and race differences as based on "nature," that is, on innate, hereditary abilities. The opposite view is taken by those who argue that men and women, as well as whites and blacks, are born with equal abilities, but that social customs determine how those abilities will be developed or not developed, that is, what kinds of habits will be induced. This is the "nurture" standpoint. Not raw natural ability, but how that ability is nurtured, is responsible for differences between the sexes and the races.

We must keep in mind that habits are very important. They, rather than operative powers, are in some measure under our control. What talents and abilities we inherit is a matter of chance, how we use our talents is up to us. And because the use of our abilities generates habits, and because habits can become so strong that they amount to what is popularly referred to as "second nature," it is easy to understand how important habits are. In fact, it is hardly an exaggeration to say that, apart from physical size, almost the entire difference between an hour-old infant and a mature adult consists of habits.

A note on maturation. Empirical psychologists have devoted a great deal of research to what is called learning theory. "Learning" has come to refer to any change in behavior brought about through experience. These changes are what Aristotle places under the heading of habit. Learning theory is complicated by debates concerning a phenomenon referred to as "maturation," and here we encounter some of the obscurity surrounding the distinction between habits and operative powers.

The problem can be illustrated by a concrete example. Among the abilities or powers of the normal human adult is that of sexual reproduction. Inanimate objects such as radios and pencils lack the ability which living things possess of being able to reproduce their kind. It is a commonly known fact, however, that the human being must reach a certain stage of development (puberty) before it is capable of procreating. How shall we understand the newborn infant, therefore? As possessing the power to reproduce, though a power that requires a certain amount of further development before it can be exercised? Or as possessing merely the potentiality to someday acquire the power to reproduce, which latter only truly begins to exist at puberty? In other words, just when does the operative power actually come into being?

This may seem like a merely semantic problem, except that behind it lie issues involving much more than mere semantics. Piaget's theories on cognitive development, for instance, involve the issue of critical periods. We know that the newborn infant is simply incapable of conscious reasoning at that early stage. The development of sophisticated capabilities requires the prior acquisition of elementary ones, just as the ability to acquire an understanding of calculus demands a previous understanding of simpler mathematical sciences. (Moralists are attentive to this phenomenon of maturation, for they argue that a certain level of experience must be reached before the human person is able to exercise genuinely free choice.) There are, apparently, critical moments in the course of human development, periods which are optimal for the nurturing of particular abilities. If the individual is deprived for too long of the stimuli necessary for this nurturing, it is either difficult or impossible to later on acquire the particular ability (habit) in question. Thus, it is easier to learn a second language when one is younger, and it is nearly impossible to acquire the habits of human socialization if one is isolated from civilization beyond a certain age. (Consult the histories of so-called "feral" children, i.e. children discovered living in the wilderness after the manner of wild animals).

There are two other especially difficult areas involving maturation. The first relates to the question: at what point does the human person begin to exist? If possession of the powers of reason and free will constitutes the essence of humanness, and if these powers are either not actually but only potentially present at birth or else are never actualized, then it might force us to revise the opinion that the newborn infant or the feral child is truly human. It might also lend support to the view of those who argue that in some sense the powers do not pre-exist the activities but are nearly identical with habits, since both are generated by the environmental stimuli that trigger the relevant act-responses.

At any rate, the only *conclusive proof* that a power is present is the actual performance of the related acts. Therefore, any argument that the powers actually exist at a time when the related acts cannot be performed must amount to a more or less reasonable inference. It is this difference between conclusive proof and reasonable inference that accounts for the inconclusiveness of the dispute between those who maintain that the fertilized ovum is fully human because it already possesses the root powers of reason and will and those who argue that the growing individual only becomes truly human at a later stage because it does not initially possess these distinctively human powers. Either opinion is, at best, *reasonable inference* and open to the possibility of being mistaken.

A note on the IQ. Another area in which maturation plays a significant part in deciding how to apply the concepts of power and habit is that of intelligence quotient (IQ). Some argue that the difference in IQ averages demonstrates the genetic superiority of certain groups over others. Such differences can be interpreted in various ways, however. First of all, it must be determined whether IQ tests reveal an innate intellectual acuity (relating to the root operative power not fully developed) or one's acquired competence (the area of habit) or a kind of hybrid, a combination of both concepts. Secondly, the theory that an ability left uncultivated beyond the optimal period of maturation can never be developed to its fullest leaves open the possibility that different IQ scores are traceable, not to genetic factors (innate powers), but to environmental opportunities (relating to the acquisition of habits).

Those are not the only issues involved, of course. Statistics involve 'measuring' groups. In discussing group differences, therefore, one would also have to keep in mind that differences in 'general' intellectual acuity are not necessarily synonymous with differences in essential humanness and that the average score of a group tells us nothing about a particular individual within that group.

E. The final concept is that of agent. Aristotle used a variety of words to signify this concept. At times he used the term "substance," at times "subject," at times "the individual." In the final analysis, the term is fairly indefinable, because it is so elementary and basic.

It is best understood by thinking of it in relation to the other four concepts. If the act is whatever someone or something is doing, then the someone or something doing the act is the agent. Objects are those things that the agent's act is directed at or bears upon. Powers are those underlying innate mechanisms whereby the agent is able to perform acts or operations. And the modifications created in the powers by an agent's repeated acts are what Aristotle calls "habits."

Apply these concepts to the following example: "John uses his mind to calculate the product of twenty-eight and fifty-six" = John (agent) uses his mind (power) to calculate (act) the product of twenty-eight and fifty-six (object). Aristotle would classify whatever memorized bits of information John used under the heading of "habit," since knowing something is an acquired mental skill.

The agent is thus, in many respects, the most basic of the concepts, because the reality it represents is basic to all the other realities. Destroy the agent, and all the acts, powers, and habits vanish with it. (Of course, if objects have their own being, they can survive an agent's destruction.) The realities described by the five concepts are very different kinds of beings. Aristotle emphasized this difference by his distinction between substances and accidents. Substances, i.e., individual things such as horses, people, trees, etc., have a being of their own. They are not *parts* of other things the way someone's reason or imagination is a part of that person. Nor do they exist *in* something else the way that the shape and size of a book exist in the book. On the contrary, powers, habits, and acts, cannot exist of themselves. He considered them to be modifications, qualities, attributes, and—in neo-scholastic English—accidents. That is, they are 'things' that cannot exist 'on their own,' but only as parts of or properties inherent in substances*. For example, you can never have sight existing on its own. There must always be someone, some *agent* or substance, that has the *power* of sight that enables it to exercise the *act* of seeing. (*It is convenient to begin thinking of substances as 'things that can exist on their own,' even though the full truth is much more complicated.)

The point makes good sense when one's attention is first drawn to it, but it is not always easy to keep it in mind. The reason for this probably lies in our common linguistic practice. Some have said that Aristotle links substances with the subject of a sentence: a substance is not *said of* a subject (as when we say "generous" of a subject, as in "John is generous") because it *is* the subject. However, it is common linguistically for us to turn any noun into the subject of a sentence. Just notice that, above, in speaking of acts, powers, habits, objects, we have used many sentences in which those terms occupy the position of grammatical subjects. We can, unless we are careful, think of them as if they were also beings in their own right, that is, substances. We can say that a man's eye saw an entire scene and unconsciously think of the eye as if *it* were an agent. Aristotle replies that it is not the eye that sees, however, but the man or woman who is using the eye(s). The conclusion is simply that we cannot decide theories on the basis of our ways of talking. We must use our intelligence to continually ask what sense our talk makes. We must make our talk fit our thought.

Applied to the self. We saw earlier in this chapter that the word "self" is given different meanings by different authors, even by the same author in different contexts. That is, the word is used to signify distinct concepts. This is not the place to consider the various uses of the word in any great detail, but it is possible, using the concepts presented in this chapter, to give a brief introduction to some of the distinct meanings of the term. (They will be dealt with in more detail in subsequent chapters.)

William James begins his chapter on "The Self" (Chap. 12 of *Psychology: Briefer Course*) by mentioning two selves, the self as knower and the self as known. The self as known, in James' view, is one of the things the self as knower is conscious of, that is, part of a passing state of consciousness. We will treat James' view at greater length in the next chapter, but from what has been said, it is apparent that James' self as known can be nothing else than an object of knowledge.

The contents of consciousness, the totality of the immediate objects of awareness (if Part One is correct), include sense-data, images, feelings, concepts, and the like. Some of these "refer" to the world outside us, but many of them "refer" to ourselves. James distinguishes these elements in our self as known into what he calls "the material me," "the social me," and "the spiritual me." The material me consists of my body, my clothing, my family, home, property, and the like, the social me includes all of the images which other people have of me, and the spiritual me embraces all of those innermost parts of my conscious being. But James restricts himself in this chapter to the stream of consciousness, so that these various me's are to be understood, not as parts of objective reality, but as parts of our inner, subjective world, hence as psychic or intentional objects.

If we consider our various thought-objects from the viewpoint of what they represent rather than from the viewpoint that they are parts of our subjective reality, we can make further distinctions.

One may strive to restrict his notion of a person to that person's acts or behavior. This concept of the person's total repertoire of behavior is regarded by some as the concept of that person or of that person's self. This is the origin of one use of the term "self," whereby it stands for what we have called "acts."

Many psychologists are interested, not in the actual behavior so much as in the patterns that the behavior manifests over a length of time. This is the source of those definitions of the word "self" which refer to things such as "functionally unified systems of responses." When these patterns of behavior are regarded as innate, they refer generally to the category of what Aristotle calls "powers." When they are considered to be acquired or learned, they more appropriately come under the heading of "habits."

None of these uses of the term "self" is so important for us as the last, namely, that whereby the term stands for the agent or what W. James calls "the self as knower." Many psychologists explicitly refrain from dealing with the question, "What is the nature of the self as knower?", preferring to concern themselves with empirical matters and to relegate this question to philosophy. This was pretty much the position that James adopted in his *Psychology: Briefer Course.*

By contrast, this is precisely the subject of our inquiry. When you ask, "What kind of being am I?", the hope is that you will be attempting to understand that being which you refer to with the reflexive pronoun "I." This is something very different from any of the above-mentioned "selves," apart even from any or all of your passing states of consciousness. James writes:

> The passing state (of consciousness) we have seen to be the very embodiment of change. Yet each of us spontaneously considers that by "I," he means something always the same. This has led most philosophers to postulate behind the passing state of consciousness a permanent Substance of Agent whose modification or act it is. This Agent is the thinker; the "state" is only its instrument or means. "Soul," "transcendental Ego," "Spirit," are so many names for this more permanent sort of Thinker. (PBC, p. 207)

Is the *self* a body, a soul, neither, both, etc.? For us, that's our focus. That question here is the same as the question, "Is the *human being* a body, a soul, neither, both, etc.?" Also the same as the question, "Is the human *person* a body, a soul, neither, both, etc." Also the same as "Am *I* a body, a soul, neither, both, etc.?" Here, those terms—self, human being, person, I—all refer, in the context of those questions, to the same being.

The contradictory answers to that question (or those questions) are what we will take up now.

CHAPTER III

THE PHENOMENALIST ANSWER

The first theoretical answer to our question that we will consider is that which is sometimes referred to as "phenomenalism." Very succinctly, phenomenalism denies that you are a self, if by "self" we mean a perduring, substantial agent, as that term was defined in the previous chapter. Rather, this theory maintains, you are a stream of consciousness, a process (acts), or a cluster of sense-data and images.

Before describing the theory in any more detail, it will be helpful to spend a moment on some preliminary matters. The reason is that it is difficult for the novice in philosophy to even understand what the theory says. It is more difficult to understand how any sane person can believe the theory. These difficulties can be overcome with a bit of practice, however, especially if two lessons are learned. The first is nothing more nor less than epistemological dualism. The second is the difference between observation and inference.

In Part One, we studied epistemological dualism. This is the view that we have no direct acquaintance with any realities outside our own consciousness. All that we do have direct awareness of are our own concepts, images, sense-data, feelings, and the like. Our thoughts, reveries, sensations, moods, emotions, etc.—our total experience—undergo constant change. William James coined an apt phrase to describe this immediate reality of ours, "the stream of consciousness."

For our purposes, we will take David Hume and William James as the two leading proponents of phenomenalism. In order to understand either the actual phenomenalism of Hume or the provisional phenomenalism of James, simply keep in mind that neither of them approached our question about the self from the standpoint of naïve common-sense realism. They both proceed from something much closer to epistemological dualism.

But not exactly the same as epistemological dualism. That theory argues that there are two worlds, the inner world that we directly experience, and the outer world whose existence and nature is known only indirectly, by inference. Phenomenalism drops the outer world, at least its 'substance' aspects.

Recall the distinction between observation and inference. It is closely related to the distinction between evidence and theory. In science, much of what is regarded as proven fact is inference or theory.

Some people, for instance, regard evolution as a fact. But, no one alive was present at the beginning of time, no one alive observed the evolution of galaxies, planets, continents, or living species, no one alive observed—not even according to the most naïve common-sense realist—any events except those that have taken place since his/her birth. Evolution, if it did occur, is not known on the basis of observation, nor is it evidence for other theories. Rather, it is a theory or inference, proposed as an explanation for things which are difficult to explain by any other theory, such things as geological strata, fossil remains which have been dug up, variations within present-day living species, etc. These latter serve as evidence for the theory of evolution. According to epistemological dualism, in fact, even the geological strata, fossil remains, and living species are only inferred, since they exist outside everyone's consciousness and have never been observed.

Phenomenalism is an even more austere outlook than epistemological dualism, for the phenomenalist refuses to indulge in any inferences which are, strictly speaking, impossible to verify. Since it is strictly speaking impossible ever to get outside one's consciousness or mind in order to see whether things in the objective universe are like the concepts we have of them inside our mind, (i.e., we cannot verify these concepts), the phenomenalist refuses to even admit the existence of the epistemological dualist's external, objective universe. This leaves him with only the stream of consciousness. This stream is cut up or sliced up into distinct clusters of sense-data, images, and the like, and ordinary, everyday names (e. g., "apples," "body," "tree," "house," etc.) used to signify these clusters.

It is this very last fact that causes most of the problems students encounter when trying to understand phenomenalism. They read paragraphs that would often make quite good sense to a common-sense realist, even to an epistemological dualist. Up to a point! Then, suddenly, the paragraph that was speaking of people, animals, trees, apples and oranges, seems to deny objective reality. This is because those words, all along, were being used to represent, not what ordinary people mean by them, but—as was stated—clusters of sense-data, images, and the like.

Phenomenalists do, however, admit the legitimacy of inferences, but only the right sort of inferences. They will not allow inferences concerning unexperienced and unexperienceable realities, but only those concerning realities that, because they are similar to previously or presently experienced realities, might have been experienced in the past or may in principle be experienced in the future.

Applied to our question about the self, we find the following results. If the phenomenalist uses the term "self," the term can only be used to refer to the whole or part of one's stream of consciousness, for that is all that is ever observed. No inferences can be made to some self as knower or as agent, since that is in principle unexperienced and unexperienceable.

Let us now illustrate the theory by direct reference to the writings of Hume and James.

W. James, in his *Psychology: Briefer Course*, adopts a provisional phenomenalism for the most part. Merely "for the most part", though, because there are many pages on which he adopts what can only be called the *epi*phenomenalist view. (That view will be considered in a later chapter.) At the very end of his chapter on the stream of consciousness, James writes that that stream is organized in ways determined by each person's choosings and habits of attention, but that the organization for one person is much the same as the organization for another person, because their choosings are usually so much alike:

> There is, however, one entirely extraordinary case in which no two men ever are known to choose alike. One great splitting of the universe into two halves is made by each of us; and for each of us almost all of the interest attaches to one of the halves; but we all draw the line of division between them in a different place. When I say that we all call the two halves by the same names, and that those names are "me" and "not-me" respectively, it will at once be seen what I mean." (PBC, pp.17, 19, & 187)

This passage, written more than eighty years ago, seems to fit well with contemporary research in infant psychology. Though the infant displays various instinctive responses to external stimuli, there is no evidence that the infant has any congenital awareness of a *me* (his own subjective reality, what is doing the responding) as distinct from the *not-me* (the stimuli from the external world). If someone reaches out and lifts the newborn's hand so that the two arms, the infant's and the other person's, both occupy the infant's field of vision, there is no evidence that the newborn recognizes one as belonging to it and one as not so belonging. It is only with time and experience that the infant learns to sort out what belongs to it (James' *me*) from what does not belong (the *not-me*). Incidentally, it is also only with time-and experience, as Piaget has shown, that the infant begins to realize that things do not disappear when they are no longer within the field of vision. For the thoroughgoing phenomenalist, though, both halves of the universe are merely parts of the stream of consciousness, not anything beyond or outside it.

This applies even to the self. In the very next chapter, James begins with the following paragraph:

> Whatever I may be thinking of, I am always at the same time more or less aware of myself, of my personal existence. At the same time it is I who am aware; so that the total self of me, being as it were duplex, partly known and partly knower, partly object and partly subject, must have two aspects discriminated in it, of which for shortness we may call one the *Me* and the other the *I*. I call these 'discriminated aspects,' and not separate things, because the identity of *I* with *me*, even in the very act of their

discrimination, is perhaps the most ineradicable dictum of common-sense, and must not be undermined by our terminology here at the outset, whatever we may come to think of its validity at our inquiry's end. (PBC, p.189)

What is the nature of this "I"? James later on speaks of the *I*, the self as knower, as being an agent rather than an object. But if all he is willing to admit is the stream of consciousness, he ought logically to deny the existence of any I, since the agent is not part of the stream of consciousness. This, in fact, is what he does go on to do, in a manner which is at first extremely confusing but which is simple semantic legerdemain.

First, following a lengthy description of the various "me's" (mentioned in the last chapter), he takes up the description of the "I." After discussing and rejecting several of the traditional arguments in favor of an agent or substance, he writes:

> The logical conclusion seems then to be that the states of consciousness are all that psychology needs to do her work with. Metaphysics or theology may prove the Soul to exist; but for psychology the hypothesis of such a substantial principle of unity is superfluous. (PBC, p. 214)

Still, he is unwilling to do without any "I" or knower whatever, even in psychology. And so he goes on to say that, since the *I* is what must know all the rest of the stream of thought, we can attach the name to "a *thought*, at each moment different from that of the last moment, but appropriative of the latter, together with all that the latter called its own" (PBC, p.225). We can, that is, adjust our use of the terms "I" or "self as knower," no longer use them to refer to some perduring, unchanging agent or substance, and instead call a *thought* "I" or my "self." His final sentence in this chapter reads:

> And in this book the provisional solution which we have reached must be the final word: the thoughts themselves are the thinkers." (PBC, p.226)

You are not a body, then. You are not a soul or spirit. You are a thought, a thought which each moment becomes, along with all that it knows (objects), the object of a later, newer, thought or *you*.

David Hume, a famous philosopher who died more than seventy years before James was born, had a slightly different version of what a person is. In a well known passage from his *Treatise of Human Nature* (Book I, Part IV, Section 6), Hume wrote:

> Setting aside some metaphysicians . . . I may venture to affirm of the rest of mankind, that they are nothing but a bundle or collection of different perceptions, which succeed each other with an inconceivable rapidity, and are in a perpetual flux and movement." (Flew, p. 189)

He introduces an analogy to make his point clear. (In reading the passage, translate Hume's word "mind" into "person.")

> The mind is a kind of theatre, where several perceptions successively make their appearance; pass, re-pass, glide away, and mingle in an infinite variety of postures and situations. There is properly no simplicity in it at one time, nor identity in different; whatever natural propension we may have to imagine that simplicity and identity. The comparison of the theatre must not mislead us. They are the successive perceptions only, that constitute the mind; nor have we the same distinct notion of the place, where these scenes are represented, nor of the materials, of which it is compos'd. (Flew, p.190)

Picture your mind as the stage on which your sense-data, memories, thoughts, feelings, and the like, appear, play their part, then yield to other players. Then, immediately, *erase the stage*. This leaves you with James' stream of consciousness. Only now, Hume's knower is not, like James', a single ever-new thought. For Hume, there is either no thinker, or the thinker is the whole present stream of consciousness.

Why are such radical positions taken by James and Hume? Their reasons are intimately tied up with their epistemologies, i.e., with their theories concerning knowledge and certainty. Hume is famous for his thoroughgoing application of an epistemological principle, what we may call *"the radical empiricist principle."* According to this principle, all of our ideas come from experience (the mind being originally a blank tablet), so that if any alleged idea cannot be traced back to experience, it is an imposter and must be thrown out of one's philosophy. Strictly speaking, Hume would not say that the alleged idea is an imposter, but that the word standing for the non-existent idea is either meaningless and to be discarded or else should be attached to a real idea.

Now it is Hume's and James' contention that, so long as human experience is what it presently is, *it is impossible ever to have any direct awareness of a substantial agent* as the older philosophers and theologians had spoken of. This is another central point of the well-known passage from Hume's *Treatise of Human Nature* referred to earlier. A few sentences from this passage make Hume's position clear:

> There are some philosophers, who imagine we are every moment intimately conscious of what we call our self, that we feel its existence and its continuance in existence; and are certain, beyond the evidence of a demonstration, both of its perfect identity and simplicity . . . Unluckily all these positive assertions are contrary to that very experience, which is pleaded for them, nor have we any idea of self, after the manner it is here explained . . . It must be some one impression, that gives rise to every real idea. But self or person is not any one impression, . . . and consequently there is

no such idea . . . For my part, when I enter most intimately into what I call *myself*, I always stumble on some particular perception or other, of heat or cold, light or shade, love or hatred, pain or pleasure. I never can catch *myself* at any time without a perception, and never can observe any thing but the perception. (Flew, pp.188-189)

For Hume, since we have no direct experience of an agent that possesses perfect identity and simplicity, we can have no such idea, and the term "self" is meaningless if understood to stand for such an idea. We can, however, take the word and assign to it a new meaning. We do experience the collection of *separate* perceptions, so Hume attaches the term to the perceptions, to which James opposes the *stream* of consciousness.

James adopts the position he does because his aim is to lay the groundwork for psychology as a strictly empirical science. If the method of the empirical sciences is to accept only Hume's "experience" as a valid test for any proposed theories, and if a substantial, perduring agent or self can never be experienced, a scientific psychology must either renounce any reference to such a thinker-self or else it must have a thinker that can be observed. James prefers the second alternative, hence he selects what he considers the most acceptable substitute, a present thought!

The strengths of the phenomenalist position are greater than most students suppose, but they must be carefully pondered, since at first the position appears so violently opposed to our deepest belief about our self. That "deepest belief" is that we are each a perduring, continuous being, a being that remains the same—in some basic sense—from moment to moment, from year to year. This belief, which is a strong conviction, will be examined more in detail in a later chapter on brain-mind identity.

But even one's unsophisticated, common-sense understanding of the issue is sufficient for recognizing the phenomenalist position as a radical departure from our ordinary belief about our self.

If one accepts epistemological dualism, this step by itself carries one a long way toward grasping the difficulty Hume and many others felt when trying to justify their common-sense belief in a perduring, substantial self.

Suppose the self is one's body. Now, one's body may exist, but one can never directly experience it. (Representationalism) What one does experience are only various sense-data which grow into one's body-image. Nor can we see our bodies in the mirror, indirectly as it were. The mirror-images are just additional images. (Take a moment sometime to look into a mirror and to notice how much your face-image looks like *a real, flesh-and-blood face*, as real as any face—or face-image!—you will ever sense.) Both one's body-image as well as mirror-images are, recall, objects of consciousness. The self as knower, as perduring agent, can never be identified with these objects of which it is aware, since it is that which is aware of these objects. If we use an analogy and picture acts of awareness or knowledge as issuing or springing forth from the knower, then we must realize that the knower can never, as it were, step out in front of itself and allow the act of awareness to bear directly upon it. The knowing self will always be standing back viewing whatever objects are out in front of it.

The only alternative would be for the knower, in some mysterious fashion, to bend its gaze back upon itself. This is just the analogy that lies at the root of a word often encountered in certain philosophical and psychological writings, the word "reflection." The English word comes from a Latin word that means, literally, "bending back." Is such a bending back possible? Even more, whether or not it is possible, do we experience any such thing?

The radical empiricist principle. Consider the problem. If we are serious in asking whether such a thing is possible, it is necessary to avoid slipshod thinking. We must realize that it cannot be just any part of ourselves that does this bending back. It is not our eyes that look back, nor our hands, nor our feet—not according to any theory whatever! If our eyes cannot literally see us in the mirror, they are also unable to stretch out several inches or feet, bend around, and look back at us. If they could, they would see a body with empty eye-sockets! (It is worthwhile mentioning such things, though no one is tempted to think them, for it helps to highlight the problem.)

If any part of us is doing the bending back upon ourselves, it must be either our brain or some other knowing "part." Who is there who would claim to be aware of his/her brain directly looking back and to be certain—intuitively certain and not certain on the basis of logical argumentation—of the fact? If it is not the brain, but your mind, intellect, reason, soul (these are the most common alternative suggestions), the same question must be asked: who can claim to be aware of his/her mind, etc., directly looking back, and to be intuitively certain of the fact? Interestingly enough, not even Descartes, the philosopher who erected his entire philosophy on the famous principle "I think, therefore I am," claimed to have intuitively certain and direct knowledge of the being doing the thinking. He claimed to know indubitably that the "I" existed, but admitted that the nature of the "I", i.e., what kind of being it was, had to be reasoned to. In the end, he was forced to argue that the concept of substance is an innate concept and to make use of a self-evident principle in arguing from the existence of thinking to the existence of the thinker (the principle being that in order to think we must exist). These reflections show the difficulty involved in maintaining that we have any direct awareness of any substance or agent.

In other words, if there is a perduring, substantial self, an "I" that is not part of the stream of consciousness but is rather the being that is aware of that stream, then we can know about it only by means of an inference. Like someone who observed Robinson Crusoe's footprint in the sand and then had to infer from it the existence and nature of the unobserved creature who had made the footprint, we must use the observed stream of consciousness as our clue to the existence and nature of an unobserved substantial self. We must construct a theory or explanation on the basis of our only available evidence, namely, our inner world, and extrapolate or project our knowledge beyond this inner world. In James' words, we must do what he refused to do, that is, "postulate behind the passing state of consciousness a permanent Substance or Agent"—a very speculative undertaking at best!

Unlike those philosophers willing to carry on this venture in speculative inferring, the phenomenalists remain faithful to their *radical empiricist principle*. Because any permanent substance or agent will remain forever "behind" the stream of consciousness, forever beyond the pale of experience, they argue that we cannot infer its nature or its existence, because *we can never have any concept of it*. Any alleged name for it would be meaningless. Therefore we cannot even speak of it.

Conceptualization vs inference. Note well what follows! There is a subtle but crucial distinction in the phenomenalist argument. *We must make a distinction between having a concept and making an inference.* i) One can have a concept without making any inference, but one cannot make an inference without having a concept. A concept is an idea of something, whether it be of a river, a mountain, an infant, or a chair. Traditionally, we say that concepts are represented by single words, as they were in the just-previous sentence. ii) An inference, on the other hand, is a judgment that such-and-such is so or that it is not so, and is traditionally held to be represented by a declarative sentence made up of several words rather than by a single word.

An example of the distinction is as follows. You certainly have a concept of Santa Claus. You may entertain that idea without making any inference or judgment about it. Or you may make a judgment. At one time, presumably, you made the tacit inference, "Santa Claus exists," while at the present time you presumably accept the inference, "Santa Claus does not exist." You cannot, however, make any inference at all about Santa Claus unless you have an idea of him.

Along the same lines, then, notice the difference between the 'man Friday' and Robinson Crusoe and your situation vis-à-vis your permanent self. Friday already knew—if we adopt the common-sense point of view—what a human being was, i.e., already had a concept of a man. He did not acquire the idea of the man, Crusoe, from the footprint. Rather, the footprint was evidence enabling him to make the inference that some other human being was on the island with him, for he had seen footprints made by human beings in the past and had not seen them made in any other way. You, on the other hand, have no concept of a permanent substance, because—according to the phenomenalists—you have never had the experience of one, and ideas must all come from experience. Your phrase "permanent substance or agent" is as empty and meaningless as "begrod" or "gubble", though the familiarity born of years of hearing the phrase and using it have blinded you to the fact.

As mentioned earlier, the phenomenalists do allow for some inferences. From your actual experience, past or present, you may legitimately infer more experiences *similar* to those that you have had in the past.

Consider the inferences you make *as you watch a movie*. If there are two people engaged in a fight and one of them picks up a rock, you can infer that the person will pull back the arm with the rock in it and then hurl the rock at the other person. Such an inference would be as valid (in this case, perhaps only solidly probable) as a similar inference made while watching an actual fight. Notice, however, that during the movie, you are witnessing only pictures on a screen, not real people and real rocks. Your inference is also only about future pictures on the screen, and not about real people and real rocks. So, too, with the real fight, if phenomenalism is correct: your inferences are from present sense-data to future, anticipated sense-data.

As will be seen in subsequent chapters, those who reject phenomenalism do so by challenging certain basic parts of the theory. Some reject the phenomenalists' rejection of direct common-sense realism (as well as epistemological dualism). Some maintain that we do have some sort of obscure intuition of substance, either of external substances or of the permanent self, though we must reason to its precise nature. (Aristotelian-Thomists) Others argue that not all of our concepts come from experience, but that certain ones, among them the concept of substance, are innate. (Descartes) Others claim that our mind is so constituted that it must think in terms of substances and their attributes, including the substantial self and its states of consciousness (Kant), just as we must speak in sentences with the subject-predicate form (language philosophers). These thinkers often conclude that we can discover solid grounds for believing that our thinking corresponds in some way to objective reality.

This is not the place to discuss the shortcomings of phenomenalism, however. Those will be taken up as we move on to other views. It is unlikely that any but a handful of readers will be tempted to adopt the theory. The majority of thinkers, in fact, reject the pure phenomenalist position for one reason or another, though one suspects it is chiefly because it is so radically opposed to our deepest common-sense conviction about our perduring self.

But, though the majority will not positively subscribe to the pure phenomenalist position as if it fully accounted for reality, there are many who adopt it as a provisional philosophy. Convinced as they are of some of the initial premises of phenomenalism, and aware of the difficulty of being certain of anything beyond the stream of consciousness, they remain agnostic about the metaphysical makeup of the human being.

It is this provisional phenomenalism that the student will most often encounter, particularly in the writings of twentieth-century psychologists and/or personality theorists. We will bring this chapter to a close, therefore, by illustrating the kind of provisional phenomenalism frequently encountered today.

Mention was made earlier, for example, of Gordon Allport. He is the author who asked, "Is the concept of self necessary?" Here is his conclusion:

> We return now to our unanswered question: Is the concept of self necessary in the psychology of personality? Our answer cannot be categorical since all depends upon the particular usage of "self" that is proposed . . . . So far as psychology is concerned our position, in brief, is this: all psychological functions commonly ascribed to a self or ego must be admitted as data in the scientific study of personality . . . What is unnecessary and inadmissible is a self (or soul) that is said to perform acts, to solve problems, to steer conduct, in a transpsychological manner, inaccessible to psychological analysis." (*Becoming*, pp. 54-55)

Reminiscent of James' position? Quite obviously. So, too, is the position of Harry Stack Sullivan who wrote, among other things:

> What the personality does, which can be observed and studied only in relations between personalities or among personalities, is truly and terribly marvelous, and is human, and is the function of creatures living in indissoluble contact with the world of culture and people. In that field it is preposterous to talk about individuals and to go on deceiving oneself with the idea of uniqueness, of single entity, of simple, central being . . . The conceptual system has grown up which finds its subject matter not in the study of personality, which is beyond reach, but in the study of that which can be observed; namely, interpersonal relations. And when that viewpoint is applied, then one of the greatest difficulties encountered in bringing about favorable change is this almost inescapable illusion that there is a perduring unique, simple existent self, called variously "me" or "I," and in some strange fashion, the patient's, or the subject person's private property . . . . No great progress in this field of study can be made until it is realized that the field of observation is what people do with each other, what they can communicate to each other about what they do with each other. When that is done, no such thing as the durable, unique, individual personality is ever clearly justified." ("A Theory of Interpersonal Relations—the Illusion of Personal Individuality," in Ruitenbeek, 1964, pp.142-143)

The accent in these passages is on functions (Allport) and on interpersonal relations or—more basically—interpersonal doings and communicatings (Sullivan). Both would come under Aristotle's heading of act. Still, though the flux that is basic here consists of fields of action rather than streams of perceptions, there is the same explicit denial of an underlying substantial agent-self. It is possible to find many similar examples of such views in the writings of recent psychologists.

One must be careful in interpreting such passages, however. A close inspection of the surrounding context often reveals either certain offhand comments or else between-the-line implications that tell another story. Quite frequently the existence of individual substances is not being denied entirely. Sullivan, for example, clearly believes that human beings are originally biological organisms and later are altered biological organisms, namely, biological organisms that have acquired various habits of behavior. But, since these theorists are more concerned about behavior, especially the clients' perceptions of the behavior, and since their interests are pragmatic or practical rather than metaphysical, they either take James' example and relegate the issue of the person's metaphysical make-up to philosophy or theology, or else they simply assume as obvious the fact that a human is a highly evolved biological organism. To the extent that they adopt the former alternative, we can describe their position as provisional phenomenalism. Insofar as they choose the latter option, their position is materialism (which will be discussed in the following chapter).

CHAPTER IV

MATERIALISM IN GENERAL

Materialism as a genus. "Materialism" is the name we will give to any theory which argues that the human being is basically a single, unified entity, and that this entity is presently, at least as far as we know, an individual of the most highly evolved species of living organisms. There are several varieties of materialism, and there are many serious disagreements among them. In this chapter, however, we will select three of the major forms of materialism and treat them as if they are simply variants of the materialist answer to "What is a human being?" These three are: Radical Behaviorism, Mind-Brain Identity Theory, and Epiphenomenalism.

Because these are only three of the possible varieties of materialism that we could examine, it will be helpful to state the reason for our choice. It is quite simple. *They differ most basically in their interpretations of "consciousness."* By selecting just these three types of materialism, types that agree fundamentally in their view of the nature of the human being but disagree about consciousness, we will gain a great deal by clarifying the concept of the vital activity that constitutes the evidence for answering the question, "What is a human being?"

Before taking up the specific variations of materialism, a few words must be said about the materialist approach in general. That is, before discussing their differences, it is well to know what the variant theories have in common.

Contemporary materialists are strongly influenced by the physical sciences. When they look out at the universe, their eyes see a world in change. Change is everywhere, on the macroscopic as well as the microscopic scale. This change has a beginning, a development, and an end: birth, lifetime, and death.

A very common view among cosmologists is what is called the "Big Bang Theory." According to this theory, there was a moment in the far-off past when all of the matter in the universe was densely packed into a single "atom." That atom exploded, and matter was sent hurtling in every possible direction. Some of it evolved into galaxies, planetary systems formed around stars in some or all of the galaxies, and at least on one planet various life forms spread and evolved. Individual living things die after a period of post-natal development, occasionally entire species die out, individual stars die after exhausting their energy supply, and someday our entire universe will "die." The matter that constitutes it will be dissipated into the night of infinite space.

It is in that overall picture that materialists situate the human being. Each person is born from a long line of ancestors, a line that includes, at its earlier stages, two-legged pre-hominids, four-legged land creatures, aquatic animals, simple organisms of no more than a few cells, unicellular specks, and—originally—inanimate molecules.

In addition, materialists generally agree that either material things are the only kinds of things that exist or else that whatever other kind of reality exists comes ultimately from material things and totally depends on them. Material things come first. That huge atom, far instance, if the Big Bang Theory is correct. Only the epiphenomenalist materialists believe that there exists something non-material, namely, the "stuff" of consciousness, but they assume that it has emerged from and depends entirely on matter.

Materialists also agree in taking quite seriously modern research on the human brain and central nervous system. Only in recent times have scientists begun to comprehend the magnificence of the brain. This very small object, weighing little more than three pounds, wholly unimpressive to the naked eye, is easily the most complex and marvelous piece of "machinery" in the known universe. It is the control center of the larger "mechanism," what is ordinarily called the human body. Like a computer, the brain gathers information from its vast communications network, processes it, then relays orders back to those parts of the body that serve it. This means, then, that a person's external behavior, open and observable to the onlooker, is being initiated and coordinated by hidden processes occurring within the central nervous system. The materialists generally concur at this point.

Avoiding pseudo-problems. Western thinking about the nature of the human being has been cast, traditionally, in terms of "the body-soul problem." There are many thinkers who regard this tradition as a hindrance that must be eliminated before we can think clearly about our selves. However natural and obvious the existence of bodies and souls may seem to us, it is not uncommon to read statements such as the following:

> The mind-body problem is one of the oldest snarls in philosophy. Plato's distinction between natural phenomena and their true essence has remained a source of confusion for 2400 years, and his creation of a world of mind as opposed to a world of matter may be regarded as his most dubious contribution to western civilization. In one form or another, his notion of the human body as a physical entity existing in space and the mind as a nonmaterial entity coexisting with the body has plagued everyone who seeks to explain the actions and conduct of man. (C. Fincher, *A Preface to Psychology*, 1964, p. 4)

There is not only considerable justification for statements such as these, but it is of positive value for us to try and understand the position expressed by them. Doing so is not difficult. All that is necessary is to stop a moment and ask, what are the interrelations between the following three things: the body, the soul, and the person or self (i.e., that which is expressed by the pronoun "I" or "you"). Before reading the next few paragraphs, take a moment to examine your own ideas on these items.

How would you answer the question, Do you believe you have a body? Most people unhesitatingly nod their assent. Do you have a soul? In olden times, most Westerners would have answered this question in the affirmative also, though the majority would confess that the existence of the soul is not as obvious as that of the body.

How would you answer the next question: What is the "you" that has a body and a soul? Perhaps you have a wristwatch and a pocket calculator. Is your relation to this second pair of things similar in any respect to your relation to the first pair? If so, what are you?

Perhaps it makes more sense to say that you *are* your body. After all, if someone kicks your leg, you might ask him or her to stop kicking your leg, but it is understood that it is you being kicked. You would never accept the excuse that it is only your leg being kicked, not you! Or is your body only *part* of you, since your soul is also part of you. You, then, are the combination of soul and body.

Does this solve all of the problems? Not entirely. People who believe they are body-plus-soul usually believe that their soul will live on after the body's death. How would you answer the question, Do you believe that when you are dead and buried, your soul will live on in the after-life? If you are tempted to answer, "Yes, I believe so," you may have immersed yourself in the difficulty Plato long ago pointed out. An affirmative answer to such a question implies, first, that you are your body (did you notice "when *you* are dead and buried?"), and secondly, that you cannot, therefore, live on in an after-life. Those who have devoted a great deal of time to thinking about such things and who do believe that the human being is a combination of body and soul have suggested that the more correct answer to the above question is: "At death, I will continue to exist, since I am my soul, but I will be incomplete inasmuch as I will lack part of what truly belongs to me, namely, my body, just as would be the case if I lost an arm or a leg."

Now, having read the above paragraphs, can you say that your usual notions about body, soul, and self, were perfectly clear? Do you believe they are perfectly clear now? Whatever your answer may be, those few paragraphs should be sufficient to enable you to surmise just how much confusion surrounds most people's ideas re body, soul, and self.

The problem runs even deeper, however, as the critics point out. It is very difficult for people not to think of the body and the soul as two distinct things. What kind of things? Refer back to Aristotle's elaboration of our five common-sense concepts. Can body and soul be distinct acts? Distinct powers? Distinct habits? Distinct objects? A bit of serious thought should make it clear that none of those are suitable answers. The most usual answer is that body and soul are two different substances. And, even though this answer creates a severe theoretical difficulty, it fits quite well with the facts most people use to justify their belief in the distinction between body and soul. Take these last two points in reverse order.

First, what are the reasons most people believe that two distinct things, body and soul, exist? Certainly, we do not *feel* as if we are two distinct things. We experience ourselves as a single being. It is the same "I" who walk, run, eat, study, take exams, converse with my friends, make decisions, and the like. Certainly, I can say that, in some sense, there are different parts to me: two hands, two arms, two legs, etc. I can easily point to just one of those parts. But, if I were asked to point to my body, what would I point to? *Would you not point to every part of yourself, from head to toes, if you pointed to your body?* What part of you, then, is your soul and where is it situated? Can you, concretely, *feel* your soul (as you feel your hands or feet or head) in any part of you? Unless you already had been told that there exists a soul, would it ever occur to you to think of a thing like that which you cannot feel or experience?

Secondly, what are the reasons people ever began believing in a soul? Traditionally, there have been *two arguments* people have found most persuasive, and materialists contend that modern science has clearly invalidated both of them. (We will bypass what may have been the earliest argument, historically, namely, apparitions of the dead in the dreams of their survivors.)

Common arguments for the soul. The first and most common argument rests upon the fact of death and *the difference between the living person and the corpse.* Death is a change that is at once both momentous and very slight. It is momentous and overwhelming: most people fear death more than anything else, and there is no loss so great as the death of a dear one. Yet, to the naked eye, it is very slight: between the living person and the corpse, there is little if any detectable change other than the fact that the living person moves and the corpse does not. But cessation of movement does not constitute death, else moments of sleep would be death. Even permanent cessation of movement is only a *sign* of death. The real change is not an externally visible one. The corpse has the same shape, color, weight, size, features, and the like, as the living person.

At first, that is. Decomposition does set in and change everything. But decomposition is not the same as death. Decomposition occurs only gradually. Actual death is brief, and the change that is death is an internal one. Even so, it is not simply internal in the sense that it occurs beneath the skin and hence is unobservable. So far as naked-eye observation goes, there are no more changes in the inner bodily organs than there are in the external bodily appearances.

These facts being what they are, it occurred to some that there must be something, some real life-giving factor, present in the living person yet absent from the corpse, a factor responsible for the change, for the whole difference between the living person and the corpse. This something must be invisible and intangible. Couple this thought with the fact that the dying person gives out a final, lengthy exhalation, a last breath that is invisible, and we have one of our arguments—very crudely expressed—for the existence of the soul. The soul is that factor, the invisible biological principle of life or life-principle. It is worth noting that in some ancient languages, the word for "life" is the same as the word for "breath." From here it is a short step to the idea of a life-principle, a soul as invisible and intangible as breath.

The second common argument for the existence of the soul is based on *consciousness*. After humans had begun to ponder more deeply on such things as emotion, imagination, memory, and thought-conscious experience—it occurred to them that *the seat of consciousness* must be something invisible and intangible. Chairs are not conscious, moss is not conscious, arms, legs, shoulders, and other fleshy parts of our selves do not think, remember, or experience passion. Consequently, it became commonly accepted that "matter cannot be conscious." Since we are conscious, there must be some non-physical part of ourselves that makes it possible.

The soul, then, must exist in order to account for these two real enough facts: life and consciousness.

Both arguments suggest that body and soul are separable and can exist independently of each other, at least temporarily. The body, if mummified, could be preserved for a long time, and already centuries before Christ we find Plato examining the question, Just how long can we expect the soul to exist on its own? This ability of the two to exist apart is the reason why, earlier, we said that most people regard the body and soul as two substances.

This opinion creates a severe theoretical difficulty, one that has already been alluded to in passing. To maintain that body and soul are two distinct substances is extremely difficult—most would say impossible—to reconcile with our deep-seated conviction that we are a single being (substance), a conviction based on our *experiencing* ourselves as single unified entities. How can two substances be a single substance? To the critics of the body-soul schema, the answer is clear: they cannot. We experience ourselves as unified beings. We are unified beings. The body-soul theory that splits us into two beings must therefore be false. (See Appendix A.)

Especially, materialists insist, must the body-soul theory be rejected once we realize how outmoded are the arguments given above for it.

First, contemporary materialists generally agree with Descartes who argued that the difference between a living person and a dead body is not the presence or absence of a soul, but a physical difference as real as that between a watch which is in good working order and the same watch when it is broken. (See Flew, p.138) Modern science, relying on the microscope and other means of research, has given us knowledge to replace our former ignorance. At death, there are massive breakdowns in our cells and organ functions; these breakdowns may be imperceptible to the naked eye, but they're not imperceptible to the eyes of science. "Death" is the collective name for those breakdowns, once they become irreversible.

Secondly, while it is true that many material things, e. g., chairs, moss, arms, legs, and shoulders, are not capable of thought, memory, or emotion, yet when the material thing in question is the brain, we can quite easily explain consciousness by it, without needing any recourse to a nonmaterial soul.

Again, many claim, it is science that we have to thank for this realization. To the naked eye, the brain is insignificant. Even Lucretius, an earlier materialist, overlooked the importance of the brain. (See Flew, p. 86) But once again recent discoveries have removed our earlier ignorance.

It is for such reasons as these that so many contemporary philosophers and psychologists view all reference to separate bodies and souls as misleading. There is no evidence to support a distinction between visible-tangible parts of our selves and invisible-intangible parts. Any perpetuation of talk about bodies and souls should be avoided, for it creates problems where there are none. It generates *pseudo-problems*. Those who perpetuate body-mind theories are, according to a majority of materialists, deserving of the scorn poured upon them by Gilbert Ryle's attack on the "Ghost in the Machine Theory" (See Flew, pp. 245, ff).

Conclusion. This chapter is merely an introduction to the materialist outlook on the human being. In many respects, the theory is refreshingly uncomplicated—in the general outline presented here. It gives us a solid basis for incorporating modern scientific discoveries into our outlook. It eliminates, not only the radical departures from common sense that we saw in phenomenalism, but even the perplexities which body-mind theories introduce us to.

We may, if we like, say that the materialist theory regards the human being as a body, pure and simple, and denies the soul. This is not necessarily misleading. But what is gained by saying that you are a body? Why not omit the word "body" and simply say that you are a visible, tangible, living, breathing, conscious being? This conveys everything (and more!) that is conveyed by "you are a body." Keep problems to a minimum.

In the next three chapters, we will examine the three varieties of materialism. They disagree radically concerning consciousness. It is our personal conviction that it is how these theories, or any others, account for the facts of subjective conscious experience that will determine how acceptable they are. Or how unacceptable.

CHAPTER V

MATERIALISM I:

RADICAL BEHAVIORISM

Preface. In what follows, we will be speaking of a somewhat idealized theory. It is not a theory that any real author espouses in every detail the way it is described in this chapter. First of all, we will be dealing with only a few portions of the position called Radical Behaviorism. Secondly, though there are many authors who hold theories that are conveniently designated by this title, they frequently disagree with one another. We will ignore the disagreements. Finally, people who publish a great deal often write things at one point that contradict what they have written at other points. It may even happen that someone writes, in the same publication, things that are generally regarded as inconsistent by readers.

This chapter, then, will focus on what is the most characteristic approach which one group of writers adopts when discussing consciousness, that is, conscious or psychic experience. It will be up to the student, once he or she has grasped this and some of the other approaches to be discussed later, to take note of the modifications which particular authors introduce into their own presentations of Radical Behaviorism and to make his or her own judgments about the validity of any particular presentation.

B. F. Skinner, once named "the most influential figure in modern psychology" (*New York Times Magazine*, March 17, 1968, p.2 p.27), was generally regarded as the leading contemporary spokesman for Radical Behaviorism. In his 1974 work, *About Behaviorism*, he made quite clear the Radical Behaviorist's view of the human being:

> A behavioristic analysis rests on the following assumptions: A person is first
> of all an organism, a member of a species and a subspecies, possessing a genetic

endowment of anatomical and physiological characteristics, which are the product of the contingencies of survival to which the species has been exposed in the process of evolution. The organism becomes a person as it acquires a repertoire of behavior under the contingencies of reinforcement to which it is exposed during its lifetime. (*About Behaviorism*, 1974, p. 228)

Skinner presents a view of the person in which we discover habits (repertoire of behavior), powers (genetic endowment of anatomical and physiological characteristics), and a substance or agent (an organism). This much the theory has in common with other materialistic views of the human being. As indicated earlier, it differs from those other views in its account of consciousness. Rather than plunge immediately into this account, it is advantageous to review something of the early history of psychology conceived as a scientific discipline.

Short historical background. Until the latter half of the nineteenth century, psychology was not regarded as a branch of knowledge distinct from philosophy, but rather as a subheading of the latter. What we today call the separate science of physics, which had been in a similar position two hundred years earlier, had only gradually emancipated itself from philosophy by attempting to base itself upon a new, "empirical" method, distinct from what was regarded as the speculative method of philosophy. In the latter half of the nineteenth century, pioneering explorers determined to make psychology scientific, a branch of knowledge existing on its own, distinct from philosophy. To do so, they had to create their own special method, modeled as far as possible upon the astoundingly successful method of the physical sciences.

The setting for this creation of a scientific rather than philosophical psychology was Leipzig. There, in 1879, the "physiological psychologist," Wilhelm Wundt (1832-1920), established the first experimental laboratory for psychological research at the University of Leipzig. Wundt, like the majority of these pioneering experimental psychologist, was something of a dualist. He believed that in the human being there are two distinct kinds of processes that occur in step with each other but that must be studied by different methods.

The one kind of process consisted of the *physiological events* occurring within the person's body. These were already being studied by the science of physiology, which relies on the experimental, observational methods used by the physical sciences.

The other kind of process consisted of the *phenomena of consciousness*: sensation, imagination, and feeling. These were to be studied by the method of introspection.

The history of psychology as an experimental science became very complicated after its inception at Leipzig. Since histories of the subject are available, anyone interested in the subject may consult them for the details. *But one major item in that history is essential for understanding the radical disagreements about 'psychology as an experimental science.'* That item is the kind of evidence gathering called "introspection."

Introspection is a special form of knowledge. The term literally means "looking inward." Its opposite would be "looking outward," and the appropriate term for it, if there were one, would be "extrospection." (The terms parallel "introversion" and "extroversion").

Introspection is the looking-within that enables us to be immediately aware of our own states of consciousness. Because one's own states of consciousness are private, the only person with direct access to them is their owner. Thus, introspection gives you knowledge of your own states of consciousness that no one else has or can have. Others can know *about* your states of consciousness, i.e., can infer them from your behavior or from your verbal reports. But you alone have immediate acquaintance with them. You could not, even if you wanted to, open your mind to others and permit them to directly experience your states of consciousness.

John Locke (1632-1704), insistent that all of our ideas come from experience, deserves great credit for distinguishing 'experience' into sensation and reflection. Sensation, he said, is 'looking outward' experience, whereas reflection is 'looking inward.' The latter is the source of such ideas as being conscious, remembering, thinking, emotions, and so on, ideas of things that cannot be seen, heard, smelled, etc. (*William James on the Stream of Consciousness* discusses these issues at great length.)

Psychology, then, conceived as the study of states of consciousness and as an experimental science resting its theories about experience on factual evidence, had to employ reflection, or what it came to be called, "introspection." Consequently, Wundt and his colleagues employed only those subjects in their laboratories who could be trusted to become proficient and reliable introspectors.

The key for understanding Radical Behaviorism is this history of methods, specifically the gradual abandonment of the introspective method and an increasingly exclusive reliance on the observational methods already employed by the physical sciences. For, as the history books relate, it was not long before controversies between professional psychologists sprang up. Introspectors began to disagree about the most fundamental matters. They disagreed about the nature of the objects directly introspected. Introspectors in one laboratory reported results that differed from results reported by introspectors in other laboratories. Finally, they began to disagree about the very definition of psychology as a science, some rebels arguing that the study of consciousness, in isolation from the biological organism which consciousness existed to serve, was artificial and sterile. By themselves, these controversies were no cause for alarm. What did become the cause, if not for alarm, at least for discouragement and frustration, was the gradual realization that the psychological method of the new science, introspection, was unable to settle these controversies. This put the fledgling science in a precarious position. It seemed to some as if it might die before it was out of its infancy.

Slowly, a few psychologists, then a few more, gropingly worked their way toward a new approach to psychology. The majority of these re-formers had felt the impact of the theory of evolution (Darwin's *Origin of Species* was published in 1859), according to which we humans are simply highly-evolved animals. Consequently, the dualism of the early experimenters simply lost its hold on their thinking. Conscious processes were viewed as one link in the chain of interactions occurring between the organism and its struggle to cope with its environment. Psychology ceased to be the study of states of consciousness for their own sake. Those states were now studied in the context of the much larger picture of biological evolution.

That larger picture had to be explored by "extrospection." Researchers had to carefully observe and record the different environmental stimuli and the corresponding reactions of the organism. This growing reliance of psychology upon objective observation rather than subjective introspection increased the confidence of the experimenters in their findings. The new approach involved sense observation of public events. One individual's observations could be checked by other observers, in contrast to the situation in which each introspector worked alone on his or her own private experiences. The new method, in fact, was the same as that which had been so successful in physics and biology. Its adoption led to a change in the definition of psychology. Less and less was it the study of states of consciousness. More and more, it became the study of behavior.

The final 'official' conversion to Radical Behaviorism was announced by the American psychologist, John Watson (1878-1958). Watson had earned his doctoral degree in psychology with a dissertation based on research with animal subjects. When working with animals, introspection is not used even a little, since the animals quite obviously do not make reports on their inner experiences. Rather, one uses exclusively the objective method. Watson asked, "Would it not be possible to study human subjects in the same manner?" Of course it's possible. Psychologists should restrict themselves to studying how humans behave under various environmental conditions. They should put aside introspective reports of private psychic events. Watson's answer was clearly and forcefully expressed in a 1913 article:

> Psychology as the behaviorist views it is a purely objective experimental branch of natural science. Its theoretical goal is the prediction and control of behavior. Introspection forms no essential part of its methods, nor is the scientific value of its data dependent upon the readiness with which they lend themselves to interpretation in terms of consciousness . . . The time seems to have come when psychology must discard all reference to consciousness; when it need no longer delude itself into thinking that it is making mental states the object of observation. ("Psychology as the Behaviorist Views It," *Psychol. Rev.*, 1913, 20, p. 158)

Several years later, Watson went further. No longer content to regard consciousness as simply off-limits to a strictly scientific psychology, he now argues that there's no such thing:

> (Consciousness) has never been seen, touched, smelled, tasted, or moved. It is a plain assumption just as unprovable as the old concept of the soul . . . He then who would introduce consciousness, either as an epiphenomenon or as an active force interjecting itself into the physical and chemical happenings of the body, does so because of spiritualistic and vitalistic leanings. The Behaviorist cannot find consciousness in the

test tube of his science. He finds no evidence anywhere for a stream of consciousness, not even for one so convincing as that described by William James. He does, however, find convincing proof of an ever-widening stream of behavior. (J. B. Watson and W. McDougall, *The Battle of Behaviorism*, 1929, pp.14, 26)

The last sentence holds the key to understanding Radical Behaviorism. Consciousness is out, behavior is in. Where formerly the experimenter was chiefly the introspector and his subject-matter his own private, conscious experience, the experimenter is now the cool, detached observer and his subject-matter the public, physical behavior of biological organisms, human or otherwise. This fact, namely, the substitution of external behavior for internal consciousness as the subject-matter of behaviorist psychology, is the clue for understanding the Radical Behaviorist's treatment of consciousness.

Radical Behaviorism and "consciousness." Newcomers to behaviorism are apt to find the last statement paradoxical in the extreme. On the one hand, it is stated that behaviorism eliminates consciousness from its subject-matter, even denies its existence. How then can this serve as a clue to behaviorism's account of consciousness, if there is nothing to give an account for?

The answer is that the Radical Behaviorist, while continuing to use the *language* of consciousness, in effect redefines it. He continues to *speak* in the old, familiar ways, but *what he is speaking about* is something very different from what ordinary, plain folk think he is speaking about. (See the Appendix to this chapter.) Until one grasps this very simple fact, one finds oneself easily confused. After one grasps it, there is no unusual difficulty whatever in understanding the behaviorist.

As a first step in acquiring an ability to think the way a behaviorist does, conduct an experiment in your imagination, the type which Einstein described as a "thought experiment." Picture yourself living in a world that appears in every respect identical to the one in which you presently live. (Incidentally, it will probably not have escaped your notice that the behaviorists do not begin with epistemological dualism but with common-sense direct realism.) Imagine that everything in this world behaves, i.e., acts or operates, in exactly the same ways that things behave in your present world.

Make only two changes. Imagine, first, that all living beings, from the smallest unicellular organisms to adult human beings, are totally unconscious, lacking all feelings, thoughts, daydreams, and the like. Since that will probably strike you as an impossible situation—how can they be awake and driving around if they are unconscious?—add to your fictional script one additional character, namely, a supremely intelligent and powerful Spirit who has control of everything in your world. In short, a super-puppeteer! You have no awareness of the puppeteer, of course. It is introduced only to help you in case you have some initial difficulty in constructing your scenario. The second change—a huge one—is to imagine that you have absolutely no access to your own feelings, thinking, and the like, so far as these are private to yourself.

Now, picture yourself growing up in the midst of this puppet-world. At first, you respond to things in the completely reflex way that the newborn infant does. Gradually, however, you begin to be programmed by your environment to acquire various forms of conditioned responses. You acquire certain patterns of leg behavior (you learn to stand, walk, run), certain patterns of arm, hand, and finger behavior (you learn to eat, to play the piano, to sew, and the like), and you learn patterns of verbal behavior (you learn to talk). This last is most important for our present purposes. Talking, making certain kinds of sounds, is a form of behavior and, according to the Radical Behaviorists, is as much governed by environmental conditioning or contingencies of reinforcement as any other form of behavior.

At first, you learn to respond to the sight of a certain individual by making the sound, "Mama." Skinner would explain the process as follows. An infant (you) at first makes many different sounds. At some point in time, one of the noises emitted either is the sound, "Mama," or is sufficiently like it, whereupon one of the organisms nearby will reward the infant (you) with a kiss, a smile, an appropriate sound, etc. This increases the probability that the infant will emit this same verbal behavior the next time it is in a similar environmental situation (the next time it sees its mother). This is the manner in which you acquire the ability to respond correctly in all sorts of different situations to all sorts of different objects. "Respond correctly" means that you behave in the appropriate manner, and that means that you make the sounds that others living around or near you make in similar situations. Later on, your repertoire of verbal behavior will become as enormously complex as it is today.

Do not, however, think of "learning to speak" as involving some kind of knowledge or insight or mental recognition. (Throughout this chapter, interpret these "mental terms"—knowledge, insight, mental recognition—in the sense you are used to, not in the behaviorist sense.) That is, you do not gradually *notice* that a particular sound, "Mama," occurs quite often at the same time that you see your mother, and then somehow *realize* that there is a connection. You do not later on learn to apply old words to new objects because you somehow *recognize* some similarity, as when you say the word "doggie" the first time you see a kitten. Nor is it that you have an insight or intuition when you finally learn to say "doggie" only in the presence of the old kind of four-legged creature and "kitty" in the presence of this new kind. You are simply learning—acquiring—new and more 'appropriate' forms of verbal behavior. (Of course, do not forget to later replace all of the mental-term terms used in this paragraph, namely, notice," "realize," "recognize," etc., with "you are conditioned.")

Obviously, if you are brought up in Germany, where the puppeteer makes the puppet-people around you utter different sounds from those made by the puppet people in America, you will learn to make different sounds in certain environmental situations. What determines the correctness of the way you speak then? Not insight, intuition, knowledge, mental recognition. Simply the particular forms of behavior people display. You will be rewarded if you emit the sounds customary among the group you live with or punished if you emit non-customary sounds.

If you have followed the script to this point, you are now ready to take the final step toward understanding Radical Behaviorism's general approach to "consciousness." Quotation marks are used quite deliberately. We are now going to be discussing, not consciousness (which does not exist), but words or language. One special type of word, one special part of our language. That is, one part of our repertoire of verbal behavior. Among the various sounds that we become programmed to use is a very special class of sounds that came to be described as "mental terms." Mental terms are words and phrases such as "consciousness," "knowledge," "see," "imagine," "intelligent," "becoming angry," "being excited," "being in pain," and the like. Gilbert Ryle's list of "mental-conduct concepts" can be added to the mental terms mentioned here. (See Flew, p. 259) These will be our chief concern in the next paragraphs.

You might wish to know how the Radical Behaviorist explains the meaning of such terms. This is a misleading way of thinking, though. It is much better if you ask, "How does the Radical Behaviorist explain how we learn to use these words, i. e., how do we get to make these sounds in the appropriate (namely, customary) environmental situations?"

The answer is quite simple. You learn to make them the same way you learn—I mean, acquire—all the rest of your conditioned behavioral responses: by imitation and/or conditioning. Gilbert Ryle's work, *The Concept of Mind*, is an ingenious behaviorist's lengthy explanation! of the kinds of behavior to which mental terms (those of the English language, that is) apply.

Some illustrations may help. Consider, first, that the people around us display a very large spectrum of diversified behavior or—better, perhaps—behavior-patterns. A happy person acts in a way quite different from the way a sad person acts. A proud parent beams when a son or daughter receives a diploma, a very different kind of behavior from that of a mother who has just caught her child raiding the forbidden cupboard. We are programmed in such a manner that we learn to make the sound "happy" for the first type of behavior-pattern, "sad" for the second, "proud" or perhaps "pleased" for the third, and "angry" for the fourth. There is no need to introduce any inferences or any introspection in order to account for these programings or conditionings.

Now, pick up the thread of the puppet-show. You have, let us say, never yet *felt* anger yourself. But the puppet which has all the external features of your real mother may enter the room and find that you have broken a very expensive vase. The puppet sends you to your room, at the same time saying such things (making such noises) as "Mommy is very *angry* at you; when you make mommy *angry*, you are bad. Mommy *angry*!" The puppet may even make these sounds in a very loud manner (may scream), may add some four-letter sounds (may curse or swear), may stamp its feet or bang its fists on something or physically strike you. Some time afterwards, still before you have personally experienced—felt!—anger, you may see the puppet-mother behave in the same fashion in the presence of the puppet-father. If your puppet-sister, in the next room with you, makes such sounds as "Mom is very angry at Dad," it will become more and more likely that you will begin to respond to such behavior-patterns on the part of the puppet-people by exhibiting some verbal behavior which includes the sound, "angry."

In the same way, you learn to use the sound "hurts" when you see someone crying and holding their bruised knee while saying "Hurts," "excited" when you observe someone jumping up and down with a smile on his face and saying "Wow, am I ever excited!", etc.

There is a minor feature of the behaviorist account of "consciousness" which must be taken note of. It concerns what are called "dispositions." Mental terms are often used in situations in which no activity is being observed. For instance, it is easy to imagine pointing at someone who is quite calm on the surface and say, "You can bet that Mr. Jones is boiling mad right now."

In this case, your statement refers, not to *actual* behavior (he is not, after all, shouting, throwing things, hitting anyone, etc.), but to "dispositions" to do those things. This, in turn, must be translated. A "disposition" is not some mysterious inside state. To say of someone, "He is disposed to act in an angry manner," is to make a probability statement. It is a quasi-prediction about probable future behavior. When you make the statement, you are warning your listener not to be surprised to see Mr. Jones explode into angry behavior at any moment. You're saying that it's *probable*.

Needless to say, this is a very sketchy effort to facilitate your grasp of the general thrust of Radical Behaviorism's account of "consciousness." As we stated earlier, the behaviorist, though denying the existence of consciousness as it is ordinarily understood, does not stop using the vocabulary of "consciousness." It might be less confusing if he did. Instead, he redefines those terms, using them to refer to something other than what we are common-sensically accustomed to thinking they refer to. Ryle's book, in fact, is nothing more than an attempt at a massive re-education (re-programming) of the reader, urging him to surrender his mythical views of consciousness (which mythical views Ryle confesses are as prevalent among plain folk as among professional philosophers) and to understand (a paradox there!) what his mental terms really refer to.

Applied. Having employed the thought-experiment about a puppet-world, you may now go beyond it. But how? How can you build a bridge from that imaginary picture to the real world? All that is necessary is to make a few slight alterations. To begin with, consciousness remains "out"! Discard the puppeteer, who is no longer necessary. Just change the puppets into biological organisms, like dogs or trainable circus animals, whose reality is supposedly explainable by the laws of physics and chemistry. In the view of most materialists, there is no radical difference between such things as the biological organisms known as human beings, on the one hand, and bits of moss or sand, on the other. There is just a larger variety of chemical ingredients arranged with enormously greater complexity in the human organisms.

The relatively recent construction of computers equipped with feedback features whereby they are said to monitor and adjust their own states, as well as with features that are said to enable them to 'learn from experience,' has convinced many that the time is coming when computers will imitate human behavior so well that we will have to apply mental terms to them as well, i. e., they will "be conscious." The literature on whether computers are conscious, for instance, is already extensive. For instance, in a postscript to a paper written by him years earlier in which he had criticized the idea of calling Turing machines "conscious," one author confessed:

> This paper can be taken as a statement of the difficulties in (and was written partly as a reaction to) Turing's extension of behaviorism into the computer field. Since writing it, I have come to see that there are ways of handling many of these difficulties . . . I now believe that it is possible so to construct a supercomputer as to make it wholly unreasonable to deny that it had feelings. (M. Scriven, in *Minds and Machines*, 1964, p. 42)

Computer technology has progressed amazingly since 1964. Already in 1978 an essay in a popular weekly reported that the best computers "can be wired up to learn by experience, follow an argument, ask pertinent questions and write pleasing poetry and music." (*Time*, Feb. 20, 1978, p. 59)

The message is this. You needn't tinker much at all with the thought experiment. The reality of the human person—according to materialists—is physics, chemistry, electronic circuitry, and observable behavior, not very different from a puppet-person. Whatever you do in transforming the picture into a view of the real world, do not put consciousness back in! No one has more strenuously made that point than Gilbert Ryle. The old notion that, besides the bodily side of the human being (which Ryle refers to as "Theatre A") where there occur events that can be investigated by eye and instrument, there is a non-bodily "Theatre B," in which occur mental events known by introspection only to the individual subject, is nonsense. Belief in a soul inside the body is mocked by Ryle as "the Ghost in the Machine" myth. Every respectable behaviorist will repudiate the 'ghost' and thus resist the temptation to imagine that mental terms refer to invisible processes.

Skinner invited his readers to find a substitute for the traditional body-soul theory. His advice is good evidence for the claim that his view of the real world is similar to the picture of an imaginary puppet-world. Even "thinking" is the name for observable behavior!

> A much simpler solution is to identify the mind with the person. Human thought is human *behavior*. The history of human thought is what people have said and done. Mathematical symbols are the products of written and spoken *verbal behavior*, and the concepts and relationships of which they are symbols are in the environment. Thinking has the dimensions of *behavior*, not a fancied inner process which finds expression in *behavior*. (*About Behaviorism*, 1974, p. 130; emphasis added)

"But surely," you protest, "at this very moment, I am thinking about this theory. And my thinking is not anything that anyone can see. It is not a form of physical behavior. Even if it were possible to explain my speaking about other people's behavior by means of mental terms, I am not at this moment speaking—I'm thinking!—and what I am thinking about (my thinking!) is an activity of my own, unobservable to anyone else. Thinking about my own thinking—that cannot be physical behavior in response to physical behavior."

But it is. "Thinking without speaking" is speaking, in fact. It is speaking under one's breath, that is all. Gilbert Ryle, a cleverer behaviorist explains:

> Theorising is an activity which most people can and normally do conduct in silence. They articulate in sentences the theories that they construct, but they do not most of the time speak these sentences out loud. They *say them* to themselves . . . This trick of *talking to oneself in silence* is acquired neither quickly nor without effort; and it is a necessary condition of our acquiring it that we should have previously learned to talk intelligently aloud and have heard and understood other people doing so. Keeping our thoughts to ourselves is a sophisticated accomplishment. It was not until the Middle Ages that people learned to read without reading aloud. Similarly a boy has to learn to read aloud before he learns to *read under his breath.* (Ryle, in Flew, pp. 260-261; emphasis added. See B. Knox, "Silent Reading in Antiquity," *Greek, Roman, and Byzantine Studies*, Winter 1968, pp.421-35, for a rebuttal to the myth Ryle appeals to.)

> What Ryle calls "speaking to oneself in silence" Skinner calls "covert (verbal) behavior."

> Usually, however, the term refers to completed behavior which occurs on a scale so small that it cannot be detected by others. Such behavior is called covert. The commonest examples are verbal, because verbal behavior requires no environmental support and because, as both speaker and listener, a person can *talk to himself* effectively. (*About Behaviorism*, 1974, p.114; emphasis added)

Here concludes the exposition of the Radical Behaviorist account of "consciousness." Consciousness as naïve people think of it is denied. Only organisms and their behavior exist, so those words in the dictionary that we call "mental terms" must refer to some kind of behavior. Our ability to use those mental terms is itself a form of acquired behavioral patterns. Even our own thinking is a form of behavior. Covert to be sure, behavior nonetheless.

Strengths of Radical Behaviorism. What many young philosophy students will probably feel to be a strength of this view is its return to direct common-sense realism. According to the latter theory, you can reach out and make direct contact with the objective universe and with other people. You need not worry about how to get outside your own mind and its contents.

166

You have never been locked inside. You've been outdoors from the beginning. All the reality that is worth knowing is, in principle, observable by means of your ordinary five senses or those extensions of our senses, e.g., the telescope, microscope, etc.

Radical Behaviorists also have it in their favor that our initial acquisition of language is, indeed, conventional programming rather than insight and understanding. The infant in Germany, as was mentioned, learns to make one series of sounds, the infant in American a different series. Does either infant think before it decides to use one type of sounds rather than another? Certainly not. The customs of the infant's 'social environment' are responsible.

The same is true of many whole expressions. The youngster in America grows up saying "It is warm outside" or "It is cold outside," while the youngster in France learns to say "Il fait chaud" ("chaud" means "hot") or "Il fait froid" ("froid" means "cold"). Can either youngster answer if asked what is the "it" or "il" that is warm or cold? That is, why do English-speakers say that the 'it' *is* warm or cold, while the French-speaker says that the 'il' *makes* warm or cold?" Why do even astronomers, who have long since adopted Copernicus' theory, which holds that the earth rather than the sun moves, continue to say "The sun will rise at such-and-such a time tomorrow morning?" These and a thousand other questions about the way we speak are answered by the word "Programming" instead of the word "Insight."

The same is true, far more than we initially suspect, of our use of mental terms. Certainly the child can learn to use the term "angry" by observing its parents' behavior even before experiencing its own anger, just as Dennis the Menace can speak of "love" long before reaching puberty.

Another way of putting the same point is this. Language, many people insist, is a public and social affair. The way we learn how to name moms, dads, dogs, books, stars, desks, rivers, mountains, and the like, is to observe them at the same time that the conventional terms are spoken in our presence. If we hear a word and do not know what it refers to, someone can point to the object. What reason is there for denying that this is the same way we learn to use mental terms? How can we learn what mental terms refer to if no one can point to those referents, i., e., if they are all private and hidden? The behavior of others does play a strong role in our acquisition of those terms, and that behavior is open and observable. We definitely do *not* learn the meaning of these terms by observing the activity going on in anyone else's brain. We simply cannot observe brain activity.

For many contemporary thinkers, the strength of Radical Behaviorism does not lie in these somewhat fragmentary arguments, however. It rests, for experimental psychologists, on a conviction that grows stronger and stronger as they train themselves to practice the strictly objective method, a conviction that there simply is no such thing as consciousness, because there is no evidence whatever for it. They reach a point where it just seems obvious that Watson was right in what he said many years ago: "He then who would introduce consciousness . . . does so because of spiritualistic and vitalistic leanings," leanings which are the inherited cultural residue of pre-scientific ages.

For many professional philosophers, Radical Behaviorism's strength lies in the fact that it can be incorporated into a broader approach called "Linguistic Philosophy"—which term would embrace such "schools" of thought as Logical Positivism, Analytic Philosophy, and Ordinary Language Philosophy. These broader theories are too complex to discuss here, but anyone who wishes to fully explore Radical Behaviorism's philosophical underpinnings would eventually have to become familiar with those broader theories. The arguments mentioned here—about the use of mental terms, rather than about words' meaning or the concepts signified by them—are suggestive of the broader Linguistic Philosophy, and may give you an idea of its general approach. (See, for instance, Ryle's discussion of the "Category-Mistake" in Flew, pp. 254-258.)

Contemporary obfuscation. The history of 'scientific' psychology does not stop with John Watson or B.F. Skinner. But these thinkers and others like them have had an enormous impact on subsequent psychology as a whole. For example, during much of the twentieth century, it became almost heretical for a psychologist to define his discipline in any other way than as "the science of behavior." That influence is easy to spot.

For instance, a large number of later psychologists use the term "behavior" to refer, not only to external or observable behavior, not only to dispositions to behave (physically), but to all of the mental processes that Watson said do not exist! A 1987 edition of a text opens with the sentence, "Psychology is the study of the behavior of organisms," but has chapters on memory, awareness, attention, thinking, reasoning, even motivation, that is, on what goes on inside a person. In other words, consciousness has crept back in.

Some behaviorists have even restored the term "introspection" as one way for researchers to gather information. But *this* introspection cannot be used by researchers, only by subjects whose verbal behavior the researcher observes!

> People can describe and label their inner experiences and report them to an observer. In contrast to other animals, humans, through verbalization, can provide valuable clues to psychological events . . . Subjects may report what they are thinking, feeling, and wishing, and what has characterized their attitudes in other situations in the past and present. (Lazarus, 1979, p.10)

Subjects engage in verbal behavior, the psychologist observes it! Lazarus is typical of those psychologists today who describe themselves as "cognitive behaviorists," but who are really old fashioned behaviorists at heart. They are like George Mandler who clarified what Lazarus obfuscated:

> . . . no cognitive psychologist worth his salt today thinks of subjective experience as a *datum*. It's a construct . . . *My* private experience is a datum for me as I make up

168

my theory of the world. In constructing my own world, my experience is a datum. But science has as a major requirement its shared public aspect.

. . . *Your* private experience is a theoretical construct to me. I have no direct access to your private experience. I do have direct access to your behavior. In that sense, I'm a behaviorist. In that sense, *everybody* is a behaviorist today. (G. Mandler, in B.Baars, *The Cognitive Revolution in Psychology*, p.256.)

Albert Bandura spelled out with admirable clarity the materialist ontology of the typical cognitive behaviorist:

Human agency does not imply psychophysical dualism. Thoughts are higher brain processes rather than psychic entities that exist separately from brain activities. Ideational and neural terminology are simply different ways of representing the same cerebral processes. ("Human Agency in Social Cognitive Theory," p.1175; 1989)

Philosophers have contributed greatly to the obfuscation. Their greatest 'contribution' goes under the name, "functionalism." Very elaborate 'verbal behaviors' named "physicalism," "reductive materialism," etc., have been invented to answer the question, "What reality(ies) are you talking about?" Already in 1984, J. Margolis wrote a brief but still useful introduction to the way functionalists invented a way of 'talking around' the question:

Our arguments against reductive materialism and behaviorism are essentially designed to separate the analysis of mental and physical properties from the issue of accepting or rejecting Cartesian or ontic dualism . . . Still, if mental phenomena are (1) real, (2) really distinct from (not reducible to) the purely physical, and (3) capable of exerting causal influence, then dualism is compatible with these three propositions.

Functionalism is the name usually assigned to theories that subscribe to these three propositions at least—without either favoring or precluding dualism. (*Philosophy of Psychology*, p.48; Jaegwon Kim's *Philosophy of Mind* is a more recent survey of the proliferating species of ontologies and vocabularies.)

All that can be said today is that the student who must deal with contemporary psychological and philosophical writings must keep in mind the various meanings which can be given to all of the terms used and decide from the context which of those meanings are the relevant ones.

Appendix to Chapter Five. A few pages back, the statement was made: "He (the behaviorist) continues to speak in the old, familiar ways, but what he is speaking about is something very different from what ordinary, plain folk think he is speaking about."

A distinction must be made between two forms of behaviorism. One form was known as "**Methodological Behaviorism**" and was advocated by those who, while not denying the possible existence of consciousness, did not believe it could ever be included as legitimate subject-matter for strictly scientific psychology. According to them, only genuinely behavioral studies qualify as strictly scientific. The study of consciousness was in effect handed back to philosophy. Those who are determinedly hard-nosed about it, regard many branches of today's psychology, such as clinical psychology and personality theory, as less than scientific.

The other form of behaviorism is **Radical Behaviorism**. This was the view taken by those who did not simply restrict themselves to behavior and ignore consciousness, *but denied it altogether*—if "consciousness" is defined as something private in principle and non-physical in nature. Radical Behaviorism was sometimes referred to as "Metaphysical Behaviorism," since it was more than simply a method adopted for studying a carefully circumscribed area of reality. It included a metaphysical premise, a statement about reality itself. It stated, namely, that the reality of the human being includes nothing but what is physical or material.

Consequently, the Radical Behaviorist would hesitate to say that, when he speaks about people thinking or musing or being angry, he is speaking about something different from what other people are thinking about. He would prefer to say either that those other people are unknowingly speaking about behavior or that they are speaking about nothing! He would contend that he is not redefining terms so much as simply pointing out the only possible correct interpretation of them.

This is another of the critical turns-in-the-road where the student must decide who, the Radical Behaviorist or a critic, is more faithful in their account of the facts. Which facts will, or ought to be, your own experience above all.

Nevertheless, the approach that this chapter takes in introducing Radical Behaviorism to the student is the most practical one. Whether the proverbial "man in the street" is right or wrong in the belief that mental terms refer to inner, private events, that is what he believes, as can be shown quite readily by means of a few Socratic questions. And this chapter is written for one type of man in the street, namely, the student presumed to be encountering behaviorism for the first time.

CHAPTER VI

MATERIALISM II:

BRAIN-MIND IDENTITY THEORY.

Preface. The second version of materialism is the Brain-Mind Identity Theory, the favorite of today's neuroscientists. Like behaviorists, neuroscientists come in as many varieties as behaviorists. (See "Contemporary Obfuscation" at the end of the preceding chapter.)

The presentation of it in this chapter will be an idealized one, as was our presentation of Radical Behaviorism. There is probably no single person who has combined all of the ingredients of the theory, exactly as they are presented here, into their own version of materialism. But there are more and more thinkers who agree with the broad outlines we will be presenting and with at least some of the specific ingredients to make it representative of their positions.

Like Radical Behaviorism, the Brain-Mind Identity Theory views the human being as a member of that most highly-evolved biological species, *homo sapiens*. It also regards the behavior of the human animal as controlled by the central nervous system. In fact, once you have clearly understood the theory in some detail, you may wonder just how important is the difference between the two versions of materialism, so similar are they in their accounts of the make-up of the human being!

> The *significant difference* between these two versions of materialism consists in the interpretation they give to "consciousness" and similar terms. The Radical Behaviorists, we have seen, argue that such terms should be used to refer to observable behavior or to predict its probability. Mind-Identity Theorists argue that the terms refer to events or processes occurring in the brain. That is major difference between the two, stated most succinctly.

171

Notice that both parties admit the reality of what the other argues for. B. F. Skinner in no way doubts the reality or importance of the central nervous system. Though restricting his own research to the outside of the organism, he assures us that he does not believe in . . . "an empty organism. A great deal goes on inside the skin, and physiology will eventually tell us more about it." (*Beyond Freedom and Dignity*, 1971, p. 186). Nor do the Identity Theorists deny the reality of the organism's behavior.

Moreover, neither of them question the close link between the two. Omitting for the moment the role of the environment, we can say that brain processes and external behavior are related as cause and effect. If we wish to describe their disagreement in these latter terms, we can say that Radical Behaviorists believe that mental terms refer to the effects of brain processes, whereas Brain-Mind Identity Theorists contend that those terms refer to the causes of the behavior. For this reason, the Identity Theory is sometimes referred to as a "causal theory of mind."

This is enough for the moment on the difference between Radical Behaviorism and the Brain-Mind Identity Theory. We will return to their disagreements later, after outlining in a bit more detail the view that the Identity Theory proposes as an account of consciousness.

The argument. As mentioned above, this theory states that mental terms refer to brain processes. Unlike the dualists, for example, who believe that some or all of our psychic activities—thinking, imagining, remembering, feeling, sensing, etc.—are nonphysical and therefore radically different in nature from the physical processes taking place within the brain, this theory maintains that there is really only one single set of events. This single set of events is experienced in two separate ways and described by two distinct "languages." But, according to supporters of The Identity Theory, recent scientific research—as well as other facts and considerations—has shown us that our common-sense notion that the events themselves are also separate is a mistake.

The following passage will give an idea of the kind of identity which this theory claims to discover between physiological processes and psychological experiences. The passage itself does not directly treat of brain processes, but its clarity and vividness make it a good introduction to Identity Theory. Only minimal effort will afterwards be required to extend the account to brain processes. The author of the passage is speaking about affective states (emotions) and claiming that they are identical with events occurring within the physical organism.

> Since the action in affective behavior is rather difficult to observe, understanding it is not as easy as understanding overt reactions such as key pressing. In fact, mysticism [sic!] has held tenaciously to this department of psychology with the result that these reactions have been thought of as "states," "mental states," "states of mind," and so forth . . . It is our contention that affective behavior may be treated as concretely as any of the most overt acts. Let us assume that a human animal is born as transparent

as a jellyfish. Imagine at what a disadvantage such an organism would be! By using a number of provocative stimuli, one could observe dramatic shifts in its activity. Now the spleen muscles clamp down and push out a tremendous amount of reserve blood into the circulatory system. Such changes in the distribution of the blood supply effect blushing and paling. Increased or decreased lung action is immediately observable as our transparent animal becomes excited or calm and relaxed again. Provoke him again, and you can comment literally, "Your blood pressure is rising, old man!" At still another time the heart rate (pulse) is sharply and suddenly increased. Tear secretion and sweat-gland action occur. Stomach and intestinal contractions are speeded up or inhibited . . . Our hypothetical animal could not have a single affective secret from us. Everything would be aboveboard and immediately observable. But humans are not transparent, and therein lies the crux of the matter. Just because they are not is no reason why we should become mystical and introduce "minds" into the picture to confuse us further. These visceral acts need not be considered as bodily changes either "accompanying" or "causing" feelings. The gland, skin, and visceral activities *are* the psychological responses of the organism! That's all there is; there is no more." (N.H. Pronko, *Panorama of Psychology*, pp. 390-391).

What is said here about the identity between visceral acts and affective states is what the Brain-Mind Identity Theory says about all psychological processes and brain activities. They are two names for one and the same set of events.

The word "brain," in the label chosen for this version of materialism, is important, for it helps to keep this theory separate from other theories also referred to as "identity theories." There is, for instance, a loose form of identity theory according to which the processes may be distinct, but the person undergoing both is one and the same. This version (see J. O'Connor, *Modern Materialism: Readings on Mind-Body Identity*, 1969, p.15) is somewhat compatible with dualism. It can be read as saying that the person who experiences inner, psychic processes (in his soul) is identical with the person who has corresponding physiological processes going on (in his body).

The theory which is our concern in this chapter focuses on the brain, for it contends that the brain is the seat of all consciousness. There are, however, other labels for this same theory. Some authors use "Mind-Body Identity" to refer to what we are calling "Brain-Mind Identity." Others speak of "Central State Materialism" (the reference is to the central nervous system, of which the brain is the chief part, and its states) or "Dual Aspect Theory" or "physicalism" or simply "Identity Theory." (Anyone who wishes to learn about some of the numerous and subtle disagreements which divide even the advocates of strict Brain-Mind Identity will find a good introduction in O'Connor's anthology.)

Some further points must now be made in explaining the approach of Brain-Mind Identity theorists to consciousness. First of all, it is helpful if we recall the distinction between acts and objects. The Identity Theorists we will discuss are interested in acts of consciousness, and not so explicitly in objects. This presents difficulties that will appear later on, but will be passed over now. Thus, it is sensation as a psychic *activity*, but usually not the *objects*, which are identical with brain processes. The case is the same for other types of consciousness: it is remembering rather than its object, imagining rather than its objects, thinking rather than its objects, that are identical with brain processes.

So far as the *objects* are concerned, Brain-Mind Identity Theorists simply deny the existence of nonphysical or nonmaterial objects of consciousness. For instance, they tend to be common-sense realists when the objects of sensation are discussed. In Part One, a passage from Bertrand Russell was quoted in which he argued that when Dr. Watson (discussed in the last chapter) watches rats in mazes, what he experiences are events within himself. Identity Theorists would by and large agree with the retort of Hilary Putnam who wrote:

> Analogously, a mechanical Russell (if we constructed a computer which "said" what Russell had said) might" argue" that" all I ever observe is my own vacuum tubes." Both "Russells" are wrong—the human being observes events in the outside world, and the process of "observation" involves events in his brain. But we are not therefore forced to say that he "really" observes his brain. (See Flew, p.296)

The important point to note is that the seeing is an event inside us (involving eye, retina, optic nerve, and brain), chiefly the end-processes in the brain-cells, whereas the objects of seeing are mountains, rivers, trees, chairs, people, etc., outside us.

In order to be thorough going in the denial of nonphysical objects of consciousness, the Brain-Mind Identity Theorist is forced to engage almost as extensively in language "therapy," i. e., revising ordinary ways of speaking, as the Radical Behaviorist was. As was true in our presentation of the approach of the latter, so here: our explanation of the way Identity Theorists employ language analysis must necessarily be of an introductory nature.

Recall for a moment some of the experiences used by the sense-datum theory to support its conclusion that the immediate objects of sense-awareness are non-physical in nature. An example is the experience of after-images. The sense-datum theory maintains that after-images exist. Now consider how U. T. Place, a Brain-Mind Identity Theorist, handles the experience of after-images.

First, he explains the predicament he would be in, were he to accept the sense-datum account:

> If we assume, for example, that when a subject reports a green after-image, he is asserting the occurrence inside himself of an object that is literally green, it is clear we have on our hands an object for which there is no place in the world of physics. In the case of the green after-image there is no green object in the subject's environment corresponding to the description that he gives. Nor is there anything green in his brain. (See Flew, p. 285)

In short, the only world that would have room for such entities would be a nonphysical one.

Place implicitly builds his argument in the following manner. Admittedly, there are two different but similar experiences involved: seeing a green patch of light and seeing a green after-image. Keep in mind, however, the way in which we learn to describe our experiences. We do not, as children, just begin one day to speak about sensations, feelings, and the like. We learn to describe our experiences by reference to physical objects (and their properties), viz., those physical objects which give rise to the experience. In order to learn how to speak of the experience of "seeing after-images," we must first learn to speak of the experience we have when there actually is what we believe is a physical splash of color present before us. The experiences, viz., what goes on in our brain in the two cases is the same, but whereas there is a real object for the one case, there is none for the other. However, we carry over the description from the one case to the other. We carry over our way of speaking of the normal experience to the experience that occurs without the normal physical object's being present.

> In other words, when we describe the after-image as green, we are not saying that there is something, the after-image, which is green, we are saying that we are having the sort of experience [in our brain] which we normally have when, and which we have learnt to describe as, looking at a green patch of light. (Flew, p. 286)

The same effort to rid us of nonphysical objects of sense-awareness is what has led other philosophers to recommend a liberal use of "it appears" or "looks" or "seems" or "feels as if" language to replace the factual "it *is!*" that frequently—according to them—creates pseudo-problems.

The materialist denial of non-physical *objects* of consciousness is applied not only to the objects of sensation but also to the objects of remembering, believing, and thinking. *The same tool of alleged 'language-clarification' is used.* Since, according to materialists, it is impossible for non-physical entities to exist, we must learn how to rephrase our everyday statements. Or, if such rephrasings are too cumbersome (Place's restatement of "seeing a green after-image" is an illustration of just how cumbersome!), we must simply be more sensitive to the traps that our everyday way of speaking lays for us and be more determined to avoid the mistakes they lead us into. It is easy to find examples. Think of the mistake a person would make if, because someone said that Jones had put in a brief appearance at last night's party, they concluded that Jones and his appearance are distinct entities and wondered what the people at the party did with Jones' appearance after he left. Or of the mistake of someone who, because Copernicus called his servant to the window to see the beautiful setting of the sun, claimed that Copernicus therefore didn't accept his own theory that the sun was at rest. Or of the mistake of someone who, hearing that a friend had come home in a flood of tears, decides that he will come home that way himself next time instead of using his car. (For this last example, see Ryle, in Flew,

p. 258.) Similarly, it is a mistake for us to believe that if, for example, we recall last Sunday's dinner, there must be some non-physical ghost of that dinner "present, before our mind," since the physical dinner can no longer be found in the physical world. And a mistake for us to believe that if thought occurs in the brain, then the brain has a thought. "This would be like thinking that if my invitation to dinner is in my pocket, then my pocket has an invitation to dinner. One bad joke deserves another." (N. Malcolm, in 0' Connor, 1969, p. 81) For some more examples of 'linguistic analysis,' pro and con, see R. J. Swartz, *Perceiving, Sensing, and Knowing*, 1965.

The second "further point" needed to explain the distinctive approach of Brain-Mind Identity theorists to consciousness is this: they hold that we become aware of our psychic processes by introspection. This, more than any other fact, is the difference between Identity Theorists and Radical Behaviorists. Place writes:

> Modern physicalism . . . is behavioristic. Consciousness on this view is either a special type of behavior . . . or a disposition to behave in a certain way . . . In the case of cognitive concepts like "knowing," "believing," "understanding," "remembering" and volitional concepts like "wanting" and "intending," there can be little doubt, I think, that an analysis in terms of dispositions to behave is fundamentally sound (See Ryle's *Concept of Mind* and Wittgenstein's *Philosophical Investigations*). On the other hand, there would seem to be an intractable residue of concepts clustering around the notions of consciousness, experience, sensation, and mental imagery, where some sort of inner process story is unavoidable. (Flew, p. 276; emphasis added.)

What Place and the Brain-Mind Identity Theorists refer to by this "inner process story" is the activity of the brain. The Radical Behaviorist argues that, since we learn to use the language of consciousness without ever observing brain processes, how can anyone observe them, given the obvious fact that they are hidden from the onlooker by the skull that encloses the brain? Mental terms cannot refer to any inner process. Identity Theorists reply to the difficulty by reinstating introspection in their account of consciousness. But they do not believe that this reinstatement requires the older dualist theory that there are two separate sets of events, one physical, the other non-physical.

Earlier, it was mentioned that, according to Place, the single, self-identical set of brain processes are experienced in two different ways and described by two different languages. We can now explain this. To begin with, brain processes can be experienced either by the brain's possessor through introspection or by a second party through objective investigation. (The first, introspection, was common long before the latter, perhaps eons before, since it is only within the last century that the brain's processes have come within the range of the scientist's methods of investigation.) For instance, picture to yourself the scene in which a woman lies on the operating table, undergoing brain surgery. The surgeon applies a probe to some portion of the exposed brain. He is able, in some degree, to "observe" with eye and instrument what is going on in the patient's brain. The patient, who remains awake during this type of surgery, reports what she, from the inside, experiences in response to the surgeon's probing. The same set of events is being witnessed by two different people, by two different means. In Place's phrasing, 'the operations for determining the nature of one's state of consciousness are radically different from those involved in determining the nature of one's brain processes.' (See Flew, p.282)

However, though there is only one set of events involved, the two different people learning about them do not observe or experience them as being the same. The events seem very different to the two people. Not even specialists in brain science are ever tempted to describe inner processes, known to them through their own introspection, in terms of neurons, cortex, amygdala, and the like. In Place's terms, "a closer introspective scrutiny will never reveal the passage of nerve impulses over a thousand synapses." (Flew, p.282)

Test this for yourself. Close your eyes and try to notice things occurring in your brain. No matter how hard you concentrate, you will never be able to determine whether there is a more activity in the left or the right side of your brain, more activity at its surface or in its interior areas, just what percentage of your neurons are firing at any given moment, etc.

Were it possible to learn about brain processes, neurons, synapses, and such, by means of introspection, we would not have had to wait until the nineteenth and twentieth centuries to begin making real progress in brain research. Nor do scientists entertain any expectations that introspection will ever replace the objective methods of science for learning the secrets of the brain. The only things that an introspector can experience are what are described by some as "raw feels," or what we've called "sense-data." (N. B. No one can tell you what is the nature of the states of consciousness as they appear to their owner. You must discover this for yourself. By introspection. Of your own inner states of consciousness. Part One again.)

Because of the fact that the two persons encounter the same brain processes under such dissimilar appearances—or, in different terms, since the same brain processes present such wholly dissimilar faces to the introspector and the brain researcher—we have evolved two separate languages for talking about this single set of events. Centuries ago, the terminology of consciousness was established as a part of the world's languages as a means of referring to the inner activities encountered by introspectors. Only recently have brain researchers established their own terminology as a tool for discussing the findings of scientific investigations into the structure and functioning of the brain.

These two facts, the dual appearances and the dual languages, pose a problem for the Identity Theory. The Radical Behaviorists could argue that there is only one set of realities, viz., external behavior, to which two languages—the language of behavior and the language of mental terms—referred, and they could "prove" that there was only one set of realities involved because there was only one set of observations involved, viz., sense observations, which observations quite obviously could discover *only* the external behavior, identical with itself. In light of the two facts explored above, though, how can the Identity Theorist prove that there is only one and the same set of events involved?

Dualists, as well as Epiphenomenalists, argue that the nature of what is discovered by introspection and the nature of what is discovered by brain research are so wholly dissimilar that they must be accepted as evidence of two distinct sets of events. Because the Identity Theorists accept that evidence (the dissimilarity), they must find some way of ruling out their opponents' conclusion (dual events) and establishing their own conclusion (identical events).

In order to pave the way toward making their own position seem plausible, the Identity Theorists draw our attention to real-life situations in which common sense claims to discern two realities but in which scientific investigation shows there is only a single reality with two appearances. Perhaps the most frequently cited case is what astronomers refer to as the Morning Star and the Evening Star. At certain periods, an observer can pick out a particularly bright star that appears in the sky at dawn. Later on, though, it can no longer be seen in the morning. However, at about the same time, a very bright star begins to appear in the evening sky. These stars, so notable because of their brightness, came to be known as Morning Star and Evening Star. Only later was it realized that the two 'stars' were really one and the same *planet*, appearing above the horizon at different times of the day at different periods of the year. (Venus is the brighter, Mercury the dimmer, of the two different-time-appearing 'stars.')

Another example is that of clouds and fog. Clouds are very familiar to young people. Fog is only slightly less so. We can easily imagine that a young person standing in a valley and watching clouds drift along high in the atmosphere and then blindfolded and whisked to a spot in the midst of a thick ground-fog would never be tempted in the slightest to identify the two kinds of reality. It is occasionally a considerable length of time before people familiar with both clouds and fogs realize the identity involved. As Place points out, the reason is that the observed appearances are quite dissimilar:

> A good example here is the case of the cloud and the mass of droplets or other particles in suspension. A cloud is a large semi-transparent mass with a fleecy texture suspended in the atmosphere whose shape is subject to continual and kaleidoscopic change. When observed at close quarters, however, it is found to consist of a mass of tiny particles, usually water droplets, in continuous motion. (Flew, p. 280)

A third example is that of lightning and electrical discharges. People were familiar with both lightning and electricity for quite some time before Benjamin Franklin's famous experiments established their identity. The Brain-Mind Identity Theorists use these cases in order to establish the quite legitimate argument that the mere existence of diverse appearances is not by itself a proof that there are two distinct realities responsible for them. It is conceivable that a single reality or a single set of events can give rise to the two dissimilar appearances. Therefore the dissimilar appearances of conscious experiences known by introspection and of brain processes known by objective observation may be two appearances of a single set of events. This, the Identity Theorist admits, is something that must be argued for. The identity is not one that can be achieved by simply redefining one's terms. Nor is it intuitively self-evident: the word "consciousness" and the phrase "brain process" do not mean the same thing, even if they may possibly refer to the same thing, just as the word "tomato" and the phrase "something that grows on a plant" do not mean the same thing though often, in the right contexts, both refer to the same entity. The identity is a concrete, empirical hypothesis ("a reasonable scientific hypothesis," according to U. T. Place—see Flew, p. 277), which—if it is correct—points to what the Identity Theorists call a "contingent fact."

What grounds are there for believing that the hypothesis is correct? It is to that question that we turn in the next section.

Strengths of Brain-Mind Identity Theory. The arguments brought forward by the Brain-Mind Identity Theorists are of several varieties. We may characterize some arguments as "negative," in the sense that they are directed against other theories. Every theory proposed to explain the nature of the human person or the nature of consciousness involves some especially nagging difficulties, and there is nobody upholding one theory who does not to some extent do so because the favored theory appears to involve fewer or less serious difficulties than the alternatives. There are also what might be termed "logical" or "apriori" arguments. These are arguments based on certain assumptions which seem quite plausible, even though they cannot be conclusively proven. They may even seem to have a connection with empirical facts, but the "facts" rest as much on the assumptions as the latter rest on the facts. Finally, there are arguments which we might label "factual," inasmuch as they are held to be solid experimental or experiential confirmations of the theory. This is an abstract classification of arguments and must not be taken as much more than an attempt to provide some rationale for the order in which they will be presented here. The types are bound to overlap, since the rejection of other theories is based on what are taken to be facts that favor this theory, and—as mentioned—there are difficulties even in separating apriori arguments from facts. (Do not forget the lesson of Part One: one man's facts are another man's inferences. One man's facts may even be regarded as outright errors by another. Etc.)

1. Radical Behaviorism's account of what our mental terms refer to, namely, to patterns of external behavior, is held by Identity Theorists (and by most other theories as well) to be a serious error. The denial of introspection flies too strongly in the face of universal human experience. Not only do each of us have direct, introspective access to our own states of consciousness which no one else has, but we often rely our ability to keep our states of mind from becoming known to anyone else. Spies, for instance, could not do their job, would even face execution in many cases, were they unable to prevent others from knowing what they believe, remember, plan etc. Other people can observe spies' behavior-patterns, though. So the two things must be distinct. Criminals, naughty boys, pathological liars, and Lotharios can be acutely conscious of the discrepancy between what they are saying and what, at the very same moment, they are thinking, and with practice they can deceive their hearers who have access only to the external

behavior. Bertrand Russell once commented, in reference to a well-known spokesman for the behaviorist view, that the man must not have had any tactful friends.

Nor does the behaviorist's appeal to "dispositions" provide a satisfactory account of our application of mental terms to persons who are not at the moment displaying any overt behavior. Consider a passage from Skinner's *About Behaviorism*:

> Watching a chess game, we may wonder "what a player is thinking of" when he makes a move. We may mean that we wonder what he will do next. In other words, we wonder about his incipient or inchoate behavior. To say, "He was thinking of his rook," is perhaps to say, "He was on the point of moving it." (p.114)

Anyone who has ever played a game of chess *knows* that more is going on than this vague "probability" of doing something like moving a rock. Reaching out one's hand to make a move is accompanied by interior thinking.

Skinner and Ryle both recognize this. That is their reason for speaking of "covert behavior," "speaking to oneself in silence." (See Flew, p. 260.) What is notable about this retreat is the fact that, first, it restores the "private access of the owner to his own 'consciousness'" (which term refers to behavior, though in this case covert behavior). The entire behaviorist program started out as an attempt to rid psychology of the troublesome and annoying nuisance of private events accessible only to their private owners. Now, though, we find that those events formerly referred to as states of consciousness—have sneaked back, though the designating of them as "behavior" rather than "conscious states" may easily lead the unwary into overlooking the return. And also into accepting as "obvious" an identification which is highly controversial. For, without any argumentation to back. it up, this assimilation of the private events ("speaking to oneself is silence") to public behavior is nothing less than question-begging, verbal sleight of-hand (sleight-of-mouth?).

Added to this linguistic ploy is the clever use of a metaphor to aid in avoiding a genuine problem. Referring to the inner process (i.e., to thinking, knowable by introspection) as "speaking to oneself in silence" is as egregious an instance of resorting to a misleading metaphor as any that the behaviorists have accused their opponents of. One cannot literally be speaking and silent at the same time. Speaking in silence is *not speaking*! It isn't even whispering! (Remember, the chess player is performing this "behavior" with his lips tightly shut.)

Though Skinner and Ryle carefully avoid bringing the matter up, others have recognized the problem, but have defended the appropriateness of the metaphor by noting that thinking *is* often accompanied by very slight movements of the speech muscles. And this is true enough, for one of the obstacles that must be overcome in learning to speed-read is "silently going through *some* of the motions of speaking."

Only, not even this "behavior on a microscopic and covert scale" is the same as thinking. Speaking, whether aloud or "silently," is behavior caused by and distinct from the thinking that occurs in the brain (according to the Identity Theorists) or in the mind (according to dualists).

The facts supporting this contention of the opponents of Radical Behaviorism are too numerous to list. Consider just a few. That thinking is distinct from all exercise of the speech muscles is shown by our ability to employ the speech muscles in reading aloud from a text—or even to recite something by heart, such as the Pledge of Allegiance, a poem, a prayer, or the like—and yet to be thinking of something wholly unconnected with the text or memorized words. (We give this thinking various names: "being distracted," "daydreaming," "looking ahead," etc.) Secondly, to see whether thinking is distinct from even the most covert muscle twitches, some researchers paralyzed their speech muscles with the drug, curare, and proved to themselves that such paralysis did not, in fact, prevent their interior thinking. (Something similar occurs in cases of radical motor aphasia.) And, lastly, consider the LSD experiences reported by John Lilly and others, the out-of-body experiences of those medically declared dead, the experiences of those in states of deep meditation: frequently, there is not the slightest trace of behavior in these cases, yet there are often inner experiences so overpowering that people's lives have been radically changed by them.

The behaviorist, faced with such facts, retreats even further, postulating that something must be going on here which is not radically different in essence from physical behavior. At this juncture, unless he is tacitly admitting his conversion to Brain-Mind Identity Theory, the critics of behaviorism simply take leave of him, agreeing with the American philosopher, B. Blandshard, who wrote: "There is no catching the behaviorist while he plays this game." (*The Nature of Thought*, 1939, chapter 7) Interestingly, though he gives scant attention to them, B.F. Skinner does admit the existence of inner states, introspectively accessible. But he refers only to states of the body—muscles, inner organs, joints, and so on—while excluding states of the brain which, he points out, is especially devoid of sensory neurons by which we might monitor them.

2. Brain-Mind Identity Theorists also have a reply to the behaviorist's argument—borrowed from the Linguistic Philosophers—that language is a social or conventional device designed to make possible inter-subjective reference to things, and that this is only possible if the things in question are public and observable to others, an argument bolstered by reference to the way in which we first acquire our familiarity with mental terms.

But, while it may, indeed, be true that children first learn words for publicly observable realities and even that we first learn to use mental terms such as "angry," "excited," "pay attention," and the like, by connecting them with observable behavior-patterns, this is not the end of the matter. The day comes when we experience, within ourselves, that feeling called "anger" and the state called "excitement." And, if Dennis the Menace ever reaches puberty, he will know that people use the word "love" to refer to more than hugging and smooching. Hence, mental terms, originally attached to publicly observable behavior, are later extended to private, introspectable experiences.

3. Without elaborating on the point, we may remark here that many will regard as a "plus" for Brain-Mind Identity Theory its acceptance of the direct realist epistemology, i.e., its position that we are in direct contact with the objective physical world. Identity Theory shares this strength—if such it is—with Radical Behaviorism, in contrast to phenomenalism, some forms of epiphenomenalism and dualism, and idealism.

None of the foregoing arguments, by itself, demonstrates, the validity of the Identity Theory. The first two 'strengths' are shared by all the theories except Radical Behaviorism, the third is shared by many, including Radical Behaviorism. This fact provides an opportunity for stating explicitly what should by now have become apparent to anyone interested in deciding what is the most acceptable theory concerning the human being. That decision must rest, no matter what theory is finally settled on, not on one or two arguments or facts, but on *the best combination of arguments and facts*—together with a judgment as to which theory involves the fewest unexplainable problems.

4. One of the most frequently encountered arguments offered in support of Brain-Hind Identity takes the form of a postulate or—some critics would suggest—a "pious hope." The Australian philosopher, J.J.C. Smart, has expressed this postulate as well as anyone:

> It seems to me that science is increasingly giving us a viewpoint whereby organisms are able to be seen as physicochemical mechanisms: it seems that even the behavior of man himself will one day be explicable in mechanistic terms. There does seem to be, so far as science is concerned, nothing in the world but increasingly complex arrangements of physical constituents. All except for one place: in consciousness . . . So, sensations, states of consciousness, do seem to be the one sort of thing left outside the physicalist picture, and for various reasons I just cannot believe that this can be so . . . The above is largely a confession of faith. (in O'Connor, 1969, pp. 34-35)

The fact of scientific progress in explaining things in terms of physics and chemistry is offered as a reason for the apriori assumption that science will eventually explain everything in terms of physics and chemistry. Many Radical Behaviorists maintain an identical act of faith. In fact, it is not too much to say that materialism has gained favor almost in direct proportion to the advances of modern science. On the premise that the strict sciences can deal only with physical or material reality, all non-physical states of consciousness—as argued for by phenomenalists, epiphenomenalists, dualists and idealists—are simply "pronounced non-existent." A phrase has even been coined for these non-existent immaterial states: "nomological danglers;" meaning that—if they did exist—they would dangle, would be unconnected and unconnectable to the growing body of scientific laws (nomos=law).

5. Without a doubt, however, the strongest case for Brain-Mind Identity Theory comes from the successes of contemporary brain research. In Chapter Four, it was mentioned that

one of the reasons people believe in the existence of a soul (mind) distinct from the body is the belief that purely material things are incapable of consciousness, thought, feelings, and the like. Since we introspectively know that we have thoughts, feelings and the like, traditionalists argued that there must be something non-material in us (the soul) which makes this possible. This argument is rejected by Identity Theorists on the grounds that it rested on pre-scientific ignorance about the brain. We now know, it is claimed, that this small, uninteresting-looking gray mass is the most spectacular physical object known to science, a marvel whose near-magical capabilities dwarf all the magnificent creations of twentieth-century technology combined.

This is not to say that our forebears were wholly unaware of the connection between the brain and consciousness. More than two thousand years ago, the Greek physician Hippocrates, the man remembered as the author of the Hippocratic oath, wrote:

> Men ought to know that from the brain, and from the brain alone, arise our pleasures, joys, laughter and jests, as well as our sorrows, pains, griefs, and tears. Through it, in particular, we think, see, hear, and distinguish the ugly from the beautiful, the bad from the good, the pleasant from the unpleasant. (Flew, p. 32)

And the man sometimes referred to as "the father of modern philosophy," Rene Descartes (1596-1650), put forward the theory that the body is an intricate mechanism controlled entirely by the brain. Even so, many years were still to elapse before scientific technology developed the instruments necessary for launching a serious investigative assault on the brain's actual workings.

Before that happened, it was still possible for philosophers to argue that there were some psychic processes which did not directly involve the brain. (For an example, see the passage from Aquinas in Flew, pp.102-4.) Even Descartes, in spite of his belief about the brain controlling the body, also believed that the brain was itself to some extent under the control of a non-material soul or mind.

What has really changed as a result of modern brain research is this.

The older claims about the brain being the seat of mental activities were in large degree merely guesses, guesses which were open to challenge from those who could not accept that something thoroughly physical was responsible for the entire range of human experiences, even our highest artistic and spiritual creations. Now, those older claims about the brain have been more and more transformed into demonstrated facts. Neurologists have pinpointed specific control centers in the brain, can now trigger muscle-activities, emotions, memories, and the like, by the accurate application of small electric charges to appropriate spots in the brain, can enable the brain to acquire control over itself by means of biofeedback mechanisms, are discovering ways to bypass defective sense organs such as the eye and ear in order to restore vision and hearing to the blind and deaf, can even split the brain to create distinct centers of consciousness. The gaps in our knowledge of the brain, gaps which dualists could seize upon to support their belief in the soul, are increasingly being filled in by science's progress. The day is nearing when the gaps will be completely eliminated, wiped out.

Such is the claim of the Brain-Mind Identity Theorists. When the day does arrive, it will be superstitious stubbornness to cling to a belief in the soul, to maintain in effect that two complete explanations for the same facts—brain and mind—are better than one. The principle of parsimony, known as Ockham's Razor, dictates that when the day arrives that one explanation of all the relevant facts is sufficient, other "explanations" should be abandoned. And the decision as to which complete explanation is to be retained is easy: retain the one for which we have solid empirical evidence, viz., the scientific account, in preference to one spun out by ivory-tower philosophers in the pre-scientific era. Any other decision would be ludicrous, as ludicrous as the behavior of the peasants who were unable to accept the scientific account of the steam-engine as sufficient to explain the railway-train's motion and who therefore postulated a ghost-horse in addition to the steam-engine. (See the tale of the peasants as told by G. Ryle, in Flew, pp. 245-248.)

Conclusion. Such in brief, is the theory of Brain-Mind Identity. This theory's account of conscious experience is infinitely more compatible with common sense than that given by Radical Behaviorism. It acknowledges the existence of an "inside story" and accepts as legitimate our ineradicable intuitive conviction that each person has, by introspection, a kind of "reflective," privileged access to his/her own inner states of consciousness. It maintains that, though earlier generations did not suspect the fact, those inner states of consciousness which "feel" so unlike bodily states (at least this is true of our purely "mental" activities, viz., thinking, remembering, and imagining), are none other than the brain processes which scientists are now so busily engaged in exploring.

What is the value of studying this alternative version of materialism? After all, a moment's reflection brings home to us a most important point. This picture of the human being is, in essence, identical with that presented by the Radical Behaviorists. When J. J. C. Smart writes that "there does seem to be, so far as science is concerned, nothing in the world but increasingly complex arrangements of physical constituents" (see argument 4 in the preceding section), he is referring to human beings as well as to the rocks at our feet. The difference between the two versions of materialism is a difference in their account of just one out of the many features of our behavior, namely, the way we learn the language of mental terms and what those terms refer to. Radical Behaviorists claim that the brain controls the body, but that the introspector does not have any better access to his own brain than the brain researcher, perhaps not even as good an access. The Identity Theorist *claims* that the brain controls the body and that the introspector does have a better access to it—*but only to its inner appearance!* The theories agree on all else: the ontological make-up of the human being, its evolutionary coming-to-be, the eventual reduction of psychology and biology to physics and chemistry, even the final destiny of the human individual, namely, dissolution. Neither theory leaves the slightest room for a discussion of immortality, a personal existence beyond the present life. To a critic of both theories, the endless squabbles over the precise interpretation of mental terms, the possibility of eliminating the language of consciousness entirely in favor of the brain-process language, the different logical varieties of "identity," whether Brain-Mind Identity is a necessary or a contingent truth, whether it is appropriate (not "true" in the older sense, but "appropriate"—since correct speaking, as measured against social convention rather than insight) to speak of computers as being conscious or not: to a critic, such controversies seem to merit the frequently-voiced criticism of twentieth-century philosophical controversies, namely, that they revolve around relatively trivial, inconsequential issues.

Still, there are two practical values in studying the difference between the theories. Both relate to consciousness, which we have referred to as the crucial evidence for determining the nature of the human being. The first practical value is that a study of the difference between the theories should sharpen one's sensitivity to the difference between conscious experience and external behavior. The two are radically distinct. One is ordinarily the cause in some sense, the other is the effect. Whatever the behaviorist may say, the angry behavior which is displayed is *not* the internal anger which is felt. As mentioned earlier, the contemporary behaviorists have allowed in at the back door what was thrown out the front door by earlier behaviorists, namely, private conscious states, only now disguised as "covert behavior." The study of Brain-Mind Identity Theory is valuable inasmuch as it wakens us to the deception and restores the distinction between internal consciousness and external behavior.

Incidentally, this value represents a bonus for those who may someday be engaged as counselors, mental-health therapists, teachers, clergymen, and the like, that is, those who work with people in real life and not only with rats or pigeons in laboratories. Though the contributions of the medical, biological, and behavioral sciences are often of great help in treating people's difficulties in living, it is often the realities of the inside story which matter most. No one has better expressed the vital difference than the psychologist, Henry A. Murray:

> I can hardly think myself back to the myopia that once so seriously restricted my view of human nature, so natural has it become for me to receive impressions of wishes, dramas and assumptions that underlie the acts and talk of everyone I meet. Instead of seeing merely a groomed American in a business suit, traveling to and from his office like a rat in a maze, a predatory ambulating apparatus of reflexes, habits, stereotypes, and slogans, a bundle of consistencies, conformities, and allegiances to this or that institution—a robot in other words—I visualize (just as I visualize the activity of his internal organs) a flow of powerful subjective life, conscious and unconscious; a whispering gallery in which voices echo from the distant past; a gulf stream of fantasies with floating memories of past events, currents of contending complexes, plots and counterplots, hopeful intimations and ideals. To a neurologist such perspectives are absurd, archaic, tender-minded; but in truth they are much closer to the actualities of inner life than are his own neat diagrams of reflex arcs and nerve anastomases. A personality is a full Congress of orators and pressure-groups, of children, demagogues,

communists, isolationists, war-mongers, mugwumps, grafters, log-rollers, lobbyists, Caesars and Christs, Machiavelli and Judases, Tories and Promethean revolutionists. And a psychologist who does not know this in himself, whose mind is locked against the flux of images and feelings, should be encouraged to make friends, by being psychoanalyzed, with the various members of his household. (Murray, in *J. of Soc. Psych.*, 1940, pp.160-61)

The Brain-Mind Identity Theory at least leaves the door open for someone to take the inside story seriously.

Only the student's own growing sensitivity to the contrast between the inside story and external behavior can protect him against being deceived by claims that are contrary to facts. As mentioned earlier, Skinner concedes the possibility of introspection, in a move that goes contrary to the historical development that led to behaviorism. In his 1974 work, *About Behaviorism*, he even discusses the importance of the inside story! After listing some of the reasons it is important, he goes on:

> There may seem to be a more compelling reason for probing the feelings of others. If it is "not the behavior that counts but how a person feels about his behavior," the discovery of feelings should be the first order of business. But how a person feels about his behavior depends upon the behavior and upon the conditions of which it is a function, and we can deal with these without examining feelings. When we are helping people to act more effectively, our first task may seem to be to change how they feel and thus how they will act, but a much more effective program is to change how they act and thus, incidentally, how they will feel.
>
> In a behavioristic analysis knowing another person is simply knowing what he does, has done, or will do and the genetic endowment and past and present environment which explain why he does it. (pp.193-194)

Thus, what is given with one hand (sentence or paragraph) is retrieved by the other. Nevertheless, Skinner claims that Radical Behaviorism is superior to Methodological Behaviorism because the former, by including and admitting the importance of inner events, restores "some kind of balance" (p.18) between objective observation and self-observation of inner, *biological* states of the organism. (See below.) But measure the claim against the facts. Let someone study Skinner's books and articles, then study the impact they have had on readers. Ask whether the net result is—as claimed—a nice balance between the objective and the subjective. Brain-Mind Identity Theorists and other critics of Radical Behaviorism rightly insist it is not.

The second practical value in studying the contrast between the two theories lies in the increased awareness such a study should foster of the difference between external observation and introspection. This distinction between these acts corresponds to the preceding distinction between their objects, and the sensitivity to the one distinction ordinarily develops simultaneously with a sensitivity to the other.

The topic of introspection is both simple and complicated. It is entirely simple, insofar as the ordinary man-in-the street (or woman) knows with complete assurance, though in an unsophisticated, pre-scientific way, the difference between introspection on the one hand and observation-and-inference on the other. Nevertheless, so many questions have been raised about introspection, its nature and its necessity, that twentieth-century psychology and philosophy have generally tended to deny it, its distinction from other forms of observation, and/or its usefulness. So prevalent has been the influence of behaviorism in psychology and 'language analysis' in philosophy that anyone who takes introspection seriously is made to feel like a believer-in-fairy-tales. To give but one example of the way in which a professional psychologist turns common sense on its head, let us quote a passage from an article by Donald O. Hebb:

> In our culture, we take it for granted that each of us knows his own mind directly and can describe its operations. To doubt this capacity for introspection, this ability of the mind to observe itself, is to invite incredulity. Yet the evidence is clear that this capacity does *not* exist.
>
> Our belief in it is of quite recent origin . . . I propose that introspection is an illusion so strongly established that it amounts to *hallucination*. ("The Mind's Eye," in *Psychology Today*, 1969, 3, pp.55-68. A brief, but useful, account of the historical background for this negative attitude of contemporary psychology and philosophy can be found in chapter nine of G. E. Myers' work, *Self*, 1969.)

A book might be written on the subject, but that is not required for the readers of this text. Without a considerable background in psychology and/or philosophy, the reader of this text is likely to have few if any of the usual intellectual or theoretical difficulties with introspection. The difference between introspection and observation, central to the argument of Identity Theory against behaviorism, will probably appear rather obvious once it is pointed out. This is attributable to the fact that your intuitions have not yet had time to be smothered by speculative difficulties. In fact, it is this author's belief that no intellectual or theoretical difficulties about introspection can ever undermine one's pre-scientific intuitions as long as the latter are sufficiently cultivated from the outset, and that the most serious problems concerning introspection arise, not from speculative theory, but rather from attitudinal habits.

Tests. Reflect a moment on our pre-scientific intuitions concerning introspection and observation. There are many different ways of bringing out their difference, but perhaps the easiest is to discuss it in relation to our use of the senses. If asked to say which of the following questions you could answer without using your senses (sight, hearing, smell, taste, touch/feeling) and which, on the contrary, require their use, would you have any hesitation about which questions fall into which category?

A-Is it raining outside?
B-What is the first word on this page?
C-Is there an alarm going off anywhere near where you are?
D-Are you afraid of flying in airplanes?
E-What is the exact time right now?
F-Do you prefer ice-water or coffee or something else with your dinner, if you're eating steak?
G-Do you believe in personal immortality?
H-Do you know what year World War II ended?

If you judge that A, B, C, and E, would require the use of one of your five senses (chiefly sight or hearing) and that D, F, G, and H, do not, you know the difference between observation (by means of senses) and introspection (without). With reference to the first group: you'd need to look out the window or listen, to discover whether it is raining; to look at the top of the page to find out what is the first word there; to listen for the alarm; and to glance at your watch or a clock (or listen for the reply if you ask someone else) to learn the exact time. But to know whether you are afraid of flying, you don't need a mirror (sight), or a stethoscope (hearing), nor would you have to place your hand somewhere—to your head? heart? knees?—to feel, nor would it help to sniff or swallow. You need none of your senses. And the same is true of the other three questions. Either they are not answerable at all, or if they are, then it is by means of introspection.

Naturally, it is necessary to have learned certain skills in order to distinguish observation from introspection. First, we have to have learned to speak. Infants can answer none of those questions, because they have not yet learned to speak. (Or to think.) Hence, to be able to introspect demands, as a prerequisite, that we have acquired a very complex skill: an ability to think and speak. Secondly, just as we must learn to sort out the various elements that go into the reports we make of our sense observations, it is necessary to have learned how to sort out the various elements that go into reports of our introspections. For example, if you were tempted to think you'd need your senses to answer the last question, you were probably thinking the sense needed was sight and that you'd need it to check the date in some book. Your mistake would consist in not distinguishing two different questions from each other: "When did World War II end?" and "Do you know . . . ?" You may learn the answer to the first question by looking in a book (sight). But how can you learn the answer to the second question?

Suppose you answer "Yes, I know the date," but then add, "It was in 1946." This answer would be incorrect, since the WW II ended in 1945. Does this error undermine the argument for introspection? Consider, you *thought* you knew (state of mind) the date. Yet you didn't.

To solve problems such as this, it is necessary to unravel further some of the factors involved. There are at least three items in your answer that must be kept separate. First, there is, in your mind, a knowledge of the proposition, "World War II ended in 1946" (some might rephrase this and say that you have in your mind the idea that the war ended in 1946). Secondly, there is your subjective feeling of confidence that that proposition corresponds to the facts. And, thirdly, there is the objective discrepancy between your belief, the proposition which you embrace so unquestioningly, and objective fact. All that you can know by introspection alone is what relates to ingredients number one and two: you know without any of your five senses whether or not you have an answer in mind and whether you are confident that it is accurate. Number three is not decided by introspection. And, finding out that you were wrong may cause your confidence to be replaced by hesitation or doubt the next time you are asked. But it cannot change the fact that, if you *felt confident* this time, you felt confident.

Interestingly enough, some philosophers seem unable to distinguish simple matters such as these. Pragmatists, for example, often think that the second-to-last question cannot be answered by introspection. Here is their reasoning. We have a proverb that "actions speak louder than words." In accordance with this, it is well known that, from someone's assertion that they believe something, we deduce that certain actions should follow. If someone really believes smoking is bad for one's health, we expect that person will refrain from smoking. If someone believes that tomorrow's exam is important, we expect he or she will stay home and study. Similarly, we expect those who really believe in hell to adopt an appropriate mode of living. Pragmatists use such considerations to justify their definition of "belief": it is that upon which we are *prepared* to act. From there, belief came—by turns—to be identified with the *actions* we are prepared to act upon, and then with the *habits* which prompt those actions. There is far more confusion involved in this approach to belief than can be dealt with here. It is sufficient to remind ourselves of the following distinctions: belief is distinct from action, as well as from the intensity of or confidence in a belief. Failure to distinguish belief and action is identical with failure to distinguish thinking and behavior, so we need pay no more attention to this confusion. Refusal to distinguish belief from its strength amounts to semantic finickiness: just how strong does a belief have to be before it counts as a belief? The fact is that pragmatists have an overly idealistic view of human nature: they expect all of our habits, drives, mental associations, desires, etc., to be integrated and consistent.

The fact that mere mortals are bundles of conflicting pulls and pushes—desires to lose weight, together with desires to eat, desires to live longer, together with desires to smoke, desires to pass tomorrow's exam, together with desires to go to a partly tonight, etc.—does not fit easily into the pragmatist's rigid "system." If the foregoing discussion is confusing, retain only this. Allow people to convince you that there are many things related to your beliefs (future actions, habits, incompatible feelings, even other incompatible beliefs, etc.), but do not allow them to tell you that you do not believe what you know you do. You may later change your belief, but that will be a change. Saying that you believe that smoking is bad for your health may not be reflected in your action of continuing to smoke, but if you know you believe you're risking your health, do not allow anyone to tell you that you don't believe it.

The considerations which follow are added simply because the subject of introspection is so vitally important to the entire approach of this text to the question, What is the nature of the human being? If you feel confident about introspection, there is no necessity to read further. Regard these as further notes that can be referred to, should you encounter confusing objections in your other reading.

First, those philosophers and psychologists who have taken time to study introspective awareness have pointed out that, when we are engaged in observing something with our senses, our sense observation is accompanied by an unusual kind of *implicit self-awareness*. "Self-awareness" must not be taken to mean that we can gaze on our naked self, just the thing David Hume stressed is impossible. It refers to an awareness of something pertaining to the subject, whether it be the contents of one's subjective consciousness, one's own psychic acts, or some other implicit phenomena.

An example will help. Imagine yourself sitting in a comfortable chair, wholly absorbed in a novel or a TV program. If the novel or program were absolutely all that you were aware of, you would be unable to reply to someone who comes and asks you, "What have you been doing for the past five minutes?" But you *can* answer "I have been sitting here reading," and it is only because, while you were absorbed in attending explicitly to the novel or program, you were *implicitly aware* of yourself being thus absorbed. Wilder Penfield reports how astonished he was the first time one of his patients reported a "flashback" when he, Penfield, touched the patient's cortex with an electrode. Surely, as he was performing delicate and dangerous brain-surgery, Penfield was concentrating on the patient and the operation and not explicitly keeping tabs on his own internal reactions. But he was concomitantly aware of those internal reactions and this enabled him later on to tell about them. Thus, our observing is accompanied by a non-explicit awareness of the observing. (Further reading on these matters may be found in the writings of phenomenologists on consciousness, of W. James on the fringes of consciousness, of the scholastics on self-consciousness, etc.)

Secondly, even when psychologists with behaviorist leanings do concede the existence of introspection, their accounts are guided by theoretical presuppositions rather than close attention to experience. Introspection is presented as a form of sensation. Its only distinguishing feature is that it is sensation of events inside the skin. Donald O. Hebb writes:

> Each of us has private information about the activities within his own skin: imagery, pain from headache, hallucination and so on. But this information—which is indeed private because it is not available to another observer—is nonetheless provided by the mechanism of perceiving the world around us. It is not the result of introspection. ("The Mind's Eye," *Psychology Today*, 3, 1969, p.56)

Hebb's final comment is not to be worried about, being a matter of personal, semantic preference. He does not like the word "introspection," that is all. For the most part, "the mechanism" he is speaking about is just what B. F. Skinner referred to above. Here is how Skinner explains what is meant by saying that "this information is provided by the mechanism of perceiving the world around us," i.e. the sensory mechanism:

> We respond to our own body with three nervous systems, two of which are particularly concerned with internal features. The so-called interoceptive system carries stimulation from organs like the bladder and alimentary tract, from glands and their ducts, and from blood vessels. It is primarily important for the internal economy of the organism. The so-called proprioceptive system carries stimulation from muscles, joints, and tendons of the skeletal frame and from other organs involved in the maintenance of posture and the execution of movement. We use the verb "feel" in describing our contact with these two kinds of stimulation. A third nervous system, the exteroceptive, is primarily concerned with seeing, hearing, tasting, smelling, and feeling things in the world around us, but it also plays an important part in observing our own body. (*About Behaviorism*, pp. 24-25)

This passage is from Chapter 2, and Skinner later reassures us that it is a complete explanation for introspective self-knowledge: "so far as we know, self-observation must be confined to the three nervous systems described in Chapter 2" (ibid., p. 238).

It is because Hebb, Skinner, and others have embraced this theoretical empiricism (empiricism is the theory that holds that sensation is the only source of reliable factual knowledge) that they must tie introspection to sensation. It is also why Skinner and Ryle identify "thinking" with twitches of the speech muscles, which can be detected by proprioception.

In fact, this theoretical premise is the ground on which Skinner bases his refusal to accept the Identity Theory's identification of consciousness and brain processes. The Identity Theory contends that when we introspect, what we are aware of are—in spite of appearances to the contrary—brain processes. Skinner denies that we can be aware of brain processes because we have no sensory neurons charged with monitoring the brain. His view allows only for information that originates at the outer ends of the afferent neurons that end far from the brain, not information from within the brain itself.

That this is contrary to experience is seen from the fact that you can think, remember, imagine, and the like, even when the objects of your thinking, remembering, imagining, etc., are not based on information now coming from the peripheral nerve endings. If you can think, with no speech muscle twitching, about whether you believe in immortality or not, your experience is something for which the behaviorist has no room in his theoretical framework. The Brain-Mind Identity Theory at least gives a better account of the introspective experience.

Thirdly, while it is true that many exaggerated claims have been made for introspection—among them the claim that *reports* of introspective awareness are infallible—it does not follow that, if introspectors disagree, there is no such thing as introspection. Yet, this illogical argument is often encountered.

> The mind does not observe itself. No two trained introspectors could agree in their descriptions of what they found unless they were members of the same school,

brought up as supporters of the same theory. This by itself is almost conclusive evidence that they were not observing, but making theoretical inferences. (D. O. Hebb, "The Mind's Eye," p.55)

Examine Hebb's logic by asking what disagreements prove. After all, if disagreements between 'reporters' is an argument against introspection, then sense observation does not exist either, for sense realists, intraorganic-object theorists, nerve-impulse theorists, sense-datum theorists, gestalt psychologists, etc., all disagree about sense-observation's object. Again, the fact that people disagree is no proof that no one of them is right.

Besides, as was mentioned earlier, one must learn a language before reporting any experience, objective or introspective. Because there are special difficulties in learning a vocabulary for private experiences—it is rather astonishing that we do so well—it is not surprising that one laboratory or school would train its subjects in the use of a language different from that of other laboratories or schools. Once the language is learned, there is considerable agreement, not total but considerable, on introspected phenomena.

Fourthly, the statement was made earlier that the most serious problems about introspection are attributable, not to speculative theory (though that is involved), but to attitudinal habits. A study of Radical Behaviorism and of its rival, Brain-Mind Identity Theory, offers an opportunity for an important lesson. There is a danger—for anyone—in cultivating, exclusively, the objective, observational 'attitude' of the physical and behavioral sciences, of strenuously attempting to avoid relying on any evidence but what is available to the senses, that is, to eye, ear, and hand. The danger can be described in a single phrase: *intellectual blindness*. None of the features of non-sensory conscious experience—thinking, remembering, imagining, deciding, etc.—has the sensuous appearance of the objects of sight, hearing, smell, taste, touch/feeling. As a result of adopting the mental attitude or posture of focusing entirely on sense experience, one's native ability to be sensitive by introspection to the "inner story" can easily atrophy.

It was to allow the student time to cultivate a strong awareness of his or her own "inner story" that this course began the way it did. Recall that it began with the most basic common-sense *conviction*, namely, that "reality" should be defined as "whatever exists, period!"—that is, "reality" should mean "whatever exists independently of what anyone thinks about it, even whether anyone thinks about it"—and then showed the representationalist conclusions that follow from a sustained examination of the contradictions between (i) that *conviction* and (ii) both our non-sensory thinking and our sensory experience. Part One was designed to explain why Russell was right when he wrote, "Naïve realism leads to physics, and physics, if true, shows that naïve realism is false." And why Einstein was right when he referred to naïve realism as "a plebeian illusion."

And to allow students to do more than simply take epistemological dualism on faith.

CHAPTER VII

MATERIALISM III: EPIPHENOMENALISM.

Transition. Epiphenomenalism is the only half-sensible alternative to the all-out materialism of Radical Behaviorists and Brain-Mind Identity theorists. As will be seen, it treats consciousness as something both real and, at the same time, distinct from physical behavior and physical brain activity. It makes no attempt to redefine the term "consciousness" in order to make it mean something that no ordinary person takes it to mean.

That claim assumes that "ordinary person" refers to people who would never think "having a stomach ache" refers to moaning and groaning behavior (as Radical Behaviorists do) or that it refers to some activity going on in their brain (as Brain-Mind Identity theoriests do). Yet, because more and more educated people—as a result of media influence—have become aware of the role of the brain, the result is that many 'ordinary persons' have now gotten in the habit of unreflectingly assuming that consciousness is activity going on in their brain. It is for that reason that the epiphenomenalist materialists who do not feel that their thoughts, dreams, and emotions are 'nothing but' brain doings are open to a theory that has room for both modern scientific discoveries about the material world as well as for the unique nature of conscious experience.

That theory is epiphenomenalism. Adherents of this view take a small step in the direction of immaterial reality. They admit that consciousness or what we experience by introspection is something that is not material in the ordinary way we think rocks, chairs, trees, and biological organisms are material.

A bit of history. Epiphenomenalism was quite popular in the late nineteenth century. Idealism and traditional dualism had been the reigning philosophies of the day. As a result, many philosophers and scientists, still under the influence of dualism and yet strongly impressed by the increasing evidence in favor of evolution, proposed an alternative theory as a means of reconciling the two. Their solution, called "epiphenomenalism," is the view that, when matter has reached the high degree of organization found in the nervous system, particularly the brain, consciousness is produced or emerges as a by-product.

But, whether the view is called "epiphenomenalism" or "emergentism," the basic idea is similar. The name is not as important as the idea behind it. That idea was expressed most famously by Thomas Huxley (1825-1895) as follows:

> When we speak of the actions of the higher animals being guided by instinct and not by reason, what we really mean is that, though they feel as we do, yet their actions are the results of their physical organization. We believe, in short, that they are machines, one part of which (the nervous system) not only sets the rest in motion, and co-ordinates its movements in relation with changes in surrounding bodies, but is provided with special apparatus, the function of which is the calling into existence of those states of consciousness which are termed sensations, emotions, and ideas. I believe that this generally accepted view is the best expression of the facts at present known . . . To the best of my judgment, the argumentation which applies to brutes holds equally good of men; and, therefore, all . . . states of consciousness in us, as in them, are immediately *caused* by molecular changes of the brain substance. (Emphasis added. "On the Hypothesis that Animals are Automata and its History," 1874; see Flew, pp.202 and 204).

About twenty years later, William James wrote *Psychology: Briefer Course*, in part of which he expounded the same thesis.

> The immediate condition of a state of consciousness is an activity of some sort in the cerebral 'hemispheres. This proposition is supported by so many pathological facts, and laid by physiologists at the base of so many of their reasonings, that to the medically educated mind it seems almost axiomatic . . . (James goes on to mention several such facts.) Taking all such facts together, the simple and radical conception dawns upon the mind that mental action may be uniformly and absolutely a function of brain-activity, varying as the latter varies, and being to the brain-action as *effect to cause*. (W. James, 1890; see Flew, pp.206-207, emphasis added.)

The crucial claim for both Huxley and James is that there are *two distinct realities* to consider. There are the activities of the brain, on the one hand, and consciousness, on the other. And, though James elsewhere argued against the view he presented in the preceding passage, it explicitly endorses Huxley's view that the brain and its doings ("the mind is what the brain *does*") are the *cause* of consciousness which is an *effect*.

One of epiphenomenalism's chief attractions is that it attempts a marriage of biology and psychology, of evolution and epistemological dualism. Epiphenomenalism agrees with both

Radical Behaviorism and Brain-Mind Identity Theory that far back in time matter alone existed. Out of the primeval chaos have come galaxies, solar systems, our planet, and eventually primitive, then more complex living organisms on our planet. Epiphenomenalism would also agree with the other forms of materialism that the earliest and least complex living organisms were little more than bio-chemical automata.

Where epiphenomenalism parts from out-and-out materialism, however, is in its contention that at some point in evolution there appeared the small beginnings of a very different kind of phenomenon: non-material consciousness. Huxley, one of the most famous of nineteenth-century advocates of Darwin's theory of evolution, notes the difference—even in highly evolved animals—between less and more developed consciousness (effects):

> The brutes, though they may not possess our intensity of consciousness, and though, from the absence of language, they can have no trains of thoughts, but only trains of feelings, yet have a consciousness which, more or less distinctly, foreshadows our own. (See Flew, pp.201-202.)

Once again, with the recognition that states of consciousness are distinct from brain states, the epiphenomenalists are on the side of the metaphysical dualists, for they are arguing that there is not just a single kind of reality (purely material) in our universe, but two quite distinct types of reality (material beings and immaterial states of consciousness).

Epiphenomenalism is not a full-grown dualism, however. It maintains that, though psychic *states*—namely, sensations, feelings, and ideas—are distinct from matter, they are only one step up from nothingness. They are not *substances*, not full-blown agents existing in their own right. They are 'by-products' whose nature is analogous to a puff of smoke, the flame of a match, or one's breath on an icy morning. They totally depend upon, and take their being from, the organism and the functioning of the organism's central nervous system. When the central nervous system ceases functioning, the states of consciousness cease to exist. They dissipate into nothingness. The organism and its nervous system are, together with other material substances, the only substantial beings in existence. Dualists, on the contrary, believe that, besides purely material beings and the psychic entities which are states belonging to some of them, there also exist immaterial *agent-substances* called by such names as "soul", "mind," "psyche," etc.

In line with its position that, though immaterial *states* of consciousness exist, but not immaterial substances, epiphenomenalism maintains that brain states are the cause of psychic states, but not vice-versa. *The cause-effect relation is a one-way street.* Just as the smoke of the locomotive accompanies but in no way contributes to the locomotive's functioning, so states of consciousness accompany but in no way contribute to the functioning of the brain. This is a second point on which epiphenomenalism is unlike dualism.

Having thus briefly set forth the highlights of epiphenomenalism, we can turn to the arguments that can be marshaled in its favor.

Strengths of epiphenomenalism. Epiphenomenalists can claim that their approach enables them to incorporate the strong points of materialism and yet to avoid the dogmatic denial of consciousness as such.

First of all, because epiphenomenalism agrees with materialism, it is able to incorporate the entire body of scientific knowledge about matter. Matter is the source of everything, and to the degree that science is able to account for the functioning of matter and material systems, epiphenomalism can, too. It is true that psychic entities are not material, but they have no causal power to effect anything or to disrupt any of the laws of physics—including the laws of thermodynamics—the discovery of which is the proud achievement of modern science.

Secondly, like Radical Behaviorism, epiphenomenalism also allows for the study of the environment and the behavior of material organisms within that environment.

Thirdly, like Brain-Mind Identity, epiphenomenalism recognizes the value of introspection as a respectable kind of observation. It refuses to sweep under the carpet the evidence each one of us has that we have direct, introspective access to our own states of consciousness, an access quite distinct from the access we enjoy, via our external senses, to external behavior. In this, it concurs with our instinctive common sense convictions. If I have a headache, for instance, only I can feel that headache, even though someone may learn that I have it, either because I tell him or because he observes that I exhibit certain behaviors.

Epiphenomenalists can claim, fourthly, that their account is more in keeping with the evidence of direct conscious experience than the Identity Theory, for they believe that states of consciousness are in fact very different from brain states. Identity Theorists admit what seems obvious to any reflective observer, namely, that introspectively experienced states of consciousness seem very different from observable brain states—*if, indeed, the latter are observable at all.* This last point is so important that it is worthwhile for us to pause briefly and dwell on it.

The brain. Consider the usual objective view of the brain and its states. Like the other parts of the body, the brain is composed of cells. It is estimated that there are approximately 100 billion cells making up the brain, though even higher estimates of the number have been mentioned. Of these, approximately ten billion are specialized neurons, the remaining nine-tenths being glial cells (from the Greek word for "glue"). The latter are often thought to serve merely a subordinate role in support of the neurons. It is the neurons or nerve-cells, making up fifty percent of the brain's mass, that are most important. Each of the neurons has a nucleus and hundreds of branches that enable it to link up with other cells, enough branches to link them with perhaps half a million others!

Scientists do not merely analyze the body and its parts (such as the brain) into cells, however. Cells are themselves composed of smaller elements. Billions of molecules are required to form a single neuron. It is estimated that each neuron, in addition to all of its other components, contains perhaps as many as 20 million RNA molecules. In turn, individual molecules are often so complex that they require thousands of "ingredient" atoms.

But the brain is not merely a static entity. It also performs many activities. In other words, we must not focus on the brain's structure alone, but must include some notion of its dynamics. In explaining the brain's functioning, scientists have compared it to an electrical system, but one whose electricity involves chiefly chemical interactions, often referred to as an electro-chemical mode of functioning. For simplicity's sake, we can say that each neuron is capable of carrying an electrical impulse from one place to another, and then of transmitting that impulse—via chemical substances called "neurotransmitters"—to other neurons.

The above description provides some basis for reflecting upon the objective nature of the brain, that is, the nature of the reality that the scientific investigators discover when carrying out research on the brain. They can dissect the brain, study the various elements that enter into its structure, analyze those elements chemically or physically, and give us the results of their analysis. The result? They approach the brain as simply one more of the billions of material objects which make up the physical universe, that universe which also contains stars, planets, rivers, forests, skyscrapers, television sets, and the like. Like those other material objects, the brain is made up of the same building blocks, namely, the atomic elements listed in Mendeleev's table of elements.

It stands to reason then that the brain, along with the other parts of the body, is fashioned ultimately from the food that the organism consumes and that the food comes one way or another from the soil, the air, and the sun's radiations.

Similarly, the functioning of the brain is fundamentally no different from that exhibited by many of those other material objects which are called, collectively, "the universe." The electrical functions of the brain are measured with the same type of instruments used in measuring any kind of electrical functions: voltmeters, ammeters, oscilloscopes, and the like. Individual chemical activities that occur within the brain can, in principle, be duplicated in a laboratory test-tube. Etc.

Consciousness. Epiphenomenalism repairs *the greatest weakness of the Brain-Mind Identity theory.* Keeping the above facts in mind, ask yourself whether those who study the brain with the methods of science, *while at the same time scrupulously limiting themselves to what they learn by those methods,* would ever in a thousand years of such investigation learn what you *feel* when you are hungry or angry, or what you *dream* while you are asleep, or what you *experience* when you remember yesterday's anger or last night's dream?

The answer is crystal clear. *No. No, not in a thousand years.* Not in a million years. There is absolutely no room for even the slightest measure of doubt. You may have all of the skills of Pavlov, Sherrington, Eccles, Luria, Penfield, Pribram—geniuses in the brain sciences—combined, and all that you will ever learn about will be atoms, atoms combined into molecules, molecules combined into neurons, neurons combined into structured brain, a brain which—on the basis of its electro-chemical properties and functions—is able to control a complex organism in its interactions with a complex environment.

In other words, with no knowledge at all of atoms, molecules, neurons, the brain, electricity, or chemistry, you can know how hunger and anger and headaches feel. You can know what dreaming is like. You can remember yesterday's anger and thus know what remembering is like and how different it is from actually feeling anger right here and now. Not only could you know these latter things, but for thousands of years prior to 'modern science' people *did* know them without knowing anything about how the brain connects with the feeling of hunger, or dreaming, or remembering anger.

> **In fact, the early introspecting psychologists knew about the feelings of hunger and anger and about dreams and about remembering as well as or better than contemporary scientists who also may know all about the brain.**

With those facts in mind, recall U. T. Place's important claim. Not all of one's subjective experience, not even the most thorough and expert analysis of subjective experience, will provide so much as a shred of information about one's brain. As Place phrases it, "a closer introspective scrutiny will never reveal the passage of nerve impulses over a thousand synapses." (Flew, p. 282)

Now add something that even the Identity Theorists admit, viz., the fact that states of consciousness and brain states *seem* to be different. That leads to an appreciation for this fifth strength of epiphenomenalism, its recognition that states of consciousness and brain states *are* different!

Three errors that must be avoided. The first is *anthropomorphism*. Anthropomorphism is the attributing of human qualities to nonhuman agents. This error is extremely easy to commit, hence it is also very common. Some of Walt Disney's movies illustrate the process with utmost clarity. A child can go to see *Bambi* or *Dumbo* and quite unquestioningly believe that deer and rabbits and elephants and birds—in short, all kinds of animals—have feelings and ambitions and thought processes just like their own. Of course the child is actually seeing, at best, only sequences of still photographs on a movie screen, still-shots that succeed one another so rapidly that it creates the impression of motion, so that a triple illusion is occurring: the child believes it is seeing moving figures rather than sequences of still-shots, animals rather than pictures, and finally animals with a consciousness like its own.

But it is not only unsophisticated children who make the error of believing they observe something that's not there to be observed. An increasing number of adults are so impressed with the truly spectacular advances in the area of digital processing that they can be seduced into believing that computers are conscious, whether they are named "Deep (or Deeper) Blue" and can defeat the best human chess players, or named "Watson" and can defeat humans in *Jeopardy*, or that they can even have—according to Raymond Kurzweil—"a spiritual life." But this is assuming that, because an assembly of wires, transistors, integrated circuits, etc., can be attached to a printer and make it type little black marks on paper which resemble the black marks a human being could produce with a typewriter or attached to a voice synthesizer that makes sounds like those that humans make, therefore the computer has the subjective experiences* human beings have. (*The key issue here is this: How can anyone learn what "subjective experience" means. We must admire the ingenuity of modern digital computing, but what Huxley said about animals—"What proof is there that brutes are other than a superior race of marionettes, which eat without pleasure, cry without pain, desire nothing, know nothing, and only simulate intelligence as a bee simulates a mathematician?" (Flew, pp.196-97)

By the same anthropomorphic reasoning, shouldn't one say that a pocket calculator can reason and remember, that a vinyl record remembers and loves and suffers heart-break, and that a television set really wants to sell you Gillette razors and Cadillac cars and Budweiser beer! In fact, the pocket calculator's circuitry does nothing more than shuttle electrical impulses back and forth, store magnetic charges, and light up tiny light-emitting diodes. The vinyl record has nothing to it but grooves with deliberately planned unevenesses. And the television set is only electronic circuitry to spray a fluorescent screen with a moving beam of electrons in response to electromagnetic radiations generated by some far-off transmitting station. Merely multiplying the number of circuits which can carry electrons and the number of elements for storing magnetic charges so as to create a machine that will imitate more and more types of human behavior should never seduce an intelligent observer into thinking that an inanimate machine is anything more than an inanimate machine. Unless he or she enjoys the type of fantasy that made Walt Disney wealthy.

The second dangerous error is the fallacy of believing that *"correlation equals identity."* The Identity Theorists are victims of this fallacy. They confuse identity and relation (particularly the cause-effect relation).

When we speak of identity in the strict sense, we are saying that, appearances to the contrary, there is only a single reality or process or set of processes involved. When a suspect is placed on trial for a crime, the jury is to decide whether or not the suspect and the perpetrator of the crime are one and the same person. The jury, in other words, is to decide whether the two designations, "suspect" and "perpetrator," refer to one person (in which case the suspect will be pronounced guilty) or whether they refer to two distinct persons (in which case the suspect is innocent and the search for the real criminal must continue).

Identity, then, is not a relationship. For there to be a relationship there must be two separate things between which the relationship exists. Relationship is thus something like a bridge. But when there is identity, there is only a single *reality*. There may be two separate *concepts* of a single thing, such as the concept the jury forms of the prisoner on the stand and the concept it forms of the criminal. But the two concepts—when actual identity exists—point to, refer to, one and the same individual.

The third dangerous error is the fallacy that *correlation equals causality.* The cause-effect relationship always involves two separate beings. One is the cause, the other is the effect. Examples of the cause-effect relationship are parent to child, tree to its image in the eye, author to book, watchmaker to watch, and—an example which U. T. Place mentions—the moon's stages to the levels of the tides (see Flew, p. 282). In some instances, a cause-effect relationship may be present along with other relationships as well. For example, there may also be a relation of similarity between a parent and a child, as there is between the tree and its image in the eye of an onlooker.

Students easily confuse cause-effect and identity. When they learn how retinal images of external, similarly-contoured objects are caused by those external objects, students have been known to say, "Of course, the tree is only an image in my eye." Of course, nothing! The tree, which is far too large to be in anyone's eye, is still outside. The tree and its image are two entirely distinct entities.

Our everyday language, designed for the practical or pragmatic purposes of daily living and not for the meticulously accurate description of reality, contributes to our confusion. Someone shows us a photograph and points to a portion of it. "There's your grandfather, in the second row, third from the left." But of course, what they are pointing to is not your grandfather (who is possibly long since dead) but patterned pigments on a piece of paper.

Finally, similarity or sameness is not identity. For instance, the word *"same"* is a very useful but dangerous word, for it is used in entirely distinct contexts. If you are told that two people have read the same book, what do you take that to mean? It can mean utterly different things, namely, that two people each picked up and read distinct members of a pair of perfectly similar books owned separately (in which case you have a relationship) or that two people each read a single book owned conjointly by them (identity). We can easily be misled unless we are alert.

Conclusions re epiphenomenalism. Epiphenomenalism is as unacceptable as any other form of materialism. First, epiphenomenalists claim that our feelings, thoughts, and decisions are utterly useless. They are fleeting by-products of the physical world where only physical things can be genuine causes. Consciousness is powerless to cause changes even in the brain. According to Huxley, causality is a one-way street. The brain causes totally powerless consciousness that causes nothing. (See Flew, pp.27-28.)

Worse, epiphenomenalists leave unanswered the question, "When I think, what does the thinking?" and "When I feel pain, what feels the pain?" They ignore questions about the agent that thinks, imagines, remembers, feels, etc. Like other materialists, epiphenomenalists might claim that the conscious agent is the brain itself. Patricia Churchland gave a lecture series, "Our Brains, Our Selves," at Notre Dame University many years ago. The phrase, "Our brains, our selves," is now the title of several internet web sites. As readers were informed by *Time* magazine in 2007, "You have a liver; you have your limbs. You are your brain" (1-2907, p.59). In his 2002 *The Synaptic Self,* J. LeDoux narrowed matters down even more, so that we are our synapses.

Unfortunately, any claim that we *are* our brains, and that brains do our thinking, are nothing less than reversions to pre-scientific and, in truth, anti-scientific naïve realism. Albert Einstein referred to such naïve realism as "a plebeian illusion."

Nor was Einstein alone. Richard Restak, Steven Pinker, Richard Dawkins, and Stephen Hawking have made similar admissions. "First, a fundamental principle: The brain exists in order to provide an internal representation of 'reality.' Quotation marks are employed here in deference to the fact that no creature, including ourselves, can ever know any other 'reality' than the representations made by his brain." (R. Restak, *Brainscapes*, pp.3-4) "Plato said that we are trapped inside a cave and know the world only through the shadows it casts on the wall. The skull is our cave, and mental representations are the shadows. The information in an internal representation is all that we can know about the world." (S. Pinker, *How the Mind Works*, p.84) " . . . we hardly realize what a complicated business seeing is. Objects are 'out there', and we think we 'see' them out there. But I suspect that really our percept is an elaborate computer model in the brain, constructed on the basis of information coming from out there, but transformed in the head into a form in which that information can be used." (R. Dawkins, *The Blind Watchmaker*, p.34) "According to the idea of model-dependent realism introduced in Chapter 3, our brains interpret the input from our sensory organs by making a model of the outside world . . . . These mental concepts are the only reality we can know." (S.J. Hawking, *The Grand Design*, p.172)

Once again, we must recall Part One of the course. How do we discover that we have no access to anything except the contents of our own stream of consciousness? Bertrand Russell summed it up. "Naïve realism leads to physics, and physics, if true, shows that naïve realism is false." (Introduction to *An Inquiry into Meaning and Truth*)

No one has ever experienced the physical world. Most of all, no one has ever experienced his or her own brain. How certain, then, can materialists be regarding their naïve-realist starting point?!

A postscript re all materialisms. Materialists claim that science is 'on their side.' In 1967, Jonathan Harrison* published a short piece, "A Philosopher's Nightmare: or, The Ghost Not Laid." In it, he used modern neuroscience to challenge materialists in the twentieth century much the same way Berkeley did in the eighteenth. Harrison theorized that, if a brain were hooked to a sufficiently powerful computer that fed the brain the same input assumed to be fed by the body's five senses and was able to 'read' the brain's interpretations and desires, the brain's owner would automatically believe it was experiencing and interacting with a physical world. "A consistent hallucination is as good as reality" in this case. Think of today's interactive computer games. (*Gilbert Ryle, one of the philosophers Harrison challenged, was the editor of the journal, *Mind*, and he refused to publish the piece! Harrison then gave it to the Aristotelian Society to publish.)

Transition. With epiphenomenalism, we come to the end of the materialist views of human beings. Epiphenomenalism provides an excellent jumping-off point for studying the more adequate views, beginning with the idealism of George Berkeley. Why? Because epiphenomenalism recognizes the reality of something that is different from matter, that is, different from whatever it is that materialists think constitutes the essential nature of rocks, tables, bones, and so on. It recognizes consciousness. It recognizes that, in this world, there is something more than, over and above, and in addition to matter in all of its (non-appearing!) appearances.

Huxley acknowledged the basic insight of Descartes' representationalism. In his famous essay, he discussed Descartes' claim that animals are merely biochemical robots or machines devoid of consciousness, then admitted that no one can prove Descartes wrong. With regard to the possibility that animals are "a superior race of marionettes," he added:

> It must be premised that it is wholly impossible absolutely to prove the presence
> or absence of consciousness in anything but one's own brain, though, by analogy, we
> are justified in assuming its existence in other men. (Flew, pp.196-97)

But it is not only impossible to prove the presence of consciousness outside our own mind (not brain!), it is also not possible to prove the existence of anything, *animals included*, outside our mind's stream of consciousness, unless . . .

. . . unless, as George Berkeley had argued, those 'things' are really groups of sense-data and images *inside* our stream of consciousness. What is not merely something in our mind's stream of consciousness is our very own human self, our mind or soul. We'll turn now to Berkeley's better belief about humans.

CHAPTER VIII

BERKELEY'S IDEALISM

The first major alternative to Descartes. "What am I?" is the question. Descartes' answer was, "I am a soul that thinks." Plus a body! He even argued with Princess Elizabeth of Bohemia that the soul and the body actually made up one being, a man or woman. She argued that his two views couldn't both be true.

That is, although Descartes first claimed he was a soul, distinct from any body, he also argued in *Meditation VI* that we can be certain we have one. For proof, he noted that God created us in such a way that we grow up instinctively believing that some of the things in our mind, namely, pain, hunger, and thirst, are indications that we have a body that needs attention. God—being infinitely good and honest—would not have created us with this instinctive belief if it could be false. He went so far as to claim, about bodies, that they "have never been doubted by anyone of sense."

But, in *Meditation VI,* he went further, and this is what led to the argument with Princess Elizabeth:

> Nature also teaches me by these sensations of pain, hunger, thirst, etc., that I am
> not only lodged in my body as a pilot in a vessel, but that I am very closely united to it,
> and so to speak am so intermingled with it that I seem to compose with it one thing.
> (Descartes, R., *Discourse on Method*, trans., Haldane-Ross, p.192)

Descartes' successors, too, were unconvinced. For instance, how can we have an idea of something we never experience? When John Locke studied Descartes, he rejected the idea that we can have such innate ideas as that of physical substances. He claimed that most of our ideas are combinations of simple ideas, and insisted that all of those simple ideas come from personal experience. But, since none of those simple ideas are ideas of substances, Locke's attempt to explain our concept of never-experienced substances failed.

Locke was succeeded by a brilliant young student, George Berkeley, who was bolder enough to embrace the logical conclusion to Locke's failed attempt. Berkeley agreed with Locke that our ideas are complex combinations of simple ideas. But he argued that those combined ideas are not just ideas *of* such things as apples, books, trees, etc., outside our mind, the idea-combinations *are* the apples, books, trees, etc., that we think we perceive. They exist only in our minds. According to Berkeley, there are no never-sensed physical bodies outside our minds.

> It is evident to anyone who takes a survey of the objects of human knowledge, that they are either ideas (1) actually imprinted on the senses, or else such as are (2) perceived by attending to the passions and operations of the mind, or lastly (3) ideas formed by help of memory and imagination, either compounding, dividing, or barely representing those originally perceived in the aforesaid ways . . . Thus, for example, a certain color, taste, smell, figure, and consistence, having been observed to go together, are accounted one distinct thing, signified by the name 'apple.' Other collections of ideas constitute a stone, a tree, a book, and the like sensible things . . . (Berkeley,G., *Principles of Human Knowledge*, par.1)

Berkeley re the self. What is it that perceives these idea-combinations? Here is where we encounter *the greatest disagreement* between the epiphenomenalist, Huxley, and the matter-denying idealist, Berkeley:

> 2. But besides all that endless variety of ideas or objects of knowledge, there is likewise something which knows or perceives them, and exercise divers operations, as willing, imagining, remembering, about them. This perceiving, active being is what I call *mind, spirit, soul,* or *myself.* By which words I do not denote any one of my ideas, but a thing entirely distinct from them wherein they exist, or, which is the same thing, whereby they are perceived; for the existence of an idea consists in its being perceived. (*ibid.*, par.2)

Like both Descartes and Locke, Berkeley did not doubt that there must be some cause for the contents of his mind. Since there are no physical bodies to cause the sensations, it must be God putting those sense-data directly into our minds from moment to moment. In fact, Berkeley used the recent 'scientific' discoveries of Galileo, Descartes, and Newton to attack all the atheists who tried to use those discoveries against belief in God. He used those same discoveries to show that it is the materialists who are the 'believers.'

18. But though it were possible that solid, figured, movable substances may exist without the mind, corresponding to the ideas we have of bodies, yet how is it possible for us to know this? Either we must know it by sense or by reason. As for our senses, by them we have the knowledge only of our sensations, ideas, or those things that are immediately perceived by sense, call them what you will; but they do not inform us that things exist without the mind, or unperceived, like to those which are perceived. This the materialists themselves acknowledge. It remains therefore that if we have any knowledge at all of external things, it must be by reason, inferring their existence from what is immediately perceived by sense. But what reason can induce us to believe the existence of bodies without the mind, from what we perceive, since the very patrons of matter themselves do not pretend there is any necessary connection betwixt them and our ideas? I say it is granted on all hand (and what happens in dreams, frenzies, and the like, put it beyond dispute) that it is possible we might be affected with all the ideas we have now, though there were no bodies existing without, resembling them. (*ibid*, par. 18)

Berkeley's challenge to materialists. There it is: " . . . it is possible that we might be affected with all the ideas we have now, though there were no bodies existing without, resembling them"! If the only things we experience are the effects produced in our minds, then we do not experience their external causes. How can we know the nature of those causes, then? Only by guessing, that is, by inferential reasoning, not by the senses themselves. In that case, there are two possibilities, both of which Descartes had discussed in *Meditation VI*. The sensations are produced either by our body via our brain or they come directly from God.

Descartes rejected the idea that God causes our sensations but then makes us believe that the color, shape, feel, and so on, that we experience in our mind are caused by physical things outside our mind. If that were true, it would be deceiving us and God didn't give us any way of discovering the deception. Berkeley realized that God not only does deceive us, but that God *did* give us the ability to discover the deception. After all, God gave Berkeley the ability to discover it!

Hence, Berkeley opts for the "God is their cause" alternative to Descartes' idea that physical things cause the sensations in our mind. His clinching reason? He went back to the Greek Aristotle's idea that "nature does nothing in vain." Of course, it's not nature that is in question. For Berkeley, the term "nature" refers to sense-ideas caused by God. Just suppose, he writes, that God rather than nature or physical bodies cause the sensory ideas in our mind. What then?

If therefore it were possible for bodies to exist without the mind, yet to hold they do so, must needs be a very precarious opinion; since it is to suppose, without any reason at all, that God has created innumerable beings that are entirely useless, and serve no manner of purpose. (*ibid*, par.20)

In other words, why would God create physical things we'll never experience so they can produce the sensory ideas we do experience, (i)when—even if bodies did exist, no one will ever experience them—no one knows how bodily things could create non-bodily ideas in our mind, and (ii)when God can simply create the ideas directly, without additionally creating matter? What intelligent God would create something (unsensed matter) so useless and so unnecessary?

In short, Berkeley challenges the materialists to face the question: "Why do you believe that your faith in never-experienced matter is preferable to faith in a never-experienced God?"

CHAPTER IX

TWO-SUBSTANCE, SHARP DUALISM

Beyond St. Thomas to Descartes

An introduction. Berkeley and many other great thinkers concluded from modern discoveries that there is no material world. But how certain can anyone be the material world doesn't exist?

Descartes thought he could prove it does exist. He thought God wouldn't have created us to instinctively believe that a material world existed if, in fact, none did. He concluded that, even though no one ever experiences physical things, they still do exist. How can we prove they don't?

Just being uncertain something doesn't exist is not the same as thinking one can prove it doesn't. For instance, many (most?) atheists will admit they have no demonstrative proof that God doesn't exist. If, then, there are no demonstrative proofs that matter doesn't exist, why not simply say we are uncertain?

Berkeley insisted however that, if we cannot sense something, we therefore cannot have an idea of it, and if we cannot have an idea of a body, we cannot even think an intelligible thought about such a blank 'something' or 'X' named "matter."

It is obvious, however, that we do have ideas of rocks, trees, squirrels, and human bodies. And we all believe they exist independently of us, that is, that they existed before us and can even now exist while we are completely asleep. Hence, because Berkeley's argument against the existence of material bodies is invalid, we will not deny their existence. For the final answer to "What am I?", we will retain the common-sense belief that some kind of physical or material things exist. However . . .

We'll *also* adopt the most recent 'scientific' theories about the nature of physical things, including our own body. They're not at all like what we grow up thinking they're like. (This answer to "What am I?" is part of a larger belief-system, one more fittingly named "quintalism" than "dualism." See the final chapter below.)

Materialism is not a scientific answer. "What am I?" is the question. What's the answer? In the last twenty-five centuries, many answers have been given to this question. At the present time, an increasing number of educated people believe there is only one respectable answer, the materialist one they call "scientific." That answer is, "Like you, I am a highly evolved animal."

Materialists, recall, believe that the only reality that exists is matter. For them the word "matter" is a collective name for galaxies, stars, planets, oceans, rocks, trees, squirrels, and lastly human beings. Such people are almost universally naïve realists, so that what they use "matter" as a collective name for are things they believe can be seen and touched: rocks, trees, squirrels, and so on. (But not stars, too hot to touch!)

Three earlier chapters have explored the three most influential versions of that widely held materialist answer to the question, "What am I?" To repeat, that answer is "At present, I am a biological organism, a member of the most highly evolved species of animal on this planet."

A major aim of this course is to explain to you why that it is not a good scientific answer to "What am I?" It's a pre-scientific, naïve-realist answer. In fact, the only truly scientific answer is "I am an immaterial conscious being."

Thesis: A human being is an immaterial conscious being.

This chapter will pull together the evidence previously described and explain how strictly logical reasoning leads *from* that evidence *to* the scientific answer.

More background history. The two most famous thinkers who concluded that you, I, and each other human being is an immaterial conscious being were Plato and Descartes.

(Another reminder concerning terminology. For many centuries, it was customary to use the word "soul" as a short name for "a spirit" or "an immaterial conscious being." St. Thomas often used "intellect" as a synonym for "(human) soul." Descartes used "mind" instead of "soul," since, to many ears, "soul" sounds too much like a religious idea.)

Begin with Plato. In his dialogue, *Phaedo*, he gathered together all of what he regarded as the best arguments to prove that human beings are non-bodily souls. As usual for Plato, he puts his views into the mouth of Socrates. The clearest and most emphatic statement of the thesis is found at the end of the dialogue. Plato has Crito, a devoted follower of Socrates, ask the question, "How shall we bury you?" Here is what Socrates replied: "In any way you like; but you must get hold of me, and take care that I do not run away from you." Then he explained what he meant:

> I want you to be surety for me to him now, as at the trial he was surety to the
> judges for me: but let the promise be of another sort; for he was surety for me to the

judges that I would remain, and you must be my surety to him that I shall not remain, but go away and depart; and then he will suffer less at my death, and not be grieved when he sees my body being burned or buried. I would not have him sorrow at my hard lot, or say at the burial, Thus we lay out Socrates, or, Thus we follow him to the grave or bury him; for false words are not only evil in themselves, but they infect the soul with evil. (Plato, *Phaedo*, trans. Burnet, 115 C-E; in Flew, 70-1)

The idea is clear. It's not possible to bury people, because persons are souls and bodiless souls are not the kind of thing that can be buried. Only the body, after it has died, can be buried. But the soul will continue to exist, apart from the body. (Plato repeated this view that humans are immortal souls in various other dialogues, e.g., *Meno* and *Republic*.)

What led Plato—or Socrates—to the belief that the soul is not just distinct from the body, but that it will continue to exist after the body dies? The *Phaedo* presents several reasons or arguments. *The best argument begins with the claim that 'learning is recollection.' It is based on facts that can be learned by conducting a (present!) careful inventory of the contents of the mind,* that is, by a review of the knowledge we possess.

Plato—or Socrates—claims that some of what we know, some of our knowledge, could not have been acquired during our current embodied lifetime. That's because the only *new* knowledge acquired during this lifetime is acquired by means of the body's five senses. However, in addition to our ideas of sensed particulars, that is, such individual things as men, horses, lovely sunsets, etc., we also have ideas of such perfect things (Plato calls them "essences") as absolute goodness, unalloyed truth, complete beauty, etc., things accessible only to our soul's intellect or reasoning part, and not to our body's senses.

Plato's explanation? He said that we must have acquired our knowledge of such invisible and intangible essences before we came into our current body. We must have brought that knowledge with us when we came into this world. It follows logically that, to acquire that knowledge, we must have preexisted the body we are now living in. And, if we could exist without this body once before, there is no reason why we can't do it again.

Aristotle and Aquinas followed Plato at least in one respect, namely, in giving careful attention to thinking, to human knowledge, and thus to ideas that we unquestionably possess. In Aristotle's treatise on the soul, we find a mysterious passage relating to human understanding. After stating that "it is evident enough that the soul is inseparable from the body" (Flew, p.78), Aristotle adds, "But perhaps intellect is something more godlike and unalterable." (Flew, p.76) The implications of this dark passage were hotly debated during the Middle Ages and the Renaissance. The best guess is that Aristotle was thinking about our knowledge of what came to be called "universals." St. Thomas most certainly followed Aristotle in giving huge importance to this kind of knowledge, namely, of universals. Universal concepts are immaterial (the reasoning is complex and need not be dealt with here), therefore our intellect, the soul's power whereby we know universals, must be immaterial as well. But . . .

Both Aristotle and St. Thomas wrote at length about human souls, but they vigorously opposed Plato's deduction that we *are* souls and that our current body is not even an essential part of us.

Aristotle was convinced that all material substances, including non-living and living ones (us, too), are composites of soul *and* body, or—more technically*—composites of substantial form and primary matter. (*See the appendix regarding "Change.")

St. Thomas Aquinas embraced and improved this matter-form or hylo-morphic view of humans. But, like Aristotle, he muddied the issue by continually using the body-soul vocabulary rather than the more accurate matter-form terminology. The result of insisting that the human being is a single substance composed of two non-substance, matter-form 'principles,' and at the same time speaking of souls and bodies makes for a 'fuzzy dualism.'

The body-soul distinction became even more entrenched in people's thinking as a result of the *Christian belief in human immortality and an end-of-the-world resurrection of the body*, a belief gained by reflection on the Gospels and Epistles. Obviously, the visible, tangible body can exist by itself after the person has died. At least for some time. Hence, if there is any 'part' of us that is immortal, it will be something invisible and intangible, different from the visible, tangible body. That something had to be the intellect-endowed soul. The result of the Christian faith was that, during the later Middle Ages, the idea that we human beings are a combination of soul and body became 'the' tradition.

Until the early 1600's. That is, until Descartes!

Descartes. Descartes is called "the Father of Modern Philosophy." The fact that any distinction between philosophy and science is mythical, Descartes should also be known as "the Father of Modern Science." He used the discoveries that today we gather under the umbrella term, "Modern Science," above all physics and physiology, to reinstate Plato's philosophy, most importantly, Plato's theory that humans are non-material souls related in some way to particle-constituted, material bodies.

Descartes deserves special credit for replacing the biased, traditional, "body-soul" or "body-mind" approach to "What is a human being?" by the far less presuppositionless "What am I?" approach. To repeat, he was successful because he used what we call "scientific" facts to prove that no one has ever experienced anything physical, including one's own body. What if bodies don't exist? Then what could I say I am? Well, even if I'm not yet sure what I am, the all-important fact to keep in mind is, "At least I'm sure that, whatever I am, I exist!"

"Oh, yes, and I'm a thinking being." Like Plato, Aristotle, and St. Thomas, Descartes kept the all-important fact of human thinking and knowledge at center stage. That is why, instead of first assuming that humans are or have bodies and asking whether or not souls exist, Descartes began as Plato did by inventorying his thoughts and beliefs. In *Meditation One*, he asked, "Which of the thoughts I now have can I be absolutely certain, beyond the shadow of any doubt, is a true thought?" His answer: "It's the thought that I exist!" (St. Augustine had a similar insight, but he did not recognize its center-stage significance.) Here is how Descartes reported his history-changing insight:

> For a long time I had remarked that it is sometimes requisite in common life to follow opinions which one knows to be most uncertain, exactly as though they were indisputable, as has been said above. But because in this case I wished to give myself entirely to the search after Truth, I thought that it was necessary for me to take an apparently opposite course, and to reject as absolutely false everything as to which I could imagine the least ground of doubt, in order to see if afterwards there remained anything in my belief that was entirely certain. Thus, because our senses . . . I resolved to assume that everything that ever enters into my mind was no more true than the illusions of my dreams. But immediately afterwards I noticed that whilst I thus wished to think all things false, it was absolutely essential that the 'I' who thought this should be somewhat, and remarking that this truth 'I think, therefore I am' was so certain and so assured that . . . I came to the conclusion that I could receive it without scruple as the first principle of the Philosophy for which I was seeking. (Descartes, *Discourse on Method*, trans. Haldane-Ross, p.101; also see Flew, pp.130-31)

"I think, therefore I am" is one of the most famous lines in world literature. Apply his thought. Persons are real. At least one. That's you yourself. You are not a fiction. If you are thinking (obviously, if you understand what you're reading, you are!) and you create the wrong concept of yourself, that will be a fiction. You, however, aren't. You can't be non-existent and still think!

But, is that by itself enough to answer the question, "What kind of thing am I?" Descartes knew that most of his readers would still be in the habit of thinking their body was more certain than their soul. And so, in *Meditation II*, he immediately added this warning to himself and them:

> But I do not yet know clearly enough what I am, I who am certain that I am; and hence I must be careful to see that I do not imprudently take some other object in place of myself, and thus that I do not go astray in respect of this knowledge that I hold to be the most certain and most evident of all that I have formerly learned. That is why I shall now consider anew what I believed myself to be before I embarked upon these last reflections; and of my former opinions I shall withdraw all that might even in a small degree be invalidated by the reasons which I have just brought forward, in order that there maybe nothing at all left beyond what is absolutely certain and indubitable. (Flew, p.131)

What, then, did Descartes decide he was? We are what Plato concluded: thinking things. Beings that think. And what is thinking?

What of thinking? I find here that thought is an attribute that belongs to me; it alone cannot be separated from me. I am, I exist, that is certain. But how often? Just when I think; for it might possibly be the case if I ceased entirely to think, that I should likewise cease altogether to exist. I do not now admit anything which is not necessarily true: to speak accurately I am not more than a thing which thinks, that is to say a mind or a soul, or an understanding, or a reason, which are terms whose significance was formerly unknown to me. I am, however, a real thing and really exist; but what thing? I have answered: a thing which thinks. (Flew, p.132)

We do not only think and reason. We will, we imagine, we feel. *And we even have sensations*, at least of pain, hunger, thirst, and the like. (Flew, p.133) That is why "thinking" for Descartes is a very broad term. It includes any conscious act, that is, any act that we perform while we are conscious.

But, still, the most important fact is that we have thoughts. So, which are true and which are false?

Representationalism again. With those considerations in the back of our mind, we return full circle again to Part One of this course, that is, to representationalism, epistemological dualism, the two-world theory. According to Descartes (and the modern thinkers cited at the end of the last chapter), the only evidence we have for anything are representations in our mind. The thoughts, feelings, sensations, etc., inside our minds are evidence for themselves. Our evidence for inferring or reasoning about anything outside our minds is what we find inside our minds.

In *Meditation III*, Descartes treats everything in our minds as ideas. He distinguishes them into innate (inborn) ideas, ideas we create with our imaginations (fictions), and ideas that seem to come via our senses from things outside of us (sensations). If we are like him, we should be able to notice similar distinctions among the contents of our own minds.

Once again, however, the big question becomes, "Which of the things in our mind give us truth about what is outside our mind, outside the perimeter of our own stream of consciousness?"

Now as to what concerns ideas, if we consider them only in themselves and do not relate them to anything else beyond themselves, they cannot properly speaking be false; for whether I imagine a goat or a chimera, it is not less true that I imagine the one than the other. We must not fear likewise that falsity can enter into will and into affections, for although I may desire evil things, or even things that never existed, it is not the less true that I desire them. Thus there remains no more than the judgments which we make, in which I must take the greatest care not to deceive myself. But the principal error and the commonest which we may meet with in them, consists in my judging that the ideas which are in me are similar or conformable to the things which are outside me; for without doubt if I considered the ideas only as certain modes of my thoughts, without trying to relate them to anything beyond, they could scarcely give me material for error. (*Meditation III*, trans., Haldane-Ross, pp.159-60)

Here's an easy way to remember the fact that Descartes is highlighting: *we understand more than we believe.* We understand thoughts and ideas about such non-existent things as Santa Claus, square circles, three-headed dragons, and the like, but we do not assent to them. The same point was made in Part One, where the distinction between having an idea (thought) and assenting to it was described.

Science. The reason for us in the third millennium to know some essential history about disputes regarding the nature of human beings is this. Ideas of "scientific knowledge" and what constitutes it have changed radically during the past two and a half millennia. The first two great sciences in the West were Plato's version and Aristotle's version. While St. Augustine's thought dominated Western thinking, Plato's philosophy was regarded as scientific knowledge. After St. Thomas decided that Aristotle's science was superior to that of Plato, Aristotle's philosophy and/or science dominated experts' thinking.

Until, that is, Copernicus, Galileo, and their successors. Descartes was the first to use their newer, more contemporary physics and physiology for his grand unifying system. He proposed a new science to replace Plato's and Aristotle's. One of the major things he repudiated was Aristotle's and St. Thomas' matter-form, hylo-morphic theory. He replaced it with a straightforward dualist, that is, body-soul distinction. Descartes converted 'fuzzy dualism' into 'sharp dualism.'

Soul & body: two central idea-thoughts. Recall that our question is "What am I?" Descartes was in no doubt whatever about the fact that he had two ideas in his mind, the idea of a soul and the idea of a body. After all, he was familiar with the writings and thoughts of his predecessors who, from the time of Socrates & Plato onward, had debated the nature of human beings, especially of souls and of bodies.

After Descartes died in 1650, huge debates erupted about whether or not the words "soul" and "body" have any genuine meaning. George Berkeley (Chapter VIII) adopted Descartes' view that no one has ever had direct experience of bodies. He claimed therefore that it is impossible to have such an idea. For him, an apple is a collection of ideas in the mind, and the same thing would have to be true of a human body. David Hume replied that, since no one has ever experienced a soul, that makes it impossible for anyone to have an idea of soul! Any words that do not stand for ideas are meaningless sounds or ink marks!

Debates about which words signify genuine ideas or concepts and which words do not became especially contentious during the twentieth century, when claims and counterclaims swirled around the question, "Whose talk is devoid of meaning, literally meaningless, hence non-sensical, and whose has genuine significance?"

Then, in 1979, Richard Rorty, reflecting on the previous three centuries' worth of incredibly detailed pro and con disputation, drew the obvious conclusion: "Everybody understands everybody else's meanings very well indeed." (*Philosophy and the Mirror of Nature*, p.88)

Descartes himself had been aware of the problem. Following tradition, he held that words for which there are no corresponding ideas, are meaningless. He solved the problem about "body" and "soul" (and thus about "substance") to his own satisfaction in *Meditation III*, where he claimed that the ideas of an infinitely perfect Being (God) and his own self (soul) are innate or inborn ideas, that is, ideas admittedly not acquired from sense experience or from imagination.

The origin of ideas. Now, in this third millennium, questions about the origin of our ideas, thoughts, or knowledge—and sensations—have become the most important questions of all. But the full answer to such questions requires a complete, grand unifying theory of everything in general and of the most important things in particular. In this chapter of *Philosophical Psychology*, we have time for only a few of the particulars from the grand unifying theory of everything named "quintalism."

From here on, however, Rorty's declaration will be explicitly adopted. No matter how we get our thoughts and ideas, *if we have them, we have them.* This is the most important lesson of Part One. The opposite view, namely, that we cannot claim to have an idea unless we can first prove how we obtained it, has been named *"the genetic fallacy."* The fallacy is analogous to finding a dime on the sidewalk and doubting whether or not it's a dime unless it can be proven how it got there.

Still, questions of origin are important. And one way to find the true answer to origin questions is to rule out the false ones. That is why, accepting, as given facts, the ideas, images, and sense-data making up the contents of our stream of consciousness, *Part One eliminated the two most common answers* to "How did those contents get into our mind?" (i) First, the belief that we get ideas via language from other people was shown to be false. (ii) Second, the belief that we get ideas of physical things by directly sense-experiencing (seeing, hearing, etc.) them was shown to be false.

A third answer, that of Plato, will be set aside. That is, Plato's idea that we acquired ideas from a previous, bodiless stage of existence will be set aside the way Aristotle, St. Augustine, St. Thomas, Descartes, Locke, and others who did not believe in reincarnation, set it aside. Berkeley, too, set aside the theory of reincarnation when he claimed that the contents of our mind all come, in this lifetime, from God. That alternative theory about the origin of our thoughts, too, will be set aside unless or until any alternative explanation(s) can be falsified.

Back to "What am I?" However, our immediate concern here is to find out "What am I?", not to ask "How did things get into my mind?" Therefore, we will set aside for *now the* 'origin' question in order to see what the mind's contents can tell us about what kind of beings we are.

Having examined two ridiculous theories about the nature of consciousness (radical behaviorism and brain-mind identity), we can build on the better answer of the epiphenomenalists. They at least recognized that consciousness itself is not material or physical the way that tables, trees, and toenails, or the way organs, cells, and neurons are. That recognition—the nonmateriality of our stream of consciousness—is an essential part of the evidence for the nature of a human being, for the answer to "What am I?"

From here on in this chapter, only two more answers will be discussed: St. Thomas' fuzzy-dualist view of human beings and Descartes' sharp-dualist revision of that view.

First, why St. Thomas? We begin with the views of St. Thomas, for two reasons.

Reason #1. Because the theological and philosophical theories of St. Thomas are often regarded as the most important medieval and pre-modern science or philosophy and because they are still viewed as the high-point of 'the Catholic intellectual tradition.' For that reason, it makes sense for us to focus attention on his view of the human being.

Reason #2. Because of the importance of common sense. All higher learning, including Descartes' own higher learning, can only be built on the platform of everyday common sense, that is, everyone's original belief-system. Aristotle 's science, *perfected by St. Thomas*, is the absolute best explicitation of our mostly-tacit common-sense philosophy. (Notice that Flew, pp. 76-81, includes comments by St. Thomas on Aristotle's text!) By studying St. Thomas' answer(s) to "What am I?", we can become very clear about our everyday, common-sense view of our selves. It also makes it easier to see why his view is unsatisfactory: he has two answers to "What am I?" and one of his answers contradicts the other.

To repeat, St. Thomas' full account of human nature is unsatisfactory, because it contains a glaring, fundamental contradiction. He attempted to adhere to everyday common sense, while also adopting the physical theories of Aristotle. This led him, in effect, to propose two *contradictory* answers to "What is a human being?" Answer #1 is "Like any human being, I am a single, unified matter-form substance, a composite of soul and body, neither of which is a substance able to exist on its own." Answer #2 is "I am a thinking soul, a substance, capable of existing on my own, independently of my body."

St. Thomas, Aristotle, and Plato. To begin with, St. Thomas embraced Aristotle's science and held that we are rational animals, unified corporeal substances made up of form and matter. He fully embraced the two parts of what had become accepted Christian teaching. (i) Humans have* bodies, and therefore are living, embodied, reasoning substances who must lead a moral life in this world. (ii) But humans are also immortal, which means that, besides bodies, we have* souls. After the death of our bodies, the soul 'part' of us (but not the whole 'us') will exist as bodiless substances, incomplete until re-outfitted with bodies on the final day of the general resurrection of all humans. (*The fallacy of asking what we 'have' instead of what we 'are' was discussed earlier in Part Two.)

Here is where St. Thomas parted company with Plato. Plato did not regard the body as an intrinsic or essential part of human beings. For him, bodies are as extrinsic to souls, i.e., to us, as ships are to piloting sailors or cars to their drivers. St. Thomas believed, as Aristotle did, that the true way to begin understanding human beings is to understand them as part of nature, as one more kind of visible, tangible, corporeal substance composed of two 'principles,' primary matter and substantial form, neither of which can exist separately. Thus, for Aristotle, there is no possibility for the substantial form, the soul, to exist after the human being of which it is a 'principle,' i.e., a non-substance component, dies.

But on the issue of immortality, St. Thomas parted company with Aristotle. He claimed that a disembodied soul is more than just a non-substantial form of a visible, tangible, corporeal substance. It is also, itself, a substance in its own right, one that can exist after the death of the??? The death of what? *Will it be the death of the human being or only the death of the body?* The answer to that question depends entirely on the answer to "What is a human being?" It is here that St. Thomas wanted to have things both ways. It is here that his answers contradict each other.

The key to recognizing the glaring contradiction is to focus on the question, "When I am thinking, what is doing the thinking?"

When I am thinking, what is doing the thinking?

St. Thomas fully agreed with Plato and Aristotle who emphasized thinking or reasoning as the essential difference between humans and beasts. Whatever else we may be, we humans are rational thinker-understanders. Hence, the question we put to St. Thomas is this: "When we are thinking, what is it that is doing the thinking?" It is his answers to this question that directly contradict each other. His first answer: "It is the soul-body (or matter-form?) composite, the man or woman, the total human being, that thinks." His second answer: "It is only the immaterial soul that thinks."

Both answers involve the five-concept model that was presented earlier. When we ask "What is doing the thinking?", we are asking "What is the agent?"

The five-concept model again. In trying to unravel the mysteries of human existence, St. Thomas relied heavily on the five-concept model which he derived from his study of Aristotle who 'put into words' the largely unspoken, tacit assumptions of everyday common sense. Those five concepts, explained earlier, are act, object, power, habit, and agent.

What acts do we humans exercise? If we rely on everyday common sense, there are two types. There are (i) *physical*, behavioral acts. We walk, breathe, eat, write, and talk. We need a body to do those things. And there are (ii) *psychological*, conscious acts. We see, hear, feel, imagine, and think. Sensing, according to Plato, Aristotle, and St. Thomas, seems to require eyes, ears, etc., that is, organs of the body.

If we follow Descartes, we match the acts with the two parts of human beings, bodies and souls, each of which for Descartes is a substance. Only the physical acts are performed by our body, all of the psychological acts are carried out by our soul. The body may have a role in producing our 'adventitious' and 'fictitious' ideas, according to Descartes, but bodies themselves, as such, are 100% devoid of consciousness.

One major problem for St. Thomas is his idea about sensing. He was a naïve realist about that. Worse are his contradictory answers to the question, "What agent does the thinking?" Let's examine his views carefully.

(Note. All of Aquinas' answers to "What conscious agent does the sensing and thinking?" are based on the principle, "Agere sequitur esse," that is, "Action follows being," that is, "The nature of activities is consequent upon the nature of the being that exercises them." Physical activities must be performed by material agents. Non-material activities can only be exercised by agents that are immaterial, spiritual beings.)

The unity of your conscious agent-self. You are one, single, unified being. Begin zeroing in on the scientific answer to "What am I?" by reflecting on a *crucial feature of your present experience*, viz., its unity.

Wiggle your toes. You feel them. Isn't it obvious that your toes are part of you? Where do your toes end and the rest of your feet begin? Can you feel any dividing line? Open and close your eyes. You feel the opening and shutting. Can you do it while you are wiggling your toes? Can you feel and notice both things happening at once? If so, is there one part of you that feels the wiggling toes and a separate part of you that feels eye muscles opening and closing? Or is it one and the same you? Can you feel any dividing line between your toes and your eyes? Or is it one and the same you, the same agent, who does all of your sensings, no matter how different they are?

Next, can you do the wiggling, blinking, and noticing, while also thinking? In fact, don't you have to first understand the sentences in these paragraphs, that is, think!, in order to carry out any of these sentence-instructions? Of course, you do. And it's one, single, unified you that is doing all the different kinds of activities. If you study Plato's dialogue, *Theatetus*, you will see that you just reflected on the same questions Socrates was asking more than two thousand years ago.

Every waking, mature person, at every moment of his or her life, is in a similar real-life situation, namely, the situation of being one, single agent actually experiencing several things at once.

Like Plato, various thinkers have emphasized this 'unity of consciousness.' For instance, Edmund Husserl began Chapter 3 of *Ideas* this way: "I am aware of a world, spread out in space endlessly, and in time becoming and become, without end . . . . I can let my attention wander from the writing-table I have just seen and observed, through the unseen portions of the room behind my back to the verandah, into the garden, to the children in the summer-house, and so forth . . ."

William Calvin described this remarkable unity of consciousness in the eleventh chapter of *A Brief History of the Mind*: "I am conscious (aware might be the better word), of the chair supporting me as I read. I notice the sunlight from the window behind me. It is quickly fading and a blast of wind is rattling the trees . . . ," etc.

The neuroscientist, Richard Restak, described it in Chapter IV of *Brainscapes*: "As an example, consider my present situation: while I am typing these words I am also dimly aware of the traffic passing outside the window in front of me, the sound of Mozart playing in the background, and the feeling of being slightly chilled in the early morning grayness."

If your conscious experience constitutes the totality of the evidence you rely on to find the true answer to "What am I?" (and it is that totality), the question you must ask is, "What is the unitary, single conscious agent capable of simultaneously feeling, seeing, noticing, *and especially thinking*?"

Aristotle's answer would be, "There must be one, single, unified substance-agent capable of exercising all of those acts simultaneously." This is the source of one of St. Thomas' answers to "What thinks?"

> Or we may reply that to operate per se belongs to what exists per se. But for a thing to exist per se, it suffices sometimes that it be not inherent, as an accident or a material form; even though it be part of something. Nevertheless, that is rightly said to subsist per se, which is neither inherent in the above sense, nor part of anything else. In this sense, the eye or the hand cannot be said to subsist per se; nor can it for that reason be said to operate per se. Hence the operation of the parts is through each part attributed to the whole. For we say that man sees with the eye, and feels with the hand, and not in the same sense as when we say that what is hot gives heat by its heat; for heat, strictly speaking, does not give heat. We may therefore say that the soul understands, as the eye sees; but it is more correct to say that the man understands through his soul. (Flew, p.104; "per se" means "through or by itself." *Summa Theologiae*, I, 75, 3, ad 2)

" . . . but it is more correct to say that the man understands through his soul." In other words, what 'rightly' thinks is not the soul, but the body-soul or matter-form human being. That goes with St. Thomas' belief that it is more correct to say that *the man*, the soul-body composite, sees with its eyes and feels with its hands. It is clearly metaphorical to say "My eyes do my seeing, my hands do my feeling." It is clear that I do both the seeing and the feeling. This 'I' is, according to St. Thomas, a matter-form composite. The composite alone is a substance. It is what exists per se. Neither of the 'principles,' the primary matter or the substantial form, can exist apart from its opposite co-principle.

This 'experienced unity of consciousness' is a fact that St. Thomas appeals to in his *Summa*, Part I, question 76, article 1.

But if anyone says that the intellectual soul is not the form of the body, he must first explain how it is that this action of understanding is the action of this particular man; for each one is conscious that it is himself who understands . . . . it is one and the same man who is conscious both that he understands, and that he senses. But one cannot sense without a body; therefore the body must be some part of man. (Blackfriars translation)

According to that approach, the logical conclusion must be that, because it is the one, same you who sees, feels, and does your thinking, you are not a soul, but a matter-form composite. That's what does your thinking. And when that matter-form composite ceases to exist, the thinking substance ceases to exist.

But now, rename the *non-substance* substantial form "the soul," argue that the soul is a substance and not only a form, and the 'you' who does your thinking is what Plato and Descartes argued, an immaterial soul. Aquinas uses this claim to 'prove' that the soul can exist without any primary matter or body. The reason is that the soul is a substance, a subsisting being per se.

It must necessarily be allowed that the principle of intellectual operation which we call the soul, is a principle both incorporeal and subsistent . . .

Therefore the intellectual principle which we call the mind or the intellect has an operation per se apart from the body. Now only that which subsists can have an operation per se. For nothing can operate but what is actual: wherefore a thing operates according as it is; for which reason we do not say that heat imparts heat, but that what is hot gives heat. We must conclude, therefore, that the human soul which is called the intellect or the mind, is something incorporeal and subsistent. (Flew, pp.103-04; *Summa Theologiae*, I, 75, 2)

Now ask again, "What does your thinking?" You, of course. What must you be in order to be a thinking being? You must be an immaterial soul, a substantial agent.

Still, as St. Thomas also admitted, it seems to be the one, same 'you' that sees, feels, etc., and that thinks and understands. But that's wrong. It can't be *one* same you, because the you that performs the acts must be *two* different you's! It is the human-being 'you,' the total body-soul composite substance, that senses, but only the soul 'you' that thinks. This becomes even more clear from what Aquinas wrote next. In *Summa Theologiae* I, 75, 3, he distinguishes his view from the ancient materialists who held that the living body both senses and thinks, and from Plato who said that the soul does them both:

The ancient philosophers made no distinction between sense and intellect, and referred both to a corporeal principle . . . Plato, however, drew a distinction between

219

intellect and sense; yet he referred both to an incorporeal principle, maintaining that sensing, just as understanding, belongs to the soul as such. From this is follows that even the souls of brute animals are subsistent. But Aristotle held that of the operations of the soul, understanding alone is performed without a corporeal organ. On the other hand, sensation and the consequent operations of the sensitive soul are evidently accompanied with change in the body, thus in the act of vision, the pupil of the eyes is affected by a reflexion of colour; and so with the other senses. Hence it is clear that the sensible soul has no per se operation of its own, and that every operation of the sensitive soul belongs to the composite. Wherefore we conclude that as the souls of brute animals have no per se operations they are not subsistent. For the operation of anything follows the mode of its being. (Flew, p.105)

"Every operation of the sensitive soul belongs to the composite." St. Thomas, like Aristotle, wrote long before the modern discoveries regarding the correlation between conscious activities and the actions of different parts of the brain. Those correlations involve, not only the senses, but thinking, emotions, moods, etc. If what today's neuroscientists and others believe, viz., that every conscious human act depends on the activity of the body's brain, then what St. Thomas wrote in the preceding entry regarding *animal* consciousness would seem to disprove the claim that the *human* intellect can operate per se. It can only be the body-soul or, better, the matter-form composite that exercises all conscious acts. (St. Thomas says that, for now, the intellect needs imagery provided by the body's 'internal senses,' but images are as non-material as sense-data.)

So, how many you's are there? Dozens, perhaps hundreds, of expert followers of St. Thomas* think there is no contradiction in his two answers to "If you answer *most precisely or correctly, what does the thinking?*" Like St. Thomas himself, they argue that there is an overlap.* The soul is not a substance, but a non-subsistent form of a substance (when talking about a man or woman), but it is also a substance and not only a non-subsistent form (when talking about thinking). When switching from one claim about the soul-form to the other ("it is the form of that which acts" vs "no, it is that which acts"), it is necessary to switch the words to indicate the switch in the expressed beliefs. Hence St. Thomas' constant switching from "We could say . . ." and "Or we can say . . ." to "Rightly" and "More correctly." In fact, a close study of St. Thomas' *Summa Theologiae* will reveal what a master of improvisation St. Thomas was! (*The improvisation continues. See, for instance, the just-published 2010 *Proceedings of the American Philosophical Association.* Its last entry is "Is Anyone Else Thinking My Thoughts? Aquinas' Response to the Too-Many-Thinkers Problem.")

Here, once again, are the contradictory conclusions that would follow, if St. Thomas' views were correct. (i)It is the 'man' (male or female), the total, *body-soul* 'you' that senses, but (ii)*only the soul 'you'* that thinks but cannot sense. Your certainty that it is the one and only agent-you who thinks *and* senses must be an illusion, according to Aquinas. Once the one you—or your body?—dies, you will no longer be able to sense or feel anything. You (a soul) will, however, be able to think and will. When the thinking 'you' regain your body at the time of resurrection, you will be a man or woman again, able to see, hear, etc., as well as think.

However, St. Thomas insisted that during the time you are only a soul, *you will no longer be a human being*, that is, a man or woman. Just in case you think St. Thomas' premises do not lead to a denial of the mature human experience of a unity of consciousness, a denial of your right-now certainty that the you *feeling* this book and *seeing* this page is the one, same, and *only* you that is *thinking* about all of this, he explicitly admitted that between death (of what?) and bodily resurrection you will not be a human being but only a soul:

> Whether the soul is a man? I answer that "the soul is a man" can be taken in two senses. First, that a man is a soul; though this particular man, Socrates, for instance, is not a soul, but composed of soul and body. I say this, forasmuch as some held that the form alone belongs to the species; while matter is part of the individual, and not of the species. This cannot be true, for to the nature of the species belongs what the definition signifies; and to natural things the definition does not signify the form only, but the form and the matter* . . .
>
> It may also be understood in this sense, that this soul is this man; and this could be held if it were supposed that the operation of the sensitive soul were proper to it, apart from the body; because in that case all the operations which are attributed to man would belong to the soul only; and whatever performs the operations proper to a thing, is that thing; wherefore that which performs the operations of a man is man. But it has been shown above that sensation is not the operation of the soul only. Since, then, sensation is an operation of man, but not proper to him [since animals, too, can sense], it is clear that man is not a soul only, but something composed of soul and body.——Plato, through supposing that sensation was proper to the soul, could maintain man to be a soul making use of the body. (Flew, p.105-06; *Summa Theologiae*, I, 75, 4; bracketed phrase added. Somewhere else, St. Thomas claims that the separated soul has a relation to the now no-longer existing body! [*At this point, Aquinas introduces a distinction between the 'signified' matter that individuals have and the 'common' matter belonging to 'the species considered in itself,' all of which involves complexities beyond the scope of this text. For a glimpse of those complexities, see A. Maurer's translation of St. Thomas' small masterpiece, *On Being and Essence*.])

What's more, because St. Thomas believed that human souls depend on their relation to a particular body for their distinct, individuated identity, he had to claim that the departed person (soul? but not man or woman!) has to retain its relation to the dead body in order to retain its numerical identity. A. MacIntyre, a contemporary Thomist, repeats this truly incredible claim: "Even a soul separated from its body by the dissolution of that body at death still derives its identity from its relationship to that body, so the relationship between soul and body and between mind and body is not, as it is with Plato and Plotinus, contingent and accidental. (Because bodies, after death [a substantial change] no longer retain their numerical identity and even decompose, those who try to explain this 'relation' call it "transcendental.") To reinforce this impossible view, MacIntyre follows other Thomists and cites St. Thomas' commentary on the Epistle to the Corinthians: "even if soul achieves well-being in another life, that does not mean that I do . . ." for "soul is not the whole human being: my soul is not me." (MacIntyre, 2009, pp.81-82) However, St.Thomas' commentary is a Homeric nod that is trumped by St.Luke's report of what Jesus promised the 'good' thief: "This day thou shalt be with me in paradise." (St.Luke 23:43) Jesus did not say "This day, thy soul wilt be with mine."

Question. Do you think that the you who feels what seems to be a body and sees what seems to be a page in a book is the one, same, only you who is thinking? Do you think it is experientially impossible that the you who feels what seem to be your hands holding this book and the you who sees what seems to be a page in a book is different from the you doing the thinking you're now doing?

Unless you're different from everyone else, your answer will be "Yes to both." Now, in agreement with even St. Thomas' description of what 'a man (or woman)' experiences, make a mental note of your present experience. Get in the habit of asking your self the above questions. Then realize that, whenever you want to be sure you know the true answer to "What am I?", you can do so by reflecting on this experience and re-asking these questions anytime you want to.

What St. Thomas didn't know and couldn't have known, you can. You have access to well-stocked libraries, which means that you can learn about the fantastic discoveries of the past four centuries and then incorporate them into your worldview, i.e., your personal philosophy.

Descartes died in 1650. Before him, such great thinkers as Aristotle and St. Thomas had no knowledge of the central nervous system, no realization that each of the external senses feed the brain afferent nerve impulses without which no sense-data will be produced in the mind. (Aristotle believed the brain was a blood-cooler.) It was only the post-Aquinas revival of the ancient atomism that led Galileo, Descartes, Newton, Locke, and then Berkeley, to realize that all the things we sense, from color to heat and cold, are effects produced in the mind, and not—as naïve-realist common sense assures us—qualities of physical bodies outside of us. In other words . . .

In other words, the question, "Do I have a body?", is a question that Aristotle and St. Thomas—and even Plato!—would have regarded as preposterous, the mark of a mad philosopher.

But, with what we know now, or can learn now if we are open to it, the true answer, "No!", becomes so logically inescapable, that the author of *Phantoms in the Brain*, psychologist V.S.Ramachandran, has insisted that "*Your own body is a phantom*, one that your brain has temporarily constructed purely for convenience." Of course, Ramachandran cannot mean that your real, unexperienced body is a phantom, since then your brain too would be a phantom, unable to create a phantom body! That is, it is not the body that is a phantom. It is the mass of proprioceptive sense-data named aches, pains, tensions, wigglings, 'body' movements, etc., that constitute the phantom. Recall the discussion of phantom-limb experiences discussed first by Descartes and referred to in Part One.

But, besides the 'phantom body,' whatever really exists correlative to the concept of a physical body is not actually a physical human body. (This is easier to understand than to believe.)

Here is the point in the argument when it is necessary to take account of what physicists have discovered in the last four centuries about the physical world, if one exists.

That is, what else did neither Aristotle nor St. Thomas know that Descartes realized? They did not understand that, if *never-experienced* matter or bodies of any kind do exist (a fact no one can prove), they are utterly unlike what we common-sensically believe they are like. There is no single, whole, human body.

Begin by comparing what you think of blood to what you'll see if you view 'it' through a high-power microscope. (Pretend microscopes exist.) As Locke already noted in the 1600's, "Blood to the naked eye appears all red; but by a good microscope, wherein its lesser parts appear, shows only some few globules of red, swimming in a pellucid liquor; and how these red globules would appear, if glasses could be found that yet could magnify them one thousand or ten thousand times more, is uncertain." (Locke, *Essay*, Bk. II, ch. XXIII)

Then, understand that every organ in your body is composed of separate cells. The separateness is especially true of neurons, thought to 'make up' the brain. As Richard Restak wrote regarding a twentieth-century debate between Golgi and Cajal, "Today, we know that Cajal was correct. With increasingly sophisticated stains that would have appealed to Cajal the artist, brain scientists over the ensuing fifty years have demonstrated that neurons in reality are separate cells that communicate with each other but are never in direct physical contact. This rules out the view that nerve impulses pass through the brain like water through a system of pipes." (*The Brain: the Last Frontier*, pp.164-65) Believing as materialists do that fifteen or fifty billion separate, unconscious neurons can be 'put together' to form a unified conscious brain is as absurd as believing that eleven unconscious football players, heaped together, constitute one conscious team.

> **Repeat (because it is so important): Believing as materialists do that fifteen or fifty billion separate, unconscious neurons can be 'put together' to form a unified conscious brain is as absurd as believing that eleven unconscious football players, heaped together, constitute one conscious team.**

What's worse for neuroscientists is twentieth-century physics. If taken seriously, it forces us to acknowledge with rigorous logic that not even cells or neurons, not even molecules or atoms, are single entities. Start with Eddington:

> When we compare the universe as we had ordinarily preconceived it, the most arresting change is not the rearrangement of space and time by Einstein, but the dissolution of all that we regard as most solid into tiny specks floating in the void. That gives an abrupt jar to those who think that things are more or less what they seem. The revelation by modern physics of the void within the atom is more disturbing than the revelation by astronomy of the immense void of interstellar space. The atom is as porous as the solar system. (A. Eddington, *The Nature of the Physical World*, p.1)

Just how porous the atom is (actually how non-existent, because only the subatomic bodies exist) can be grasped from what Selig Hecht wrote in *Explaining the Atom* (p.64):

> In the atom of hydrogen the single electron is near the outer rim of the atom. If its nucleus were enlarged to the size of a baseball, its electron would be a speck about eight city blocks away.

An equivalent sphere with a diameter of sixteen city blocks would be empty except for a baseball and a tiny BB. If all of the protons, electrons, and neutrons in your body were squeezed together, so that no empty space separated them, the total mass would be smaller than the head of a pin. Here, then, is what William James wrote more than a century ago about our fictitious! concept of a unified brain:

> The 'entire brain process' is not a physical fact at all. It is the appearance to an onlooking mind of a multitude of physical facts. 'Entire brain' is nothing but our name for the way in which a million of molecules arranged in certain positions might affect our sense . . . . Their aggregation into a 'brain' is a fiction of popular speech. (*Principles of Psychology*, V.I, p.178)

Hard as it is to believe, and it would be simply *too* hard if it were not for the brute logic of it, the inexorable conclusion that comes from modern discoveries is that *you are a soul* living in the midst of the virtual-reality 'world' that is your personal, private stream of consciousness. Outside your stream of consciousness there may be a physical world, but—in the words of Eddington, the physicist who carried out some famous observations to determine whether Einstein's general relativity theory was correct—"the most arresting change is . . . the dissolution of all that we regard as most solid into tiny specks floating in the void."

No one can be certain, however, since it is impossible to prove that *anything* physical exists.

Two approaches to "You are a soul." There are two ways to prove and/or defend one's belief, one positive, and one negative. One can either show why one's own belief is true, or one can show why other beliefs are false. The same is true regarding the different ways to prove or defend one's answer to "What am I?"

First, there is the *positive* approach based on the immateriality of our intellect's objects, used by Plato, perfected by Saint Thomas Aquinas, plus the unity of consciousness, also first used by Plato. In order for us to understand immaterial objects, such as essences and universal concepts, we must be souls able to exist without matter. This chapter's sharp-dualist view agrees with Plato and St. Thomas. In fact, given the immateriality of sense-data, this chapter's answer to "What am I?" goes even farther: everything we experience, whether by intellect or sense-experience, is immaterial, hence the whole conscious human being is an immaterial, substance-agent.

Second, there is the *negative* approach. The preceding evidence shows the error of the materialists. But it also refutes the false half of St. Thomas' answer. Why? Because no such things as unified human bodies, including brains, exist. This negative approach uses a combination of representationalism (no one has ever experienced anything physical) and modern sub-atomic physics (no bodies, if any exist, are larger than subatomic particles). Here are a few more sources for this conclusion:

> From that day in 1911, when Rutherford described the inside of the atom, our whole idea of matter has been changed. The atom, formerly likened to a solid billiard ball, has become a transparent sphere of emptiness, thinly populated with electrons. The substance of the atom has shrunk to a core of unbelievable smallness; enlarged a thousand million times, an atom would be about the size of a football, but its nucleus would still be hardly visible—a mere speck of dust at the center. (Otto R. Frisch, *Atomic Physics Today*, p.13)

> The new atomic model was definitely planetary. The surprising thing of the planetary model was how small the nucleus appeared. If the golf ball-sized atom was once again inflated, this time to the size of a modern sports arena or football stadium, the nucleus of the atom would be the size of a grain of rice. (Fred A. Wolf, *Taking the Quantum Leap*, p.75)

> Now how do we know this is true if we can't see it? What proof have we that matter is made up of these quintillions of infinitesimal particles? Robert Millikan, one of the world's most noted physicists, said, "We can count the exact number of molecules in any given volume with more certainty than we can count the population of a city or a state." . . .

An atom is the smallest part of an element that can exist either alone or in combination with other particles. There are more atoms of hydrogen in a pail of water than there are drops of water in all the oceans of the world combined. So small is the diameter of an atom that half a million atoms piled, one on top of another, would not even equal the thickness of this page! The volume of the average atom is about 1.56 X 10^{-25} of a cubic inch, which means that there are approximately fifteen-thousand-six-hundred-billion-million-million atoms to a cubic inch. Of course, such a number is totally incomprehensible, yet in spite of its inconceivable minuteness, the atom is mostly empty space! Its entire mass is packed into its nucleus which, believe it or not, is one trillionth the size of the atom itself. This is very fortunate. If the atom were all nucleus without any space in it, a glass of water would weigh as much as a two-ton truck and you would weigh as much as half a dozen locomotives . . .

Because they are so incredibly close to the nucleus these electrons make approximately 10,000,000,000,000,000 revolutions around it every second . . . (Jerome S. Meyer, *The ABC of Physics*, pp.22, 34-35)

A bar of gold, though it looks solid, is composed almost entirely of empty space: The nucleus of each of its atoms is so small that if one atom were enlarged a million billion times, until its outer electron shell was as big as greater Los Angeles, its nucleus would still be only about the size of a compact car parked downtown . . . . Nor, to return to the old classical metaphor, does a cue ball strike a billiard ball. Rather . . . on the subatomic scale, the billiard balls are as spacious as galaxies, and were it not for their like electrical charges they could, like galaxies, pass right through each other unscathed. (Timothy Ferris, *Coming of Age in the Milky Way*, pp.288-89)

In every single drop of sea water, there are fifty billion atoms of gold. One would have to distill two thousand tons of such water to get one single gram of gold . . .

If we magnify the atom to the size of a football, the nucleus would be but a speck in its center and the electron, still invisible, would be revolving around its surface. Similarly, if we picture the atom as large as New York's Empire State Building, the electron, the size of a marble, would be spinning around the building seven million times every millionth of a second. There is relatively more empty space in the atom than between the planets in the solar system. (Bernard Jaffe, *Crucibles: The Story of Chemistry*, p.83)

For each proton in the nucleus, there was a negatively charged electron, gyrating around the atom's core at a distance 50, 000 times the diameter of the nucleus. If a hydrogen atom's nucleus were the size of a tennis ball, its electron would be two miles away. (J. Boslough, "Worlds Within the Atom," May 1995 *National Geographic*, p. 654)

Many people find this, not just hard to believe, but impossible. In fact, a recent class of students found Myers' claim, "So small is the diameter of an atom that half a million atoms piled, one on top of another, would not even equal the thickness of this page!", just that: impossible.

Take a moment to view this page from its edge and ask yourself whether you find it credible. Then reflect on the conclusions of Part One: even if a book, pages, and your hands do exist, they are not what you see and feel. The whole of the *sensed* 'world' is the sense-data component of your personal, private, stream of consciousness. When you think about books, pages, and hands, you are thinking about what you do not sense, what you have never sensed. Ask yourself whether you find such facts credible?

William James did. Which leads us to the next and final chapter in this course.

(An addendum. What about animals? According to Aristotle and St. Thomas, they can perform psychological acts of sensing, even if they cannot think or reason. According to Descartes, they can do neither, for all consciousness is immaterial. If modern physics is true, animals have no bodies or brains, for neither exist. If any—never seen!—animals did exist, they too would be souls. If animal souls, and not body-soul animal composites, did any seeing, hearing, feeling, etc., then animal souls would also be immortal. Those who believe in transmigration *should* treat what appear to be cows in India's streets with the same respect given to [dead] ancestors.)

CHAPTER X

JAMESIAN QUINTALISM

Introduction. The previous chapter referred to the necessity of having a complete, grand unifying theory of everything in general and of the most important things in particular in order to have scientific certainty about any particular, lesser theory.

While the 'first edition' of *The Philosophy of Human Nature* (the original title of this book when it was in mimeograph form) was being written, it was impossible to finish it with these post-epiphenomenalism chapters. The reason was simple. That first version was written during a period when I was not bold enough to decisively accept certain conclusions and therefore had not worked out my own grand unifying theory of everything with those conclusions in place.

During the thirty five years since those mid-seventies, I finally understood William James, the most brilliant psychologist who ever lived, the one who solved the most important problem of all, namely, how to think about and thereby how to describe in words a complete thought. That made it possible to 'finish' the system.

This is not the place for presenting that final, grand unifying theory in any detail. That's been done in several other recent writings. In this final chapter, I will summarize how I think James might answer the question, "What is a human being?", IF I could persuade him to change his mind on just one, single issue: "Do souls exist, distinct from their three-component streams of consciousness?" I will then situate that answer within the outline of a broader, quintalist system of thought.

Quintalism. Aristotle and St. Thomas believed there are four *basic* kinds—or *genera*—of things in this universe. There are material and immaterial things. Among each genus, there are innumerable *species*. Among material things there are inanimate stars, planets, moons, rocks, etc., and innumerable species of living plants and animals. Among the immaterial spirits, there are human souls, angels, and God. (Experts do not agree on the degree to which Aristotle's concept of a First Mover is similar to St. Thomas' concept of God.) Human beings straddle the gap between material and immaterial beings.

Descartes boldly sliced the entire universe of things into just two basic kinds of things, material and immaterial ones, with no diverse species in either category. For instance, he held that material things are all just differently arranged particles and that a dead body differs from a living one the same way a broken machine differs from a working one.

Finally, Berkeley-type idealists and ordinary-type materialists each believe in only one of Descartes' two different kinds of things.

According to quintalism (think of quintet, quintuplets, etc.), there are five different types of realities. First, there are the souls and spirits believed in by Plato, St. Thomas, and Descartes. Humans, angels, and divine beings are all souls or spirits, i.e., immaterial, conscious beings. Secondly, presume for now that there are physical things. None of them, however, are larger than subatomic particles. The other three kinds of things are components of the stream of consciousness, namely, immaterial: sense-data, immaterial memory-images of sense-data, and immaterial complete thoughts.

The reason for insisting that the last three items are different from each other is to make it utterly clear that *thoughts are not images.* James was in the habit of distinguishing only percepts and concepts as components of the stream of consciousness, and it defeated his efforts to create his own grand unifying theory of everything.

James and souls. During James' lifetime, the dominant 'philosophy' in the universities was one that he opposed: 'monist idealism.' Like Berkeley, monist idealists believe there is only one kind of reality, viz., immaterial reality. But, unlike Berkeley, they also believe there is really only one numerical (countable) being, period. Their view might be summed up by saying that only 'the infinite Absolute' exists, and that everything else, including our selves, are parts of 'the Absolute.' We are not beings distinct from 'the Absolute,' and we cannot perform actions with any kind of independence. What seem to be our distinct selves and our independent acts are illusions.

James vehemently disagreed. Two years before his death, he told an audience in England,

> I am finite once for all, and all the categories of my sympathy are knit up with the finite world as such, and with things that have a history . . . I have neither eyes nor ears nor heart nor mind for anything of an opposite description, and the stagnant felicity of the absolute's own perfection moves me as little as I move it. (Lecture II of *A Pluralistic Universe.*)

One of the ways James tried to help his readers escape or avoid the monists was by constantly drawing attention to immediate experience. He made it a 'first principle' postulate for his final theory, which he called "radical empiricism."

Radical empiricism consists first of all of a postulate . . . The postulate is that the only things that shall be debatable among philosophers shall be things definable in terms drawn from experience. [Things of an unexperienceable nature may exist ad libitum, but they form no part of the material for philosophic debate.] (Preface to *The Meaning of Truth*.)

The reason for introducing the subject of monism and James rejection of it is this: it is partly responsible for his attempt to pretend that any individual's *experienced* stream of consciousness is the singular, individual, personal self. We do not have any direct experience of a soul, hence no direct experience of our self. (What would it be like?!) And certainly, no one experiences some larger, world-sized Absolute Self! All that we experience is our personal, private stream of consciousness, no matter how absurd that sounds.

Here is James' description of it:

To sum up now this long chapter. The consciousness of Self involves a stream of thought, each part of which as 'I' can 1) remember those which went before, and know the things they knew; and 2) emphasize and care paramountly for certain ones among them as '*me*,' and *appropriate to these* the rest. The nucleus of the '*me*' is always the bodily existence felt to be present at the time. Whatever remembered-past-feelings *resemble* this present feeling are deemed to belong to the same *me* with it. Whatever other things are perceived to be *associated* with this feeling are deemed to form part of that *me*'s *experience*; and of them certain ones (which fluctuate more or less) are reckoned to be themselves *constituents* of the me in a larger sense,—such as the clothes, the material possessions, the friends, the honors and esteem which the person receives or may receive. This me is an empirical aggregate of things objectively known. The *I* which knows them cannot itself be an aggregate, neither for psychological purposes need it be considered to be an unchanging metaphysical entity like the Soul, or a principle like the pure Ego, viewed as 'out of time.' It is a *Thought*, at each moment different from that of the last moment, but *appropriative* of the latter, together with all that the latter called its own. All the experiential facts find their place in this description, unencumbered with any hypothesis save that of the existence of passing thoughts or states of mind . . . . (*Principles of Psychology*, V.I, pp.400-01)

What are you, then? According to what James wrote in that Chapter X of his *Principles of Psychology*, you are a thought. But, like Descartes, what James meant here by "thought" is *the entire stream of consciousness*. The non-self 'things' that James says you experience are what Berkeley said, groups of sense-data or qualities in that same stream of consciousness!

In fact, the 'objects' of our perception, as trees, men, houses, microscopes, of which the real world seems composed, are nothing but clusters of qualities which through simultaneous stimulation have so coalesced that the moment one is excited actually it serves as a sign or cue for the idea of the others to arise. (*Principles of Psychology*, V.I p.555)

Trees, men, houses, etc., are "clusters of qualities" in our mind. That is why James could write that "the clothes, the material possessions, the friends" that are part of our 'world' are "parts of the *me*"! Our field of consciousness 'contains' everything that we experience and nothing more.

Nothing, that is, except certain important 'senses' that he described in his 1901 *Varieties of Religious Experience*:

> A conscious field *plus* its object as felt or thought of *plus* an attitude towards the object *plus* the sense of a self to whom the attitude belongs—such a concrete bit of personal experience may be a small bit, but it is a solid bit as long as it lasts; not hollow, not a mere abstract element of experience, such as the 'object' when taken all alone. It is a *full* fact, even though it be an insignificant fact; it is of the *kind* to which all realities whatsoever must belong; the motor currents of the world run through the like of it; it is on the line connecting real events with real events. (Lecture XX)

James' idea that you, I, and each other human person is a (stream of) thought or field of conscious experience is, of course, utterly at odds with our everyday common sense. We are the distinct-from-the-stream, *perduring agents* who experience sense-data, are aware of memory-images, and understand the thoughts. Unless, before we experienced them, sense-data, memory-images, and thoughts were just floating around, untethered and un'had' by any conscious agent, and unless they floated in (and out of) the knower's mind, then it is clear that they come into being only after there is a conscious agent able to 'have' them. We have to exist before we can acquire knowledge or experience anything. Our *concept* of our 'self' may be made up of memories and sense-data, but the *actual self* that we are is not. Parallel to the difference between God and our concept of God, there is a distinction between our self and our concept of our self.

What's more, if James had been right about 'the Self,' those 'senses' to which he drew attention would all be illusions. Unless there are things outside our field of consciousness, among which things is the agent-self that experiences and thinks and is the 'arbiter who seems to sit aloft' and decides which thoughts to embrace and which to reject, those 'senses' would point to nothing. Here again are the senses, *so central to common sense*, that we experience:

> A conscious field *plus* its object as felt or thought of *plus* an attitude towards the object *plus* the sense of a self to whom the attitude belongs—such a concrete bit of personal experience may be a small bit, but it is a solid bit as long as it lasts . . .

Take a few minutes to reflect on that powerful "sense of a self." One way to feel its full impact is to ask your self questions about your self. For instance, have you ever thanked God for creating *you*? There are billions of other people. Imagine that God had created those billions, but never got around to creating you. You might have never existed. Or ask yourself whether you've ever been thankful you were born to the parents you have, rather than to some other parents. Or a thousand years ago, or five thousand. Or in a different country and civilization. Is it conceivable to you, as it seems to be for millions of other people, that you have lived another life or two—or a dozen lives—before this one? Would you still be you, if every last one of your memories were stripped from you? (Locke got confused when he tried to answer that.) And, if you are a soul (you *are*), how can even God tell one invisible, faceless soul from another?

The 'common-sense principle.' Here we come upon the reason for insisting, early in Part One, on what was called "the common-sense principle." *No conviction of common sense will be surrendered unless there are preponderant reasons for doing so.* Nothing is more obvious in our everyday thinking as the sense that reality does not depend upon our knowing it. Nothing is more obvious than the fact that we all believe in things we have never experienced, beginning with the other side of the moon, billions of other human beings, the inside organs of our own skull, etc.

In other words, it was James' rejection of 'the common-sense principle' and his embrace of the radical-empiricist 'postulate' that led him to reject the existence of the soul as the true answer to "What am I?" However, two years before his death, he admitted that the conviction that we ourselves are distinct agent-souls could not be permanently denied:

> Some day, indeed, souls may get their innings again in philosophy—I am quite ready to admit that possibility—they form a category of thought too natural to the human mind to expire without prolonged resistance. (W. James, *Pluralistic Universe*, ch.5)

What's more, he himself referred to some of the most important evidence that we humans are souls. First, there is his recognition of the experienced unity of conscious experience and lack of unity in the so-called "brain," and the *perplexity* that this recognition gives rise to:

> Such a figment [the 'unified brain'] cannot serve as the objectively real counterpart to any psychic state whatever. Only a genuinely physical fact can so serve, and the molecular fact is the only genuine physical fact. Whereupon we seem, if we are to have an elementary psycho-physic law at all, thrust right back upon something like the mental-atom-theory, for the molecular fact, being an element of the 'brain,' would seem naturally to correspond, not to total thoughts, but to elements of thoughts. Thus the real in psychics seems to 'correspond' to the unreal in physics, and *vice versa*; and our perplexity is extreme. (Epilogue to the *Briefer Course*)

In fact, in an 1887 book review, James had already made the same point, adding that the fictitious nature of the brain has logical implications regarding the mind or soul, that is, the spiritual ego:

> It is only when we seek to go beyond the empirically given correspondence of thought and brain state, and to express it in more elementary terms, that we get entangled: 'Total brain-state' is not the name of a physical fact at all; and this may end in leading us to considerations which force the notion of a spiritual ego, in spite of its barrenness, on our belief. (*Essay, Comments, and Reviews*, p.402; James wrote this review before *The Principles of Psychology*.)

That, of course, is the point. We must 'go beyond the empirically given,' and the empirically given doesn't include the brain, only the psychic! But, not only does the 'empirically given' not include any brain, there is no brain and no human body of which a brain would be only a part. Like it or not, all of modern physics shows that, if there is any physical world at all, it is not empirically given and it *contains nothing larger than subatomic particles.*

The ultimate question. "What, then, is the source of your present stream of consciousness?" Either there is no cause (Hume), or it is your brain (no such thing exists), or—as Berkeley concluded—it is God. James himself, so clearly sympathetic to Berkeley's philosophy, once at least showed his sympathy for a conclusion, similar to Berkeley's:

> The perfect object of belief would be a God or 'Soul of the World,' represented both optimistically and moralistically (if such a combination could be), and withal so definitely conceived as to show us why our phenomenal experiences should be sent to us by Him in just the very way in which they come. All Science and all History would thus be accounted for in the deepest and simplest fashion. (*Principles of Psychology*, Vol.II, p.317)

Ten concluding notes. As mentioned above, this final chapter can do little more than point in the direction of a larger unifying theory, thus to other more inclusive writings. Having introduced the thesis that our streams of consciousness come 'warm' from the hand of God, it would be very unsatisfactory to end the course and this text without at least a few indications of what can be found, regarding God, in those other more inclusive writings.

1. What we mean—or should mean—when we say that one thing causes another has been debated endlessly during the past twenty-four centuries.

St. Thomas, following Aristotle, wrote about four 'causes,' and his present-day disciples continue that tradition. The universal way of presenting those four causes begins with a material object, such as a table or house, etc. To say that it has four 'causes' should mean only "How many things must you learn about in order to fully understand it?" Four. You should know what it is made of (the 'material cause'), what is its form or structure (the 'formal cause'), what made it come to be (the 'efficient cause'), and what's its purpose (the 'final cause'). However, the only everyday meaning of "cause" is what Aristotle and Aquinas called "efficient cause."

When we ask "What is the cause of our stream of consciousness?", we are asking about the efficient cause, about what produces or gives rise to sense-data, etc.

Once again, the answer is either "Nothing," "The brain," or "God." Apply the process of elimination. (i) No common-sense person would say "Nothing, I just have sensations, etc., and they come literally from nothing and nowhere." Only skeptics come close to that when they say "No one knows and no one can know." (ii) Though today's neuroscientists or other materialists believe "The brain" is the answer, that is ruled out for the simple reason that modern physics shows that James was right more than a century ago when he wrote that brains do not exist, that the concept of a unified brain is a "fiction of popular speech." (iii) The only remaining alternative is "God."

2. How does God cause our consciousness? God does it by creating. James ended his quest for a unified theory by asking the question, and he included "by creation" as one possibility:

> Nevertheless, within experience, phenomena come and go. There are novelties; there are losses. The world seems, on the concrete and proximate level at least, really to grow. So the question recurs. How do our finite experiences come into being from moment to moment? By inertia? By perpetual creation? Do the new ones come at the call of the old ones? Why do not they all go out like a candle? (*Some Problems of Philosophy*, ch.III, end)

"By perpetual creation" is the right answer. But that only deepens the mystery. How can something be created from nothing? And obviously our 'finite experiences' are what James calls them, "Novelties", created from nothing! We never have any sensation twice; the second one is always brand new, however similar it is to previous ones. For, as James notes, each new moment of experience is different at least by this, that it contains a memory of the last moment(s).

Once again, the Rorty Rule must rule here. We are capable of *understanding* the thought, "Conscious phenomena do not pre-exist our experience of them, they are not made from pre-existing stuff, rather they are created brand new," even though we are not capable of '*seeing*' what kind of 'stuff' is a thought, and even though we are not capable of 'seeing' why the total visual field of colors has a side 'facing' us but no opposite side, etc. Knowing seems always to end in bafflement.

Thus, everything in our stream of consciousness is created new, from moment to moment, by a cause that is capable of creating.

3. The continued existence of a sensed object requires continued creation. Study St. Thomas and Descartes and you will learn that they had a name for this continued creating: "conservation in being." It is what James alludes to with his question, "Why do not they all go out like a candle?"

Divine creation differs from human creation. We can take material, make a hat with it, and store it away in a closet. Unless something destroys it, it will continue to exist. That is not the case with things created by God. After something is created by God, it will 'go poof' if God 'takes the divine eye off it' or abruptly halts the conserving-creating.

4. The view that God can create a world, toss it off into space, and let it go on its merry way without any further divine input is an age-old view called "deism." The deist view is similar to the idea that we humans can make things that operate automatically. Instead of watching the back yard and turning on the lights if an intruder approaches, we have motion-sensitive lights that will turn on automatically when an intruder arrives. Instead of watching the thermometer to know when the house temperature reaches seventy degrees, we set the thermostat to turn off the furnace automatically at seventy degrees.

According to the deists, God 'wound up' the world and then let everything happen according to the 'natural laws' that God built into things. God can now sit back, relax, and just watch history unroll. Automatically. On its own. Except, of course, when God intervenes to create a miracle. And except if we humans have free will enabling us to have some input of our own into that history.

5. Even if there is a physical world, how could it possibly cause anything immaterial? How can discrete, colorless, subatomic particles produce color? How can discrete, non-colliding, silently-moving subatomic particles produce heard sound? The reason no one has discovered an answer to such questions is because those subatomic particles can't produce color, sound, etc. Period!

Even if neurons existed, why would similar input from dissimilar afferent neurons cause such utterly different effects as colors, sounds, pains, tickles, etc., depending only on the part of the brain that they reach? Why would homogeneous tiny electric currents do the same? Even Huxley admitted that no one has a clue. His only reason for not worrying about such lack of answers was simple. He said no one understands *any* example of alleged causality!

Still, even if there are physical things, they are all subatomic in size. Like planets, the electrons move at dizzying speeds and in endless ways. Instead of asking how they can cause anything, ask what causes them to do the only thing they can do: move and stop moving according to incredibly complex laws! Before Copernicus, people believed that, to explain why planets continue moving, there had to be something continuously acting and moving them, otherwise, they'd stop moving. Today's thinkers have no other 'scientific' answer to the movement of anything than "They just do it."

Of course, some thinkers believe there are four 'natural' forces that make things move. Only those who remain under the 'plebeian illusion' of naïve realism believe there are such things as forces. David Hume pointed out, first, that no one has ever sensed a force, and, second, that we acquire our concept of force from our experience of 'muscular tension,' as when we try to pull apart two powerful magnets. As for gravitational force, theories about 'it' are themselves endless.

Most people don't even make the obvious distinction between the *force* of gravity and the *law* of gravity! (See, for instance, the "Interlude" in *William James on Morality*.)

6. One of Descartes' successors was N. Malebranche, a predecessor of Berkeley. He proposed a famous theory called "occasionalism." According to him, God is the sole cause of everything in nature. When the occasion calls for it, God makes this or that to happen. This means that God replaces all other answers to "What causes such-and-such?"

For instance, Aristotle and St. Thomas held that what causes the planets to move the way they do is bodiless spirits, angels if you wish. Of course, God gives the angels their ability to move planets, which makes God the 'primary' cause and the spirits 'secondary' causes. Aristotle and St. Thomas also regarded us humans as 'secondary' causes of things. The carpenter causes the table. The murderer causes the fatal wound that kills someone. We can even cause other people's thoughts, which idea is behind the claim that every lie is immoral, since the essence of language is to communicate true thoughts to each other.

Reflect, however, on the idea of communication. In our common-sense thinking, it happens when one person causes ink marks on paper (writing) or causes sound waves in the air (speaking). Both assume that it is via physical things that one person can 'give' another person a thought.

Part One of the course showed the error in that analysis of communication. We, relying on our prior knowledge, interpret seen ink marks and heard sounds. But where does that prior knowledge come from? Descartes showed that it does not come from our senses. Berkeley says that sensed colors, sounds, etc., come from God, but he failed to insist that our ongoing thoughts must be coming from God as well. This helps to understand the real mystery of occasionalism. How does God know which thoughts to supply to whom and when?

Christians, like Malebranche and Berkeley, already are fervent believers in occasionalism on a limited scale. Why else do they pray, often in church and in groups, that God will inspire world leaders to devise plans for world peace and dozens of other good things? They trust that, on the occasion of their praying, God will make things happen in other people's minds. When two people communicate, God 'reads' the mind of one person and furnishes the appropriate thoughts to the other person's mind. That is occasionalism.

St. Thomas, in Part 1 of Book III of *Summa Contra Gentiles*, chapter 69, argues against occasionalism. What fact(s) does he use for his argument? Only one, repeatedly, again and again. It is, he writes, more fitting or reasonable for God to share causal power with his creatures than for God alone to do all the causing. He uses an argument from 'fittingness.'

The issue, however, is not what St. Thomas or anyone else thinks is fitting. The question is, "What are the facts?"

7. Related to the issue of occasionalism is the familiar 'solution' to the problem of evil, the problem that inspired the *Book of Job*. If God is both all-powerful and all-good, how can we explain the fact that an all-powerful God does not do what good human beings would do, *if they could!*, prevent all suffering? Why, for instance, does God not prevent the horrific things humans do to one another, e.g., war, torture, murder, etc.? The most usual 'solution' is that God permits evil in order to give us humans free will.

God does not permit anything. That is the same old deist philosophy. God does not stand by and watch what we humans will or won't do. God is not only right there. Whatever is done, is done only because God does it. Even the Neo-Thomists held that no secondary cause, whether soldier, torturer, or murderer, can do anything without an input from God, the first cause of everything.

The 'solution' is not reached by avoiding the facts, but by doing hard thinking.

8. Stephen J. Hawking made the news this year with the publication of a new book entitled, *The Grand Design*. In it, he writes that the universe's creation did not require the activity of God. In place of God, he points to the laws of nature. According to what he calls "M-theory,"

> . . . ours is not the only universe. Instead, M-Theory predicts that a great many universes were created out of nothing. Their creation does not require the intervention of some supernatural being or god. Rather, those multiple universes arise naturally from physical law. (pp. 8-9)

He especially likes gravity. The law, not the force!

> Because there is a law like gravity, the universe can and will create itself from nothing in the manner described in Chapter 6. Spontaneous creation is the reason there is something rather than nothing, why the universe exists, why we exist. It is not necessary to invoke God to light the blue touch paper and set the universe going. (p.180)

But what reality do 'the laws of nature' have? Literally, they don't exist. They are concepts created by our minds to describe what things have done in the past and to predict what they can be assumed to do in the future.

The things that exist are persons, their multi-component streams of consciousness, and subatomic particles. When we speak of the laws of nature, we are—or should be—thinking about what those things that exist do. The question then becomes, "Why do they do what they do?" Laws do not answer that question. Laws pose the question.

The most important laws of nature are what we can call "correlation laws." John Hospers composed a brilliant passage that illustrates such laws and points to the question, "Whence the laws?", specifically, the question Hawking ignores.

> In practice we come rather quickly to laws which cannot be explained further. Laws about atomic structure are typical of such laws. Laws of psycho-physical correlation are another example. Why do I have a certain colour-sensation which I call red, indescribable but qualitatively different from all others, when light within a certain range of wave-length impinges upon my retina, and another indescribably different sensation which I call yellow when rays of another wave-length strike the retina? That this wave-length is correlated with this visual experience seems to be sheer 'brute fact'—a law which cannot be explained in terms of anything more ultimate than itself . . . . Like so many others, this point may seem logically compelling but psychologically unsatisfying. Having heard the above argument, one may still feel inclined to ask, 'Why are the basic uniformities of the universe the way they are, and not some other way? Why should we have just these laws rather than other ones? I want an explanation of why they are as they are.' I must confess here, as an autobiographical remark, that I cannot help sharing this feeling. I want to ask why the laws of nature, being contingent, are as they are, even though I cannot conceive of what an explanation of this would be like, and even though by my own argument above the request for such an explanation is self-contradictory. (J. Hospers, "What is Explanation?", in *Essays in Conceptual Analysis*, ed. Antony Flew, 1956)

It would be hard to find a more powerful testimony than Hospers' to the common-sense 'concept' or conviction regarding efficient causal influence. It would also be hard to find a better example of the kind of self-imposed blindness—"I cannot conceive . . . ," and "by my own argument above the request for such an explanation is self-contradictory"—that Rorty exposed. All we can say is, "Too bad for your argument." If Hawking could *conceive* of a creative god whose existence he then denied, surely Hospers could as well.

9. As for "What makes the subatom-size electrons behave as they do?", Cecil Schneer was able to conceive of an answer:

> [. . .] if the electron is to lose energy in radiation, how is it kept from spiraling in toward the nucleus? And if the atom in a stable state is not to emit electromagnetic radiation—and most atoms do not unless excited—then the electron cannot move in the positive field surrounding the nucleus. But in that case, what is to keep it from falling into the positive nucleus like a meteor into the sun? The electron must revolve about the nucleus to generate the centrifugal force to counterbalance the attraction of the nucleus. But if it moves, it emits radiation and so moves less and less, and the

atom collapses. And if it does not move, the atom still collapses. The objection to the perpetual motion of the electron was the same that had been made to Copernicus' motion of the earth. Where was the force to maintain the motion of the earth? Where was the energy to maintain the motion of the negative electron in a positive field? The prime mover could not, surely, be expected to attend individually to all electrons in all atoms. (C. Schneer, *The Evolution of Physical Science*, p.349)

"The prime mover" refers, of course, to God. If God doesn't move them, then either nothing does or else it is some kind of force. But, though we may have concepts of them, forces are as fictitious and non-existent as laws of nature. And, James would add, as fictitious as brains.

10. If the two basics of Descartes' revolutionary worldview—representationalism and atomism—are true, why does God first make us learn and believe in common sense's naïve realism?

The first answer must be that God's plan calls for us to be morally good. St.Paul says that all the rules for that are summed up in the great command, "Love your neighbor as yourself." (Romans 13:8-10) Common sense is not only enough for that. Our *common-sense naïve realism is essential*, if we are to have an idea of which neighbors our decisions affect and an idea of which decisions will likely cause pleasure or cause pain.

But God's plan also calls for us to be scientists, trying to enjoy learning the truth about this universe we live in. Francis Bacon described this part of God's plan for us:

Whereas of the sciences which regard nature, the divine philosopher declares that "it is the glory of God to conceal a thing, but it is the glory of the King to find a thing out." Even as though the divine nature took pleasure in the innocent and kindly sport of children playing a hide and seek, and vouchsafed of his kindness and goodness to admit the human spirit for his playfellow at that game. (F. Bacon, *The Great Instauration*; Preface)

Relative to the desire for scientific certainty rather than simple faith, Descartes wrote a letter to a friend whose wife had died in which he confessed as much:

I think I know very clearly that they [our souls] last longer than our bodies, and are destined by nature for pleasures and felicities much greater than those we enjoy in this world. Those who die pass to a sweeter and more tranquil life than ours; I cannot imagine otherwise. We shall go to find them some day, and we shall remember the past; because we have, on my view, an intellectual memory which is certainly independent of the body. And although religion teaches us much on this point, I must confess a weakness in myself which is, I think, common to the majority of men. However much we wish to believe, and however much we think we do firmly believe all that religion teaches, we are not commonly moved by it as when we are convinced by very evident natural reasons. (*Descartes: Philosophical Letters*, trans. A.Kenny, pp.134-35)

The truth frees us in many ways. It frees us from ultimate worry and despair. The other day's news reported an increase in the number of elderly people consulting specialists in geriatric psychiatry for help in dealing with depression. Could it be partially attributed to growing doubts about immortality, doubts created by the incessant repetition of the myth that science has replaced religious faith with proven facts? Consider the boast that one of Descartes' biographers made regarding neuroscience's direction.

> In the twenty-first century, this is how the last battle for the human soul will go. Materialists will discover more and more about how the brain works. Mentalists will never be able to show how an independent mind works. One day, one hundred, two hundred years down the line, everyone will finally realize that the materialists have won and that the mentalists have lost this last battle for the human soul. When humankind finally faces the fact that the mind is the brain, that there is no independently existing mental soul to survive the death of the body, that none of us chirpy sparrows is immortal, when Descartes's ghost in the machine finally fades away and his animal machine is triumphant, then there will be a revolution in human thought the like of which none has gone before. (R. Watson, *Cogito, Ergo Sum*, p.327)

The *better science* of Descartes, James, and others, that is, the better science presented in this course, will—if more people embrace it—show Watson's error and restore the traditional peace of mind that St. Paul wrote about.

> . . . grace be to you and peace from God our Father. We give thanks to the God and Father of our Lord Jesus Christ, praying always for you; for we have heard of your faith in Christ Jesus and of the love that you bear towards all the saints because of the hope that is laid up for you in heaven. (Colossians 1:2-5)

Evident natural reasons—reached by hard thinking—can convert faith into science.

CHAPTER X-b

WHY THIS LAST IS 'THE' SCIENTIFIC ANSWER

Each reader is 'on her own.' Or 'on his own.' William James, in his divinely inspired description of each thinker's status-quo situation (one that changes, moment by moment), made the obvious point that we are each our own 'supreme arbiter' of what we will or will not believe. Here is that description:

> The truth must be admitted that thought works under conditions imposed *ab extra*. The great law of habit itself—that twenty experiences make us recall a thing better than one, that long indulgence in error makes right thinking almost impossible—seems to have no essential foundation in reason. The business of thought is with truth—the number of experiences ought to have nothing to do with her hold of it; and she ought by right to be able to hug it all the closer, after years wasted out of its presence. The contrary arrangements seem quite fantastic and arbitrary, but nevertheless are part of the very bone and marrow of our minds. Reason is only one out of a thousand possibilities in the thinking of each of us. Who can count all the silly fancies, the grotesque suppositions, the utterly irrelevant reflections he makes in the course of a day? Who can swear that his prejudices and irrational beliefs constitute a less bulky part of his mental furniture than his clarified opinions? It is true that a presiding arbiter seems to sit aloft in the mind, and emphasize the better suggestions into permanence, while it ends by dropping out and leaving unrecorded the confusion. But this is all the difference. The *mode of genesis* of the worthy and the worthless seems the same. The laws of our actual thinking, of the *cogitatum*, must account alike for the bad and the good materials on which the arbiter has to decide, for wisdom and for folly. The laws of the arbiter, of the *cogitandum*, of what we *ought* to think, are to the

former as the laws of ethics are to those of history. (*Principles of Psychology*, I:552; "ab extra" = "from outside")

" . . . a presiding arbiter seems to sit aloft . . ." No one knows anything that she or he has not personally learned and not forgotten, and no one can believe something she or he does not know. (Or *think* she or he knows.) But above all, each of us is our own presiding arbiter, our own 'judge and jury of one,' regarding what we do or do not believe.

Free will. If there is any law to guide us presiding arbiters, it is the 'law of ethics' that tells us we *ought* to seek the truth. The law of ethics or morality assumes that we are able to freely choose what to believe and what not to believe.

But there have been and still are thinkers—psychologists and philosophers alike—who believe that our 'sense' of freedom regarding what we choose is an illusion. Their view is called "determinism." If they were right, i.e., if their belief were true, it would be impossible for us to learn our belief-options and then to make a decision based on weighing the evidence. It would make it impossible to make any kind of free moral decisions.

Some determinists cite experiments conducted by Benjamin Libet* to argue 'scientifically' that we are flesh-and-blood robots whose brains, like computers, are composed of atoms and molecules that have no more freedom to 'disobey' the laws of physics and chemistry than a computer as a whole has. (*A recent work that explores Libet's research as well as the entire variety of opinions regarding the issues is a 2011 anthology of essays compiled by Bob Doyle. It is entitled *Free Will: The Scandal in Philosophy and How You Can End It*.)

William James wrestled with the issue during his twenties, but finally rejected determinism. In his diary, he wrote, "My first act of free will shall be to believe in free will."

Scientific? Why belabor the obvious fact that each of us is 'on our own' in what we believe? It's because I'm claiming that Jamesian quintalism is not only the true answer to "What is a human being?", but that it is THE scientific answer. One person objected to subtitling this book as THE scientific answer, as if there are other genuinely scientific answers. But what is science? Can an error, a false belief, be scientific? Not according to my belief about what is science. And each of us is on our own in regard to that topic, too. Anyone familiar with *What Is This Thing Called Science?*, by A.F.Chalmers, or with any other book detailing some of the contradictory opinions about the one and only correct meaning of "science," knows that there are so many, many contradictory opinions vis-à-vis "the one and only correct meaning of 'science'," that whoever claims to have the one and only scientific theory about anything must explain what they mean by "science." There are no collective, disembodied, public bodies of knowledge floating around or anchored in a library book, regardless of whether they are named "philosophy," "theology," or "science." However, as explained in *The Wonderful Myth Called 'Science,'* there is a better use for the term "science":

. . ."science" as the name for a disembodied 'thing' is a myth. All knowledge is private knowledge belonging to some individual knower. The degree to which a person's personally acquired knowledge is true and is part of a system of other true beliefs—a system broad enough to account for all the relevant evidence—is the degree to which a person's worldview, philosophy, or belief-system deserves to be called "science," that is, a tapestry of tested and true personal opinions. (p.34)

That is why this text's answer to "What is a human being?" must be assessed within the entire network of tested and true answers to fundamental questions, i.e., within the context of Jamesian quintalism, a rival system that grew out of a critical rethinking of common sense. (See *William James on Common Sense: Foundation for all Higher Learning*, a lengthy presentation of the necessity mentioned by W. Kohler in *Gestalt Psychology*.)

Because you, like me, have your own philosophy or individual worldview or belief-system already, rethinking your common-sense answer to that question requires that you re-view those two pillars of common sense: the naïve-realist view that you have direct access to such material things as bodies and brains, as well as to microscopes, X-ray machines, etc. (a view Einstein called "a plebeian illusion"), and the view that brains actually exist (a view that modern physics has disproven). This text has concentrated on the facts and reasoning that show why those two aspects of common-sense's naïve-realism are false, and why representationalism and modern 'atomism' are true. Others have taken their turn trying to discover "a tapestry of tested and true personal opinions." Now it's your turn.

Still, it is probable that there will be readers who believe 'psychology' is science and that some things believed by contemporary psychologists are relevant facts ignored and possibly inconsistent with what is claimed in this text. Consider just two such facts.

The 'split-brain' phenomenon. The second greatest shock I've had in the last fifty years came when I read an account of Roger Sperry's experiments with patients who, to be delivered from epileptic seizures, submitted to brain surgery that severed the corpus callosum, a thick set of nerve fibers connecting the two halves of their brain. According to the first account that I read, the result was that the patients did obtain relief from their seizures, but also discovered 'that someone else was inhabiting their body'! Inasmuch as each hemisphere of the brain 'controls' the behavior of the opposite side of the body, Sperry's experiments seemed to prove that there were, in effect, two separate brains controlling different parts of the body. As a result, so the account concluded, there were now two persons living in single bodies. (A good account can be found in S.Springer and G.Deutsch's *Left Brain, Right Brain* and C. Sobel's *The Cognitive Sciences*, pp.97-101)

But does anyone believe another human being, with an ability to understand and answer questions, can be created out of nothing as a result of surgery on another person?!

As could be expected, the resulting outpouring of speculations about how to fit the surgery's effects into a coherent theory concerning the nature of the human person led to profound disagreements. For instance, after studying the disagreements, Sobel concluded that recent research plus current theories leave us with a puzzle:

> Unlike the jigsaw puzzles we play with on rainy days, however, this puzzle lacks a correct theoretical framework at the outset, and there are no convenient straight edges to help identify it . . . . The framework one chooses determines how and where one looks for answers. (pp.95-96)

That is the sober fact that you must cling to. *You are on your own* to make up your own mind. And which answers you choose will depend, not on isolated fact-claims*, but on what overall belief-system you make your own. (*As some explainers point out, there have been conflicting descriptions of the subsequent experiments carried out with the help of the split-brain patients.)

Further help is available in Daniel Robinson's *The Mind*, an anthology that has essays by Derek Parfit (who seems to believe the surgery produces three entities, two of which at least are not persons), Grant Gillett (who argues that Parfit has it wrong), and Robinson himself. Springer-Deutsch summarize Robinson's conclusion as follows:

> Philosopher-Psychologist Daniel N. Robinson of Georgetown University argues that issues pertaining to the unity of consciousness are largely unaffected by split-brain data. He reminds us that the issue is older and deeper than contemporary commentators generally acknowledge, and that historical versions of the dispute reveal insights and confusions similar to those now filling the pages of contemporary journals. Much of the confusion has to do with questions of definition—words that have quite different meanings are used interchangeably, leading not only to confusion, but to subtle deceptions. (*Left Brain, Right Brain*, p.335)

In his essay, Robinson put his finger on two of the most important reasons for getting the facts straight about the unity of consciousness *and the unity of the person*. In both moral philosophy and jurisprudence, the identity of a person supposed to have done some action is crucial: "one must establish that the actions in question proceeded from that person's intentions and no other's." Moreover, "the entire history of Judeo-Christian religious teaching is animated by the same theory of individual responsibility, personal identity, and the irreducibility of the unique self." (Robinson, *The Mind*, p.345)

Multiple Personality Disorder. For most readers, the literature on multiple personalities—for instance, stories about Frankenstein, Jekyll and Hyde, Eve (Three Faces of Eve), and Sybil—is more familiar than technical treatises about the results of split-brain surgery. The result is that most people believe there really is such a thing as individual humans having more than one personality. A well-informed discussion of the history and varieties of such cases, of the possible causes, and of the radically different interpretations of the entire subject is Ian Hacking's *Rewriting the Soul*.

Two important questions must be asked about MPD (acronym for Multiple Personality Disorder), also known as DID (Disjunctive Identity Disorder). First is the same problem that Robinson identified in regard to split-brain cases, viz., definitions. Psychologists do not agree on either the definition *or the reality* of personality. Although S. Maddi (see his *Personality Theory*) claims that it is practically insane ("mad" is his word) to deny the reality of personalities, others have a better sense of what is really going on:

> PERSONALITY. Personality is not purple! Nor is it red, yellow, blue, or pink, square, sweet, loud, or hard. It is not an it. Personality is an idea that caught on some time in the history of our language. No one ever saw it, smelled it, tasted it, heard it, or touched it. If someone tries to sell you some at $1.98 per pound, he ought to be locked up. If you buy some, you ought to be! It is not an it—it is an idea that caught on. It caught on because the idea of personality has helped men make sense out of their own behavior and the behavior of people around them. In some respects the concept of personality is like the concept of force in physics or valence in chemistry. In the technical terminology of the philosophy of science these ideas, by definition unobservable, are called hypothetical constructs. These constructs—like force, valence, gravity, personality—help us make sense out of our world. They help us understand the myriads of events constantly occurring about us. These constructs enable us to bring some order and simplicity to the fantastic complexity the environment constantly presents to our millions upon millions of sense receptors. (M. Doherty & K. Shemberg, *Asking Questions About Behavior: An Introduction to What Psychologists Do*, p.7)

The issue of hypothetical constructs or pragmatic fictions should be far better known than it is at present. A convenient introduction to the subject can be found in *Logical Fictions*, also published by iUniverse.

Mental illness in general. Human beings, endowed with minds and a rich array of emotions, should be viewed as almost infinitely complex. We are not fleshy robots, as materialists seem to think. How mysterious we are soon becomes apparent for anyone who reads the almost endless stories of unusual human experiences. The more one becomes familiar with those almost endless stories of unusual *and extremely varied* experiences, the more cautious one should become when confronted with attempts to categorize people.

For instance, at first all of us think in terms of very simple categories. The simplest of all in the present context is "sane" and "crazy." However, in modern times, specialists entrusted with the task of helping 'crazy' people become 'sane' have found it convenient to invent ever-more-detailed categories of 'crazy' or mentally ill people. Those categories have been collected and published in a series of books named *The Diagnostic and Statistical Manual* or

DSM. Over the years, there have been several editions of the DSM. DSM-IV listed 410 mental disorders. The DSM-II listed 145 disorders, up from the original, 1952 edition's list of only 60 categories. Sixty to one hundred forty-five to over four hundred. The increase raises a very simple question: do the new categories indicate really brand new kinds of mental disorders, or were those disorders simply undiagnosed until recently? Opinions differ.

Opinions differ about everything. Recent research into using chemicals (drugs) to treat mental disorders has convinced many that 'mental' disorders are actually 'brain' disorders. Many psychologists embrace the idea that mental-illness classifications* should be viewed—in many cases, at least—not as indicators of invisible, underlying illnesses, but as acquired patterns of visible behavior that can be remedied by behavioral and/or cognitive-behavioral therapy. In an effort to force attention away from unprovable speculation to the realm of the immediately observable, Thomas Szasz wrote a widely-read book, *The Myth of Mental Illness*. As for the present diversity of opinions, a thorough, accurate, and even-handed treatment of the issues at stake is *The Perspectives of Psychiatry*, by P.McHugh and P.Slavery. (*In 1988, a rival to the DSMs was published: *Behavioral Assessment: A Practical Handbook*. It had a third edition.)

To understand how difficult, really impossible, it is to fully grasp the mystery of the human mind, ponder this question: "Is alcoholism a disease or illness, or is it a matter of strong habit or addiction?" First, what is an alcoholic? A drunkard? Someone who presently drinks too much alcohol on a regular basis? Someone who rarely drinks to excess, but who cannot consume even one alcoholic drink without losing control and drinking to excess? Suppose a person who, in the past, drank too much alcohol on a regular basis but who, after a long time in AA, has not touched alcohol for years: is such a person still an alcoholic, but for now a 'recovered alcoholic'? Who is and who isn't an alcoholic?

If it is a disease, as so many were taught to believe, what does 'disease' mean in this case? If there are no viruses (a cold), no bacteria (tuberculosis), and no uncontrolled cell growths (cancer) involved, what would this 'disease' consist of?

And if it is a strong habit or addiction, who can tell what that means? We use "habit" as the name for various repeated behaviors that were not present at birth. Is a habit anything more than a shorthand way of referring to those behaviors? Wouldn't that mean that someone who goes to sleep and is not exercising any of those behaviors loses the habit during that period of time? If people who are totally asleep still do possess all their habits, what is it that they possess? Behaviorists, confronted with this question, latched onto the term "disposition." But if sleeping persons have a disposition, Just what is *it* that they have?

A caution. Never ignore the truth that "Truth is stranger than fiction." The December, 2000, issue of the *Atlantic Monthly* carried an article entitled "A New Way to be Mad." The author reported on apotemnophilia (or BIID, Body Integrity Identity Disorder), a disorder that led two individuals to have their perfectly healthy legs amputated. Both claimed that they were "much happier" after having their legs cut off. Yet the psychiatrists who examined the men declared them "competent." Competent?

In a March 25, 1997, the *New York Times* reported on Hearing Voices Network, a group of persons who traditionally would have been diagnosed as schizophrenics, but who argue that they are not mentally ill because they are able to fit their voices into their otherwise normal lives. Normal?

More than one psychiatrist has noted that we all have a touch of abnormality or insanity. What, then, is the absolute baseline for being 'norm-al'? A study of statistics will furnish the answer.

A recommendation. Make friends with William James, easily the greatest student of the human psyche that this country or any other country ever produced. At the end of Chapter X of his 1890 *Principles of Psychology*, William James described the phenomena we now call "abnormal psychology." Then in 1896, he delivered a series of lectures on the subject. He never published those lectures, but they were skillfully reconstructed from James' notes by Eugene Taylor. Charles Scribner's Sons published Taylor's reconstruction in 1983 under the title, *Exceptional Mental States*. James' own exceptional mind is evident immediately when we read this statement from his first lecture: "Sleep would be a dreadful disease except for its familiarity"! (Taylor, p.15)

A recent three-volume presentation of James' philosophy* explains what James thought, but also shows how to correct some of the missteps that are partly the reason why his psychology, though often praised, is rarely studied and insufficiently appreciated in this new millennium. (*James on common sense, on the stream of consciousness, and on morality.)

A conclusion. The purpose of this addition to Chapter X is to emphasize that the key question is "What kind of being am I?", a question that can be generalized as "What kind of being is a human being?" (Unless you are a reincarnated butterfly!) *Not all of the split-brain research or exceptional mental states can obviate the need for answering that key question,* or the need to incorporate in that answer all of those modern discoveries we often refer to collectively as "modern science."

If there is a bottom line to this entire text, that's it.

EPILOGUE

Do you make any difference to the universe? Somerset Maugham wrote of himself that "It would have made small difference to the universe if I had never existed." Was he right? In other words, does any of us humans matter? Does any of us make a contribution to world-history?

The Christian view is that each and every individual person has more value than the whole animal kingdom and all of the physical universe. Each one of us has a unique contribution to make to world-history. William James concurred. He believed that what we contribute begins with our free-will decisions and their effects, even if all of those effects are created by God in consequence of our decisions.

Take for example the long history of 'the human search for truth.' Of course, the only reality or realities to which that phrase refers are the plural searches for truth conducted by individual humans. Each and every one of us must take responsibility for our own decisions about truth, decisions that will affect the lives of other humans. James discussed the search for truth in his most famous lecture, "The Will to Believe." He wrote that lecture in response to "The Ethics of Belief," by William Clifford.

Clifford used his essay to prove what can be called "Clifford's Commandment." He declared that "It is wrong always, everywhere, and for everyone, to believe anything upon insufficient evidence." Though James severely qualified Clifford's view, he began his response by largely agreeing with it:

> [. . .] When one turns to the magnificent edifice of the physical sciences, and sees how it was reared; what thousands of disinterested moral lives of men lie buried in its mere foundations; what patience and postponement, what choking down of preference, what submission to the icy laws of outer fact are wrought into its very stones and mortar; how absolutely impersonal it stands in its vast augustness,—then how besotted and contemptible seems every little sentimentalist who comes blowing his voluntary smoke-wreaths and pretending to decide things from out of his private dream! (*The Will to Believe*, p.7)

249

The ethics of belief is nothing less than the Golden Rule. If we want others, viz., our neighbors, to pass on to us truth rather than error, we in our turn must pass on to others truth rather than error. But we can, unfortunately, pass on error rather than truth. As Clifford observed,

> It is not only the leader of men, statesman, philosopher, or poet, that owes this bounden duty to mankind. Every rustic who delivers in the village alehouse his slow, infrequent sentences, may help to kill or keep alive the fatal superstitions which clog his race. Every hard-worked wife of an artisan may transmit to her children beliefs which shall knit society together, or rend it in pieces. No simplicity of mind, no obscurity of station, can escape the universal duty of questioning all that we believe. (W.Clifford, in *The Ethics of Belief Debate*, ed., G. McCarthy, p.22)

And we can't pass on the truth if we don't learn the truth!

What logically follows from that? Just this. Whatever your present habits of thought, you have not only the ability to change your mind. You have the *moral obligation* to reexamine your present thought-habits to see which of them may be false, which of them you *ought* to change your mind about. That will be hard. James, great psychologist that he was, explained why in the passage cited in Chapter X-b, the passage that ends with this:

> The *mode of genesis* of the worthy and the worthless seems the same. The laws of our actual thinking, of the *cogitatum*, must account alike for the bad and the good materials on which the arbiter has to decide, for wisdom and for folly. The laws of the arbiter, of the *cogitandum*, of what we *ought* to think, are to the former as the laws of ethics are to those of history. (*Principles of Psychology*, I:552)

Repeat: If you suspect that any of your previous beliefs have been mistaken, you have not only the ability but the obligation to change your mind. The laws of what you *ought* to believe are to the laws of what you *have been thinking* till now (the laws of history) are 'the laws of ethics.'

Reexamining your present beliefs and being open-minded to new ones, so that you can pass on truth, will take effort. James ended his chapter on "The Will" with the following reflection:

> I must say one word about the extraordinarily intimate and important character which the phenomenon of effort assumes in our own eyes as individual men. Of course we measure ourselves by many standards. Our strength and our intelligence, our wealth and even our good luck, are things which warm our heart and make us feel

ourselves a match for life. But deeper than all such things, and able to suffice unto itself without them, is the sense of the amount of effort which we can put forth. Those are, after all, but effects, products, and reflections of the outer world within. But the effort seems to belong to an altogether different realm, as if it were the substantive thing which we *are*, and those were but externals which we *carry*. If the 'searching of our heart and reins' be the purpose of this human drama, then what is sought seems to be what effort we can make. He who can make none is but a shadow; he who can make much is a hero . . .

Thus not only our morality, but our religion, so far as the latter is deliberate, depend on the effort which we can make. "Will you or won't you have it so?" is the most probing question we are ever asked; we are asked it every hour of the day, and about the largest as well as the smallest, the most theoretical as well as the most practical, things. We answer by consents or non-consents and not by words. What wonder that these dumb responses should seem our deepest organs of communication with the nature of things! What wonder if the effort demanded by them be the measure of our worth as men! What wonder if the amount which we accord of it be the one strictly underived and original contribution which we can make to the world! (*Principles of Psychology* V.II, pp.578-79)

What better way to end this work as well?

APPENDIX A

Common-Sense Concept(s) of Change

The Neo-Thomist Analysis

A. The Generic Concept

Preface 1. According to Bertrand Russell, Einstein, and your author, "Naïve realism leads to physics which shows that naïve realism is false."

Preface 2. There are two things to know. First, if Aristotle or St. Thomas were asked, "What exists?", the answer would be unequivocal. There are substances and accidents. Substances are things that can exist in themselves, whereas accidents are things unable to exist on their own. A rock is a substance. Its color, shape, and size are accidents. You can find an introduction to this common-sense view in Aristotle's *Categories* and his *Metaphysics*. The second thing to know is that the substance-things we experience with our senses change.

One of the most noticeable things about the world as we ordinarily think about it is the fact that things change. There is a tremendous difference between (i) the painting of a landscape, which—no matter how vivid it may be—is yet in reality perfectly still and unchanging, and (ii) the actual landscape, filled with living creatures, whose appearance alters from season to season. The world is in no way a wax museum piece, but is constituted by things in continual flux. Seasons change, the weather changes, objects move or are moved from place to place, living things are born, grow and die, etc.

A three-part concept. All of these changes differ from one another in some way. But is there anything common to them? Is there any abstract, general idea or pattern of "change"?

There is. And this general idea seems to be constituted of three distinct points or elements, the subject that undergoes the change, the state before the change, and the state afterwards.

First, the subject of the change. To begin with, there must be some thing that changes, or, as it is sometimes expressed, there must be something that perdures (continues to exist) throughout the process of change.

This is what differentiates change from mere removal-followed-by-substitution. For instance, if a lamp is sitting on a desk and someone, after removing it, replaces it with an ash-tray, we would not say that the lamp changed into the ash-tray. Not even if, like a magician, the person carried out the substitution too fast for the eye to detect it. (Even though there is no transformation of the lamp into an ash-tray involved here, there are some changes obviously occurring, viz., transfer of things from place to place.)

The perdurance of something common that is the subject of the change also serves to distinguish change from annihilation-followed-by-creation. For instance, imagine that suddenly the lamp was actually annihilated, and that—without any lapse of time—there was created an ash-tray in the very place left vacant by the annihilated lamp. It would be impossible to verify whether the lamp had changed miraculously into the ash-tray or whether there had actually been annihilation-creation, but the situations are nevertheless quite different. To have change, then, there must be something that perdures. We say that the match is changed into the smoke and ashes, not that it is annihilated and the smoke and ashes created in its place. This something that perdures is also referred to as a "substratum" ("what lies beneath" viz. beneath the change) and as "subject" of the process of change.

Now, the two states. These are two other parts to our general concept of change. There must be two distinct states in which the subject or substratum is found: (i) the initial state which ceases to be and (ii) the final state which comes to be. (There may be other intermediate states as well.)

For instance, the leaves change in autumn. The leaves themselves are the something-which-changes, the initial state in which the leaves are found is that of being small and green-colored, and the final state in which they are found is that of being large and golden—or red-colored, etc. When a lump of clay is fashioned into a statue, the clay is the substratum or the something-which-changes, the initial state is the lump-shape and the final state is the statue-shape. If the leaves were initially small and green and even in October were small and green, we would deny that there has been any change. (At least with respect to the size—and color-states.) Or if the lump of clay remained a lump, we would deny that there has been any change. (At least with respect to that state; its temperature might have changed.)

B. Three Species of Change

The species of change-concepts. There are at least three specifically different ways in which we think of change, and they are quite different.

254

Type #1: Accidental change. This is a type in which there is a modification of some substance ("thing" in the strong sense) which nevertheless retains its own identity and perdures—remains the same numerically—throughout the process of change or modification.

Examples of this would be: when the leaves on the tree grow in size during the summer, when a woman dyes her hair from black to blond, when a lamp is moved from one place to another, etc.

It is customary to distinguish those three types of accidental change. The first of these is sometimes referred to as "*augmentation*," which means the thing's size changes. The second example is referred to as "*alteration*" in a strict sense, since it means that the thing is altered with respect of one of its qualities. And the final example is called "*locomotion*," which merely means "change in place or location."

The examples all have this in common: the thing that changes is the substance, and the substance retains its essential self-identity throughout the change. You have leaves early in the summer, you have the identical leaves at the end. You have hair at the beginning and the numerically same hair at the end. You have a lamp at the beginning and a lamp at the end, just as you also have an ashtray at the beginning and an ashtray at the end. What has changed—to speak loosely—are the accidents or properties or characteristics, what neo-Thomists call the "accidental forms."

Type #2: Substantial change. This is a much more radical conception of change. It occurs whenever some substance changes into another substance, when the first substance perishes and a quite different one comes to be. We ordinarily believe that this is what occurs—though today's atomic physics raises questions—when something living dies and a corpse begins to exist (the living thing ceases to exist when it changes into a corpse), or when a house is destroyed by fire and turns into smoke, gases and ashes, or when food is eaten by something alive and becomes flesh and waste products.

Here, the states that succeed one another are much more fundamental. In a sense, they are not states so much as the very core of what exists before the change and what exists afterwards. They are the very essence of the first substance, and the very essence of the new one.

The best way to understand the neo-Thomist theory is to think of each change'able substance from two angles. First, each thing is *actually* something definite at the present moment. It is a human. Or a chicken. Or a tree. Second, however, it is *potentially* the other things it can become. The actuality is attributable to its substantial form. The potentiality is attributable to what is called "matter," "primary matter," and "potency." Because neither can exist apart from the other, they are called "substantial principles" rather than "substances."

For instance, in a substantial change, there is the form of the thing that exists prior to the change: the "living-human-being-ness" or the "chickenness" or the "treeness" of the living thing that dies, and the form of the thing that comes to be after the change: the "corpseness" or "macnuggetsness" or "woodness." The concept of substantial change is much more radical than the idea of accidental change.

Substantial change involves both of the substantial *principles*, primary matter and substantial form.

(a) 'Primary matter' as the substratum. What is the substratum of substantial change, i.e., the change of one substance into another? In the earlier, accidental type of change, it was the substance itself that was the substratum. Now, however, the initial substance perishes and a new one is generated from it. This poses a problem.

In Aristotle's day, it was believed that there are four basic chemicals or kinds of matter, viz., air, earth, fire, and water, which in a sense are the substrata of substantial change. But Aristotle also noted that these four themselves, though they exist as such, can change into one another; so that water becomes air (evaporates), fire becomes earth, etc. Today's physicists claim that all of the chemical elements can be changed into one another by long arduous steps, as when they are changed in the heart of the stars, where, for instance, hydrogen is transformed into helium.

What is the substratum of substantial changes? Because he did not really believe the elements existed actually, only *virtually*, Aristotle invented the idea of "primary matter" to serve as the substratum in substantial change. "Primary matter" is merely a name for something which is not perceivable, something that can be recognized only by the intellect which posits that *there must be some reality present as a substratum*, otherwise there will not be change, but only annihilation-and-creation. And, to the Greeks, annihilation and creation were simply inconceivable.

This primary matter is only a *principle* and cannot exist by itself, it has no determinate properties of its own, it is merely an otherwise-nameless reality whose existence is reasoned to by the intellect in order to provide something that will be the perduring substratum of substantial change.

(b) The second *principle* is 'substantial form,' that which constitutes the distinctive essence or nature of the thing in question. (We will pass over other complexities, e.g., the notion of privation, the notion that matter is part of the essence, etc.) The easiest way to speak of the substantial form of anything is to ask yourself the question "What is this thing most properly?", then to take the answer and add to it the suffix "ness." That will give you the name of the object's substantial form. The substantial form of the object you are reading at this moment is "paperness."

We can sum up this description of the 'substantial change' concept by saying that a substantial change occurs when one substance perishes and a new one is generated from it, i.e., when a substance loses its substantial form, and the primary matter which had been united with the substantial form acquires a new substantial form, so that the primary matter and the new substantial form together constitute the generated substance. (The new form emerges from the matter, the old one reverts back to it.)

Today, some people believe that the chemical elements are substances and remain through the process of material changes. For instance, if hydrogen sulfide (H2S) is burned (i.e., oxidized), the substances produced are sulphur dioxide and water (SO2 and H2O). Chemists may tell you that the hydrogen, sulphur, and oxygen constitute the substratum (substrata) of the change. They have perdured throughout the process. If this more recent picture is correct, what appear to be changes of one material substance into another are really instances of the third type of change, mixing and unmixing. (The internet has several sites that distinguish chemical from physical changes. Question: which, if either of them, is a substantial change? Or is the Neo-Thomist, Aristotelian theory simply out-of-date naïve realism? Yes, the last; not even hydrogen, water, exist.)

Type #3: Mixing and unmixing. Or, combining and separating. Whether this third type of change should be reduced to the first, that is, to accidental changes (of location and/or relations) is a disputed question.

This concept of change is often used to describe what happens when aggregates or artifacts with visible parts, each of which are substances, are assembled or disassembled, that is, when many natural substances are combined to form some whole or when that whole is reduced to the natural substances which constituted it. Examples will make the meaning clear. (Or at least clearer!) The workers at General Motors stand in the assembly line, each doing their own thing. What goes into the factory are thousands and thousands of individual substances, like motor blocks, pistons, axles, nuts, bolts, etc. What emerges from the factory are assembled cars. And yet, the only real change that occurs, according to many, are rearrangements of the original substances: changes in their spatial relationships to one another. The original substances (motor blocks, pistons, etc.) are not changed at all. Thus, what we refer to as a car is actually many substances. Each of them wears out individually, and each can be pulled out and replaced by some new substitute. (Think of the carburetor wearing out, or the spark plugs, or the fan belt . . . .) Each retains its own substantial form, so that, for instance, the substantial form of the tire is rubber-ness, that of each bolt is metal-ness, and so forth. There are as many substances, and therefore as many substantial forms as there are original substances. This type of change, where the original substances retain their individuality, can be termed "mixing." Disassembly of the car is "unmixing."

Other thinkers maintain, however, that when the individual substances are assembled into a car, there is generated—in addition to the many individual substantial forms—an overall "accidental" form, namely, of "car-ness."

How are these different types of change related to one another? Without making some radical decisions in one's grand unifying theory, this is a difficult question to answer. The following points might help to explain why.

C. Some Corollaries.

(a) Perhaps one of the most crucial notions is that of "one single substance." QU: When can you be certain that you are thinking of a truly substantial change? AN: When there is one substance before the substantial change occurs, but a new and essentially different one afterwards, then the type of change that occurs is a substantial change. Many feel that those things which we call "distinct things" in everyday life are to be identified as substances, i.e., trees, people, animals, trees, etc. Thus, when a tree is cut down, or when a match burns, or when a house is built, there is a substantial change. Others maintain that this answer does not take sufficient account of the complexities involved in answering the question, "When do we have a single substance?"

(b) Some maintain that what is a single substance at one level is really several substances at another level of analysis. For instance, a tree is a single substance at one level, but at a lower level it is several, namely, several cells; and each single cell is, in its turn, several substances at a lower level, namely, several molecules; and each molecule, in turn, is several atoms, etc. Similarly, with a watch. If the watch is a single substance, so also is each part, and maybe each subatomic particle of each atom. If so, then in a watch, there are several substantial forms, with different degrees or levels of being (reality). Thus, also, the disassembling of a watch does and does not involve substantial change: at the level of the watch itself, it would be substantial change, though at the level of the pieces, it is only accidental change (see "unmixing" above). Cfr. A. van Melsen, "What are the Individual Substances in Matter?", in H. Koran, *Readings in the Philosophy of Nature*.

(c) Others maintain that a distinction must be made between natural and artificial substances. Substances produced by nature are natural (trees, animals, persons, rocks, etc.), whereas those produced by humans are artificial (watches, chairs, beds). The forms of natural substances are true substantial forms, whereas the forms of artifacts are somewhere between substantial forms and ordinary accidental forms, that is, they are quasi-accidental forms. Each ordinary (or natural!) accidental form inheres in a single substance whereas the quasi-accidental form of an artifact inheres in what are several distinct substances.

(d) Others maintain that only the lowest level substances are true substances, though the exact nature of the lowest level substances is difficult to determine. Scientists are continually discovering new subatomic particles. According to this hypothesis, only the ultimate subatomic particles have the right to be called substances. This means that all other supposedly higher-level substances are actually not single substances but only many distinct ones. According to this view, most changes are mixing and unmixing.

(e) Modern physics, therefore, challenges our common-sense notions regarding the nature of material things and of the changes that they undergo. A reading of any popular book on modern physics will illustrate this fact: see, for instance, *The Restless Universe*, by Max Born, chapter one. What are we to make of the claim that mass and energy are interchangeable, or that they are different forms of a more ultimate underlying, nameless stuff, or that solid, inert objects like tables or chairs are not at all solid and inert, etc.? The subject is a large and difficult one.

(f) Genuinely critical thinkers will not be deceived. No matter what positions one takes on the issues discussed here, everyone ultimately argues in a circle. Why? Because one's most fundamental premises will be found to be part of one's individually chosen grand unifying system, mostly *tacit* except in the case of those who are genuinely critical thinkers! (There's a circular argument for you.) 8-15-72

(g) The Spring, 2009 issue of the ACPQ (American Catholic Philosophical Quarterly) carried a book review entitled "In the Twilight of Neothomism a Call for a New Beginning." Neothomism is indispensable for understanding the ontology of our original common-sense philosophy. Genuine new beginning will require a recognition that modern physics and physiology have, in the words of Russell, shown that common sense's naïve realism is false. *The Wonderful Myth Called 'Science'* explains why in great detail. Once more, the myth is the 'collective body of public knowledge.' The discoveries of Galileo, Descartes, Newton, et al, are what make it truly wonder-full.

APPENDIX B

Meaning vs Concepts

[This appendix is particularly important for two reasons. First, because it goes to the very root of Neo-Thomistic epistemology, and the inevitable suspicion that this book commits the horrific error called "nominalism." However, most thinkers ignore the distinctions between Hobbes' nominalism, Berkeley's imagism, and Kant's conceptualism. What's more, Neo-Thomists who use the term, "nominalism," generally believe in *ideas and/or concepts, which they interpret as some kind of forms.*' Thus, their adage, "The form in the mind is the same as the form in the (known) thing." That adage builds on the ancient theory which assumes that the elements of thought are distinct ideas or concepts. That ancient theory continues to have unwarranted influence, a fact clear from even a few minutes spent browsing *Concepts: Core Readings* (MIT, 1999), a 649-page collection of what Steven Pinker describes as "all the great papers on concepts."

Second, because it, this appendix, can serve as a transition from the 'concept' approach to William James's momentous and largely unrecognized *true* description of thought as continuous, partless meaning. What follows is an early, slightly-revised attempt to describe a way to realize that the unit of knowledge is not distinct ideas or concepts, but rather *the undivided MEANING of all the words* in whole sentences (propositions), paragraphs, chapters, etc. Much fuller accounts can be found in other works, especially in Chapter III of *William James on the Stream of Consciousness.*]

CHAPTER SIX. MEANING

Perhaps more than any other chapter in this book [an early effort, never published!], the present one will demand your utmost concentration. The reason is this: there is no more subtle aspect of your consciousness—precisely because of its utter "transparency"—than the aspect that I intend to point out to you now.

More than any other, this aspect of your consciousness is personal and private. Two people can hear the same noises or see the same ciphers (i.e. they can listen to the same words or they can read the same writing), but the meaning that each gets from those words will be the same or different, depending upon their particular backgrounds (all their previous habits of association and distinction), depending on their particular powers of insight, depending on their particular degree of actual attention. Yet, even if the meaning that each gets out of what is heard in common or read in common is almost identical in a particular situation, the thought of each is utterly personal.

For, someone else may have the ability to do the same thing you are doing now (i.e. think while you read); he or she may be able to think the same thoughts; but your thought is yours and the other's would be the other's. You will never get a direct look at someone else's thought, nor will they ever get a direct look at yours. If you like, you can conceal your thought, or you can say things that will cause the other to think exactly the opposite of what you are thinking.

The most usual method of communication between two human beings is via the medium of sounds or visual "signs." There are, of course, other methods of communication that can be quite effective; blind people, for instance, rely very much on the sense of touch at their fingertips.

But you notice an ambiguity already: I have spoken of consciousness, meaning and thought, but I have given no indications as to how I conceive their precise relationships. Allow me to say that the meaning I attach to these words can be gathered only from this book as a whole. The important thing for a proper understanding of "knowing" is the ability to distinguish which meaning is behind the use of any of these words in any particular context by any author whatever. Once this is had, there is no need to restrict any word to the way one particular person uses it. None of us has the authority to impose our preferred meaning on a term and to forbid anyone else to use that term differently. Therefore, you might say that my aim is to give you an insight into these realities, not to give you definitions of them.

Thought is present to you now. This chapter is based on the assumption that you have no further to look, in your pursuit of a clear understanding of thought, than your own present consciousness. As you look at each successive line of print and read, you are thinking. You can look on this chapter as a map designed to help you "locate" that thought within your consciousness.

I. TWO IDEA-or-CONCEPT APPROACHES

Plan. We will proceed by way of contrast. I will contrast two types of approach, a static type (two examples) used to introduce students to the concept or idea of ideas and concepts, and a dynamic one that, it is hoped, will introduce the concept or idea of thought that is above and distinct from sense-data and memory-images. Since one of the important things is to notice the ambiguity of all terminology that deals with these matters, it is only fair to admit that the contrast of the two types of approach discussed here as "static" and "dynamic" is also ambiguous. The main purpose of this description is pragmatic, as you will see.

This chapter presupposes the previous chapter concerning the type of contact involved in sense-perception, as well as the chapter on habits of association and distinction. I will now give you two outlines, one on how you could reach a particular idea and one on what a generalized idea is. But these are not outlines to help you understand how you could reach a particular idea beginning from when you were a child, but how you can reach it here-and-now. Your habits of association are now presumed. This will not talk about the genesis of any of your ideas, but solely about the "reactivation" of an idea you already have had many, many times in the past.

First Approach. First, try to consider in detail the various ways you could arrive at an idea of this particular book at this particular moment.

1.Imagine that someone, holding something behind his or her back, had walked into the room where you are seated, had asked you to close your eyes, then had placed something (this book) into your hands and asked you to guess what it was. You would run your hands over he surface of the object, would "weigh" it, would shake it to see if it had any "moving parts", etc. But it would take you only a moment to know that it was a book. And you would be so certain of this that it would be a shock to you if you opened your eyes and found that it was not a book.

2.Suppose you were in the same situation, but that instead of placing the book in your hands, the person ruffled the pages near your ear. It would still be easy for you to identify the object as a book.

3.Suppose they described it as "something rectangular-shaped, about eight inches long, about five wide, and about three-quarters of an inch thick, made of sheets of paper placed on top of each other in a neat pile, bound together at one edge with thread and glue, and all of them written on." Again, a moment's reflection, with so many clues, and you would be able to guess that they were speaking of a book.

4.Suppose the book were a gift, all wrapped up with tissue-paper and a bow, and you were shown the gift and asked to guess what it was. The shape and size of the wrapped gift which you were shown would give you a good lead, and perhaps only two or three guesses would be enough for you to identify it.

5.Suppose that, after having unwrapped the gift, you made a remark such as "Thank you, I have been wanting to read this ever since I saw the reviews of it." And suppose someone in the next room overheard that remark. If you asked them to guess what you had received as a gift, they would probably have little difficulty in concluding that it was a book.

If you wish to analyze your own particular idea of this particular book, you will have to take into account every element mentioned in those five paragraphs, for the particular idea is connected with a tactile perception, a noise, a series of noises (description), a visual perception, and with other ideas such as "read" and "review" (though these could be looked on as noises also). Any single one of these clues would be sufficient to lead you to the same idea: the idea of this particular book.

Second approach. The purpose of this is to enable you to examine a generalized idea of a class of objects: a generalized idea of a "book." (Generalized ideas were called "universal concepts.") Take the particular idea of this particular book that you have now and see if this same idea can be extended to other objects "essentially" similar to it. If not, see if you need a different idea for the "class." You can do this by asking what particular features must be present before an object qualifies as a "book".

1. Color: if you examined your idea of "book-in-general", you would see that it has no particular color to it. You could see a book that was red and one that was green and yet both would be "books" to you. In fact, reflecting on distinctions made in the second chapter, you can say that, as long as a book has at least *some* light-reflecting properties, it would qualify as having the necessary color.

2. Paper: neither does a book have to have a particular kind of paper in order to fit under the definition of a book: parchment, cloth-fiber, wood-pulp, all of them will satisfy the minimum basic requirements.

3. Size: the size is also a variable when it comes to defining the general idea of book. An object could be so large that only Paul Bunyon could open and read it, but it could still fit the idea of "book-in-general."

4. Contents: another variable. Notebooks which are new and as yet unwritten-in have as much right to be called books as encyclopedias.

5. Covers: not even covers or bindings can be pinned down too definitely. A paperback is a book the same way that a hardcover is. (But, e-books?)

Yet, for all its generality, your idea of book-in-general is so definite that it does not overlap at all with your idea of a cat.

Concluding considerations. In accord with this second static approach, you can now try to examine your present idea of book-in-general in order to see what sort of thing an idea is. However you decide to define "idea," your definition must take account of the above facts, otherwise it will be deficient to the degree that it ignores or brushes aside any of them as "unimportant." The trouble with most definitions of "concept" is precisely this: not so much that they are mistaken in what they affirm, but because they tend to ignore half of reality. Actual errors do result when the unexplained half is forced into a definition that cannot contain it. It is the old problem of Procrustes all over again.

Above all, in comparing the first idea of a particular book with the second idea of book-in-general, there must be a theory that covers both of them equally well. As a test for your theory, try to apply it to the following sentence: "This book and every other book in the world are identical insofar as each of them is a book." The idea of book was used in that sentence three times. The sentence makes sense. How many concepts of "book" would you say you used as you read it? One concept that fits all three uses of the word? Three separate concepts? Two concepts, one of a particular book and one of the class "book"? Can you, by your introspection, be certain which of those answers is correct, or does your answer depend to a great extent on the results that might follow if you admitted any answer different from your usual one? Any theory that cannot face the test of a concrete application such as this and clearly explain it without abstracting from any of the pertinent facts, can make no claim to being an adequate theory of "thought." No one who denies that any of the pertinent facts is truly relevant out of fear of the possible repercussions to his or her "system" can claim to have a valid system for understanding thought.

II. DYNAMIC or MEANING APPROACH

I suggest that none of the existing systematic theories of "thought" gives the entire picture. The reason is not that they are false in what they affirm, but because they are too restrictive to be able to account for all the pertinent data. I further suggest that, until the ambiguity that attaches to every definition thus far offered by philosophers is fully recognized, agreement re epistemology will never be reached.

The present approach to the "idea" of an "idea," then, will not aim at giving any hard-and-fast definitions. Rather, my aim is to aid you in noticing what is going on in your consciousness right now, so that you will then be able to recognize the degree of truth contained in all the various definitions and theories of thought thus far to be found. (Throughout here, such words as "thought", "concept" and "idea" are being used interchangeably: the meaning depends on the context.)

NOW, NOTICE WHAT YOU HAVE BEEN DOING SINCE YOU BEGAN THIS CHAPTER! NOTICE WHAT YOU ARE DOING RIGHT NOW! You have been and are . . . . seeing, and associating, and imagining, and . . .

. . . and **THINKING**.

Reflect on the following facts:

    1.Leaving out of consideration all the distractions you may have experienced, during all the time you have been sitting here reading this chapter, you have been relying on ONE KIND OF SENSE-PERCEPTION: THAT OF EYESIGHT. You have been adjusting the muscles of your eyes so that the color-patterns caused by reflected light-energy focused and projected onto your retinas would be continually shifting across the areas of those retinas. Put into ordinary, but not-strictly-scientific terms, you have been "running your eyes along" the lines of print contained on these pages.

    2.By reason of the infinitely complex habits of association which you have built up over the period of many, many years, the following phenomenon took place: as you ran your eyes along those lines of print, a certain MEANING has been automatically, unconsciously, effortlessly, spontaneously, and naturally evoked in your consciousness. During all the time you tried to concentrate your attention on the various ways in which you could find out that this book IS a book, and then on the basic requirements of an idea of book-in-general . . . , during all that time you were not paying attention to noises made by this book, no one came into the room to ask you to guess what they had in their hands, you did not ask anyone in the next room what you had gotten as a gift, nor have you been sitting here just musing to yourself. Rather, you have been sitting here INTERPRETING the black-marks that are located within a certain rectangular-shaped white-color-pattern which is caused by the light reflecting from this page of the book you are holding in your hands. You have been interpreting symbols. You have been seeing, and associating, and imagining, and . . .

. . . and **THINKING**.

    3.In fact, whether you noticed it or not, you have had many, many, many thoughts, far more than simply two ideas or thoughts, "this particular book" and "book-in-general." Return to the beginning of this chapter and look at all the different words you have looked at and understood. Notice that you can just as truly be said to have an idea that corresponds to each of those words (sets of ciphers) as you can be said to have an idea that corresponds to manyofthemtakentogether. What sense, for instance, could you get out of the following words: "perhaps than other in book present will your concentration"? That 'sentence' is made up of every other word of the first sentence in this chapter.

    What you *see* here is purely "raw material" for thought. Notice how essential *every* bit of this raw material is for your thought. Even a single letter can change the entire sense of a long sentence. The introductory sentence of this section of a "dynamic approach" would have been entirely changed if it had been written: "I suggest that _one of the existing systematic theories

266

of thought gives the entire picture." You can close your eyes and have merely the "imaginary words" corresponding to those written ciphers running through your imagination; and the same "mental" addition or omission of that single "N" will change your entire thought. This leads to many questions. Can thought possibly by only an image? Or can a theory of thought possibly leave out of account the image if you extend the meaning of "image" to take in "imagined words"? And what, then, is the image? Take the two thoughts: "none of the existing theories is sufficient" and "one of the existing theories is sufficient," and compare the images which correspond to those two thoughts. What is the nature of the images that can be so nearly identical and yet serve as underpinnings for such totally diverse thoughts?

4. Notice further that you did not have a definition of "idea" in order to understand the ideas I was trying to convey in this chapter. Nowhere thus far has there been given a definition of what I mean by idea or thought, yet I dare say that the meaning of that word in any particular context was clear enough that you did not need to have it defined beforehand. If it were necessary to define "thought" before you can use the word, then why do we not have to define beforehand EVERY word that we use? But this would be impossible, for we would have to use words to define words and it would end up in a vicious circle. The trouble with definitions is not that they are useless, but that too often, once they have been laid down, it is taken for granted that the word as defined can be henceforth used without ambiguity. Any such idea is naïve. A definition is a generalized expression that sums up a lot of detailed explanation. The value of the definition will never be greater than the accuracy and practical applicability of the detailed explanation on which it is based.

5. Notice further, that you will never, so long as you live, catch up with an actual thought. By "catch up with," I mean "by *direct* reflection and introspection." It is essential to take a dynamic approach. Analyze what you have been doing since you began this chapter. But even more, analyze what you have been doing since you began this paragraph. *Analyze what you are doing right now as you read THIS word and now THIS word.* Or take any single sentence from this chapter and analyze it. Analyze the meaning of "analyze the meaning of." YOU CANNOT CATCH UP WITH THOUGHT. For, every moment you begin to analyze a thought, it is already a past thought, even a split-second-old thought. And you are using—understanding—a new thought to analyze it. You are using—understanding—a new thought by which to analyze the old one. Your present thought (the meaning of the words you are actually reading) is simply unanalyzable until it is past. At every indivisible moment of your conscious life—such as this present one and this present one, etc.—there is some meaning in your consciousness as long as you are paying attention to something. Or even when you are distracted by something.

The heart of this chapter and the key to understanding it is to be found in that last paragraph. That last paragraph also contains the reason why no image theory will ever satisfy, no matter how essential images are to our thinking. You can make an analysis of the analysis of the idea of "analysis"; if an idea is ONLY an image, then you can have an image of an image of an image. This ends in tautology, or rather something more akin to stuttering, and is as simplistic a theory as was ever devised to explain anything.

III. MEDITATION

The present chapter should be regarded, then, more as a meditation than anything else. Unless you take time to examine your own present consciousness in an effort to verify the things that have been pointed out about it, you will always know about "thought" merely 'from the outside.'

The following is a picture which may be helpful to you in meditating upon what you are doing as you read this chapter (or as you read any book).

Picture your self looking out over a fast-flowing stream. Out beyond the banks of the stream, the water rushes by. But, floating on the surface of the water, you see a small inflated balloon. Imagine it as more or less stationary: it does not rush downstream with the water. It is supported by the water which floats beneath it; and, obviously, if the source of water were cut off, then the balloon would sink to the stream's rock-bed. But, even though the balloon remains stationary in front of you, moving neither up—nor downstream, it is definitely affected by all the variations of the surface of the stream: when the water rises in a sudden wavelet, the balloon rises; when a trough comes, the balloon takes a dip; the balloon is continually spinning and bounding, turning this way and that, as the water churns beneath it. Yet, once again, the balloon itself does not move along downstream. It floats above the water and remains more or less "just there."

Try to visualize your own conscious state as you run your eyes along the lines of print here as being made up of two principal elements: (1) a stream of ciphers (visual perceptions) and imagined words, which floats through your consciousness or which floats by your field of "attention"; and . . .

. . . and (2) **automatically evoked meaning**.

The first element is the "perceptible" element of your consciousness. By perceptible, I mean that, by intense enough reflection, you can *directly* notice it. You have no difficulty at all directly noticing the ciphers you see on the page before you. If you concentrated hard enough on the previous chapter, you can now perceive those 'inner-speech' words as they run through your imagination. These words are a stream. You are reading word-by-word or phrase-by-phrase. Even when you repeat a phrase to yourself, it is a repeated or similar phrase, not the original one itself.

But although this stream of words flows on and on through your consciousness (so that you do not remember the exact words you have read nor their exact order; they are lost in the "past" of memory), there is effortlessly, and spontaneously evoked, called-forth, in your consciousness, a balloon (a "cloud" would be a better description now, in order to give less definiteness to the "outline" or shape of it) of *meaning*, of thought; this second element is located (if you can call it that) a "wee bit above your mind's eye." I say "above," for you can never look at it directly; all you will perceive directly is the flow of words (even if you add some of your own in your reflection on what you are reading). BUT THE FLOW OF WORDS IS DIFFERENT FROM THE MEANING THEY EVOKE. You can use different words, and get the same meaning. Or you can translate the words into a different language and get the same meaning. Or, if you know the Morse Code, you can have a different perceptible element and the same meaning. Words and symbols are conventional, arbitrary. The arbitrariness of meaning is an entirely different type of thing.

The "thought" or "meaning" that floats before your attention is continually changing, being modified by this word and that, suddenly flashing with brilliance when a particular phrase brings special insight (usually because of special connotations; due to association-habits for the greater part, or to special concentration), then dipping in clarity when a word or a phrase or a sentence is hard to follow (when you must recall, call-back, the stream of words and re-listen to them), etc. And when all perceptions are missing, thought itself sinks to non-existence. Even when only the imagination works, as happens in dreams, there is still a possibility that thought can be distinct.

IV. SEVERING THOUGHT FROM IMAGES

Like it or not, too many theories of the "concept" have been tied to the unconscious analogy of the image, whether it is the image of some real perception of a thing (usually a visual shape), or the image of a word (or a string of them). By not noticing the difference between the "perceptible" (taken in the special sense in which I have used it here) and the "imperceptible" elements of consciousness, theories of the concept have "canonized" words. Thinkers have imagined that there was something sacrosanct about words, and have forgotten that words are at the service of thought.

The truth is, however, that we can have a visual perception, such as the perception of someone down the street waving to us, and can have as clear and distinct an idea of what the person means (what that signal means) as we can of anything at all. We can listen to something that someone says to us, but can—merely from certain mannerisms to which we may not even pay distinct attention—get a meaning entirely different from what his or her words tell us. ANY SINGLE ONE of our perceptions can serve as the basis for a thought, and quite a clear thought at that.

Therefore, it is essential to realize the ambiguity of the word "image" when it is taken from its primary analogue (a painting or photograph, etc.) and applied to the imagination. As so often has happened, people have spoken of the "image" as if it were perfectly clear to everyone just what this "image" was. But, "image" itself is a word: the essential thing is to know what it means.

The liberation of the power of thought that is consequent upon a realization of this fact is something like the release of power that follows upon a splitting of the atom.

V. ONE OR MANY?

Notice that, while the "flowing stream" that makes up the perceptible element of your present consciousness is divisible, the whole "cloud" of meaning that is in your mind at present is not. You can take the flow of words, just as you can take any sentence from this page, stop it, lay it out in front of you, cut it up into parts, and examine each part.

For instance, you can take just one sentence like "This is an apple," and write it out as it is written out there. You can cut it up into its parts: "this" "is" "an" "apple." You can examine each word, divide it into syllables and letters, analyze the multiple potential meanings it can have (the work of a dictionary), study its origin, write a book about your investigations, etc.

But when you look at an apple and tell someone "This is an apple," the MEANING of that phrase is not merely the sum of its parts. The meaning is something over and above them. Had you said: "Is this an apple?", the meaning would have been wholly different. Yet, if you give "This is an apple" the right inflection, it can be given the meaning of the second. When there is a discussion of the "judgment," this should be taken into account: for too long, the judgment has been looked upon as if it were the joining of two ideas or two concepts. Are they *two* concepts when the sentence containing two distinct words is here-and-now enunciated? Potentially or actually? The perceptible element of a person's consciousness when he or she makes such a judgment may be divisible (only one part of it can be enunciated at any particular moment), but the meaning-element can only be potentially divisible: i.e. it has various "aspects" which correspond to the various perceptible elements enunciated or remembered. The meaning-element itself can never be actually divided. The only *actual* meaning is that which is here-and-now in someone's consciousness as he or she is *actually* thinking. When the person has stopped thinking (has gone asleep, etc.), there may be memories, there may be collections of atoms and molecules (in books). But there is no actual meaning in existence except when someone is thinking.

Interpretation. Thought has a passive aspect to it when we are basing our thinking on *received* perceptions. When someone is talking to us and we are paying attention to him or her, or when we are reading and concentrating on it, or when we are just "experiencing": in all these cases, the meaning in our consciousness is *evoked*.

Yet, even here, there is always the possibility (and often the fact) of our actively contributing to the meaning: we are not satisfied with merely receiving perceptions, but we *interpret* them.

In either case, "interpretation"—if not taken as an act—can serve as a synonym for "meaning". We can say we "put a certain interpretation on something," or we can say it "had such-and-such a meaning for us."

Conversation is another concrete experience in which the perceptible and impercepible elements can be clearly detected.

270

1. The listening aspect of conversation: here, we are supposed to be allowing the meaning aspect of our consciousness to be evoked by the other person's words (too often we are already thinking up an answer to one part of his or her "speech" and ignoring the remainder of it).

2. The answering aspect: here, we already have the thought. We try to put it into words. The "perceptible" aspect of consciousness is now produced by us. The amazing thing is that it can be produced at will, just as we can raise our arms at will. And, if we are "alive" with our thought (when emotion lends us its catalyzing influence), we pay no heed at all to our words: they pour out in torrents.

VI. A 2011 CONCLUSION

One aspect of 'epistemology' (a fancy term better replaced by "theory of knowledge") is the fact that we can think about thinking and create theories about knowledge, even theories about theories!

What is most amazing is that, in order to criticize the Neo-Thomistic ideas about ideas and concepts, we must make use of the fiction that thoughts can be 'broken' into such parts as ideas and concepts, into subject-concepts and predicate-concepts, into simple and complex ideas, into nouns, verbs, adjectives, and adverbs, etc. The supreme marvel is that God makes it possible for us SEARCH FOR THE WHOLE TRUTH and thereby to focus on what seem to be distinct parts of our total system-beliefs and to think of them as distinct "propositions" and distinct "beliefs." We can then 'critically re-examine' this or that particular proposition or belief in the context of our entire system of beliefs and, if necessary, give it up, replace it with a different proposal or belief, etc.

As James might say, we can even imagine that thoughts are "things." That will give us matter for decades, eventually an eternity, of reflection on and marveling at one of the greatest mysteries in the universe, thought!

APPENDIX C

Time

[This appendix is part of a chapter in another unpublished ms entitled *Will You Control Your Imagination?* But the notion of time is essential for much of Part One. The original text is slightly revised.]

4. Mindset as Bundle of Habitual Expectations (III): Expectations and TIME. Whoever wishes to join or rejoin abstract theory and real-life experience must never lose sight of her or his HERE-AND-NOW. In speaking of expectations, I am referring to experience, to facets of experience and thought. But when we experience, the expectation is always NOW. That is because everything we experience is experienced NOW. In fact, it is always at THIS VERY MOMENT that we experience whatever we experience, think whatever we think, and decide whatever we decide.

Expectations, though, are not about now, but about the FUTURE. The PAST is over and done with. The most we can do is remember the past. Even that, of course, is something we can only do now, at this very moment. And, although in the past we may or may not have expected what we're experiencing right now, we cannot now do any expecting about what's going on. Only about what's going to happen sometime in the future, whether one instant from now, one year from now, one million years from now.

Keep in mind that it isn't essential that you agree with the thoughts that these ink marks will evoke in you (at least right now I expect they will do so). Before you can do that, the thoughts first must come to you and you must understand. Otherwise, you'll not know whether the thoughts I had back here on Tuesday, November 28th, 1989, were like the thoughts you are in the habit of assenting to or whether they contradict them. In fact, if this is your first time reading this chapter, you may not even be certain what to expect: whether the thoughts that will come to you in the future (as you read the pages ahead) will be like the thoughts you're in the habit of assenting to or whether—if they're as radically different from everyday commonsense as those in Chapter I were—they'll be very UNlike your customary thoughts. Just so long as you understand that these opening remarks are making use of a very simple time framework, past, present (now), and future, you have the essentials for understanding what's next:

> Our PRESENT habitual expectations regarding the FUTURE are based on our memories of the PAST, for they are generalized descriptions of what we've already experienced. (Of course, we'd not label every expectation "habitual.") Since our PRESENT mindset usually teems with PAST-based anticipations of what's to come in the FUTURE (see p.179), we need the framework of "time" to map out and understand our mindset.

The Plan for this Segment III. First, there will be a few notes on the importance of the time-framework as basic to all inquiries. But, because time doesn't exist, that fact makes it necessary to show why, in trying to answer Augustine's question, "What is time?", we must try to answer another very important question: "What is the OBJECT OF THOUGHT, when we're describing both what does not exist as well as what does exist?" Then all of that will be applied to reflections on time and related topics.

Importance. Here are some preliminary reasons why understanding time is essential for understanding anything at all:

(i) The time-framework of past, present, and future, is necessary for anyone who wishes to understand *herself* or *himself*. The easiest way to explain why is by referring to that most obvious and important fact about our concrete, real lives mentioned on page 161: we are always at some point between the moment of our birth and *the time of our death*. Moreover we are never at that point for more than an instant. If you're like me, that means that every time you ask "How much time do I have until I die?", the time you'll have between that moment and *the one that'll be called "your death"* by the coroner will be shorter than it was the last time you asked it. The purpose for mentioning specific dates throughout these pages is to increase awareness of this prerequisite for full self-knowledge. Your eyes are scanning these lines at a particular moment, and if you re-scan them it will be a different particular moment later than the first.

(ii) Whoever wishes to understand *"psychology"*—i.e., to understand what is "generally" true of all humans whatever—must have a thorough grasp of the principles involved here. If it's the old-fashioned psychology which requires an understanding of MEMORY which relates to the past, of SENSING which relates most obviously to the present, and of prediction, anticipation, or EXPECTATION which relates to the future, it is clear that notions of time are wholly pervasive. If it's the new, behaviorally-oriented "psychology" which studies behaviors which have a beginning, a course, and an end, i.e., behaviors whose "parts" never co-exist, since all the parts except the one that's presently occurring will be past (i.e., over and done with, no longer in existence) or future (i.e., not yet in existence), it is equally clear that there is no escaping the need to deal with the paradoxes of time, i.e., of the no-longer past, the not-yet future, and the never-stopping present.

(iii) Whoever wishes to understand what *history* is, what is the reality which "historians" study, where "history" exists if at all, must understand all about time. If history exists, it exists now. If history is someone's present understanding of the past, and if the past does not exist, this poses all the problems that Parmenides raised. Another way of conveying the same point is this: the first problem about "history" is not what kind of evidence historians can use in their efforts to prove which theories (e.g., about the Fall of Rome) are true and which false, the first problem is "Do historians know what they're talking about?" Do ANY of us know what we're talking about when we talk about the PAST which doesn't exist? (See "Judgments of existence," page 42, ff.)

(iv) Whoever wishes to understand *biology* must deal constantly with the time dimension of life. The very notion of biology as "the study of life" is a reification, for there is no such thing as life, only living organisms. The model for studying living organisms was noticed twenty-three centuries ago by Aristotle: every living organism has a beginning in time, a course of growth and development (maturation) that—if successful—reaches the mature adult form (structure and functioning) to be expected of a member of the "species," and finally deterioration and death. No organism is in all phases of its lifetime simultaneously, which poses the well-known issue of the teleological blueprint: what directs the presently undeveloped organism to the not-yet-existing, future adult form? Time is also involved in all discussions of biological "clocks" and life-rhythms. And when the topic of evolution is introduced as essential to biology, time as a backdrop becomes relevant for the same reason it is essential to all other kinds of history: how can we talk of a past that doesn't exist?

(v) Whoever wishes to understand *physics* must understand the issues discussed here. People aren't the only beings which behave. Physical bodies, of which Newton wrote, also behave. In fact, ever since the time of Galileo and Descartes, what is most obvious is that the most profitable way to approach the world of nature is in terms of BODIES WHICH DO ONLY TWO THINGS (BEHAVE IN ONLY TWO WAYS): REST AND MOVE. Zeno more than anyone made it clear that our commonsense notion of motion becomes a problem as soon as we try to combine it with our notions of past, present, and future: no rabbit or tortoise or arrow or bullet can be in two places at one moment, which seems to imply that at any given moment a thing is stationary, which further implies that it must be stationary at every moment, which means it doesn't ever move. Which is the very opposite of the opening lines of Max Born's *The Restless Universe*: "It is odd to think that there is a word for something which, strictly speaking, does not exist, namely, 'rest'." Whereas Born says nothing is ever stationary, Zeno claimed nothing ever moves. It would seem then that one of these authors, Zeno or Born, is violating Parmenides' dictum: What-is-not cannot exist, cannot be thought, and cannot be named. Which is it, no rest or no motion?

(vi) What is true of physics in general is even more true of *astronomy*: whoever refuses to think hard about time will never get to the bottom of things in astronomy. Not merely because Newton's physics—including his notions of time and space, both absolute and relative—is the basis for ordinary ideas about astronomical matters, but because Einstein's relativity theories underlie so much of what is currently written about such things. First, there is the postulate that nothing can move faster in time than light which needs a second to travel each 186,000 miles. This means that light is in the same boat with rabbits, tortoises, arrows, and bullets, which also take time to travel. And then there are the famous paradoxes of relativity-weirdness: e.g., time slows down when bodies approach that top velocity of 186,000mps. Time slows down?! Vis-à-vis what "yardstick"? Finally, because today's astronomy is so involved in questions about the past (e.g., cosmogony), it is also deeply immersed in the history-paradoxes.

> These will provide some indication of the importance of this particular object of thought," i.e., TIME. Because we all "get by" so well with those everyday notions of time Augustine referred to, we fail to realize how little we understand the matters involving time, particularly our ability to think so easily of the motion and rest of bodies, our memory of the non-existent past, our expectations of the non-existent future, the paradoxes involved in thinking about "the present moment," as well as the difficulty of trying to make one thing (time) out of three different things (past, present, future), none of which exist.

Notes on DESCRIBING an OBJECT-OF-THOUGHT. Any time we find (notice) ourselves thinking or talking about anything whatsoever, it is possible for us to pause and ask: "What exactly IS such-and-such (the "anything whatsoever")?" If we think of the "such-and-such" as an object—not necessarily a physical body, not necessarily a visible item, not necessarily a tangible reality, but just as an "object" in the same all-inclusive, neutral sense that we give to the term "something"—then pausing to define the word or phrase, telling what we mean by such-and-such, as well as explaining what (we believe) such-and-such an object is, will often yield what looks like a DESCRIPTION of such-and-such.* If we make an effort to put aside our presuppositions about whether it exists or not (ignore the all-important issue discussed under "judgments of existence" on pages 42, ff) as well as any explanatory theories we may have about the thing under discussion, in order to simply describe what appears or is present to us (we usually say "present to our mind" or 'present to our thought") when we repeat the object's name, we can describe this describing as a "phenomenological description of the object." (*What follows relates equally to a new 'favorite' concept, narration.)

At least that was the belief of Edmund Husserl and of the "phenomenologists" (not "phenomenalists") who accepted parts of his program called "phenomenology." Husserl's thinking has much in common with what Plato did with Socrates' discovery of the process called "definition": in various works, Plato conducted phenomenological descriptions of such objects as "virtue" and "love" and "justice," descriptions in which he believed he was describing things that, though not physically existing, were unquestionably "present" to conscious awareness.

His thinking also has much in common with Descartes" emphasis on consciousness, for being conscious of the objects we describe is clearly a prerequisite for describing them. (H.Spiegelberg's *The Phenomenological Movement: A Historical Introduction* is a fine introduction to the *many* different, disagreeing phenomenologies.)

The relation between these two things—the acts or activity of consciousness and the objects we are conscious of—can be remembered by a simple formula called the principle of intentionality or the principle of the bipolarity of consciousness: *It's not possible to be conscious of anything (an object) if there's not something to be conscious of.* (Parmenides thought of it first.) This does nothing but sum up, in shorthand style, what we all common-sensically take for granted. We don't see anything while we're conscious unless there's something to see, so that if there's nothing to be seen, we don't see. It's not possible to practice our seeing, that is, to just do some seeing all by itself, while making sure we don't see ANYthing. Repeat the same for hearing, smelling, tasting, remembering, feeling, thinking, i.e., for all those activities we do when we are awake and conscious. That way, it becomes easy to understand the meaning of the phenomenologists' principle of intentionality. It's called "intentionality" to capture the notion that the object is the thing at which the act is directed, is the thing it (the act) is intent upon. It's called "bipolarity" because conscious act and attended object are at the two opposite poles of the knowledge relation.

However, the principle of intentionality must not be applied at the level of thought IF IS ASSUMED THAT THE OBJECT IS A *DISCRETE* IDEA OR CONCEPT rather than a complete thought framed by the rest of a belief-system. (What follows addresses this point specifically.)

Though it is a fine model or picture or diagram to use when discussing our awareness of things at the *sense* level, it does nothing but perpetuate the LOOKING MODEL approach when used at the level of intellectual *understanding*. Pages 66, 126, and 152 were composed as brief essays on just this point. True, we will never escape the looking model imagery (more on this in a moment), but we must learn to free ourselves by recognizing it as an analogy that starts with a limp and—if pushed to the limit—leads to total paralysis.

We must therefore insist that things are not at all the way they appeared to Husserl, just as they were not at all the way they appeared to Plato. Or even Socrates. There is not literally any such thing as "defining," as Socrates believed. *Defining* is using word-clues to express one's complete thoughts, and the thoughts expressed are thoughts about how the "thing" or object—if any such thing exists—is related to other things or objects (if they exist). The same is true when we're *describing* something, i.e., using word-clues to express one's complete thoughts, whether the object is a Platonic essence or one of Husserl's.

But if it is essential to stop thinking of thinking as thinking of an "object," WHAT CAN BE PUT IN ITS PLACE? In line with the new picture I have been trying to cultivate throughout these pages—the picture "embodied" in the epigraph "Thoughts come to you"—we must resort to using the "verbal expression" for a (complete) thought, namely, *the meaning of a complete sentence or sentences.* By pretending that the thought which is expressed by the complete sentence is the ONLY thing we'll even pretend is an "object" of thinking, we simply preface the sentence with "<u>that</u>" and describe in full what is occurring: Person X is thinking (or understanding) *that* so-and-so did such-and-such. It is the attempt to capture this "whole thought" that makes it natural at times to say that the object (!) of thought is a FACT, since we do speak of "THE FACT <u>that</u> so-and-so did such-and-such." Thus, the object of thought is not a thing, not an object, but—when we almost MUST pretend that when we think we think of something—a fact. But, immediately, we must make a mental gestalt-shift and MAKE CERTAIN NOT to imagine that the complete thought or the fact is like a Platonic "proposition" or "fact" that floats adrift in this universe, detached from this or that particular thinking or understanding person's belief-system.

For example. "I am trying to describe understanding right now." Suppose that sentence gives you a clue to what I was thinking about when I put down that sequence of ink-marks ("sentence"). If you asked me: WHAT (object!) was I thinking ABOUT when I wrote it, I might be tempted to say "I was thinking about understanding." I might be tempted to add: "And in a moment I'll present part of a phenomenological description of it." BUT, what I should have answered is "I was thinking <u>that</u> I am trying to describe understanding right now." I'd probably add, immediately, that there is no such thing as understanding: that's a reification, a noun that seems to name a thing which is an operation. Much better to rephrase it: "I am trying to give you some clues to what I believe goes on when I understand what's really going on."

Therefore, what we're doing when we're thinking, understanding, or intellectually knowing is best pictured negatively, i.e., using a picture as a point of CONTRAST. We NEED mental pictures, images, analogies, metaphors, etc., as vehicles, that is, as accompaniments for understanding. Here, though, it is best to picture thinking and understanding as NOT looking at anything. Husserl was partly right: it is our natural tendency to discuss all conscious acts along the lines of the "act-vs-object" pattern, and the model or ideal conscious act has always been the visual act of seeing, i.e., the picture of myself looking at something in front of me. A major change in thought-habits is called for.

> THESIS XXI. It is imperative to overcome the tendency to accept the principle of intentionality as applying at the "level" of understanding as if the 'object' is an isolated *idea* or concept rather than the *meaning* of the sentence(s). To understand what understanding is, I first picture myself looking at something in front of me, then I CROSS OUT THAT PICTURE. I 'negate' it. I 'transcend' it. I understand that there is MORE than UNconsciousness, MORE than sensing, MORE than experiencing memory-images of what I've sensed. But, since understanding that understanding is not looking at something, understanding understanding is NOT looking at understanding which cannot be looked at. In fact, since understanding is not on the page-62 list, but I am, it is best to notice that the above clues suggest that, for "understanding," I reified the verb in "I understand that . . ."

Understanding what all of that means is simply not possible EXCEPT against the backdrop of, or within the context, of this entire 1001-Basic-Principle belief-system into which it fits as a link in a "circular" chain of reasoning. Having made the 1000 other commitments that form the belief-system being presented, I must find some way to deal with the final item, the "activity" of understanding, which remains unstated by the other 1000 principles. That the "statement" of this remaining item—the supreme paradox or mystery—seems like a semantic maze in the style of G.Ryle who, having made his commitments, simply "danced around" knowledge, is unavoidable.

Because the issue "What is the OBJECT OF THOUGHT?" is so difficult, and because THE INNOVATION CONCERNING IT IS THE MOST IMPORTANT IN THIS BOOK, the effort to state it clearly deserves a bit more clarification. The claim that Husserl, like Plato, was wrong can be made more understandable by the following two-step reflection on description, which will then be further clarified by using the "description of TIME" as an illustration case.

First (this will be a description of the first step), see if what follows does not conjure up some of the unnoticed aspects of "describing" something. Begin with what most of us did at some point during our early education. The teacher placed something, say, an apple or other object on the desk. Next, s/he instructed us to write a paragraph describing what we saw. We call the item on the desk "the object." It is "present" to our gaze, we see it with nothing obstructing our view. And, "back here" at the gazing or conscious end of the looking-relation is I MYSELF, seemingly in my physical being: a certain number of feet away from the object, in a certain direction (north, north-west, west . . .), etc. All of this—our own location in a classroom, our location vis-à-vis the object's location, the fact that we can see it, the teacher's instructions—is obvious to us, *consciously*, and constitutes our mindset-context for the next step which our attention is focused on: describing what we see. This step consists in setting down cues and clues for the thoughts that come to us, at least those we pick out as worth giving clues for.

Aware of it or not, all of that is part of our mindset whenever we set about the task of "focusing" or "concentrating" INTENTLY on some "object," so that we can make or compose a description (phenomenological or otherwise) of it. Pages 54-55 have already mentioned that a number of writers have quite explicitly described their starting point just that way. A quick glance at sections 27 ("The World of the Natural Standpoint: I and My World About Me"), 35 ("The Cogito as 'Act'"), and 41 ("The Real Nature of Perception and Its Transcendent Object") of Husserl's *Ideas: General Introduction to Pure Phenomenology* will show that his "natural standpoint" of lived experience is what I've called "the commonsense view" as a starting-point. For instance:

> I am aware of a world, spread out in space endlessly . . . I can let my attention
> wander from the writing-table I have just seen and observed, through the unseen

portions of the room behind my back to the verandah, into the garden, to the children in the summer-house, and so forth, to all the objects concerning which I precisely "know" that they are there and yonder in my immediate co-perceived surroundings—a knowledge which has nothing of conceptual thinking to it, and first changes into clear intuiting with the bestowing of attention, and even then only partially and for the most part very imperfectly.

But not even with the added reach of this intuitively clear or dark, distinct or indistinct *co-present* margin, which forms a continuous ring around the actual field of perception, does that world exhaust itself which in every waking moment is in some conscious measure "present" before me. It reaches rather in a fixed order of being the limitless beyond. (E.Husserl, *Ideas*, trans'd by B.Gibson; sec.27.)

Husserl's point*—an elaboration of Kant's "space as a form of perception"—merely calls our attention to a constant feature of ALL our waking moments: we "sense," even without putting it into words, that we are HERE, in this place, surrounded by a whole universe spread out in space. Because this is our psychological background whenever we're awake and "feel" as if we're oriented, not-dis-oriented, it is the psychological background for every act of "setting ourselves to describe some object," as well. (*Ignore for now Husserl's incredible blunder, that this *presuppositionless* knowledge "has nothing of conceptual thinking to it"! If it's knowledge, it's thoroughly permeated by a highly-complex conceptual worldview, however tacit.)

Once we've psychologically adopted the "about-to-describe-something" mindset or attitude, it is as easy to "describe" describing as it is to describe time, neither of which is visible or tangible, as easy as it is to describe my surroundings, my writing desk or a piece of white paper (the things Husserl starts with). It's equally easy when the object is virtue, justice, seeing, consciousness, object of consciousness, presuppositionless (sic) inspection, etc. Or even non-being, nothing, nothingness, negating, privation, absence, vacuum, void, death, and similar non-entities.

Here's what we do in each case: First, we mentally, psychologically, consciously (which synonym we use, whether a cue with fewer or more connotations for us as opposed to for other people, is of no importance here) put whatever is "NAMED" out there in front OF US, just as if it's on the teacher's desk, and paint a verbal description of it, a word-picture. (The only difference between the writing class and the art class is that in one we are to use word-clues to what we're thinking as we see, whereas in the other we're to use a painting as a clue to what we think we're seeing.) When the object's not physically there, we imagine (pretend) it is.

Secondly (what follows are many sentence-clues to thoughts about what preceded), TAKE A CLOSE LOOK AT WHAT PRECEDED. What preceded was a description of part of what happens when we describe something. In the preceding case, the "something" described, the "object" was allegedly "describing." WHAT STANDS OUT?—WHAT "APPEARS"?!—when we take that brief event (a several-minutes long description of "describing") and conduct a phenomenological inspection of it? What becomes obvious?

If you examine that several-paragraph description (word-picture) of "describing," you'll notice three things. First, it does not just talk about one "object." Although the word or clue "describing" returns at various points, it is clear that the description also included judgments about a wide variety of "related" topics. That is, it used names of dozens of other things besides "describing." This is in keeping with Thesis VII (p.52): We never understand one thing in isolation from others. This is why page 66 concluded by drawing attention to ALL the things brought into the description of something. Notice, secondly, that it WEAVES A TAPESTRY. It is a tapestry whose parts are complete thoughts, expressed by a series of complete sentences. (Four paragraphs' worth.) So far from being a presuppositionless description, the entire CONTEXT is "permeated" with commitments (e.g., that there's some describing going on—which can only be "defined" within the context of all the things which are NOT describing—and something to BE described, etc.). To show it, we must, after each sentence, ask the presuppositionless describer, "What does *that* mean?" Thirdly, and most especially, any attempt to begin FROM POINT ZERO (with no presuppositions) to do nothing but establish the sense or meaning of this or that, prior to embarking on some special "scientific" task of investigating existential facts, is doomed. Presumably we to whom the "descriptions" are offered can understand the meaning of each sentence in the description which is to help us understand the meaning of just one of the "words" out of all the words used in the description, and presumably the describer who speaks or writes the sentences also understands what all the words s/he uses mean while explaining just the one meaning being focused on. Although we can give credit to Husserl for his achievements (see p.56), he ultimately surrounded his project with an enormously complex, but completely unnecessary theoretical-fiction apparatus. Page 19's list of starting-points, as well as what follows, is relevant here.

In a word (clearly a facetious idiom), the understanding that goes on during "describing" is something we do while we're attending to something visible when there's something sensible to attend to. And when there's not, it's something we do while we're at least PRETENDING that we are looking at something, such as justice, beauty, seeing, etc. BUT the understanding is not looking. And what we understand is not an object. Not that we can wholly escape the looking picture. So accustomed are we to picturing thinking as looking that we'll almost inevitably want to ask: "What is it that we understand?" I.e., what THING is it? Once we're clear that understanding isn't looking, and that it's not a thing or object-thing we understand, we must get in the habit of controlling our imagination when we are tempted that way. We understand complete thoughts or facts, but that's only shorthand for: We understand *that* such and such. For instance, we understand *that* understanding is not looking, we understand *that* King Lear does not exist, we understand *that* "justice" is a reification created by converting "He is a just person" into "Justice is one of the things he's best known for," etc. (Of course, if we accept as a fact something that is not true, then we're in error, i.e., we're assenting to a thought that is false.)

With that two-step "reflection"—a description (of what description is and is not) and a reflection (a description of a reflection?) on it—in mind, you will understand better what is going on when I repeat the same two steps and use 'TIME' as the object of study. Or of presuppositionless (!) phenomenological description.

First (the straightforward description step), in order to understand what is meant by "TIME" it is necessary to draw another line. The first was the line described by Wm. James in the passage quoted earlier on page 86. Recall for a moment that first "line." It is one that we draw in our map of the universe. It is a spatial line. What that means is easiest understood if, as was done on page 77, we imagine the world stopped. We take inventory of all the things we believe inhabit the universe. My inventory list—with the quantities left somewhat inexact—is found on page 62. (I.e., clues to my beliefs as to what exists are found on p.62.) On one side of this spatial line are myself, my sense-data, my memory-images, and my thoughts. On the other side are the galaxies, the stars of the Milky Way, our local star called the "sun," our planet earth, the oceans, the continents—or at least all the subatomic particles that we usually say "make up" those larger bodies—and the other 5,199,999,999 people scattered over those continents, including all of *their* sense-data, memory-images, and thoughts. That is, on one side of the line is myself and all that pertains to me, on the other is everything other (than me and what pertains to me).

This second, other "line" is the one called "NOW." It is the famous line that divides time into past and future. Think of it as one of the lines found in history books, lines notched to indicate millennia, centuries, decades, etc., each of which is labeled ("2000 BC," "1482 AD," etc.). Unlike the SPATIAL line which is purely imaginary (p.230), this TIME (temporal) line is a symbol for all that is NOT imaginary, i.e., all that does exist NOW. Unlike what is on the two sides of the imaginary space line, namely, things that are real, the things on the two sides of the time line are purely imaginary. Aristotle (*Physics* IV, 10) begins his discussion of time by asking whether it even exists; among the reasons for saying it doesn't is the fact that it included parts that don't exist: the PAST which "has been and is not" and the FUTURE which "is going to be and is not yet." Though what Aristotle goes on to say is not entirely consistent, it is easy to follow, particularly for one central reason: as far as our common-sense notions are concerned, there would be no time if the world really WERE stopped dead in its tracks and nothing moved or changed. If the sun stood still, there'd be no morning and evening to make up a day, no days and nights to make up a week, no weeks and months to make up a year. If the sun didn't MOVE from skyline to heaven above and to opposite skyline, over and over and over again, there'd be no yesterday or last week or last year to make up the past, and no tomorrows to make up the future.

Aristotle tends to say there IS time, however, and the reason is obvious. As was remarked on page 81, the world is NOT stopped dead in its tracks. Things keep changing so rapidly that Heraclitus concluded nothing ever remains the same, not even for an instant. By the time we pull our foot out of the river, so much water has flowed by and there have been so many changes all up and down the river, that when we step back in a second time, it's not the same river. Hence, he concluded, it's not possible to step twice into the same river. (Now that we know how fast atoms and subatomic particles move, we can understand why Born, too, said there's no such thing as rest.) Though Aristotle believed there was some permanency in the world, he agreed with Heraclitus that in the sublunary region, i.e., here on this planet, things are constantly changing even while retaining some enduring self-identity. But in the sky is the most obvious and regular and dependable motion of all: the movement of the sun creating the rhythm of the days that form the backdrop for our "day-ly" lives. That's what makes plausible the commonsense thought: If there weren't some change or movement, there'd be no time.

Before following that up, it's worth taking a moment to notice another common-sense notion that's basic here. The LINK between "Stop the world and take inventory of what-exists"—suggested throughout these pages as the way to begin ANY project of trying to get to the real truth about ANYthing—and Aristotle's habit of beginning with substances (p.222) and the fact that so many writers begin with their writing desk or the paper they're writing on should be clear: WE BEGIN OUR THINKING WITH THINGS, not with time, not with space, but with such things or substances as writing paper, desk, house, etc. It's the way to BUILD FROM our original, Nature-given theory of everything, the one called "common sense." P. S. As we'll see, the further step which DESCARTES suggested becomes particularly helpful: Begin with the one thing which none of us can ever be wrong about when trying to find one sure answer to "What exists?" That one thing is our self, one's own SELF. I exist. That is, begin with the being that is on "this" side of the space—or world-line each of us draws for herself or himself. End of P.S.

But does time really exist? What do we mean by "the past" and by "the future" anyway? Is Aristotle correct to say they don't exist? What else does exist besides oneself? As is the case with every question that can be asked, there are not only different answers given by different thinkers, but there is no agreement—even among those who agree to use "English" clues to their thought, on what they'll mean when they use "time" words: time, past, present, future, etc. (Page 88 mentioned the names of two useful collections of diverging views.) And yet, as Augustine noted (he used totally different "words"—Latin ones—to note it), we all understand each other well enough to coordinate our everyday activities.

The answer I'll give is that neither space nor time exist in any way at all. There are only things that change, some of them by moving. We only imagine that there is some container, "space," which things supposedly exist in. Similarly we only imagine there is some other "dimension" which they supposedly change in. That is, there is no space but just those same spread-out things which "make up" the world (i.e., things to which we refer collectively by "world"). There is no time, just those spread-out things which were not always where or how they are now, things which will not always remain where or how they are now. There are only the things that exist now. The only way they exist is how they exist now.

Because it will help as a reminder and a focus for understanding the positions taken here, it is worth underlining the principle just stated.

THESIS XXII. There are things that change, some of them by moving. These things (some of which at least have not always existed) were not always where or how they are now and will not always remain where or how they are now. We can have thoughts of them as they were in the past—we can even have thoughts of things that no longer exist—and we can think that they will be thus and so in the future, but these are our *thoughts* of things, not the *things* thought of. Whatever things exist are things that exist now, the way they exist now. Time, past, present, future, motion, and change do not exist, though I use thoughts of them to think correctly about the things that do exist, move, and change.

QU: What gives me such confidence on these matters? What inclines me to make Thesis XXII a Basic Commitment and to use it as a "premise" against which to judge other proposed theories? AN: What I know about myself. This connects with the major insight of Descartes, that the greatest certainty, the MOST scientific knowledge we can have, is not about unchanging realities (see the quotes on page 212) but about a changing existent, oneself. Even if the price to be paid is that—since so much about us changes from moment to moment—we have to constantly update much of this scientific knowledge. Not all of our evidence for the non-existence of the past or future comes from what we know about ourselves. In fact, for centuries people sought elsewhere for their most basic certainties. Thousands of other facts—that no amount of sumptuous meals eaten in the past will prevent me from dying of starvation now, not all the cozy hearths I've been warmed by in the past will keep me from freezing to death now, not all the beds I've made in the past can alter the messed-up condition of the one I'm looking at now—make the non-existence of the past overwhelmingly obvious, just as all my uncertainty about whether rescue from starvation or freezing will come in soon and my awareness that a nuclear bomb could obliterate this city along with this bed before I get it made, are equal indications that it's still now and that the future isn't yet.

When Descartes prescribed a thought-experiment to cure us of our tendency to look everywhere but to ourselves for our first certainties, however, the first thing he did was suggest: Pretend there's no physical world and that you don't even have a body to feed with meat and vegetables, to warm before the crackling hearth, to make beds with. That experiment brings to light the fact that, even if I suppose Berkeley is right and no physical world exists, i.e., even if my beliefs about a starving or freezing body and messed-up bed clothes are illusions, it won't change some of the facts I know about myself.

Now, one of the most important things I know about myself involves "time." It is that most overwhelming fact of my experience, the one mentioned earlier on page 161 and more recently on page 236: My past life constantly lengthens in exact proportion to the way "the remainder of my life" shortens. There is only one of me and I'm always at just one point in my life. Whenever I conduct Descartes' suggested thought—experiment, I'm confident it is at a specific point between the first and the last times I open my eyes (if I have any). There are not thousands of me, one fitting each description of myself on successive days of my life. There's only one me RIGHT NOW: that's the me as I am RIGHT NOW. And now, a moment later, the me as I am RIGHT NOW. Whoever thinks of me as a new-born infant might be right in believing I'm among the 5.2 billion present inhabitants of this planet, but would be wrong about my age and present condition, just as anyone who thinks of me as 60 years old won't be right for a few years (if they can retain the thought that long).

From what is true about me, I generalize about others. Everyone else is just one person, too. This fits all the basics of everyday commonsense. When estimates are made of the world's population (5.2 billion), the estimators try to count each person as one. The notion that each person is to count as just one is also part of the democratic ideal for elections: one person, one vote. And whoever wants to know more about anyone of those 5.2 billion humans now living than the general facts that are true of all humans must think of them as they are at the very moment the knowing is taking place.

What would the alternative be? In addition to the PRESENT world made up of the things that fill all three of space/s dimensions (up-down, right-left, front-back), there would have to be billions of other universes, one corresponding to each segment of the PAST. How MANY billions would depend upon whether we use years for our standard "segment," or days, or hours, or minutes, or seconds, or nanoseconds, etc. In each of the segments for the past 56 years, there would be another me. Not quite a clone, for each bit of metabolism alters each cell irreversibly, and metabolism never stops. But each would be so close to the next clones that the differences wouldn't be noticeable except when some intermediates were skipped in the comparing process. Some thinkers of the past have held views similar to this, and there is a current quantum-weird view that's a close cousin of it. (See pp.19 and 172 of N.Herbert/s *Quantum Reality*.)

Because I know that there's only one me and because I know that I, not any clones, am that one, I know that those other me's—if they existed, which I haven't the slightest reason to believe—would be OTHERS, only LIKE me at best. (This, incidentally, is the basis for Lucretius' argument that, even if all my atoms are some day reassembled, it will not be me but only a clone of me, a being LIKE me, that/s reassembled.) Whoever believes anything different believes incorrectly. If I'm correct. Naturally, I'm certain I am correct, otherwise I'd either change my views or become an agnostic on the topic. Even being divine and omniscient couldn't change these facts, which is why some views of divine knowledge must be recognized as fanciful.

> Each moment of time is present to divine eternity not only as being known to it, but physically or in its being itself. John of St.Thomas has established his master's [Thomas Aquinas'] doctrine on this point very clearly. All the moments of time are present to divine eternity—in which there is no succession, and which is an instant that endures without beginning or end—because the creative ideas embrace according to their own measure, which is eternity and which infinitely transcends time, the created beings which they cause to be, the proper measure of which is the succession of time . . . "All things which here below supervene upon and succeed one another by flowing progressively into non-being, and which are diversified according to

the vicissitudes of their times, are present before this today and continue to exist motionless before it. In that today, the day when the world began is still immutable. And nevertheless the day is already present also when it will be judged by the eternal judge." (J.Maritain, *Existence and the Existent*, ch.4, sec.26; the quotation is from St.Peter Damian.)

It is clear that such descriptions are an attempt not to ascribe to the divine the same limitation we humans find ourselves in when WE want to know something: We can only know things, we say, THROUGH the medium of thoughts which are substitutes or mere "representations" of the realities that they are thoughts OF. But if we humans can think of past and future even though they don't exist—it is as easy to think thoughts of myself doing the things I did the day before yesterday as it is to think of myself sitting here now and writing this word and now this word and now this one, etc.—why should such a miraculous feat be limited just to humans? In fact, anything else would ascribe error to the divine. If I think about myself doing what I was doing yesterday and don't KNOW that it does NOT represent the one, real me right now, I'm in error. The only thoughts that are true must "keep up with the changes." (Or "with the times." A significant common-sense saying.) It is utterly mysterious how thinking can occur and how I can understand facts about realities distinct from the thoughts. Trying to fathom how a divine knower would understand certainly isn't helped by thinking such fanciful thoughts as the above. Again, my greatest confidence comes from my evidence about myself. Regardless of what others have thought in the past, I'm quite certain I am not just an eternal thought in God's mind, but a 56-year old, real, non-thought being (reality). Nor am I an UNchanging real being.

Your present experience of READING to which I've regularly drawn your attention will reinforce the truth of the basic principle for you. Consider the fact that you are reading this page and your eyes are right now scanning just these lines of print and none of those on earlier pages. If you turn back to page 200, you'll see that the first of the four questions, "What exists?", stressed that you could at least be certain that what you took to be the ink-marks on page 200 existed. But if you do turn back now to page 200, you'll only be remembering these, just as, if you'd earlier turned back to Page Six, you'd have only been remembering those on page 200. And, though 1 just thought again about pages 200 and Six, I finished composing them months ago and today (11-30-89) I'm composing this page. No one I know can read more than one page at a time, just as I cannot compose more than one at a time. Such everyday facts are the reason why we link SENSING with the PRESENT, and MEMORY with the PAST. The greatest errors are committed when we overlook the difference between (actual) sensING and (only) REMEMBERING what we sensED (see page 111).

Enough. Our tendency to overlook the obvious is the only reason we often don't notice that we are always changing, getting older, nearing the time when the coroner will fill out that death certificate. All the well-known thinkers born more than a century ago who seemed to subordinate this truth to their belief in some larger "collective" of which they imagined themselves apart—Hegel is the standard example—are dead. If they still linger on, swallowed into some everlasting whole, it's in a different way than they existed when they wrote and predicted it. Even if those who decided while alive to believe all the changes of everyday life are mere appearance were right, the appearance of them writing to say so had its brief moment and is no more:

> Philosophy affirms that the outward world is only phenomenal & the whole concern of dinners, of tailors, of gigs, of balls, whereof men make such account, is a quite relative & temporary one—an intricate dream—the exhalation of the present state of the Soul . . . are words a young Ralph Waldo Emerson wrote to his brother, but that was May 31, 1834, and the Soul has clearly moved on to later exhalations. Whoever prefers not to be convinced that the priority should be given to everyday facts of life such as these, rather than to any "metaphysical" theory such as Emerson borrowed from oriental writers via Coleridge via German-writing authors of the last century OR any "scientific" theory such as many contemporary writers borrow from physicists who've been no more successful than Einstein at avoiding the confusions suggested by "relativistic" mathematical formulae, must be left to choose from the theories sampled in Smart's, Gale's, or some other anthology. Or compose a different one.

Isn't ANY part of time real? Even if we agree with Aristotle that two of the parts of time do not exist, i.e., the past and the future, what about the present? Perhaps yesterday is an earlier today that has passed out of existence and tomorrow is a today which hasn't yet appeared on the stage of real existence, but what about today? Or, even if today's earlier hours have gone into limbo and the later ones are still on their way, what about this hour? Or this minute? Or this second? Isn't at least the present moment, NOW, real?

Our answer must be unequivocal: the present NOW—regardless of how it is thought of—is as much a purely mental, imaginary, only-thought-about thing as past and future. The three "parts" of that non-existent fiction, time, are all in the same category: mental creations. And they are created and "defined" in relation to one another, much as straight & curved, up & down, large & small, inside & outside, true & false, part & whole, or even (Ryle's) genuine & counterfeit are correlatives "defined" in terms of each other.

This is not how everyone thinks, of course. While Wm. James, in Chapter XV on "The Perception of Time," agrees that the present moment (as an extensionless instant) is a pure abstraction, he insists that we do experience a duration called "the specious present":

> Let anyone try, I will not say to arrest, but to notice or attend to the present moment of time. One of the most baffling experiences occurs. Where is it, this present? It has melted in our grasp, fled ere we could touch it, gone in the instant of becoming . . . [Reflection, though, assures us that] the practically cognized present is no knife-edge, but a saddle-back, with a certain breadth of its own on which

we sit perched, and from which we look in two directions into time. The unit of composition of our perception of time is a duration, with a bow and a stern, as it were, a rearward—and a foreward-looking end. (W.James, *Principles of Psychology*, I, 608-09.)

James" mention of "knife-edge" is a reference to the older view that the present moment is an indivisible instant, the temporal equivalent of a spatial point (this older view of a point as something with zero dimensions is now avoided, since it seems to be a description either of nothing at all or of a spirit), except that, like me, he substitutes the image of a knife-edge or line for that of a point. The picture of the present moment as a vertical line—that of something with only one dimension (up-down) intersecting a one-dimensional horizontal line—is the picture of something even thinner, of course, than a knife-edge. But, it's a picture, an image. A "SPATIALIZATION" of time (see p.90 above). Without the left half of the line which we pretend isn't right there now but is the past and the right half of the line which we pretend is the future, there'd be no horizontal line all right there in front of us AT PRESENT for the vertical "present moment" line to intersect and cut into two halves.

All these images must be ruthlessly resisted. Whereas James rejects the present moment as defined here, he does so in order to introduce a "thicker" present. His substitute present-duration is as imaginary as the razor thin present he rejects. There aren't any nows or present moments. Not of any kind whatever. There are only things (people, etc.) that exist at present or now. When they exist presentLY, exist even as we think about them, then—employing the mental or imaginary "past, present, and future" time-line that we use to remember or keep track of which thoughts about which things were earlier and which later vis-à-vis each other, or to remember which events thought about were earlier and which later—we'll say they "exist NOW" in order to indicate our belief that what we're thinking about and our thinking occur simultaneously, that neither is before or after the other, for they're occurring AT THE SAME POINT on the horizontal time-line. That is, when we speak of things as existing now, it indicates our belief that we're not thinking about things that did exist but don't and not thinking about things that will exist but don't, but rather about things that do exist. Referring to two things as "simultaneous" means that neither was, is, or will be before the other, or that neither was, is, or will be after the other as measured by our internal, mental time-yardstick, means therefore that they'll be located at the same point regardless of whether it was in the no-longer-existent past or will be in the not-yet future. P.S. The expressions "no-longer past" and "not-yet future" must not be allowed to mislead us. The past never did exist. Since there is no present that exists, there is no present that can pass out of existence, become past, or become no-longer past. There are only things which exist and may someday cease to exist. There are not even any things that don't exist yet but will, even though we can think about 'things' that never existed, don't exist, and will never exist. End of P.S.

With the preceding Basic Principles clarified, it is now safe to indulge in our habitual common-sense thinking and, like Augustine, to engage in a more or less 'phenomenological description' of the facts relating to "time." When we do, we'll find that the first and the last word will be <u>that</u> Isaac Newton's imaginary notion of "absolute, true, and mathematical time" as something that "flows equably without relation to anything external"—it's often called "duration"—unquestionably captures what we commonsensically take for granted. Everything begins with "constant or unvarying repeated events."

Let us imagine ourselves, semi-presuppositionlessly, in the place of our most primitive ancestors, the ones who surely lacked any ideas of calendars and clocks. What experiences of ours would have led us to create the idea of time? Three facts immediately come to mind. The daily rhythm of the day beginning with the appearance of the sun at one horizon and ending with its disappearance at the opposite horizon, followed by a period of darkness, then the sun's REappearance, etc., over and over, is the first notable fact of our experience related to time. Coordinated with this outer regularity is our personal rhythm of waking, sleeping, waking, sleeping, over and over again. But, whereas we can interrupt our pattern of sleeping and waking, nothing seems to alter the regularity of the sun's behavior. The second unvarying pattern is the roughly twenty-eight day cycle of the moon's four phases. Dividing that cycle by four gives us such a convenient seven-day "week" that ancient legends and even sacred literature canonized the custom. Finally, the longer period measured by the changing seasons must have begun to emerge in our ancestors' consciousness—particularly after farming began and "when to plant?" became an urgent concern—as standing over and measuring "equably" the briefer "moons" which measured the briefer "weeks" which measured the briefer "days."

Whatever UNpredictability there might be in nature that would allegedly make us begin speculating about powerful supernatural beings who (if we could just manage to get them on our side) would prevent nature's forces—floods, lightning, drought, fierce animals, sickness—from harming us, it would not change the fact that our lives would be measured by the even broader background PREdictability of years, months, and days.

The story of how our ancestors progressed from complete reliance on these natural "clocks" to the invention of the "artificial" clocks that we rely on today is a fascinating and many-detailed tale well-told in Book One of D.Boorstin's *The Discoverers* which he titled simply "Time" and in D.Landes' *Revolution in Time.* Our libraries are full of other histories which tell of all the different theories about the real nature of the "thing" which these clocks MEASURE: time itself. The first story or history has culminated in the invention of the "atomic clock" which is so accurate that, according to p.74 of the 10-23-89 issue of *Time* magazine, researchers can now measure how much the earth's gravity can slow down time: "a second every 10,000 years." The history of theories ABOUT "time" has progressed from theories which practically identify time with the movement of bodies outside our mind to theories which recognize that we measure that outside movement against a mind-related time that is entirely independent of it. The first story is too long for summary here. The second can be briefly described.

As mentioned earlier, Aristotle linked his discussion of time to the changes, esp. motions, of observable bodies. He was thoroughly entrapped by the typical Greek emphasis on circles, circles, circles as the perfect, endless(ly repeating) pattern of motion. Since the most obvious perfect, circular motion in the universe appeared to be that of the sun moving around the earth, it was natural that the sun's movement around the earth was the movement used to measure all other movements or changes in all of nature. As Landes writes, it was natural for early people to measure their lives by "daybreak, sunrise, high noon, sunset, and darkness" (p.1). It is worth noting that, in primitive times, distances were most likely measured by time: one place might be a two days' journey away, etc. If days and parts of days constituted the units of time whereby all other activities were measured, then it would be tempting to identify time with the movement of the sun.

The advances in understanding nature that we've come to refer to collectively as "The Rise of Modern Science" could not take place until some more EXACT way of measuring minutes, eventually seconds, was invented. But, in each instance, some "standard" movement or change became the measure for all others: the movement of water, drop by drop, from one container to another, the movement of sand through the hour-glass's small opening, the back-and-forth movement of the clock's pendulum, the regular advances of the spring-operated escapement wheel, and now the vibrations (9,192,631.770 per second) of cesium atoms (same *Time* article).

Closer analysis, though, shows that such movements of physical objects, no matter how "regular," really are NOT time. At best, they are only our methods for "measuring" time (if it exists), and which rhythmic movement or change we select is purely arbitrary. Eventually, we discover that, if there is such a thing as time, it is entirely independent of the motions we arbitrarily select as "instruments" for measuring it. It is only a short step from there to discovering that thoughts about time are precisely that: THOUGHTS that come to us, what we understand. We also discover that there is no such thing as the time we have the thoughts about. In other words, our thoughts about time, the time we think about, as well as the thoughts whereby we measure it, are purely psychological or mental things, not physical at all. The pathways of analysis from what's physical to what's in the mind are many. They all converge on one fact: Without minds, there'd be no time, no thoughts or questions about time, and no measure of time.

The one analysis most often used to turn our thoughts to some inner sense of time is also often left incompletely analysed. We know that there are experiences that drag by and others which fly. Often, this psychological fact is used as if it indicates there are two kinds of time, real or objective time and psychological or subjective time. But this isn't right. The only reason for realizing that the "subjective impression" is something noteworthy is the assumption that it's an illusion.

To begin with, every MEASURE of "how much time" something took requires a mind to COMPARE two things: what's measured and the yardstick it's measured against. When we say an experience (listening to a boring lecture) dragged by—e.g., "It seemed like it was three hours long"—we mean that our overall "impression" was that the experience was LIKE other experiences which begin with the hour hand on one number and end with the hour hand on the third-later number. If an enjoyable evening flew by—"It seemed like only an hour"—we mean that our overall impression was that this experience was LIKE other experiences that ended with the hour hand only one number later. Why we bother to use "SEEMED" rather than "was" is because the lecture "really" only took an hour and the evening "really" took three. We're comparing subjective, psychological "experiences" with (a)other past experiences measured by movements of a clock or watch and with (b)contemporaneous, present movements of a clock or watch.

But that's an incomplete analysis, however, because it omits to mention a BASIC BELIEF OR ASSUMPTION: that the clock THIS time was not really moving faster or slower than it did on those earlier occasions. If the clock ran three times faster on those earlier occasions which both seemed and were three hours long than it did during the lecture (or if the clock ran three times slower during the lecture), then our subjective impressions would be correct. "Hour" after all is only a description—for us who rely on clocks and watches—of what happens while the clock's hour hand is moving from one number to the next. The same thing is true of the enjoyable evening.

In other words, Newton was right: we assume that the REGULAR, REPEATED movements or other changes on which we rely to measure time must—if they're to be reliable the way we ASSUME (incorrectly, if our watch-hands' revolutions, the sun's circling, the earth's rotating, or the atom's vibrations fluctuate in speed)—are constant as measured against some UNVARYING or "equably flowing" background measure that no one's ever observed, that physicists have tried in vain to "verify." The most famous attempts were the Michelson-Morley experiments.

The key to all of this is a THREE-ITEM distinction. There are the things we want to measure, time-wise (lectures and enjoyable evenings). There are the things we use to measure them time-wise (clocks and watches). And there is our understanding of what we mean when we say "We have no way to prove that the second item, the thing we use to measure other things, itself 'runs' at an absolutely uniform, unvarying rate, i.e., without ever speeding up or slowing down." The first two things, what's measured and what's used to measure it, are both things we think of as physical and common-sensically think of as accessible to our senses. The third is neither, and is completely unknowable except for beings to whom thoughts come: ourselves.

Understanding the first two things is easiest. From the days of our earliest ancestors until Copernicus, people used what they believed was the movement of the sun around the earth to measure everything else. Since Copernicus, the custom has been reversed, and we today believe it is the earth's rotation on its axis every twenty-four hours that is the most basic time-measure of all. Except if we happen to live in a technologically-advanced country where people organize their activities according to the movements of clocks and watches, and then the clocks and watches become the standard measuring devices and everything else is measurED by them. But watches are just 3-D physical objects like the earth and sun. In the same way that ink-marks are only ink-marks (regardless of how different people react to the sight of them), so there are just moving or changing things (nothing "static" and unchanging would be useful for us to "tell time" with), and all three move in repetitious fashion, over and over again, at unvarying rates. WE ASSUME. It is that assumption—that a regular repetition can be perfectly regular—that has led people to constantly look for one. For the Greeks and our Western World ancestors, there seemed to be no reason to doubt that sky-bodies operate on perfectly regular, daily schedules: the sun takes exactly the same amount of time to return to any exact PLACE of the imaginary circle (path, orbit) it follows or creates while revolving around the earth, just as the moon and other planets do. In our time, few of us doubt that the earth takes exactly the same amount of time to return to any particular position vis-à-vis the sun as it (the earth) performs its daily spinning pirouette. The same thing would apply to yearly cycles: the sun, which "moves south" during the northern hemisphere's summer and slightly "back north" during the winter, or the earth whose axis wobbles just slightly, keep returning to any selected "original" position at exact intervals. But—as mentioned earlier—the daily and yearly cycles are useless for measuring the rate of acceleration for cannon balls dropped from the tops of towers (e.g., at Pisa) or to measure the lifetime of some kinds of subatomic particles. Hence the invention of clocks and watches. They weren't perfect, for they were continually "gaining" and "losing" time. Until recently, that is, when more and more perfect clocks and watches have been invented that are assumed to fluctuate by no more than the smallest fraction of a second per day. The Aug/Sept issue of *Technology Review* mentioned on p.12 that "the latest atomic clock will err by less than a second in 3 million years."

> Still, *that almost-perfect non-fluctuation is assumed*, for the simple reason that the measurements of one thing's perfect regularity—that thing can be circling sun, rotating earth, swinging pendulum, twisting watch wheel, vibrating quartz crystal, oscillating atom—will always have to be some other thing's regularity. But if EVERYthing, *what measures and what's measured*, slowed down together or speeded up together or fluctuated together, we'd never know because we don't have anything ELSE to observe while comparing THEM to it.

That's the reason for adding to the two observable or noticeable items, one of which is measured and the other of which is used for measuring what's measured, a third item, namely, a "background" understanding of the fact that we must assume UNVARYING regularity or constancy in the measuring item. Newton invented what we now must recognize as a metaphor to capture this background understanding, the metaphor of something "flowing" equally, to which "something" he gave the name "absolute, true, and mathematical time." His metaphor—so beautiful that it has captured the imaginations of physicists and other readers for generations since—is a metaphor for something wholly inaccessible to our senses, something that we can become explicitly aware of only by hard thinking.

Recognition that we have this background understanding is reached by the same kind of analysis Plato furnishes in the *Phaedo* (sec.73, ff) to bring us to the realization that we carry with us an understanding of "perfect equalness" and that no matter what sense-observable pair of things we describe as equal (somewhat equal, almost equal, perfectly equal), we apply to them this background "sense" of perfect equalness. Plato's conclusion, that we cannot possibly get this thought of perfect equalness FROM the things we sense, since they are always IMperfectly equal (do we get the idea of a mouse from seeing a tree?), is parallel to this case: we don't get our sense of perfectly equal intervals of time FROM the reappearance of the sun, FROM the return of the pendulum, FROM the successive ticks of the clock, FROM the re-crossing of "12" by any of the watch's hands, since it is precisely about THEM that we ask "Are they equal?" Our mental "yardstick," the thought of what's perfectly equal, is no more part of the things of which we ask "How perfectly equal are they?" than the yardstick is part of the carpet about which we're asking "How long is it?"

A note on relativity theories. (More exactly, a note on various authors' VARIOUS interpretations of Einstein's relativity theorIES.) Because time is a topic at the very core of any interpretation of relativity formulae—which, in themselves, are meaningless ink-marks, in the same category with what is on Page Six or any other piece of paper in the whole world—and because what is discussed above and below relates to ANY AND EVERY thought about "time," it is appropriate to insert a brief note on how the conflicting interpretations of those formulae connect with these reflections on that non-entity, time. Whoever would like to have his or her thoughts "stretched" on the topic of time can find the wherewithal in the many popularizations of Einstein's theories. Everyone has his or her favorites, and my own preference is M.Gardner's *The Relativity Explosion* (the 1976 revision of his already masterful *Relativity for the Million*). A.Eddington's *Space, Time and Gravitation* is an older classic. Einstein's own *Relativity: The Special and General Theory* (in 1952, three years before his death, he added a fifth appendix to the 15th edition of this 1916 work) has fewer everyday illustrations and is more difficult than either of those; in addition, it—like several interpretations—is laced through with an epistemology closely related to the no-longer-popular theories of the logical positivists. (As Einstein himself confessed to Heisenberg.)

There are two key principles that are of the utmost importance for the correct interpretation of relativity formulae, just as they are for interpreting anything else. The first is: separate fact from fiction (both useful and useless). The second is: abstract revisions of some parts of commonsense derive their only empirical support from other parts of everyday commonsense.

As for the first, whoever reads ANYthing on relativity theory (or "quantum physics) would profit by first reading Einstein/s and Infeld's *The Evolution of Physics* (part I at the very least) in order to get in the right frame of mind, one expressed with perfect succinctness by M.Kline in the remark quoted earlier on page 43: "The greatest science FICTION stories are in the science of physics." (Let it be noted: this is not unique to physics.) In the *Evolution of Physics*, we find the following passage which reflects a theme Einstein repeated over and over during a long career spent reflecting on just why it is that the mathematically expressed laws of our physics seemingly allow us to understand something of reality:

Physical concepts are free creations of the human mind, and are not, however it may seem, uniquely determined by the external world. In our endeavor to understand reality we are somewhat like a man trying to understand the mechanism of a closed watch. He sees the face and the moving hands, even hears its ticking, but he has no way of opening the case. If he is ingenious he may form some picture of a mechanism which could be responsible for all the things he observes, but he may never be quite sure his picture is the only one which could explain his observations. He will never be able to compare his picture with the real mechanism and he cannot even imagine the possibility or the meaning of such a comparison. But he certainly believes that, as his knowledge increases, his picture of reality will become simpler and simpler and will explain a wider and wider range of his sensuous impressions. He may also believe in the existence of the ideal limit of knowledge and that it is approached by the human mind. He may call this ideal limit the objective truth. (A.Einstein and L.Infeld, *The Evolution of Physics*, p.31.)

It would be difficult to find a clearer expression of representationalism: each one of us must deal not only with a nature but also with other people who are out beyond our direct access, with realities of which we must form our own inner maps and theories, which we constantly test against our sense-impressions. From the passage cited on page 190-91, it is clear that Einstein regards sensuous impressions the way everyone from Galileo to Kant did, viz., as effects IN us of OUTside causes we cannot get even so much as a peek at.

A key phrase to keep in mind when reading works on relativity theory, therefore, is THEORETICAL FICTIONS. Those who embrace relativity theories become used to the notion that our everyday commonsense notions are "unscientific" and need to be replaced by "more scientific" approaches. Once we realize that "commonsense" is the name for THEORY (Thesis XIX, p.180), it follows that those mistaken commonsense notions are themselves theoretical fictions. What is not noticed, frequently, is that the "scientific" replacements are equally fictitious. When that's not recognized and these "scientific" replacements have become HABITS of thought, they come to seem as self-evident as the fictions they replaced. What is also not noticed is that these replacement fictions float like so many stringless balloons unless they're firmly attached to everyday commonsense experience.

Gravity is an excellent example for understanding what is meant. The force of thought-HABITS is illustrated by our initial reaction to the claim that gravity does not exist. As a result of unnoticed but routine "reinforcement" by what we hear and read, our belief that gravity is what makes a vase fall when it slips from our grasp seems so obvious that we almost gasp in disbelief the first time we're told that some physicists believe there's no such thing as the force of gravity. That would not have fazed people who lived before Newton. To them (and to us when we were very young), it would have seemed equally self-evident that it was the vase's weight—heaviness—that made it fall. But is there really any such thing as "the force of gravity"? The fact that the writers quoted earlier on pp.147-49 use it as a standard example of a construct would suggest that there isn't. Or at least that those authors think there isn't. Here is what M.Kline, referred to above, thinks.

> Contrary to popular belief, no one has ever explained the physical reality of the force of gravitation. It is a fiction suggested by the human ability to exert force. The greatest science fiction stories are in the science of physics. However, mathematical deductions from the quantitative law proved so effective that this procedure has been accepted as an integral part of physical science. What science has done, then, is to sacrifice physical intelligibility for the sake of mathematical description and mathematical prediction. (M.Kline, *Mathematics and the Search for Knowledge*, p.122.)

Kline contrasts mathematical description to physical intelligibility and says physics (physicists) sacrifice the latter for the first. It is preferable to say that some physicists believe they've sacrificed physical intelligibility for mathematical description, but even more preferable to say that it is absolutely impossible to have mathematical description or prediction without some minimum of "physical intelligibility."

In fact, popularizers of relativity theory—as well as professional "physicists" in their professional writings—strain to find physical counterparts to which they can apply the quantitative formulae. And it is here that the contradictions, disagreements, and science fictions become obvious. Some writers continue to treat gravity as a force. Some speak of gravity waves and ask whether they are propagated in time the way electromagnetic energy is or whether it is propagated instantaneously. Some discuss particles of gravity or packets of gravitational force called "gravitons," and describe experimental efforts to detect them. Others speak of warps in space, warps in the space-time continuum, worm-holes through the space-time continuum. Each of these is denied by others, much as the claim that gravity is equivalent to inertia is denied by those who believe gravity is a real force but inertia is not a force at all, much as both those claims are denied by those who believe neither gravity nor inertia are forces. Some interpretations of Einstein's relativity formulae are so bizarre that Gardner's apt description of some quantum interpretations as "Quantum Weirdness" (see *Discover* magazine for October, 1982, pp.69,ff.) suggests that these should be called "Relativity Weirdness." [A note. It helps to recall that even Newton who, in spite of his remark "I don't create hypotheses" created an entire system of them (see pt.I of Einstein/Infeld's *Evolution of Physics*), and who enunciated the "law" that governs this hypothetical entity, gravity, expressed his own thoughts with enough ambiguity to cause endless discussions about "Just what DID Newton think about gravity?" See for instance *Newton's Philosophy of Nature: Selections from his Writings*, edited by H.S.Thayer, and E.McMullin's *Newton on Matter and Activity*.]

What conclusion should we draw from these disagreements about gravity? (And this is only one of the many disagreements in the interpretations of the mathematical formulae.) The first conclusion has just been explained: all of these interpretations are loaded with theoretical fictions. The second, mentioned above, is equally important.

The second is that abstract revisions of some parts of commonsense derive their only empirical support from other parts of everyday commonsense. Unless the replacement fictions are firmly attached to everyday commonsense experience, they float adrift like so many stringless balloons.

No one can even begin to think about a space-time continuum, about warps in the space-time continuum, about the speed of light, about measuring movements of everything else against the movement of light, about twins whose metabolism and clocks run at different rates, about shrinking spaceships, about Doppler effects and red shifts, who doesn't first know about space and time separately, who doesn't know the difference between a continuous yardstick which we pretend is discontinuous by notching off sections ("cuts") at regular intervals and one that's really discontinuous (cut up), who doesn't know about the speed of tortoises and hares, about measuring the movement of everything against the movement of a tortoise or of a hare, about ordinary metabolism and clocks, about unshrinking space-ships, about the differences in the train-whistle's sound to the train's engineer and to the car-driver waiting for the train to get through the intersection, who cannot tell a telescope from a microscope, who doesn't understand the difference between a star and a white spot on a photograph, etc. That is, it is essential to keep in mind that we all begin our commonsense-theory revisions by using our common-sense theories.

It is equally essential to keep in mind that, in the interims between periods of intense speculation, we conduct our affairs the same way we did before we began to believe in relativity-related paradoxes: we eat, sleep, wake, bathe, go to the store to purchase stationery supplies so that we can take notes about relativity paradoxes, etc. Only if we can RE-join the abstractions, whether couched in the familiar ink-marks we call "prose" or the forbidding ones we call "mathematical formulae," with those interim everyday experiences (see, e.g., Reichenbach's description on pp.183-84), can we conclude we really understand what's going on.

One way to rejoin theory and experience is never to quit thinking about the question: What do I SEE? (In physics as well as in psychology: see p.227.) Just as the paradoxes of quantum theory do not arise at the level of everyday life but only in connection with alleged submicroscopic realities that are UNSEEN, so the paradoxes of relativity theory do not arise at the level of everyday life but only in connection with alleged events in the macrocosm that are UNSEEN. It is as hard to recognize this sometimes, however, as it is to recognize that what we scan while we're "reading" are ink-marks, period, so swift is our imagination to supply what we then "project" by the process referred to as "theory-laden observation" (see pp.55,ff):

> Physicists often speak of "seeing" the subatomic particles that are produced in particle accelerators. The particles can be made to interact within a device called a bubble chamber, which is a large tank that has been filled with hydrogen. As the particles pass through the hydrogen, they produce tiny bubbles. After these bubbles are photographed, the particle interactions that took place can be studied at leisure.

> But are the particles really seen? Of course not. The only things that are observed
> are hydrogen bubbles that are strung together like beads . . . The particles themselves
> are too small to be observed directly, even by the most powerful electron microscopes.
> (R.Morris, *Dismantling the Universe*, "Epilogue: How Real is 'Real'?")

To be completely thorough, we should ask: But are even the bubbles seen? Einstein, like Russell (and Descartes to Kant), would say "Of course not" (see pages 190-91). In fact, what physicists study are photographs with streaks on them. That is what must be kept in mind when reading physicists' wildly contradictory interpretations of quantum formulae. Bohr and Einstein, recall, wrangled for a quarter of a century over their contradictory interpretations.

And what do astronomers who wrestle with the paradoxes of relativity and space-time continua, etc., actually observe? Mostly photographs (though Einstein, like Russell [and Descartes to Kant], would say "Not even photographs"). It comes as a shock to most of us to be told that the modern professional astronomer hardly ever looks through a telescope. Yet the opening lines of a recent book on stars powerfully evoke the way things are in the late twentieth century.

> When day ends, the blazing sun relinquishes the sky to the pinprick glimmerings
> of a multitude of cousins. The appearances of these other suns triggers a flurry
> of activity on the night side of the globe as astronomers perform last minute
> calibrations—pushing buttons, flicking switches, and sighting through the eyepieces
> of their telescopes. Then, guided by computers, the giant contraptions of steel and
> glass begin tracking the stars. But once the telescope locks onto its target, human eyes
> seldom bother to look again. Even through the most powerful instrument, stars are
> too far away—the nearest being some 6 trillion miles distant—to show up as more
> than specks of light. What astronomers covet is not a visual glimpse of these celestial
> bodies but a more permanent record of their elusive radiation. (E.Ferrington?, *Stars,
> Voyage Through the Universe Series*, Time-Life Books.)

The direct connection between relativity-theory interpretations and these reflections on time should be obvious, then. For, when we LOOK to discover what it is we really do observe, it seems—commonsensically, at the level of everyday life—that the things we see and the way they move fits well within the commonsense notions behind Newton's descriptions of time and motion. (The notions must be freed from some of Newton's descriptions, hence the term "behind.") Nothing we SEE zooms by us with a velocity approaching that of light. It is only when such velocities are involved that the relativity formulae tempt us to doubt our common sense. The same will be said later in connection with interpretations of quantum theory, when it will become important to ask whether anything we SEE violates the law of causality by happening without a prior event, for it is only at that point in our speculation that the quantum formulae tempt us to doubt our common sense. That is why, to repeat, it is essential for us to first understand well our everyday common sense before we dive headlong into worse complications than we already face.

Of course, if Berkeley—whose views have been adopted by many physicists of last century and this—is right, the unobserved and unobservable physical world of stars and planets, space-ships and time-clocks, suns and subatomic particles, does not exist at all. Except in our imaginations. James tried to make it go away by sleight-of-hand semantics (p.119 above), but the Einstein/Infeld quotation brings the question right back: Is there ANY reality out there "behind" our sensuous impressions? The problem's there for each of us to face in our turn. We can pretend not to notice, but that's cowardly. Better to confront it boldly; that's what pp.9,ff—"The Iron Curtain Objection"—were all about, and that's why pp.190,ff, brought it back. [End of long! 'note on relativity.']

Time & laws of nature: fictions. Before leaving the discussion of Newton's metaphor of absolute time as an equably flowing backdrop to our lives, it is worth spending a little more time reflecting on how it permeates all of our "scientific theories." Some people have come to the conclusion that the triumph of "modern" science is that its practitioners have substituted the search for LAWS in place of the search for FORCES and CAUSES (see Page Six). Nothing, perhaps, better illustrates the importance of clarifying our thoughts about time than the task of clarifying our thoughts about the laws of nature.

How should we think of "laws of nature"? Clearly the expression is metaphorical. Can any of us imagine a group of atoms holding a conference to draft a set of laws for atomic physics? No more than we can imagine planets doing it, trees doing it, or insects. And, in spite of the volume of first-hand observations of our so-called "closest cousins"—chimps, gorillas, etc.—that have been carried out in this half of the twentieth century, no reports have come back of any parleys at which these cousins have discussed either tribal laws or any kind of inter-group laws. So what are these laws of nature?

At first they don't seem anything like the human laws they are analogues of. But what are human laws? Our laws can be thought of, common-sensically, as descriptions of certain kinds of behavior (killing people, driving over the speed limit, interfering with people who are exercising their rights of free speech, voting for presidential candidates not born in this country, etc.) that we are advised not to engage in. But, unlike the case with, say, the dietary laws our physician advises us to follow, we know that we are expected to "follow" these human laws OR ELSE. Or else we can expect other people called "police," others called "judges," and others called "jail guards" to engage in certain kinds of behavior described elsewhere in the "law." But our "laws" assume that we can understand language, can interpret those cues and clues to the thoughts that the "lawgivers" had in mind when they "put them on paper." That's because we have to KNOW the law (it has to be promulgated) before we can OBEY it. It is also assumed that we can DISobey the law, which is why some are elected and others appointed to "enforce" the law, i.e., to punish with either physical or psychological pain those who do not behave in the ways prescribed to and expected to be obeyed by good citizens.

BY CONTRAST, the laws of nature aren't written. The atoms, trees, insects, and animals that "obey" them couldn't read them if they were. The beings that "obey" them don't know them. And the beings that "obey" them have no choice between obeying or disobeying.

But the contrast is specious. A better way to view human laws starts with the idea of contracts, which is why it is no accident that there is a theory about the origin of human laws called the Social Contract Theory. Laws and contracts, if they exist at all, exist only in minds. Neither has ever been put on paper," only small ink-marks made by the "law-givers" and "law-yers" so they'd be able to remember what they'd agreed on. Anyone who's familiar with the history of Supreme Court Justices constantly faced with new challenges to old "interpretations" of the original ink-marks, like anyone who's familiar with what clever lawyers can do with the jot-and-tittle ink-marks will understand why trying to find the "law" in the small ink-marks is equivalent to trying to find the "meaning" in the small ink-marks. In other ~~words~~ cues and clues, everything Chapter I said about the non-existence of LANGUAGE can be repeated for the non-existence of LAWS. The reason that Wittgenstein (quoted on Page Six) is right in saying that the laws of nature explain nothing is because THERE ARE NO LAWS OF NATURE. "Laws of nature" is a cue for a theoretical fiction which we create by analogy with our thoughts about HUMAN "laws." Which would be descriptions IF such things existed. "Descriptions," too, is (or are) cues for a theoretical fiction.

But DESCRIPTION is one of the two best theoretical fictions to use when trying to understand the "laws of nature" theoretical fiction. (The other is prediction.) The laws of nature are descriptions of how things have behaved IN THE PAST. But—to borrow James' description of the present or specious-past duration (p.247)—the "laws of nature" are fictions "from which we look in two directions into time." At the same time that they are descriptions when we're looking into the past, they are PREDICTIONS of how we expect things to behave IN THE FUTURE. This notion is one of the most important of the 1001 Basic Commitments I've made, and bears underlining:

> THESIS XXIII. "Laws of nature" are shorthand descriptions of what things have done in the past and express our predictions or expectations concerning what they will do in the future.

That formulation makes clear the intimate relation between time and the laws of nature. The laws of nature are our "mental bridges" from the past where we've been, over the flowing now, into the fog-bound future that we've not yet seen. Equipped with memories for where we've been, these "laws of nature" are our guide into an unknown "Beyond," one that doesn't even exist until we step foot into it.

The link with "absolute" time becomes clear when we understand why it is so important for our predictions to "come true" at precisely EXACT times. It is because laws are SHORTHAND descriptions for events, and the events for which they are laws are REGULARITIES. We're inclined to distinguish the laws from the concrete events, inclined to imagine that somehow we can extract (by "induction") the golden kernel, the law, from the insignificant particulars that merely "exemplify" it.

But that's the Platonist in us. It's the same Platonist in us that looks for a definition of virtue "in itself," APART FROM this woman's courage, that man's honesty, that child's docility, that other child's loyalty (see p.63 above), that makes us overlook that even these "virtues," i.e., good "habits," are shorthand reifications from our descriptions of agents acting.

Why are we interested in predicting the precise time that Halley's comet will return, that the next total eclipse of the sun will be visible from this point on the globe, etc.? Because these are the actual regularities predicted by the laws concerning regularities. The law of inertia says that a body (comet, star, satellite) undisturbed by an outside force will continue moving AT A UNIFORM RATE. That means, EACH SECOND or minute or hour it will cover EXACTLY as much distance as it covered each of the preceding undisturbed periods. Notice the regularities: in a vacuum at sea level unsupported apples will be falling 32 ft/sec faster at the end of each second than they were going at the second's beginning, half of the unsplit atoms in a lump of uranium will split regularly (every 4,500,000,000 years), a cesium atom oscillates regularly (9,192,631.770 times each second), etc. And what do we use to measure those times? The watches and clocks in whose REGULARITY we place so much confidence. For good reason: the things we make our watches and clocks with, as well as the watches and clocks themselves, all obey REGULAR laws of nature. Which is the only reason we rely on them.

All of that is, of course, circular "argumentation," with one theoretical fiction created on top of others and interlocking with them. What we need to do is to sort out the facts from the fictions. Such as the fiction that there are iron-clad differences built into such ink-marks as guidelines, facts, rules, laws, inductions, descriptions, etc. The fact is that we often stop our analyses just before the point where they become interesting. Just before, for instance, we discover that so many of the things we call "laws of nature" are BELIEFS ABOUT THE FUTURE RIDING ATOP BELIEFS ABOUT THE PAST.

Hume's analysis of causality. Another approach that uncovers the same connection between laws of nature and time comes from Hume's analysis of causality, which turns out to be *an analysis of regularity rather than causality.*

Start by considering the question: What certainty do we have that the sun will rise tomorrow? I have a statistics book whose author writes: "We cannot say with certainty that the sun will rise tomorrow." In fact, the author claims that all of science's laws are only probable, that statistics is fundamental to all of science.

At first that sounds positively absurd. If we cannot be certain the sun will rise tomorrow—even Aristotle thought that view was safely in the fold of scientific truths!—then what can we be certain of? (Death and taxes is an answer our habits of expectation regularly suggest.) Does the author mean that predicting tomorrow's sunrise is akin to fortune-telling, crystal-ball gazing, or astrology? Didn't astronomers long ago change their name from astrologers to astronomers to indicate their break away from pseudo-science to real science?

Yet, what evidence DO we have for what will happen tomorrow, which is in the FUTURE? Our only evidence is what we believe has happened in the PAST. Is there anyone who claims that they've discovered the CONNECTION between past and future, that they KNOW why nature's laws won't change overnight? The most famous, detailed examination of this question was conducted by David Hume (see, for instance, section IV of his *Enquiry Concerning Human Understanding*), and his surprising conclusion was a powerful spur to one of the most famous systematic thinkers of all time, Immanuel Kant, who said Hume's examination woke him from his "dogmatic slumber." Hume's conclusion? Though he is quite content, he says, to take it for granted "THAT THE FUTURE WILL RESEMBLE THE PAST" and that "the course of things" will continue to be "regular," yet we must confess ourselves completely in the dark as to the underlying reason for it. We are in the habit of EXPECTING that it will, and each time nature fulfills our expectations that things will continue behaving as they've always done, the psychological law of habit-formation describes what happens: our habit of expecting it to happen again becomes stronger. But there's really no way to PROVE that nature will continue operating in the future by the same laws or regularities it has operated on in the past. We're "so positive" that it will, that we're shocked that anyone would even question it. But when we try to find the connection between past and future, all we have is our MEMORY (and sometimes less) of how things have behaved in the past.

Now it is precisely this ASSUMPTION about nature's regularity that is at the core of the discussion about time: each moment of ANYthing is future, whether sun's rise or clock's tick or atom's vibration. Without a guarantee about the sun's next rising, the clock's next ticking, the atom's next vibration, etc., we also have no guarantee they'll occur ON TIME: what guarantee do we have that the next light wave will emerge at the same time interval that the last one did? Once our illusion that we have guarantees about the future is brushed aside, we can see more clearly that we have been merely taking it for granted all along. We think "The only way to be practical is to assume that nature's laws won't change," and everyone else who wants just to be practical agrees. So we walk down the stairs rather than try to fly down from the window, give children silly-putty to play with rather than tri-nitro-toluene, and make sure that, if we must, we lie down over by the lambs, not near the lions. Who but a fool would assume nature's laws will change? Hume himself didn't challenge them:

> My practice, you say, refutes my doubts. But you mistake the purport of my question. As an agent, I am quite satisfied in the point; but as a philosopher [scientist], who has some share of curiosity, I will not say skepticism, I want to *learn the foundation* of this inference. Can I do better than propose the difficulty to the public, even though, perhaps, I have small hopes of obtaining a solution? We shall at least, by this means, *be sensible of our ignorance*, if we do not augment our knowledge. (*Enquiry*, sec. IV; emphasis added.)

His mindset may have been worlds apart from that of Socrates. He may have thrown in the sponge on life's questions, a thing Socrates refused to do even hours before drinking the hemlock. He may have recommended caring first for the things Socrates put last. But on the matter of acknowledging we don't know when we don't know now, the Scot's refrain is the same as the Greek's . . . .

Finally, reflecting on time would not be complete without a few words about DURATION and how believing in it can create total mental atrophy about our real human condition. What is meant by "duration" varies from person to person, from context to context. Isaac Newton, in the very passage where he defined time, called it "another name" for that equably flowing, absolute, true, and mathematical time. It is just as easy, however, to use "duration" for imaginary things diametrically opposite to what's flowing. Think of a river or a section of a river. "Duration" is the name for a high-in-the-sky view of the ribbon of time that we say wends its way below, though from where we're at it seems to stand still.

The contrast is total. The knife-edge view of a moving, razor-thin NOW dividing a non-existent past from a non-existent future is only one step from the complete truth: even the razor-thin NOW is non-existent. There are only things which are continually changing. Let me repeat the formula: (i) only things that presently exist actually exist; (ii) the things that presently exist only exist the way they are at present, that is, (iii) they weren't always the way they are now, and (iv) they won't always remain the way they are now.

The down-there-river picture is the reverse. Like the parts of a flowing river, it seems that every part of time or "duration" is real. It's all right there in front of us. People don't notice that our POWERFUL IMAGINATIONS enable us humans to constantly perform the trick which only God [see page 245] is supposedly capable of: from the platform of a motionless NOW we can take in with one glance all of time: past, present, and future. The past is off there to the left, the future off to the right, and the present is dead-center. In a way remarkably reminiscent of reading, our eyes "follow" time from left to right, exactly the way our eyes sweep across the print on pages like this one, across the signs on billboards, across the labels on soup cans, etc.

Now, imagine the river to be frozen solid, devoid of motion. Whereas in reality the very concept of motionlessness is a figment of our imagination, as Max Born observed, and whereas in reality neither our pricey camera with its thousandth of a second shutter-speed nor an Edgerton strobe can completely "stop" the speeding bullet, and whereas in reality some particles have lifetimes measured in billionths of a second, the frozen-river illusion makes it possible for us to imagine ourselves with an eternity in which to leisurely contemplate the story of temporal eternity. The more we learn about the details, the more we fill in the blanks in our imaginative reconstruction, the more apt we are to fall into Hegel's Black Hole, where we disappear and just the final, fixed picture remains. Of course, we aren't left out of the fixed picture. Can't you see us? Right there, in that tiny section labeled "Twentieth Century." No wonder his readers concluded that Hegel's "System" was the final chapter, that if it was true—and who could doubt, once they'd glimpsed the Finished Canvas?—the Zeitgeist has run its course. Parmenides would have applauded. Change is no longer real. "Change" is the name we give to those pre-enlightenment illusions of ours, and "dialectic" describes structure, not process. James Jeans compared the whole of world history to a finished tapestry and our lives to paths marked off by flies crawling across its surface.

If ever it is essential to have absorbed—even better than he himself did—Einstein's repeated warning about the power of our imaginations and the need to control them, it is when we deal with matters of those two non-entities, time and space. His epistemology is superior to Kant's (page 7, earlier), because he recognized the EXTENT of creative imagination's role even better than Kant did. It is worth noting that the following lines come from a passage where he himself contrasts his views with Kant's.

> I am convinced that even much more is to be asserted: the concepts which arise in our thought and in our linguistic expressions are all—when viewed logically—the free creations of thought which cannot inductively be gained from sense experiences . . . Thus, for example, the series of integers is obviously an invention of the human mind, a self-created tool which simplifies the ordering of certain sensory experience . . . (A. Einstein, *Ideas and Opinions*, p.33.)

His point, that our constructions do NOT come from experience, not even by induction, should hang over the entrances to ALL the classrooms in the university, not just over those where physicists lecture. But it was understandable that he spoke most often of the power of physicists' imaginations:

> If you want to find out anything from the theoretical physicists about the methods they use, I advise you to stick closely to one principle: don't listen to their words, fix your attention on their deeds. To him who is a discoverer in this field, the products of his imagination appear so necessary and natural that he regards them, and would like to have them regarded by others, not as creations of thought but as given realities. (Same source, p.264.)

But, wait. Isn't it possible that duration really does exist? As a psychological reality, though? Isn't the whole purpose of these analyses to track time FROM the physical world TO our mind? Perhaps we've merely sought duration in the wrong place, viz., OUTside of ourselves, rather than where it really is, viz., INside us. Why else do we say and understand such things as the following: "The past exists only in our mind, i.e., in our memory," "The future exists only in our mind, i.e., in our expectation," "Past, present, and future—the parts of time—do not exist OUTside us, only INside us." There are writers who've thought this way, and we must take a quick sidelong glance at their ideas.

For instance, see how easy it is to read the following passage from St.Augustine (about reciting a familiar passage) with the mindset that past and future do co-exist with the present,

IN OUR CONSCIOUSNESS. What he writes can be applied to any kind of recitation: poem, paragraph, even a sentence.

> Before I begin [reciting], my attention encompasses the whole, but once I have begun, as much of it as becomes past while I speak is still stretched out in my memory. The span of my action is divided between my memory, which contains what I have recited, and my expectation, which contains what I am about to recite. Yet my attention is continually present with me, and through it what was future is carried over so that it becomes past. As the process [of reciting] continues, memory is constantly increased—and expectation is shortened—until the whole expectation is finished. (St. Augustine, *Confessions*, Bk.XI, sec.28.)

But our mind has no more room for past and future than the universe outside does. All of our memory-images, spread-out as these faint copies of originally spread-out sense-data may be, are *present* memory-images. We don't literally hold our memories of the past in the back of our minds and our expectations of the future up front. All the "room" is taken up with the *present* ones. There's no 'space' for long recitations or any of the other things Augustine goes on to speak about . . .

Not till we appreciate fully the power of our imagination, our power to create and BELIEVE FULLY IN fiction (Einstein, p.260), will we begin to understand ourselves and how utterly, infinitely superior we are to every other kind of creature we are acquainted with (if any exist). Not till we appreciate fully the EXTENT to which we live amidst creations of our powerful imaginations, will we begin to suspect the real nature of the world and of the 'world' in which we live. Not until we put both together will we understand what's REALLY going on. What's going on is quite different from what we got in the habit of believing while we were growing up.

Addendum. Calendars and time-lines—including all the time charts we find in history books—are to the clock what written language is to spoken. "Written language" gives us temporally coexistent, fixed "symbols" for the sounds (and thoughts) that cannot be frozen any more than time. Calendars, just more ink-marks on paper, give us temporally coexistent, fixed "symbols" for the ticking of the clock (and thoughts of time). The standard calendar, with anywhere from 28 to 31 "blocks" that are read exactly the way the print on the page is read, gives us 28 to 31 abbreviations, 28 to 31 bits of shorthand, for 1 rotation of the clock's hour-hand or 24 turns of its minute-hand or 1440 spins of its second-hand. Of course, that's merely pretending. The calendar is just ink-marks on paper. What thoughts it triggers depends upon our habits of association, etc. In physics, we often use just a straight line, "read" from left to right, with short perpendicular strokes which "cut" the segments of duration so they can be labeled and counted, etc. The lines, one beneath or on top of the other, that are used as charts in the history books, are really shorthand for dozens or hundreds of "pages of the months" from one-year calendars. The lines in archaeology books are shorthand for thousands and millions of month-pages. But, then again, they're all just lines. The same line—with no change in its length, thickness, or shape—can represent the thousandth-of-a-second flight of a sub-atomic particle in a physics book, the Tudor dynasty in a history book, and the Paleozoic Era in an archaeology book. It's what our imaginations "project" onto them that we're really interested in.

The addendum brings to a close this brief introduction to the nature of the time concepts essential for creating inner scenarios of the universe's doings, so that we can (in imagination at least) get a bird's eye view of cosmic HISTORY and our own place in it, much the way that space-maps, ranging from those of the heavens to those of our home-town, enable us (in imagination at least) to get a bird's eye view of cosmic GEOGRAPHY and our own location in it. This is the fourth section of this second chapter, the third on "Mindset as a Bundle of 'Habitual' Expectations." The first dealt with habits, the second introduced the notion of how quickly we work with a vastly underestimated volume of information, and this one has tried to heighten awareness of the time dimension involved in living-into an unknown future that seems already familiar because of what we bring with us from our now-no-longer-existing past. Next, we zero in on just one feature of "what we bring with us from our past."

SELECTED BIBLIOGRAPHY

Although the text uses original publication dates for reference purposes, many citations are taken from later editions. Where these later editions have been used, they are indicated here in parentheses. (For instance, Eddington's *The Nature of the Physical World*, was originally published in 1928, but the quotation in the text is taken from the 1968 paperback edition.)

Some items that have been consulted but not cited are included for readers desiring further source material. Note, however, that—despite protests to the contrary—there have been no 'breakthroughs' regarding basic issues in the last fifty years. In fact, the usual complaint about philosophy is that there has been no progress in the last five centuries, since today's philosophers continue to debate the same old questions. The reason is obvious. Everyone begins with the same philosophy, common sense, a truth emphasized throughout this text, and everyone has to individually decide how much of common sense to retain and how much to surrender.

ADLER, M. J., *The Difference of Man and the Difference It Makes*, 1967, NY: Hold, Rinehart and Winston. (Meridian Books, 1968).

AQUINAS, St. Thomas, *Aristotle's DE ANIMA with the Commentary of St. Thomas Aquinas* trans. K.Foster and S.Humphries, 1951.

ARMSTRONG, D.M., *The Mind-Body Problem*, 1999, Boulder, Co., Westview Press.

BAARS, B., *The Cognitive Revolution in Psychology*, 1986, NY: Guilford Press.

BARRETT, W., *Death of the Soul: From Descartes to the Computer*, 1987, Garden City, Doubleday.

BARZUN, J., *Darwin, Marx, Wagner*, 1941. (Doubleday Anchor, 1958).

BAUER, F., *James Vs Darwin*, 2009, NY, iUniverse Press.

BAUER, F., *The Wonderful Myth Called 'Science.'* 2008, Antioch, Solas Press.

BERKELEY, G., *Principles of Human Knowledge*,

BLOCK, N., ed., *Readings in Philosophy of Psychology*, 2 vols., 2001-02, Cambridge, Harvard Un. Press.

CAMPBELL, K., *Body and Mind*, 2nd ed., 1984, Notre Dame Press.

CHALMERS, A.F., *What Is This Thing Called Science?*, 3rd ed., 1999, Hackett Press.

DAWKINS, R., *Unweaving the Rainbow*, 1998, Boston, Houghton Mifflin.

DESCARTES, R., *Discourse on Method*, trans. Haldane-Ross, p.101.

DESCARTES, R., *Philosophical Letters*, trans. A.Kenny,

DOBZHANSKY, T., *The Biology of Ultimate Concern*, 1967, Cleveland, World Publishing Co.

EDDINGTON, A., *The Nature of the Physical World*, 1928, NY, Macmillan (Ann Arbor Paperbacks, 1968)

EINSTEIN, A., *Ideas and Opinions*, 1954, N.Y., Dell.

FIRTH, R., "Sense-Data and the Percept Theory," in R.J.Swartz, 1965.

FLEW, A., ed., *Body, Mind, and Death*, 1964, N.Y.; Macmillan.

GALE, R., ed., *The Philosophy of Time*, 1967, Garden City, NY., Doubleday.

GALLAGHER, K., *The Philosophy of Knowledge*, 1964, NY., Sheed & Ward.

HALL, C., *A Primer of Freudian Psychology*, 1954, NY., New American Library.

HEISENBERG, W., *Physics and Philosophy*, 1958. (Harper Torchbook, 1962)

HIRST, R.J., *Perception and the External World*, 1965, NY., Macmillan.

HOSPERS, J. *An Introduction to Philosophical Analysis*, 2nd ed., 1967, Englewood Cliffs, Prentice-Hall.

JAMES, W., *Psychology: Briefer Course*, 1892.

JAMES, W., *Pragmatism and Other Essays*, 1907.

JAMES, W., *Principles of Psychology*, 2 vols., 1892.

JUNG, C.G., "The Basic Postulates of Analytic Psychology," Chapter nine of *Modern Man in Search of a Soul*, 1933. (Included in Ruitenbeek.)

KOREN, H.J. *Readings in the Philosophy of Nature*, 1961, Westminster, Md., Newman.

KOHLER, W., *Gestalt Psychology*, 1947. (Mentor Books., 1959; original 1927)

KUMAR, Manjit, *Quantum: Einstein, Bohr, and the Great Debate About the Nature of Reality*, 2008. (NY, Norton)

LOCKE, J., *Essay Concerning Human Understanding*.

LOVEJOY, A., *Revolt Against Dualism.* (Open Court, 1960)

LUIJPEN, W., *Existential Phenomenology*, 1960, Pittsburgh, Duquesne Un.Press.

MacINTYRE, A., *God, Philosophy, Universities,* Lanham, MD, 2009.

MATSON, F., *The Broken Image*, 1964, Garden City, NY., Doubleday.

MARITAIN, J., *The Degrees of Knowledge*, 1959, N.Y., Scribner and Sons. (Fourth edition, trans. under the direction of G.Phelan)

MAY, R., ed., *Existential Psychology*, 1961, N.Y., Random House.

McINERNY, R., *Thomism in the Age of Renewal*, 1966, Garden City, NY.

MYERS, G., *Self,* 1969, New York, Pegasus.

OWENS, J., *Elementary Christian Metaphysics*, 1963, Milwaukee, Bruce.

PEIPER, J., *Leisure, the Basis of Culture*, trans. A.Dru, 1952, NY (New American Library, 1963)

PHILLIPS, R.P., *Modern Thomistic Philosophy*, two volumes, 1950.

PIEFER, J.F., *The Concept in Thomism*, 1952, Bookman Associates.

RAMACHANDRAN, V.S., & BLAKESLEE, S., *Phantoms in the Brain*, 1998, NY: William Morrow and Co.

ROBINSON, D., ed., *The Mind*, 1998, NY, Oxford Un. Press

RUITENBEEK, H., *Varieties of Personality Theory*, 1964, Dutton.

ROYCE, J., *Man and His Nature*, 1961, NY., McGraw-Hill.

RUCH, F.L., and ZIMBARDO, P.G, *Psychology and Life*, 8th ed., 1971.

RUSSELL, B., *An Outline of Philosophy*, 1927. (Meridian paperback, 1960).

SEARLE, J., *Mind: A Brief Introduction*, 2004, NY: Oxford Un. Press.

SIMPSON, G.G., *The Meaning of Evolution*, 1949. New Haven, Yale Un.Press).

SKINNER, B.F, *Beyond Freedom and Dignity*, 1971, Knopf. (Bantam, 1972)

SKINNER, B.F., "The Machine that is Man," in *Psychology Today*, April 1969.

SOBEL, C., *The Cognitive Sciences*, 2001,

STRAWSON, G., *Mental Reality*, 1994, Cambridge, MIT Press.

SWARTZ, R.J., *Perceiving, Sensing and Knowing*, 1965, NY., Doubleday.

WATSON, R., *Cogito, Ergo Sum: The Life of Rene Descartes*, 2002, Boston, David Godine Publisher.

WOOLDRIDGE, D., *Mechanical Man*, 1969, NY., McGraw-Hill.

YOUR INDEX

(No index is included. That is why there is a detailed table of contents. However, you will find it convenient to make a list of some important titles and/or names *and page numbers*, if, while you are reading, you come across an idea that you will want to return to again. That is why the next few pages are left empty, except for some letters at the top.)

A-E

F-J

K-O

P-S

T-Z